The Earthscan Reader in Environmental Values

The Earthscan Reader in Environmental Values

Edited by

Linda Kalof
and
Terre Satterfield

London • Sterling, VA

First published by Earthscan in the UK and USA in 2005

ISBN: 1-84407-167-7   paperback
        1-84407-166-9   hardback

Typesetting by Composition and Design Services
Printed and bound in the UK by Bath Press, Bath
Cover design by Andrew Corbett

For a full list of publications please contact:

Earthscan
8–12 Camden High Street
London, NW1 0JH, UK
Tel: +44 (0)20 7387 8558
Fax: +44 (0)20 7387 8998
Email: earthinfo@earthscan.co.uk
Web: **www.earthscan.co.uk**

22883 Quicksilver Drive, Sterling, VA 20166–2012, USA

Earthscan is an imprint of James and James (Science Publishers) Ltd and publishes in association with
the International Institute for Environment and Development

A catalogue record for this book is available from the British Library

Library of Congress Cataloging-in-Publication Data has been applied for

Printed on elemental chlorine-free paper

Contents

Environmental Values: An Introduction – Relativistic and Axiomatic Traditions in the Study of Environmental Values

Part 1 Economic Themes in Environmental Values

Part 2 Philosophical and Ethical Themes in Environmental Values

Part 3 Anthropological and Sociological Themes in Environmental Values

Part 4 Judgement and Decision Making Themes in Environmental Values

List of Figures and Tables

Figures

Tables

About the Authors

Jonathan Baron is a Professor, Senior Fellow in the Leonard Davis Institute for Health Economics and Member of the Graduate Group in the Wharton School at the University of Pennsylvania. Baron studies intuitions that stand in the way of maximization of utility, such as those related to parochialism, the act-omission distinction and moralistic values. He is also interested in the theory of utility maximization, in methods for experimentation and data analysis and in public-policy implications of research on judgements and decisions.

T. Jean Blocker is Associate Professor in the Sociology Department at the University of Tulsa and Founding Fellow of the National Energy-Environment Law and Policy Institute (NELPI), also at the University of Tulsa, which focuses on energy, environmental and natural resource law and policy. Her areas of interest include ecology and the environment, social inequality and urban sociology.

J. Baird Callicott is Professor in the Department of Philosophy and Religion Studies at the University of North Texas. During the 2004–2005 academic year, Callicott was Visiting Professor of Philosophy, Visiting Professor of Forestry and Environmental Studies and Bioethicist-in-Residence at Yale University. His areas of expertise include classical Greek philosophy, environmental philosophy and ethics, ethical theory, history of philosophy, comparative philosophy, philosophy of science, history of ideas in ecology, philosophy of ecology and conservation biology.

Richard T. Carson is Professor and Chair of the Department of Economics at the University of California, San Diego, and Senior Fellow at the San Diego Supercomputer Center. He previously served as Research Director for International Environmental Policy at the University of California's Institute on Global Conflict and Cooperation. Carson has extensive experience in the assessment of the benefits and costs of environmental policies. His specialty is valuing non-marketed and new goods using a wide array of techniques, including contingent valuation, hedonic pricing and the household production method.

Robert Costanza is the Gund Professor of Ecological Economics and Director of the Gund Institute for Ecological Economics at the University of Vermont. Costanza's research has focused on the interface between ecological and economic systems, particularly at larger temporal and spatial scales. This includes landscape-level spatial simulation modelling; analysis of energy and material flows through economic and ecological systems; valuation of ecosystem services, biodiversity and natural capital; and analysis of dysfunctional incentive systems and ways to correct them.

Thomas Dietz is Professor of Sociology and Crop and Soil Sciences and Director of the Environmental Science and Policy Programme at Michigan State University (MSU). He is also Associate Dean in the Colleges of Agriculture and Natural Resources, Natural Science and Social Science at MSU. His research interests are in human ecology, cultural evolution, environmental values and the human dimensions of global environmental change.

Riley E. Dunlap is currently Professor of Sociology at the University of Central Florida. His areas of interest include the demographic and ideological correlates of environmental attitudes and activism, the nature of 'environmental concern', trends in public opinion towards environmental issues, and the linkage between public attitudes and opinions and environmental policy-making.

Douglas Lee Eckberg is Professor and Chair of the Department of Sociology and Anthropology at Winthrop University. He has published several articles on environmental actions and attitudes. Currently he is conducting research on the nature and scope of homicide in 19th-century South Carolina.

Stephen C. Farber is Professor in the University of Pittsburgh's Graduate School of Public and International Affairs, and Director of the Environmental Management and Policy Specialization at the University of Pittsburgh. His areas of interest include environmental and resource economics, environmental management and policy and ecological economics.

Robin Gregory is a Senior Researcher with Decision Research, Associate Director of the Eco-Risk Research Unit at the University of British Columbia and Director of Value Scope Research, Inc. His fields of specialization include stakeholder involvement in environmental and risk decisions, decision making under uncertainty, valuation of nonmarket environmental resources, risk management and perceptions of hazardous technologies, and choice and preference behaviour.

Ramachandra Guha is a historian and biographer based in Bangalore. His books include *Savaging the Civilized: Verrier Elwin, His Tribals, and India* and *Environmentalism: A Global History*.

Bruce Hannon is Jubilee Professor of the Liberal Arts and Sciences, Professor of Geography and The National Center for Supercomputer Applications (NCSA) at the University of Illinois at Urbana-Champaign. His areas of interest include modelling ecological, economic, energy systems, conservation, resource utilization and conservation, and employment impacts of changes in technology and consumption.

Robert Emmet ('Bobby') Jones is an Associate Professor in the Environment and Globalization Programme in the Department of Sociology, a Research Associate with the

Energy, Environment and Resource Center, a Research Associate with the Southeast Water Policy Center and a faculty member of the Environmental Studies Programme at the University of Tennessee. He has an interdisciplinary education in the social and natural sciences and his work examines the human dimensions of environmental change and ecosystem management. He has worked on projects related to the re-introduction of wolves to Yellowstone, salmon restoration in the Pacific Northwest, water recreation in the Columbia River Basin, water supply and amenity ('green') migration issues in Southern Appalachia, boomtown growth in the West, hazardous waste management in Washington State, land-use at the Oak Ridge Reservation in Tennessee, public support for the environment in the US, and others related to environmental justice and race.

Daniel Kahneman is the Eugene Higgins Professor of Psychology, Princeton University, and Professor of Public Affairs, Woodrow Wilson School. Kahneman is also a Fellow in the Center for Rationality at The Hebrew University in Jerusalem. Professor Kahneman and Vernon K. Smith received the Nobel Prize for Economic Sciences in 2002.

Linda Kalof is Professor of Sociology at Michigan State University. She is series editor for *A Cultural History of Animals* and *A History of the Human Body* and the journal *Human Ecology Review*. Her areas of interest are the cultural representations of human and other animals, visual sociology and nature/culture interactions.

Stephen R. Kellert is the Tweedy/Ordway Professor of Social Ecology and Co-Director of the Hixon Center for Urban Ecology in the Yale School of Forestry and Environmental Studies. Kellert's research has focused on science, policy and management relating to the interaction of people and the natural environment. His current research projects include studies of the theory, science and practice of restorative environmental design; the theory and application of the concept of biophilia; connecting human and natural systems in urban watersheds; and the biocultural basis for an ethic toward the natural world.

Jack L. Knetsch is Professor Emeritus in the Department of Economics and the School of Resource and Environmental Management at Simon Fraser University, where he has taught and conducted research in the areas of behavioural economics, environmental economics and policy analysis for the past 30 years. He holds degrees in Soil Science, Agricultural Economics and Public Administration, as well as a PhD in Economics from Harvard University, and was with public and private agencies and organizations in the US and Malaysia before moving to Canada. He has accepted visiting appointments and lectured at universities in Europe, Asia and Australia, as well as in North America. Much of his recent research has centred on policy implications of behavioural economic findings.

Sarah Lichtenstein is a founder and treasurer of Decision Research. Her fields of specialization were human judgement, decision making, risk perception and risk assessment. She is now retired but continues as an adviser and consultant to Decision Research. She has recently edited a book with Paul Slovic for Cambridge University Press on *The Construction of Preferences*.

Angela G. Mertig is Associate Professor in the Department of Sociology and Anthropology at Middle Tennessee University. Her areas of interest include environmental sociology, research methods, public opinion, social movements, animals and society, and gender and society.

Arne Naess is Professor Emeritus at the University of Oslo. He has been working with the Centre for Development and the Environment in Oslo, Norway since 1991. Naess' areas of interest include ecophilosophy and ecology, and he is perhaps best known for developing the deep ecology perspective.

Bryan G. Norton is Professor of Philosophy, Science and Technology in the School of Public Policy, Georgia Institute of Technology. He writes on inter-generational equity, sustainability theory, biodiversity policy and on valuation methods. His specialty is the integration of spatio-temporal scaling considerations into sustainability criteria.

Mark Sagoff's latest book is *Price, Principle, and the Environment* (Cambridge University Press, 2004). He is a Senior Research Scholar with the Institute for Philosophy and Public Policy at the School of Public Policy at the University of Maryland, College Park; a Pew Scholar in Conservation and the Environment; and past President of the International Society of Environmental Ethics. Sagoff has published widely in journals of philosophy, law, economics and public policy.

Ariel Salleh is Associate Professor of Social Ecology at the University of Western Sydney. Her interests include sociology of knowledge, women's empowerment and recognition of their contributions to ecological citizenship and alternative ways of knowing. She examines this in the context of global/local struggles over resources, and classic theoretical debates on reproductive labour.

Theresa (Terre) Satterfield is an Assistent Professor of Culture, Risk and the Environment in the Institute for Resources, the Environment and Sustainability at the University of British Columbia. Her areas of interest include the social study of environmental conflicts, environmental values and public policy, social and cultural theories of risk, political and human ecology, sustainability movements and the anthropology of environmentalism.

Paul Slovic is a Professor of Psychology at the University of Oregon and a founder and President of Decision Research. Slovic studies human judgement, decision making and risk analysis. He and his colleagues worldwide have developed methods to describe risk perceptions and measure their impacts on individuals, industry and society.

Clive L. Spash is Research Chair in the Department of Geography and Environment at the University of Aberdeen, and programme head for the Socio-economic Research Programme at the Macaulay Institute. Spash's research in recent years has concentrated upon environmental valuation with regard to the use and role of benefit–cost analysis, and the part played by attitudes, norms and beliefs in relation to preference formation. In addition, the use of participatory and deliberative mechanisms for environmental management has been of increasing interest. His interdisciplinary research interests cut across the disciplines of economics, ecology, social psychology, philosophy and political science.

Mark Spranca is the Director of the RAND Corporation's Center for Healthcare and the Internet and Co-Founder and CEO of Axia Health Sciences. Spranca is an expert on health behaviour and consumer health-related decision making. He has designed and evaluated health benefit decision support tools and web-based tools for patient education and chronic disease management.

Paul C. Stern is Study Director of two National Research Council committees: The Committee on the Human Dimensions of Global Change and the Committee on Assessing Behavioral and Social Science Research on Aging. His areas of interest include the determinants of environmentally significant behaviour and participatory processes for informing environmental decision making.

Kent D. Van Liere is a Senior Consultant to Population Research Systems in San Francisco.

Matthew A. Wilson is an Assistant Research Professor with the School of Business Administration, and a Research Fellow at the Gund Institute of Ecological Economics at the University of Vermont. Dr Wilson's fields of specialization include social survey methods, economic psychology, sustainable business management theory and the economic valuation of environmental goods and services.

Chapter Sources

Part 1 Economic Themes in Environmental Values

1   Carson, R. T. (2000) 'Contingent valuation: A user's guide'. *Environmental Science Technology*, vol 34, pp1413–1418
2   Farber, S. C., Costanza, R. and Wilson, M. A. (2002) 'Economic and ecological concepts for valuing ecosystem services'. *Ecological Economics*, vol 41, pp375–392
3   Spash, C. L. (1999) 'The development of environmental thinking in economics'. *Environmental Values*, vol 8, pp413–435

Part 2 Philosophical and Ethical Themes in Environmental Values

4   Callicott, J. B. (1984) 'Non-anthropocentric value theory and environmental ethics'. *American Philosophical Quarterly*, vol 21, pp299–309
5   Norton, B. G. (1984) 'Environmental ethics and weak anthropocentrism'. *Environmental Ethics*, vol 6, pp131–148
6   Naess, A. (1984) 'A defence of the deep ecology movement'. *Environmental Ethics*, vol 6, pp265–270
7   Guha, R. (1989) 'Radical American environmentalism and "wilderness" preservation: A third world critique'. *Environmental Ethics*, vol 11, pp71–83
8   Salleh, A. (1993) 'Class, race and gender discourse in the ecofeminism/deep ecology debate'. *Environmental Ethics*, vol 15, pp225–244
9   Kellert, S. R. (1993) 'The biological basis for human values of nature', in Kellert, S. R. and Wilson, E. O. (eds), *Biophilia Hypothesis*, Island Press, Washington, DC, pp42–69

Part 3 Anthropological and Sociological Themes in Environmental Values

10 Eckberg, D. L. and Blocker T. J. (1996) 'Christianity, environmentalism and the theoretical problem of fundamentalism'. *Journal for the Scientific Study of Religion*, vol 35, pp343–355

11 Dunlap, R. E. Van Liere, K. Mertig, A. and Jones, R. E. (2000) 'Measuring endorsement of the New Ecological Paradigm: A revised NEP scale'. *Journal of Social Issues*, vol 56, pp425–442

12 Stern, P. C. Dietz, T. and Kalof L. (1993) 'Value orientations, gender and environmental concern'. *Environment and Behavior*, vol 25, pp322–348

13 Norton, B. G. and Hannon, B. (1997) 'Environmental values: A place-based theory'. *Environmental Ethics*, vol 19, pp227–245

Part 4 Judgement and Decision Making Themes in Environmental Values

14 Kahneman, D. and Knetsch, J. L. (1992) 'Valuing public goods: The purchase of moral satisfaction'. *Journal of Environmental Economics and Management*, vol 22, pp57–70

15 Baron, J. and Spranca, M. (1997) 'Protected values'. *Organizational Behaviour and Human Decision Processes*, vol 70, pp1–16

16 Sagoff, M. (1998) 'Aggregation and deliberation in valuing environmental public goods: A look beyond contingent pricing'. *Ecological Economics*, vol 24, pp213–230

17 Gregory, R., Lichtenstein, S. and Slovic, P. (1993) 'Valuing environmental resources: A constructive approach'. *Journal of Risk and Uncertainty*, vol 7, pp177–197

18 Dietz, T. (1994) 'What should we do? Human ecology and collective decision making'. *Human Ecology Review*, vol 1, pp301–309

Acknowledgements

We thank Thomas Dietz for his steadfast encouragement, Amy Jean Fitzgerald for her skilful research assistance, and the Ecological and Cultural Change Studies Group at Michigan State for their multiple readings and suggestions for improvement of the introductory essay. Equal thanks go to our colleagues at Decision Research in Oregon, particularly Robin Gregory and Paul Slovic. In addition, we would like to thank Maria Isabel du Monceau and the impressive graduate students in the University of British Columbia's Resource Management and Environmental Studies programme for their ongoing conversation on the subject of environmental values. Invaluable financial support was provided by the US National Science Foundation's Ethics and Values program and from Getty Conservation Institute's symposium on *Assessing the Cultural Significance of Natural Heritage*. Any opinions, findings, conclusions or recommendations expressed here are our responsibility and do not necessarily reflect the views of the funding agency.

List of Acronyms and Abbreviations

AC	avoided cost
AC	aware of harmful circumstances
AERE	Association of Environmental and Resource Economists
AR	ascribes responsibility
CERCLA	Comprehensive Environmental Response, Compensation and Liability Act
CV	contingent valuation
DSP	dominant social paradigm
EAERE	European Association of Environmental and Resource Economists
ELM	evolutionary linguistic model
EPA	Environmental Protection Agency
ERE	*Environmental and Resource Economics*
ESEE	European Society for Ecological Economics
EVRI	Environmental Valuation Reference Inventory
FI	factor income
GDP	gross domestic product
GNP	gross national product
GSS	General Social Survey
HP	hedonic pricing
IEE	Institute for Ecological Economics
ISEE	International Society for Ecological Economics
IUCN	Internation Union for the Conservation of Nature and Natural Resources
JEEM	*Journal of Environment Economics and Management*
MAUT	multiattribute utility theory
NEP	New Environmental Paradigm
NIMBY	not in my backyard
NOAA	National Oceanic and Atmospheric Administration
OECD	Organisation for Economic Co-operation and Development
PCE	personal consumption expenditures
RAM	rational actor model
RC	replacement cost
TC	travel cost
WTA	willingness to accept
WTP	willingness to pay
WWF	World Wildlife Fund

Environmental Values: An Introduction – Relativistic and Axiomatic Traditions in the Study of Environmental Values

Terre Satterfield and Linda Kalof

If the curious were to find their way to a dictionary, she or he would discover myriad and indeed disparate definitions of value both colloquial and formal. So it comes as no surprise that the study of *environmental values* is itself an active, multifaceted and disputatious field. Journal citations with the key word 'environmental values' number in the thousands as scholars seek nuanced improvements to methodological conundrums and yet also address fundamentally important questions such as: What is value? How should it be measured and/or assigned to the natural world? Are all values commensurate, amenable to measurement across a common scale, and thus to comparison and trade-offs? Can valued environmental goods (such as an old-growth forest) be substituted by other goods (such as housing), thereby ensuring utility? And is the market a viable avenue for establishing value in the first place? This volume is devoted to helping define the meaning, representation and study of environmental values in the context of policy decisions about land management and conservation efforts. In particular, we orient this volume of essential readings in environmental values towards senior undergraduates, graduate students and practitioners, all of whom seek an understanding of the field but at the same time may be intimidated by the diversity of the literature.[1] Our secondary purpose is to outline a few of the central tensions and problems encountered in the study of environmental values, and to assist the understanding of broader practices of civic participation, governance and decision making. Finally, it must be said that this is a vast field of inquiry and that for each exemplary or novel article selected here, there were many that had to be eliminated in the interests of length, which in the end determined the price of the book you are now reading. We could not, for instance, accommodate the growing and pertinent literature on sustainability measures, specific subcategories of value (such as existence value or postmaterialist values), public deliberation practices (with one exception), or the myriad experimentations with design in the presentation of information for survey or choice processes in valuation contexts.[2] Ultimately, contributions were chosen on the basis of readability for an interdisciplinary audience, influence on the field and/or adherence to ontological and epistemological dilemmas in the definition, measurement and representation of values. Each thematic section begins with a brief introduction to alert the reader to key theoretical and methodological contributions, whereas we begin here with a broader overview and introduction to this collection and to the field of environmental values.

Valuing the Environment

The last decade has witnessed a flurry of research devoted to identifying the value of nature (broadly construed), specific environmental goods (a northern spotted owl), ecosystem services (nutrient recycling) or cherished places (Yellowstone National Park). Contributions to the literature have come from most corners of the natural, economic, social, psychological and decision sciences, as well as from philosophy and its sub-discipline, environmental ethics. Some have sought methods that reflect axioms or principles (agreed upon material or reasoned evidence from which value can be derived and ordered), while others assert the importance of relativistic or subjective approaches to eliciting (drawing out) and attributing value. Some make distinctions between held values (beliefs we adhere to), while others focus on assigned values (rankings, dollar or numeric tags that express the relative weight of one value as compared to one or more different values). Still others are concerned with the proper representation of values that are not only tangible (such as those based on the specific physical attributes and contributions of a good, for example, the board-feet of timber that can be cut from a single tree), but also intangible (such as those based on more nebulous qualities, including the inculcation of awe or the symbolic resonance of revered spiritual or cultural properties, for example, watching the sunset over the rim of the Grand Canyon). In addition, many of the approaches represented in the philosophical/ethical themes, anthropological/sociological themes and judgement/decision making themes (Parts 2, 3 and 4) seek to provide alternatives to economists' conceptualizations of value. Of particular concern is the economists' use of a contingent valuation (CV) method wherein an individual's subjective valuation of a natural good is ascertained by asking stakeholders or survey respondents to state how much they would be willing to pay (WTP) to improve the status of a particular environmental state or good – for example, to improve the habitat of an endangered species – or willing to accept (WTA) for its loss.

Two broad-stroke (though not necessarily consciously articulated) positions underpin much of the values literature. The first can be characterized as axiomatic (clear or obvious). An axiomatic, or axiom-focused, approach operates on the premise that certain categories of value are better, 'truer', more important, necessary to life, self-evident and/or intellectually defensible than all others, and these priorities should provide the basis from which environmental policy is derived. Axiomatic traditions are, by definition, expert driven, with values set by assessment, argument or measurement produced by disciplinary specialists who are not necessarily or solely attendant to the opinions of stakeholders or nonspecialists, but rather to the functioning of ecosystems or the intrinsic value of a herd of caribou. The second position – the subjectivist or relativist – is guided by the principle of expressed or revealed preference. The point for these practitioners is that there are no right or wrong preferences, only different ones. Researchers are expected to capture (but not judge or influence) these disparate perspectives during the process of drawing out the values (elicitation). Their findings are used to provide insight for those responsible for conducting benefit–cost analyses or making land management decisions.[3]

Axiomatic Traditions

Much axiomatic work on the subject of environmental values can be attributed to the multidisciplinary movement known as ecological economics. Practitioners in this field are working to identify new methods for valuation where traditional welfare or neoclassical economics cannot be depended upon to adequately capture the full range of values. Many also reject WTP/WTA approaches due to (1) the belief that concepts such as discounting (to establish the future value of a good), exchange value, and utility maximization are fundamentally flawed as they pertain to nonmarket (namely environmental) goods, and (2) the conviction that the physical world has a limited capacity to provide for the world's population and that many resources are neither limitless nor substitutable (for example, clean water). These scholars argue that new methods are needed to make better links between our understanding of the interdependency of economic and ecological systems. The 1990s saw the emergence of several economy–environment journals that encouraged the development of alternate approaches, and few benefit–cost analysts would today include 'use value' only at the expense of such variables as future generations or species survival.

Historically, social scientists generally think of their work as value free, and so do not conceive of their work as axiomatic. But, again, environmental economics, and to some extent ethics (see below), prove the exceptional case. The value of environmental goods for this group of scholar-evaluators is assessed on the basis of disciplinary givens such as the contribution of a good to the maintenance of species diversity, the functioning of an ecosystem and/or to the value attributed to particular ecosystem service. Assumed to exist are higher and lower order expert-defined values, which are amenable to measurement and provide self-evident truths as to the real value of a good. For modelling and assessment purposes, emphasis is typically placed on indicators of system integrity, health, carrying capacity or resilience. This practice can point in turn to the designation of critical habitat or draw attention to (i.e. valorize) system functions – for instance, the waste-filtering capacities of wetlands or the importance of a keystone species to the overall health of a system. A central question for most of these approaches is: What is the best indicator of value or importance to a system, and/or which indicators speak to which scale or components of a system – be that at the level of organisms; whole populations; or the larger forest, tropical, desert or other ecosystems of which these are a part (Suter, 1993)?

Prominent among the efforts by ecologists to valorize ecosystem services is the controversial adoption by Costanza and colleagues of assigning a dollar value to ecosystem services (goods not normally traded on the market). Though not reproduced here, 'The Value of the World's Ecosystem Services and Natural Capital' was published first in the journal *Nature* and subsequently in the journal *Ecological Economics* (1998). The paper contains a typology of worth based on the economic contribution (or the 'total global flow of US$ value per year') of different geographic domains (marine, riverine/lake, terrestrial, wetland, grassland, desert, tundra, urban etc.). Each domain is examined for its contribution to specific ecosystem services (e.g. gas regulation, climate regulation, water supply, nutrient recycling etc.). The authors' breakdown of services is a viable schema of ecologists' thinking on values, whereas the attention their findings draw to the functions of nature normally taken for granted is also evident. The concluding assessment by Costanza and colleagues that the total global biosphere is worth, on average, US$33 trillion per year (nearly twice the annual gross national product of the US at the time) has, however, been hotly contested. Many economists working to elicit dollar value as a measure of, and a means for, aggregating public preferences for natural goods, view this costing of the globe and the authors' selective use of a subset of WTP estimates as a slight to their disciplinary integrity. Others simply find that such time-captured static pricing of nature and/or the use of discounting principles to capture future value defy concepts fundamental to ecology, including the episodic (and occasionally catastrophic) change characteristic of ecosystems as well as their largely unpredictable and uncertain adaptations to perturbations.

A second very significant contribution to axiomatic methods for identifying environmental values is driven by the work of environmental ethicists. Ethics – in this case environmental ethics – are defined as the logical or reasoned basis for defending 'right' versus 'wrong' practice or conduct toward the biophysical world. While some argue that only humans can be moral agents (and thus can evaluate things) because only humans have the capacity for consciousness, others argue that some animals have consciousness and that ecosystems, organisms and species can be defended as possessing certain kinds of value in and of themselves (based, for example, on a good's contribution to biodiversity or ecosystem functioning). The natural world is thus considered by many ethicists to have moral standing regardless of its use to humans.

Among the ethical divisions central to this literature is that between anthropocentric versus biocentric positions and weak versus strong anthropocentricism (Norton, 1991; Rolston, 1994, 1999; Callicott, 1995). An anthropocentric ethic posits that nature's worth is derived primarily from its capacity to serve human ends. A biocentric ethic respects all living organisms; because nature is alive, it is regarded as 'good' in its own right and thus deserving of moral consideration. Many nuanced arguments exist within these broad positions. For example, is it better to inculcate an environmental ethic based: (1) on the potential human benefits of a healthy environment; (2) on the argument that nature has rights and thus its welfare should be taken into account or enshrined in law; (3) on the aesthetic attributes of nature; or (4) on the basis of a cross-human and human-to-nature ethic of egalitarianism (Merchant, 1992)? These considerations, in turn, raise several questions about humans' obligatory posture toward nature – namely, what are our obligations to the natural environment? And are those obligations derived from our obligations to ourselves and other humans, or to our investment in physical places, or from a discrete obligation to nature (Dickson, 2000)?

Regardless of any one ethicist's position on the above points, most agree that the values humans hold about nature are the root cause of environmental problems. It is assumed that current value systems reflect our disregard for nature and even our willingness to dominate nature (a position articulated by Dunlap, Van Liere, Mertig and Jones in Chapter 11 as the dominant social paradigm). This value perspective is said, in turn, to legitimize or cause our heedless exploitation of natural systems. It is further assumed that if people adopt a more ethical orientation toward the environment, environmental problems will in part be solved (Dickson, 2000, p127).

In short, ecological economists and ethicists alike labour to argue that nature is typically undervalued and that – if we become more fully cognizant of the moral qualities as well as of the material, aesthetic and spiritual benefits of nature – nature might come to be managed by humans with respect and according to a range of axiomatic principles. They valorize certain qualities of natural systems, attributes regarded as overlooked in a post-World War II epoch that prioritizes the extraction of renewable and nonrenewable natural resources.

Relativistic Traditions

Ethicists and ecologists have forced onto the values stage the relevance of a systemic/functional, biologically delimiting and morally resonant definition of value. The cross-fertilization with other disciplines of these ideas is ongoing and significant, some of which will become apparent below. It remains the case, however, that the study of environmental values for policy and land management purposes is heavily influenced by relativistic approaches or, more colloquially, by practitioners whose central goal is the monitoring of public opinion. This relativistic slant is derived in part from the deep tradition across the social sciences of 'value-neutral' approaches to human behaviour and partly because 'the individual being is seen, for all practical purposes, as the originator of preference and, therefore, of value' (Brown, 1984, p231). It is also because of the role citizen preferences play in the instigation of endangered species legislation, the growth of environmental activism and the general public support for environmentally oriented behaviour (recycling, water conservation, wilderness recreation, green consumerism, and so on). Considerable support exists today for public consultation as the basis of good governance and civil society.

Following Brown (1984) and Gregory (1999), most of the available social science valuation tools are glossed as expressed preference approaches. Brown (1984, pp232–234) argues that preference is used 'to mean the setting by an individual of one thing before another because of a notion of betterness'. This overarching category can be subdivided further still into approaches that work to identify held values (underlying values or ideals that prioritize modes of conduct and desirable qualities) and those that work to measure assigned values (the relative importance or worth of an object in a given context, which is not a characteristic of the object per se but the importance of which is derived, at least partially, from held values). Understandably, much confusion for new students of environmental values is generated by the failure of many practitioners to clarify whether one is talking about held or assigned values.

Contingent Valuation as Willingness to Pay

Expressed preference work is dominated by contingent valuation surveys employing WTP and WTA protocols (Mitchell and Carson, 1989).[4] Resting on economists'

assumption that dollars are as neutral a metric as is available for measuring value, practitioners posit a hypothetical market on which environmental improvements and losses
are exchanged for promised payment. It is further assumed that preference is akin to
the pursuit of individual human welfare or self-interest played out as a rational market
choice. Participant citizens in WTP/WTA studies are asked to state the maximum price
they would be willing to pay to obtain an improvement in environmental quality (for
example, the restoration of a bird habitat) or to state the price they would be willing to
accept given deterioration of status (for example, the loss of said habitat). Requests to
assign dollar values to such environmental goods are generally accompanied by technical information on the geophysical domain in question (such as a community
watershed) and quantitative details about the benefits (perhaps recreational or ecological) and costs (perhaps jobs lost or revenues forgone) of different policy options. Total
WTP is the product of average or mean WTP multiplied by the population to which
the decision applies (a local town, users of an environmental asset, a county, a nation
state etc.). Total WTP is then pitted, in a benefit–cost analysis, against the costed interests of other stakeholders (industry, government, competing resource users etc.).

Psychological and Social Studies of Value

Dissatisfaction with economic definitions of value and a strong tradition in the study of
attitudes and beliefs in sociology and psychology have helped fuel many alternate nonmonetary studies of value. Most of this work emphasizes a 'values held' definition.
Much of it also recognizes the escalation of environmental concern over time and across
social groups, and finds that values once thought extremely radical are held by a broad
variety of individuals and groups (see Dunlap, Van Liere, Mertig and Jones in Chapter 11
of this volume). More importantly, this body of work disavows (1) the assumption that,
taken literally, values and valuation are synonymous, that quantitative values equal, or
actually express, individual value-systems, and (2) the assumption that the public
majority endorses and is satisfactorily portrayed by rational, economic expressions of
the value of nature. Most define value as 'what we care about' (Keeney, 1992, p3), as
the 'basic motivations which guide thoughts and action' (Axelrod, 1994, p83) or following Rokeach (1973) as general goals or orienting dispositions from which attitudes
to specific items are derived (see also Stern, Dietz and Kalof in Chapter 12 of this
volume).[5]

Recall that the principal distinction between relativistic and axiomatic studies is
that for the first group the goal is to characterize the values held by the public, while for
the second group the goal is to instantiate the wisdom of recognizing some values as
more important or significant than others and, in so doing, overturn the historical force
of a human-centric, utilitarian worldview that promotes hubris towards and dominance
over nature. Yet the salient feature of two classic nonaxiomatic studies of value is the
decidedly ecocentric flavour detected in survey responses.

As early as 1978, Dunlap and Van Liere argued convincingly that a 'new environmental [value] paradigm' (NEP) was emerging to supplant the dominant social
paradigm (DSP) (Dunlap and Van Liere, 1978). The DSP is that 'constellation of values,

attitudes, and beliefs' thought to underpin key Western assumptions about the human–nature interface (i.e. limitless progress is possible, faith in science and technology is abundant, nature exists to serve humans etc.). Since then, Dunlap and his colleagues have reconceptualized the E in NEP to read 'Ecological' rather than 'Environmental' to reflect the NEP's measurement of the endorsement of an ecological worldview. The NEP explores the tolerance expressed for limits to growth, support for a greater balance between the human and nonhuman world and support for anti-anthropocentric positions. Salient among these findings is the remarkable degree of acceptance of the NEP – not only among environmentalists, which was expected, but among the general public as well.

Equally renowned is Kellert's broadly cross-cultural survey work, much of which is summarized in his book *The Value of Life* (Kellert, 1996). In Chapter 9 we reproduce Kellert's argument that all humans have an innate biological need to value the environment because of the importance of biodiversity to human physical, emotional, spiritual and intellectual wellbeing. While some scholars disagree with Kellert's assumptions about biological or biophilic predispositions to the natural world (and some find difference where Kellert finds universality – interpreting the ethnic-, income- and gender-driven differences uncovered in his book as more meaningful than does he), his typology is consistent with a number of subsequent studies and is also supported by work in other disciplines.

Each of the above studies of value warrants recognition for deviating from the framing of value as a benefit–cost problem, thereby resisting the tendency for the definition of value used (e.g. an economic one) to inscribe particular forms of discourse into the elicitation process itself. An economistic frame insinuates a market preoccupation and, more broadly, a rationalizing discourse may unintentionally exclude moral or political imperatives, despite the fact that key stakeholders often defend their claims in the most profoundly moral terms (Brosius, 1999, pp36–40). Lockwood similarly notes that many elicitation instruments fail to 'give participants any opportunity to explore different ways of expressing their values and [in the absence of alternatives] participants must offer a response that is against their preferred mode of value expression' (1999, p394). Designing better value statements for survey purposes will not likely be a resolution because the problem arises from the tendency to confuse expressions of values that refer to an individual's fundamental beliefs (held values) with operational expressions of those values in terms of context-specific objectives or the means by which desired values are realized (Kraus, 1995; Ladd and Bowman, 1995).

However well or poorly values are captured or measured, the question also remains: What converts such values into meaningful actions? This is precisely the question addressed by three further contributions to the field; each departs considerably from the direct characterization or measurement of subjective positions and instead addresses the conditions under which held values become active in public life. Stern, Dietz and Kalof address norm activation primarily in reference to involvement in social movements. They isolate those values most closely associated with involvement in environmental activism, expressed as citizen activism, the uptake of behaviours, and policy support consistent with the preservation of nature and environmentalism generally. In Chapter 8 of this volume, Salleh explores debates in ecofeminism versus deep ecology. Arguing that women's reproductive labour (which fosters a close relationship between women and nature) has been ignored in the biocentrism of privileged white men, Salleh asserts that environmental advocacy and feminism is praxis and life-needs oriented. Eckberg and Blocker (see Chapter 10) similarly challenge conventional assumptions regarding religiosity and environmentalism, widely known as the Lynn White Hypothesis (White, 1967). They find that the influence of religion on environmentalism is complex: people who identify themselves as conservative Christians are likely to be anti-environmental, whereas Christians who do not identify with conservative fundamentalism (but participate in religious activities) are pro-environmental.

The Value Basis of Judgement and Decision Making

The above contributions to the ethical, social and psychological dimensions of value have legitimized a much broader conception of the term 'value' than has been the tradition in the field. Social scientists have provided evidence for the claim that expressions of value are rooted both in utilitarian approaches to preference (which address the question: what is it that a person values or will 'pay for' because it benefits him or her as an individual?) and in ethical and de-ontological approaches (which address the question: what does a person believe to be important to the greater good that is nature and society?) (see Sagoff in Chapter 16 of this volume). The enormous advances in value identification techniques offered by these exemplary studies cannot be underestimated. However, as researchers, decision makers and policy advisers look for ever deeper understandings of value, and for greater clarification as to how values influence decision making, a concurrent and decidedly applied set of criticisms has also emerged among those who study human judgement.

Much of this work was inspired by experimental psychologists studying common judgement errors in human cognition. As already noted, it was Brown (1984) who first distinguished between values held and values assigned. The distinction is an important one because most ethicists and social psychologists believe that held values – as culturally and biologically influenced phenomena – are fundamentally stable orientations toward our social and physical world. Conversely, many experimental psychologists and decision analysts regard assigned values as ephemeral – contingent on the context in which those values (particularly those expressed as assigned prices in WTP formulas) are elicited.

The point for many decision analysts is to provide evidence for the problems endemic to WTP and WTA protocols and to offer viable alternatives to these practices. A first set of criticisms addresses the cognitive limitations that most persons exhibit when facing a value-based decision problem; a second set addresses what is known as the weak link between values and actions. In the first instance, students of judgement and decision making have found, overwhelmingly, that assigned values of the kind sought by WTP studies are highly problematic because the average respondent's cognitive ability is bounded. This bounding is due not to lack of wisdom per se but to the features of human cognition. It is simply the case that most people experience difficulty navigating the complexities involved in making judgements or assigning value in the context of those decisions. Problems arise because people routinely and unconsciously avert complexity by relying on a consistent set of biases or 'heuristics' (rules of thumb) that make information processing easier and simplify decisions. Such heuristics and biases can be an elegant means to an efficient decision, but in many cases, they lead to errors or poor-quality judgements. Cognitive difficulty can also be attributed to the features of the decision task itself. Most value studies work to identify the links between values held and the decision or policy that such values support. But it turns out that standard surveys offer relatively poor opportunities for respondents to think through the links between a value stated and an action endorsed (Ladd and Bowman, 1995; Satterfield and Gregory, 1998). Together these difficulties suggest that how a value is elicited – the way in which a valuation task is set up, worded, or *framed* – strongly influences the outcome.

Many of these problems were examined by Fischhoff (1991), who proposed a set of conditions under which 'basic' values (akin to held values) and 'stated values' can be elicited. But he also concludes than many values are labile and thus an artefact of survey design. Further prominent examples of framing effects include: the availability heuristic, which finds that people estimate the frequency of the occurrence of something on the basis of how easily they can imagine or recall an instance of it; and the gain/loss effect, which finds that decision tasks worded as a gain versus an equivalent loss are not always perceived as equivalent. The presentation of information pertinent to a decision can also impose mental fatigue and thus fog the participant's ability to juggle cognitively the many pieces of some decisions.

It is also the case that WTP studies have been criticized for producing an abundance of unusually high WTP amounts and 'protest zeros'. These are instances where study respondents resist the prevailing format by entering a zero or by offering an unrealistically high value, in response to questions about the worth of an environmental good. Quite often these entries are accompanied by margin comments reflecting the respondent's discontent with being asked to think of the environmental good in question in monetary terms. In Chapter 14, Kahneman and Knetsch explain this protest as rooted in economists' misunderstandings of the evaluator's intent. Economists supportive of WTP methods assume that value is easily and accurately assigned by the respondent, who, as a rational agent-consumer, uses that dollar assignation to express her or his preference order for environmental goods or states. A higher dollar value, it is assumed, will (1) be assigned to states (e.g. clean water) preferred over and above other states, and (2) reflect the true amount that people are willing to pay, in the same sense that if you prefer car A over car B, you're likely to be willing to pay a fixed amount more for car A. How much more depends on your income and on your subjective degree of appreciation for car A.

But if, as the works covered in this section suggest, valuations are often inexact or labile – and thus they can change as judgement conditions are altered – something other than a conventional market transaction must be taking place in the mind of the respondent. Kahneman and Knetsch's article reveals, for instance, that when survey respondents evaluate nonmarket goods, they are generally insensitive to quantity. WTP amounts do not change significantly when the value of improving one lake, versus all of the lakes in a region, is rated. The authors thus speculate that such WTP transactions are akin to contributing to a cause – they are purchasing moral satisfaction and not the good itself. These are symbolic actions that express the intensity of feelings about a good and the moral importance attributed to that good.

Baron and Spranca's contribution (Chapter 15) also addresses the problem of assigned values and protest zeros by investigating the problem of 'protected' (or non-negotiable) values. They argue that valuation exercises can be an uncomfortable experience for many participants because the exercise forces them, whether implicitly or explicitly, to make trade-offs that may give rise to moral and ethical dilemmas that are fundamentally difficult to resolve. Many people are deeply offended by or have a profound psychological aversion to trade-offs because they view a subset of trade-offs as violating norms they seek to protect or regard as sacred.

More interesting problems for those who study decision making stem from the breadth of interpretation available to a broadly stated value expression, wherein a value endorsed and an action chosen are logically inconsistent. This may occur because of the many trade-offs involved in choosing one action over and above another, by the inability to consider or imagine the consequences of different outcomes and by the subtle effects of question framing. Gregory, Lichtenstein and Slovic (1993) (as well as Sagoff) respond to this very problem by pointing to a new breed of value studies known as constructed preference work. Constructed preference approaches address head-on the fact that researchers are caught between the need for informed choice and the knowledge that relatively subtle cues can influence judgements. These approaches have redefined decision making and valuation practices as actively constructive processes that must avoid unrealistic cognitive demands by offering the decision maker conscientious supplementary and contextual help in the teasing out of good-quality judgement information. In practice, constructed preferences can be accomplished through a prescriptive and intentionally structured approach to decision problems. This in turn helps move concerns about framing effects from the passive stance of avoiding judgement errors to the active construction of an improved and appropriately defensible valuation context.

Finally, we do not mean to suggest that all decision-focused work necessarily assumes a rational actor model of human behaviour (hence, the need to rationalize the decision process through use of defensibly constructed preferences). Dietz argues instead that while benefit–cost analysis is based on a rational actor model, discursive policy analysis draws on a linguistic model of human action. In the rational actor model, individuals interact in self-interested ways (strategically, trying to maximize benefits), whereas in the linguistic model human cognition and language is central to human action. Individuals are continuously defining, redefining and renegotiating with others the contexts of action. Thus, discursive methods use conversations or group interaction to make decisions or evaluate policy, and they can also incorporate benefit–cost analysis, if all individuals agree that utility maximization is the rule that should be applied to a policy decision.

Conclusion

Sorting one's way through the environmental values literature is a nearly impossible task. Nonetheless, a few dominant trends are discernible. First, economic, and especially preference-centric/WTP, definitions of environmental values dominate the field.

Though WTP methods are not the sole focus of this volume, it is virtually impossible to discuss or understand the environmental values literature without some reference to WTP, because almost all other work is defined as against or capable of improving upon this method.

Second, much of the literature can be distinguished as either axiomatic (primarily by ethicists or ecologists) or relativistic (primarily by economists, psychologists, sociologists and anthropologists). Axiomatic practitioners do not necessarily identify themselves as such, but their work is ultimately oriented to 'right' or 'best' practices, however defined. But few scholars (with the possible exception of Norton and Hannon's article on place values which is reproduced in Chapter 13) have offered an explicit schema for enhancing one's experience or enhancing appreciation of the natural, economic or spiritual qualities of nature. This lack is due both to the newness of the field and to the timidity produced by the predominance of relativistic approaches to environmental valuation.

Third and broadly stated, relativistic approaches dominate, but problems arise from this focus on human attitudes and preferences – what people want or believe – because some values (particularly as expressions of WTP) are not clearly defined in the minds of respondents and as such are vulnerable to manipulation. Information processing errors and/or cognitive errors produced by the use of heuristics to simplify complex or unfamiliar questions are also notably common. Valuation practitioners are thus suspended between the desire to be objective and the need to (1) provide information necessary for a more informed examination of value, and (2) ensure that the task is cognitively doable.

Fourth, this conundrum has inspired an ongoing period of innovation. Many now acknowledge that if the method of elicitation affects outcome, it is better to proceed with a framework that clearly exposes the researcher's methodological rationale (be that an axiomatic or preference driven one) and renders visible the context and thinking that lead to the value elicited. Constructed preferences argue further than when valuation practices are simplified or broken down into their component parts such that participants can examine the multifaceted nature of their decision, value elicitation processes become decision-focused exercises wherein the link between a value held, a value assigned, and the support or basis for a final decision or policy is clarified.

Finally, the rebellion against cost-centric approaches is, in part, a rebellion against the overly rationalist language of WTP and benefit–cost analysis generally. The concern is that such discursive frames silence or render invisible expressions of moral conviction, enchantment, awe or the kind of spiritual reverie that underpin the many reasons we value nature.

Ultimately, all valuation exercises must clarify and defend whether they mean to be axiomatic or relativistic, whether they mean to valorize those qualities that are underrepresented or silenced, whether they mean to identify categories of value meaningful to either expert or lay populations versus elicit decisions that are value based, and whether they mean to think of valuation efforts as the summation of individual preferences or the product of group-based deliberation.

Notes

1   In the late 1990s, John Foster (1997) in conjunction with economists and ethicists produced a very fine collection of theoretical work on the subject of environmental values. We mean not to reproduce that work, though some cross-over is inevitable. Instead, we have chosen studies that are classics or summations of classics in the field and from which can be gleaned obvious guidelines for applied design and practice.

2   A good example of the dilemmas faced is the decision not to include work by Kempton, Boster and Hartley (1995), and Atran and colleagues (2002). These scholars have produced decisive work on the subject of cultural models of nature – akin to but not solely an expression of environmental values. The same could be said of Inglehart's (1995) important work on post-materialist values, as this is one of many good quality pieces on specific subcategories of value expression. Further, we were unable to explore the experimental edges of the field including but not limited to that field of economics concerned with sustainability theory.

3   A cautionary note: like any broad-stroke distinction, discussion of these two positions, the axiomatic and the relativistic, is meant to facilitate the reader's grasp of a rich and varied literature; the border between the two approaches is less clear than our portrait implies.

4   Much recent contingent valuation work has abandoned WTP methods in favour of choice processes and the costing of behaviour that is observable or revealed (see especially Farber et al, Chapter 2 in this volume).

5   For a recent review of research on environmental values emphasizing work in social psychology and political science, see Dietz et al (2005).

References

1   Atran, S. Medin, D. Ross, N. Lynch, E. Vapnarsky, V. Ek', E. U. Coley, J. Timura, C. and Baran, M. (2002) 'Folk ecology, cultural epidemiology, and the spirit of the commons: A garden experiment in the Maya lowlands, 1991–2001'. *Current Anthropology*, vol 43, pp421–450

2   Axelrod, L. J. (1994) 'Balancing personal needs with environmental preservation: Identifying the values that guide decisions in ecological dilemmas'. *Journal of Social Issues*, vol 50, pp85–104

3   Baron, J. and Spranca, M. (1997) 'Protected values'. *Organizational Behavior and Human Decision Processes*, vol 70, pp1–16

4   Brosius, P. (1999) 'Analysis and interventions: Anthropological engagements with environmentalism'. *Current Anthropology*, vol 40, pp277–309

5   Brown, T. C. (1984) 'The concept of value in resource allocation'. *Land Economics*, vol 60, pp231–46

6   Callicott, J. B. (1995) 'Environmental ethics: Overview', in Reich, W. T. (ed) *The Preservation of Species*. Princeton University Press, Princeton, NJ, pp138–172

7   Costanza, R. d'Arge, R. deGroot, R. Farber, S. Grasso, M. Hannon, B. et al (1998) 'The value of the world's ecosystem services and natural capital'. *Ecological Economics*, vol 25, pp3–15

8   Dickson, B. (2000) 'The ethicist's conception of environmental problems'. *Environmental Values*, vol 9, pp127–152

9   Dietz, T. Fitzgerald, A. and Shwom, R. (2005) 'Environmental Values'. *Annual Review of Environment and Natural Resources*, vol 30, forthcoming.

10   Dunlap, R. and Van Liere, K. (1978) 'The "New Environmental Paradigm"'. *Journal of Environmental Education*, vol 9, pp10–19

11   Fischhoff, B. (1991) 'Value elicitation: Is there anything in there?' *American Psychologist*, vol 46, pp835–847

12   Gregory, R. (1999) 'Identifying environmental values', in Dale, V. H. and English, M. R. (eds) *Tools to Aid Environmental Decision Making*, Springer-Verlag, New York, pp 32–58

13   Gregory, R. Lichtenstein, S. and Slovic, P. (1993) 'Valuing environmental resources: A constructive approach'. *Journal of Risk and Uncertainty*, vol 7, pp177–197

14   Inglehart, R. (1995) 'Public support for environmental protection: Objective problems and subjective values in forty-three societies'. *PS: Political Science and Politics*, vol 28, pp57–72

15   Keeney, R. L. (1992) *Value-focused Thinking: A Path to Creative Decisionmaking*. Harvard University Press, Cambridge, MA

16   Kellert, S. (1996) *The Value of Life: Biological Diversity and Human Society*. Island Press, Washington, DC

17   Kempton, W. Boster, J. and Hartley, J. (1995) *Environmental Values in American Culture*. Massachusetts Institute of Technology, Cambridge, MA

18   Kraus, S. (1995) 'Attitudes and prediction of behavior: A meta-analysis of the empirical literature'. *Personality and Social Psychology Bulletin*, vol 21, pp58–75

19   Ladd, E. C. and Bowman, K. H. (1995) *Attitudes toward the Environment: Twenty-five Years After Earth Day*. AEI Press, Washington, DC

20   Lockwood, M. (1999) 'Humans valuing nature: Synthesizing insights from philosophy, psychology, and economics'. *Environmental Values*, vol 8, pp381–401

21   Merchant, C. (1992) *Radical Ecology*. Routledge, New York

22   Mitchell, R. C. and Carson, R. T. (1989) *Using Surveys to Value Public Goods: The Contingent Valuation Method*. Resources for the Future, Washington, DC

23   Norton, B. G. (1991) 'Thoreau's insect analogies: Or, why environmentalists hate mainstream economists'. *Environmental Ethics*, vol 13, pp235–251

24   Rokeach, H. (1973) *The Nature of Human Values*. Free Press, New York

25   Rolston, H. I. (1994) *Conserving Natural Value*. Columbia University Press, New York

26   Rolston, H. I. (1999) 'Ethics and the environment', in Baker, E. and Richardson, M. (eds) *Ethics Applied*. Simon and Schuster, New York, pp407–437

27   Satterfield, T. and Gregory, R. (1998) 'Reconciling environmental values and pragmatic choices'. *Society and Natural Resources*, vol 11, pp629–647

28   Suter, G. W. I. (1993) *Ecological Risk Assessment*. Lewis, Boca Raton, LA

29   White, L. Jr (1967) 'The historical roots of our ecological crisis'. *Science*, vol 155, pp1203–1207

Part 1

Economic Themes
in Environmental Values

Introduction

Exploring the full range of economic thought and experimentation that has influenced the environmental values field is a Sisyphean task. Indeed, few constructs have generated more academic print and heated exchange than has the very suggestion that economic value be assigned to nature, which to many is de facto priceless and thus invaluable. Our less ambitious task for this section involves three paramount goals: (1) representation of conventional and newly emerging contingent valuation practices, well laid out by Carson; (2) an overview of the tensions between neoclassical economic approaches and the more 'classical' approach promoted by ecological economists (our debt here is to Spash); and (3) robust coverage of pertinent concepts and applications for the valuing of ecosystem services, offered here by Farber, Costanza and Wilson.

Undoubtedly, the canonical valuation text is Myrick Freeman's *The Measurement of Environmental and Resource Value* (1993). While not reproduced in this volume, it should be noted that Freeman's work is essential to those working to value nonmarket, especially environmental, goods. Importantly, the second edition of *The Measurement* also seeks to integrate both stated and revealed preferences. Freeman's influence is evident in the Carson article reproduced in this section, although the contribution's primary emphasis is a more general discussion of contingent valuation approaches. Of particular interest to Carson is the question of passive or nonconsumptive use. He rightly notes that it was Krutilla (1967) who first drew attention to passive use, often referred to as existence value or bequest [to future generation] value. Passive use includes those instances where one might vicariously enjoy a forest or simply hope that it continues to exist now and in the future without extracting or actively consuming its assets. Capturing and measuring use of this kind poses some of the most vexing problems for valuation scholars. Precisely because some value is not revealed or is difficult to discern through indirect measures (e.g. how much people spend to view the forest) or through stated preferences (willingness to pay (WTP) or similar methods), many problems of validity or technical viability arise. Carson thus helpfully lays out a simple and clear set of economic and design criteria to which a good contingent valuation (CV) study must conform, and in so doing introduces many of the points debated in subsequent chapters. Most relevant are his discussions of key maxims for evaluating the reliability of CV for passive use applications. These include price sensitivity tests, the problem of scoping or embedding effects (does price change with the quantity or scope of the good provided?), the use of open- versus closed-ended pricing scales, and/or the thorny problem of 'warm glow' effects (i.e. when survey respondents state WTP preferences based on the moral satisfaction of contributing to a cause rather their willingness to pay for a habitat improvement – a problem addressed by Kahneman and Knetsch in Chapter 14). Critical attention is also paid to contextualizing choice processes. (How much information is enough? How much is too much? What discursive forms are appropriate?) The sample or size of the population to which a problem applies is also crucial, as is the mode of survey delivery, be it mail, in-person interview or phone. The cumulative result of this elegant piece is to provide the reader with a rich picture of the kind of thought and problem solving that must underpin any good CV study.

Farber, Costanza and Wilson focus the reader's attention on the valuation task first raised by biologists: How might we recognize and thereafter value ecosystem services? Borrowing from Aldo Leopold's (1949) concept of intrinsic value as expressed in his land ethic, value for this group of practitioners is defined as 'the contribution of an action or object ... to maintaining the health or integrity of an ecosystem or species irrespective of human satisfaction' (p376). In defending this meaning of value, the authors offer a succinct intellectual history of the term, arguing for an objective (not subjective) definition that allows for the possibility of both higher order values and trade-off limitations (e.g. when one confronts an ecosystem function hence value that one cannot live without). This leads to a discussion of the classical notion of physical commodities in which values are derived from a good's properties and not simply preference or utility maximization per se. This line of argument suggests that some goods should be valued in reference to their service value *only*, a value that might in turn trump anthropocentric preferences and, more broadly, the principle of 'consumer sovereignty'. Farber, Costanza and Wilson also consider pertinent definitions of value drawn from the natural sciences, including evolutionary value (the ability to generate genetic diversity, promote natural selection or transmit genetic information); co-evolutionary value (one species' value to the survival of another); and an energy theory of value, which is logically parallel to thermodynamic principles. Finally, the principle of value thresholds is introduced thereby raising the possibility that loss of some functions may have a nonlinear effect in that small perturbations may result in dramatic changes to (or irreversible delivery of) services. Ultimately, in this contribution, it becomes apparent that the clash between ecological and neoclassic definitions of value is fundamental indeed and many now largely reject definitions of value based solely upon consumer preference.

In the last article in Part 1, Spash also turns to an intellectual history of economics and the concept of value to explore the possibilities for alternatives to mainstream economics. He argues that ecological economics is in fact a synthesis of several much older economic theories including those focused on ethics and classical political economy. He regards the ecological economics movement as begun by a cluster of economists attendant to system limits and or sceptical of the principle of ecosystem service substitutability. Yet, he is also interested in distinguishing the different practices and trains of thought within this diverse subfield. Among the distinctions are those between classical economists, agricultural economists, resource and welfare economics, and ecological economics. His article is superb for its flavour of the disciplinary upheavals captured by this field and for the implications for study of different definitions of value. Interestingly, Spash pays express attention to the cross-disciplinary fervour generated by these debates, and the ways in which ecology has fundamentally shaken if not altered the premise on which most economics and benefit–cost analysis is founded. The problem at hand, he finds, is not simply a matter of methodological adjustment but rather goes to the heart of economic orthodoxy and so renders questionable concepts such as discounting and the very moral standing of environmental goods as commodifiable in the first place. His is a provocative piece that fittingly encourages the chapters that follow, be they focused on ethics, human behaviour and morality, or cognitive biases and the limits to human-centric choice and decision processes.

Terre Satterfield and Linda Kalof

References

1   Freedman, M. (1993) *The Measurement of Environmental and Resource Value, Second Edition.* Resources for the Future, Washington, DC
2   Krutilla, J. (1967) 'Conservation reconsidered'. *American Economic Review,* vol 57, pp777–786
3   Leopold, A. (1949) *A Sand County Almanac, with Essays from Round River.* Ballantine, New York

1

Contingent Valuation: A User's Guide

Richard T. Carson

Introduction

The essence of an economic analysis is to compare *all* of the benefits of the proposed action to *all* of the costs [1], with a project said to pass a benefit–cost test if the sum of all the benefits is greater than the sum of all the costs. Such an analysis is seriously defective without monetary values for the environmental amenities and services (hereafter 'goods') affected by a proposed action. The central problem in the application of standard economic tools to the provision of environmental goods, whether indirectly through regulation or directly through public provision, is placing a monetary value on them. Because these goods are not routinely bought and sold in the market, actual cost/sales information is seldom available. Economists have developed a variety of techniques to value nonmarket amenities consistent with the valuation of marketed goods. These techniques are based upon either observed behaviour (revealed preferences) toward some marketed good with a connection to the nonmarketed good of interest or stated preferences in surveys with respect to the nonmarket good [2]. The stated preference approach is frequently referred to as contingent valuation [3, 4] especially when it is used in the context of environmental amenities. The use of contingent valuation (CV) has engendered a heated debated [5] between proponents [6] and critics [7].

A CV survey constructs scenarios that offer different possible future government actions. Survey respondents are then asked to *state* their preferences concerning those actions. The choices made by survey respondents are then analysed in a similar manner as the choices made by consumers in actual markets. In both cases, economic value is derived from choices observed either in an actual market or in the hypothetical market created in the survey.

Under the simplest and most commonly used CV question format, the respondent is offered a binary choice between two alternatives, one being the status quo policy and the other alternative policy having a cost greater than maintaining the status quo. The respondent is told that the government will impose the stated cost (e.g. increased taxes, higher prices associated with regulation, or user fees) if the non-status-quo alternative is

Note: Reprinted with permission from Carson, R. T. (2000) 'Contingent valuation: A user's guide'. *Environmental Science Technology*, vol 34, pp1413–1418, Copyright © 2000 American Chemical Society.

provided. The key elements here are that the respondent provides a 'favour/not favour' answer with respect to the alternative policy (versus the status quo), where what the alternative policy will provide, how it will be provided, and how much it will cost have been clearly specified.

Random assignment of cost numbers to respondents allows the researcher to trace out the distribution willingness to pay (WTP) for the good. The percentage of the relevant public willing to pay different amounts is determined in much the same way as a dose–response experiment in biology or medicine [8, 9]. When a parametric functional form is assumed for the WTP distribution, summary statistics such as mean and median WTP can be estimated.

WTP is one of the two standard measures of economic value. It is the appropriate measure in the situation where an agent wants to acquire a good. Minimum willingness to accept (WTA) compensation is the appropriate measure in a situation where an agent is being asked to voluntarily give up a good. Both of these measures are Hicksian consumer surplus measures and are often defined net of the price actually paid or received. Whether WTP or WTA is the correct measure depends on the property right to the good. If the consumer does not currently have the environmental good and does not have a legal entitlement to it, the correct property right is WTP. If the consumer has a legal entitlement to it and is being asked to give up that entitlement, the correct property right is WTA. For marketed goods, theoretically the difference between the two measures should generally be small and unimportant [10] as long as income effects and transaction costs are not large. For nonmarketed goods, this may not be the case [11] as the difference between WTP and WTA is also dependent upon the substitutability of the nonmarketed good for goods available on the market.

CV has been in use for over 35 years, and there are now over 2000 papers and studies dealing with the topic [12]. Illustrative applications of CV to estimated benefits include the following: increasing air and water quality; reduced risk from drinking water and ground water contaminants; outdoor recreation; protecting wetlands, wilderness areas, endangered species, and cultural heritage sites; improvements in public education and public utility reliability; reduction of food and transportation risks and health care queues; and provision of basic environmental services such as drinking water and garbage pickup in developing countries. While the most visible applications are those for natural resource damage assessments such as the *Exxon Valdez* oil spill [13], the vast majority of CV applications have been undertaken for the purpose of assisting in policy evaluations.

CV is used by most federal agencies with environmental responsibilities and by many state agencies. CV studies have been conducted in over 50 countries by government agencies and international organizations. One indication of the importance of CV can be seen by looking at Environmental Valuation Reference Inventory (EVRI), a large online database currently being assembled for policy-making purposes by Environment Canada, as a cooperative venture undertaken with the European Union, the US EPA, the environmental protection agencies of Chile and Mexico, the World Bank, and the Economy and Environment Program for South East Asia (http://www.evri.ec.gc.ca/evri/). As of December 1999, that database contained 524 studies based upon stated preferences, 255 studies based upon revealed preferences, and 123 studies based upon actual costs.

The debate over the use of CV has two major thrusts. The first one is largely philosophical revolving around whether so-called passive-use or existence values should be included in an economic analysis [14]. Economists have traditionally thought of marketed goods where it is necessary for a consumer to physically use a good to get utility from it. However, it is possible for consumers to get utility from a good without physically using it. Such uses have become known as passive-uses, and without their inclusion, goods such as a remote wilderness area have little or no economic value. The use of CV is central to this debate, as it is the standard and often the only approach that can include passive-use values. The second debate, a largely technical one, revolves around what economic criteria the results of a CV study should meet. Much of this debate concerns the merits of particular tests and whether various phenomena are anomalies from the perspective of economic theory, and if so. whether they are peculiar to particular studies or CV practices [15] or symptomatic of more general problems with CV [7]. Because CV studies range from very good to very bad, the key factors that an informed user should examine in making an initial assessment about the quality of a particular study are discussed below.

Inclusion of Passive-Use Considerations

WTP and WTA are defined without regard to an agent's motives and as such are synonymous with what has been termed 'total' economic value. For market goods, it is generally considered necessary to directly use a good, often by consuming it or physically interacting with it, for the good to have economic value to the agent. This is not the case for many environmental goods where it is possible to passively use the good.

Consideration of passive-use value in an economic analysis is due to Krutilla's [16] seminal observation that many people value natural wonders simply for their existence. Krutilla argued that these people obtain utility through vicarious enjoyment of these areas and, as a result, had a positive WTP for the government to exercise good stewardship of the land. These values have been called bequest value, look-existence value, intrinsic value, inherent value, passive-use value, stewardship value, and nonuse value. The term *passive-use* value was popularized in the important 1989 US Appellate Court decision, *Ohio* vs *Department of Interior,* which mandated that such values be included in a natural resource damage assessment to the extent that they can be reliably measured.

Without the inclusion of passive-use considerations, *pure public goods,* including overall level of air quality, national defence, and remote wilderness areas, have little or no measured economic value. Pure public goods are those for which it is impossible to exclude people from enjoying the good and from which enjoyment by one person does not degrade another person's enjoyment of the good. Pure public goods are typically, but not always, provided by government. (Quasi-public goods are those provided for by the government, like a Forest Service campground, from which it is possible and often desirable to exclude people.) The value of pure public goods cannot be assessed by traditional economic techniques because they effectively work by looking at differences in quantities of a good consumed as a function of differences in prices. For a pure public good, all people experience the same level of the good.

A CV survey can create an idealized market for a pure public good whereby respondents face a choice between two different quantities of the good. The usual example is the status quo level of the good versus an alternative level that will entail a specified cost increase. Any particular good can have both direct-use and passive-use values. The exact dividing line between direct-use and passive-use is to some degree dependent upon knowledge of physical and biological linkages and upon what activities of consumers are observed. For instance, while swimming in a lake obviously involves direct water contact, connecting the distant wetlands necessary to support a duck hunter may be difficult. Even in the quintessential example of lost passive-use, harm from the *Exxon Valdez* spill to households outside Alaska, household news-watching behaviour was influenced by spill coverage [17].

The estimate inferred from the contingent market described in the survey will generally be an estimate of total economic value (WTP or WTA). Any estimate of total economic value includes both direct-use and passive-use considerations. Efforts to disaggregate these two components, however, have been shown to be problematic [14].

There are three well-articulated viewpoints with respect to the inclusion of passive-use: (a) that passive-use values are irrelevant to decision making [18], (b) that passive-use values cannot be monetized but should be taken account of as a political matter or by having experts decide [19], and (c) that passive-use values can be reliably measured and should explicitly be taken into account [20]. The first position is hard to defend from an economic perspective. Failure to consider passive-use value is clearly inconsistent with economic theory if the objective is to maximize public welfare in any well-defined sense as pure public goods would clearly be under-supplied. The difference between the second and third position depends largely upon whether one wants the monetary value the policy-maker placed on the good to be kept implicit [21] rather than explicitly disclosed, whether one wants the preferences of experts or the public, and one's view on whether CV techniques can be reliably implemented.

Technical Issues Surrounding the Use of CV

The measure of economic value produced by a CV study should conform to several different economic criteria; various tests of these have been proposed. Much of the technical debate is over whether failure to satisfy one or more of these tests in a particular CV study is indicative of a problem with that particular CV study or of problems with CV generally. This debate exists because there is considerable variation in CV practices and results. Critics sometimes fail to see that economic theory often predicts that these practices should influence the results [15]. Furthermore, some suggested tests (especially large split-sample comparisons) are very expensive to implement; hence, all available tests are not performed in any particular study.

Concerns raised by CV critics over the reliability of the CV approach led the National Oceanic and Atmospheric Administration (NOAA) to convene a panel of eminent experts co-chaired by Nobel Prize winners Kenneth Arrow and Robert Solow to examine the issue. In January 1993, the Panel, after a lengthy public hearing and reviewing many written submissions, issued a report which concluded that 'CV studies can produce estimates reliable enough to be the starting point for a judicial or administrative determination of natural resource damages – including lost passive-use value' [22]. The

Panel suggested guidelines for use in natural resource damage assessment legal cases to help ensure the reliability of CV surveys on passive-use values including the use of in-person interviews, a binary discrete choice question, a careful description of the good and its substitutes, and several different tests that should be included in the report on the survey results. The Panel suggested several topics needing further research. Since the Panel issued its report, many empirical tests have been conducted, and several key theoretical issues have been clarified.

The simplest test corresponds to a well-known economic maxim: the higher the cost, the lower the demand. In the binary discrete choice format, this can be easily tested by observing whether the percentage favouring the project falls as the randomly assigned cost of the project increases. This price sensitivity test has rarely failed in empirical applications.

The test that has attracted the most attention in recent years is whether the WTP estimates from CV studies increase in a plausible manner with the quantity or scope of the good being provided [23, 24]. CV critics often argue that the lack of sensitivity to scope, or embedding as it is sometimes called, results from what they term 'warm-glow' by which they mean getting moral satisfaction from the act of paying for the good independent of the characteristics of the actual environmental good [23]. Several well-known examples in the literature show insensitivity to the scope of the good being valued [25]; other examples show substantial sensitivity to the good's scope [26]. There have now been a considerable number of tests of the scope insensitivity hypothesis, and a recent review of the empirical evidence suggests that the hypothesis is rejected in a large majority of the tests performed [27].

There are two difficulties with the warm-glow explanation for embedding. The first, while warm-glow is a well-defined concept in the economic literature with clear implications for giving to private charities, its relevance to public provision of environmental goods via taxation requires that agents get utility from the act of paying higher taxes [28]. The second is that the term embedding has multiple meanings as used in the nonmarket valuation literature [24]. Specifically, it has been used to refer to an insensitivity of estimates to the scope of the good being valued as well as a sensitivity of the estimates to the order in which they are valued. Under the latter phenomena, the value of a particular good tends to fall, often substantially, as it is valued further out in a sequence of goods. Having the value of the good differ depending upon the order in which it is valued is disturbing to many policymakers. However, such an effect is predicted by economic theory due to the substitution possibilities between the goods and the reduction in disposable income that occurs with the purchase of each new good [29]. This dependence on the order in which a good is valued is simply one manifestation of why political control of the agenda (e.g. the order in which issues are considered) is so important.

A major focus of the technical debate concerning CV has been on the choice of the particular format used to elicit information about the respondent's preferences. Different question formats are used. For instance, a binary discrete choice question versus an open-ended question that asks the respondent directly for their WTP for the good may result in different estimates, with estimates from binary discrete choice questions being higher than those from open-ended questions. The argument made by some is that if agents had well-defined preferences for the good, both formats should result in similar estimates [30]. The counter argument, which comes from the economic theory on mechanism design, is that incentives for truthful preference revelation are different for these two formats, and as consequence, one should expect the estimates should be different with the binary discrete choice question predicted to yield truthful responses [31] if other conditions typically associated with a referendum are met.

Another major focus of the technical debate has been comparing estimates from CV surveys to estimates from other methods [32]. Most available comparisons are for quasi-public goods such as outdoor recreation. CV estimates tend to be slightly lower and highly correlated with corresponding estimates based upon revealed preference methods such as travel cost analysis where differentials in the cost of getting to a recreation site implicitly define a demand curve for the site or hedonic pricing where the environmental good is bundled into a marketed good like a house [33]. For private goods, surveys tend to predict higher purchase levels than actually observed [34], which is the same as the result from comparing survey indications of willingness to make voluntary contributions and actual contributions to provide a public good [33]. In the public arena, however, surveys taken close to an election tend to provide quite good predictions of the actual vote [35], and when large changes are seen in the per cent favouring a ballot measure over time, it is usually due to grossly disproportionate expenditures by the measure's opponents [36].

There are several other issues surrounding the use of CV. These include the related issues of yea-saying, protest zeros, nay-saying and calibration. Yea-saying is manifested when a respondent says yes to an amount in order to please the interviewer even though the respondent's WTP is less than the amount asked about [4]. Protest zeros occur when a respondent who has a positive WTP for a good gives a response of US$0 to an question that requests an actual WTP response even though the respondent has a positive WTP for the good [4]. A variety of explanations for protest zeros ranging from rejection of the legitimacy of the scenario presented to strategic behaviour have been put forth. When asking discrete choice questions, the corresponding phenomenon is sometimes labelled nay-saying [4]. This occurs when the respondent provides a no response to an amount asked even though WTP is greater than the amount asked about. The presence of 'untruthful' responses, for whatever reason, leads to arguments that contingent valuation responses should be 'calibrated' to potentially correct for either an upward or downward bias [37]. An interesting adjunct to this issue is the issue of how to combine data from both the stated and the revealed preference approaches [38, 39] and how to perform benefit transfers [40]. Some economists and psychologists have raised the larger issue of whether respondents have well-defined economic preferences for many goods. The interested reader is directed to refs 41–43 for lively discussions and exchanges on whether such problems generally exist, and if so, how they should be handled.

Assessing the Quality of a CV Study

The first consideration in evaluating the quality of a CV study is the survey instrument. A good CV survey should have what is known as 'face validity'. The good and the scenario under which it would be provided should be described clearly and accurately, and the trade off that the respondent is asked to make should be a plausible one. The respondent should be provided with enough information to make an informed decision but not be overwhelmed with it.

Most good CV surveys contain the following: (a) an introductory section that helps set the general context for the decision to be made; (b) a detailed description of the good to be offered to the respondent; (c) the institutional setting in which the good will be provided; (d) the manner in which the good will be paid for; (e) a method by which the survey elicits the respondent's preferences with respect to the good; (f) debriefing questions about why respondents answered certain questions the way that they did; and (g) a set of questions regarding respondent characteristics including attitudes and demographic information. Estimates from studies with vaguely described goods and vaguely defined or implausible payment obligations should be carefully scrutinized for their relevance [44].

Producing a good CV survey instrument requires substantial development work [4, 44, 45]. This work typically including focus groups and in-depth interviews to help determine the plausibility and understandability of the good and the scenario being presented. The task of translating technical material into a form understood by the general public is often a difficult one. Developing a useful CV survey instrument requires the research team to clearly define what the proposed project will produce in terms of outputs that people care about in language they understand. Pretests and pilot studies are conducted to assess how well the survey works as a whole, with some elements of the survey usually needing redesign to improve respondent understanding.

Second, the particular population sampled should be the relevant one for evaluating the benefits and/or costs of the proposed project. The size of the population over which benefits and costs accrue can be one of the major factors in determining a good's economic value. For a pure public good, the economic value of a good is simply the sum of the WTP of all agents in the relevant population, since enjoyment of the good by one agent does not diminish any other agent's enjoyment of it [1].

Third, survey data are typically highly variable when trying to measure a continuous variable (e.g. income or hours worked), and CV survey data are no exception. A sample size on the order of several hundred to a couple thousand observations is generally required to achieve reasonable reliability from a sampling (confidence interval) perspective. All members of the relevant population should have a positive and known probability of being included in the sample. If inclusion probabilities are not equal, an appropriate set of weights is needed.

Fourth, consider the mode of survey administration and the survey's response rate. The NOAA Panel [22] recommends in-person interviews in part because visual materials such as maps and pictures that facilitate respondent understanding can be used. Mail and telephone surveys are dramatically cheaper and should not be dismissed out of hand. Mail surveys tend to suffer from sample selection bias, because those returning the surveys are typically more interested in the issue than those who do not. Such respondents are more likely to provide extreme WTP responses than a randomly chosen individual. Furthermore, households who move into an area tend not to be included in the original sample. Telephone surveys have severe drawbacks if the good is complicated or visual aids are needed, and response rates from random-digit-dialled telephone surveys are becoming harder to calculate due to the increasing number of computer and fax lines. A high response rate to a survey (currently in the 60–80 per cent range for the surveys of the general population) helps minimize potential problems with extrapolating to the population of interest. A variety of weighting and imputation procedures are available to help correct for the inevitable deviations from the desired sample, and there are statistical methods to help correct for sample selection bias [46].

Fifth, there are other more mundane aspects of the survey instrument and its administration that a reader should examine. For all administration modes, look at how non-respondents were treated and the effort expended to convert initial refusals. For in-person interviews, professional interviewers should be used. For mail surveys, the adequacy of the original mailing list should be examined. With respect to the unit of observation, the household is generally more appropriate if a payment vehicle like higher taxes or utility bills is used; while the converse is true of payments that take the form of entrance fees. Was the payment described as a lump sum or a continuing payment? With respect to payment frequency, a one-time payment generally produces more conservative estimates since it does not offer the opportunity to spread payments over time. A one-time payment is appropriate in cases where providing the good represents a one-time event, but not in cases, like local air pollution, for which ongoing easily visible actions must be taken. Was the respondent asked for information about WTP or WTA? WTA questions are usually much harder to successfully implement due to the need to convince respondents of the legitimacy of giving up an environmental good, but they often represent the correct property rights perspective.

We have focused substantial attention on the survey aspects of a CV study because care in handling them usually reflects care in dealing with other aspects of the study. Studies that do not follow good survey practices often produce results that are difficult to use and to interpret [44].

Most studies construct an equation that predicts WTP for the good as a function of several other variables in surveys, such as income, past recreational use, and various attitude and knowledge questions concerning the good. An equation with reasonable explanatory power and coefficients with the expected signs provides evidence in support of the proposition that the survey has measured the intended construct. If this is not the case, either the research team has failed to collect the relevant covariates in the survey, suggesting inadequate development work, or the WTP responses are random and completely useless.

CV results can be quite sensitive to the treatment of potential outliers. Open-ended survey questions typically elicit a large number of so-called protest zeros and a small number of extremely high responses. Inference about the right tally of the WTP distribution is often problematic as only a very small fraction of the population having extreme high values for a good can dramatically influence mean WTP. In discrete choice CV questions, econometric modelling assumptions can often have a substantial influence on the results obtained [9]. It is particularly critical to allow for the possibility of a spike in the WTP distribution at zero [47] and to account for income constraint on WTP [48]. Any careful analysis will involve a series of judgemental decisions about how to handle specific issues involving the data. These decisions should be clearly noted.

Finally, the distribution of economic value on a per-capita basis should appear reasonable. For estimates based on the general population rather than a specific population (like hunters), many respondents are likely to be unwilling to pay anything for the good.

For most environmental goods, WTP distributions will be quite asymmetric with mean WTP larger than median WTP, in part because the income distribution is asymmetric and in part because there is often a sizable part of the population that is fairly indifferent to the environmental good and a smaller group that care a great deal about its provision. Mean WTP is the traditional measure used in benefit–cost analysis, while median WTP, which corresponds to the flat amount that would receive majority approval, is a standard public choice criterion. There is no single 'correct' measure independent of the purpose for which it is being used. Typically, the entire WTP distribution will be of interest to policy-makers. The degree of precision necessary for the CV results to provide a useful input to the decision making process can vary substantially. In some instances only a rough order of magnitude comparison between benefits and costs may be required, while in other instances relatively small changes in an estimate may influence the preferred outcome. This consideration should be reflected in the sample size chosen and the effort put into survey design.

Conclusion

The recent debate surrounding the use of CV is, to some degree, simply a reflection of the large sums at stake in major environmental decisions involving passive-use and the general distrust that some economists have for information collected from surveys. Outside of academic journals, criticism of CV has taken a largely anecdotal form, ridiculing the results of particular CV studies, many of which use techniques known to be problematic. The implication drawn is that all CV surveys produce nonsense results upon which no reasonable person would rely. In an academic context, however, the debate over the use of CV has been more productive. The spotlight placed upon CV has matured it; its theoretical foundations and limits to its uses are now better understood. A carefully done CV study can provide much useful information to policymakers.

Much CV research, however, still needs to be conducted. Perhaps the most pressing need is on how to reduce the cost of CV surveys while still maintaining a high degree of reliability. Current state-of-the-art practices are very expensive and, hence, impractical to implement in many situations where information on the benefits and cost of environmental aspects of policies are badly needed. The cost of state-of-the-art CV surveys stems from their use of (a) extensive development work to determine how the public views the good, (b) in-person interviews, (c) full probability sampling designs, (d) large samples, (e) extensive visual presentations of the good and its method of provision, and (f) a single binary discrete choice question. Items a–e are largely survey design and administration issues. It is possible to cut development costs and time for any specific CV survey by implementation of research programmes designed at solving some of the more generic representation issues such as low-level risk [49] or large-scale ecosystems [50]. Combination telephone-mail-telephone surveys (where a random sample of respondents is first recruited by phone, mailed the visual aids for the CV survey, and then asked the CV survey question by phone) hold promise in terms of substantially reducing survey administration costs while retaining many of the advantages of a high quality in-person survey. Item f is currently the focus of substantial research. One can generalize the binary discrete choice question in two general directions: getting more information about the interval where the respondent's value for the good lies or asking the respondent about different but related goods. The first approach has long been used in CV surveys in the form of asking one or more repeated binary discrete choice questions or for the respondent's actual WTP amount. It can substantially decrease the number of observations needed for a given level of statistical precision. The second of these approaches is becoming increasingly popular in the environmental valuation literature [51] and is often referred to as choice-based conjoint analysis, a term from the marketing literature [52]. Under this approach, respondents are asked to pick their most favoured out of a set of three or more alternatives and are typically given multiple sets of choice questions. This practice can provide substantially more information about a range of possible alternative policies as well as reduce the sample size needed. Survey design issues with the choice-based conjoint approach are often much more complex due to the number of goods that must be described and the statistical models that must be employed. A drawback of both of these approaches is that they provide increased incentives for strategic behaviour on the part of survey respondents. Assessments of the trade offs involved in the use of these and other stated preference approaches to placing a monetary value on nonmarketed goods are currently underway.

Acknowledgements

Partial support for this work came from US Environmental Protection Agency Grant R-824698. The views expressed in the papers are those of the author and not necessarily those of the US Environmental Protection Agency. The author wishes to thank the reviewers for helpful comments.

References

1 Just, R., Hueth, D. and Schmidt, A. (1982) *Applied Welfare Economics*, Prentice-Hall, NY
2 Freeman, A. M. (1993) *The Measurement of Environmental and Resource Values: Theory and Methods*, Resources for the Future, Washington, DC
3 Cummings, R. G., Brookshire, D. S. and Schulze, W. D. (1986) *Valuing Environmental Goods: An Assessment of the Contingent Valuation Method*, Rowman and Allenheld, Totowa, NJ
4 Mitchell, R. C. and Carson, R. T. (1995) 'Current Issues in the Design, Administration, and Analysis of Contingent Valuation Surveys', in Johansson, P. O., Kristrom, B. and Maler, K. G. (eds) *Current Issues in Environmental Economics*, Manchester University Press, Manchester, UK
5 Portney, P. (1994) *Journal of Economic Perspectives*, vol 8(4), p3
6 Hanemann, W. M. (1994) *Journal of Economic Perspectives*, vol 8(4), p19
7 Diamond, P. and Hausman, J. (1994) *Journal of Economic Perspectives*, vol 8(4), p45
8 Cameron, T. A. (1988) *Journal of Environmental and Economic Management*, vol 15, p355
9 Hanemann, W. M. and Kanninen, B. (1999) 'The statistical analysis of discrete-response', in Bateman, I. and Willis, K. (eds) *Valuing the Environment Preferences*, Oxford University Press, Oxford, UK

10 Willig, R. D. (1976) *American Economic Review,* vol 66, pp589
11 Hanemann, W. M. (1991) *American Economic Review,* vol 81, p635
12 Carson, R. T. et al (1995) *A Bibliography of Contingent Valuation Papers and Studies.* NRDA, La Jolla, CA
13 Carson, R. T. et al (1992) *A Contingent Valuation Study of Lost Passive Use Values Resulting From the Exxon Valdez Oil Spill,* Report to State of Alaska, November
14 Carson, R. T., Flores, N. E. and Mitchell, R. C. (1999) 'Theory and measurement of passive-use value' in Bateman, I., Willis, K. (eds)*Valuing the Environment Preferences,* Oxford University Press, Oxford, UK
15 Randall, A. (1998) *Resource Energy Economics,* vol 20, p197
16 Krutilla, J. (1967) *American Economic Rev*iew, vol 57, p777
17 Farrow, S. and Larson, D. M. (1967) *AERE Newsletter* May, p12.
18 Rosenthal, R. H. and Nelson, D. H. (1992) *Journal of Policy Analysis and Management,* vol 11, p116
19 Quiggan, J. (1993) *Journal of Policy Analysis and Management,* vol 12, p195
20 Kopp, R. (1992) *Journal of Policy and Analytical Management,* vol 11, p123
21 Cropper, M. et al (1992) *Journal of Policy and Economics,* vol 100, p175
22 Arrow, K. et al (1993) *Federal Register,* vol 58, p4601
23 Kahneman, D. and Knetsch, J. (1992) *Journal of Environmental and Economic Management,* vol 22, p57
24 Carson, R. T. and Mitchell, R. C. (1995) *Journal of Environmental and Economic Management,* vol 28, p155
25 Boyle, K. et al (1994) *Journal of Environmental and Economic Management,* vol 27, p64
26 Smith, V. K. and Osborne, L. L. (1996 *Journal of Environmental and Economic Management,* vol 31, p287
27 Carson, R. T. (1997) 'Contingent valuation and tests of insensitivity to scope', in Kopp, R., Pommerhene, W. and Schwartz, N. (eds) *Determining the Value of Non-Marketed Goods: Economic, Psychological, and Policy Relevant Aspects of Contingent Valuation Methods,* Kluwer, Amsterdam
28 Chilton, S. M. and Hutchinson, W. G. (1999 *Journal of Environmental and Economic Management,* vol 37, p202
29 Carson, R. T., Flores, N. and Hanemann, W. M. (1998) *Journal of Environmental and Economic Management,* vol 36, p314
30 Boyle, K. J. et al (1996) 'Valuing public goods: Discrete versus continuous contingent-valuation responses', *Land Economics,* vol 72, pp381–396
31 Hoehn, J. and Randall, A. J. (1987) *Journal of Environmental and Economic Management,* vol 14, p226
32 Hanemann, W. M. (1995) 'Contingent Valuation and Economics', in Willis, K. G. and Corkindale, J. T. (eds) *Environmental Valuation New Perspectives,* CAB International, Oxford, UK
33 Carson, R. T. et al (1996) *Land Economics,* vol 72, p80
34 Cummings, R. et al (1995) *American Economic Review,* vol 85, p260
35 Asher, H. (1998) *Polling the Public,* 4th ed. Congressional Quarterly Press, Washington, DC
36 Cronin, T. E. (1989) *Direct Democracy: The Politics of* I· *·iative, Referendum, and Recall.* Harvard University Press, Cambridge, MA
37 Blackburn, M., Harrison, G. W. and Rutstrom, E. E. (1994) *American Journal of Agricultural Economics,* vol 76, p1084.
38 Cameron, T. A. (1992) *Land Economics,* vol 68, p302
39 Adamowicz, W. et al (1994) *Journal of Environmental Economic Management,* vol 26, p27

40 Loomis, J. (1992) *Water Resource Research*, vol 28, p701
41 Bjornstad, D. and Kahn, J. (eds) (1996) *The Contingent Valuation of Environmental Resources: Methodological Issues and Research Needs*. Edward Elgar, Brookfield, VT
42 Bateman, I. and Willis, K. (eds) (1999) *Valuing the Environment Preferences: Theory and Practice of the Contingent Valuation Method in the US, EC and Developing Countries*. Oxford University Press, Oxford, UK
43 Hausman, J. (ed) (1993) *Contingent Valuation: A Critical Assessment*. Elsevier, Amsterdam
44 Mitchell, R. C. and Carson, R. T. (1989) *Using Surveys to Value Public Goods: The Contingent Valuation Method*, Resources for the Future, Washington, DC
45 Chilton, S. G. and Hutchinson W. G. (1995) *Journal of Economic Psychology*, vol 20, p465
46 Greene, W. H. (2000) *Econometric Analysis*, 4th ed. Prentice-Hall, NY
47 Kristrom, B. (1997) *American Journal of Agricultural Economics*, vol 79, p1013
48 Haab, T. C. and McConnell, K. E. (1998) *Land Economics*, vol 74, p216
49 Beattie, J. et al (1998) *Journal of Risk and Uncertainty*, vol 17, p5
50 Kramer, R. A. and Mercer, D. E. (1997) *Land Economics*, vol 73, p196
51 Adamowicz, W. L. et al (1999) 'Stated preference methods for valuing environmental amenities', in Bateman, I. and Willis, K. (eds) *Valuing the Environment Preferences*, Oxford University Press, Cambridge, MA
52 Louviere, J. J. 'Conjoint analysis', in Bagozzi, R. (ed) *Advanced Methods in Marketing Research*, Blackwell, Oxford

2

Economic and Ecological Concepts for Valuing Ecosystem Services

Stephen C. Farber, Robert Costanza
and Matthew A. Wilson

Definitions

The terms 'value system', 'value', and 'valuation' have a range of meanings in different disciplines. In this paper, we provide a practical synthesis of these concepts in order to address the issue of valuation of ecosystem services. We want to be clear about how we use these terms throughout our analysis. 'Value systems' refer to intrapsychic constellations of norms and precepts that guide human judgement and action. They refer to the normative and moral frameworks people use to assign importance and necessity to their beliefs and actions. Because 'value systems' frame how people assign rights to things and activities, they also imply practical objectives and actions. We use the term 'value' to mean the contribution of an action or object to user-specified goals, objectives or conditions (Costanza, 2000). A specific value of that action or object is tightly coupled with a user's value system because the latter determines the relative importance of an action or object to others within the perceived world. We define 'valuation' as the process of expressing a value for a particular action or object. In the current context, ecosystem valuation represents the process of expressing a value for ecosystem goods or services (i.e. biodiversity, flood protection, recreational opportunity), thereby providing the opportunity for scientific observation and measurement.

The distinction between intrinsic and instrumental value is an important one (Goulder et al, 1997). On the one hand, some individuals might maintain a value system in which ecosystems or species have intrinsic rights to a healthful, sustaining condition that is on a par with human rights to satisfaction. The value of any action or object is measured by its contribution to maintaining the health and integrity of an ecosystem or species, per se, irrespective of human satisfaction. Some interpret Leopold's (1949) land ethic as constituting an intrinsic value system, where something is 'right when it tends to preserve the integrity, stability and beauty of the biotic community. It is wrong when it tends otherwise'. On the other hand, instrumental values reflect the difference that something makes to satisfaction of human preferences. Instrumental values,

Note: Reprinted from *Ecological Economics*, vol 41, Farber, S. C., Costanza, R. and Wilson, M. A., 'Economic and ecological concepts for valuing ecosystem services', pp375–392, Copyright © (2002), with permission from Elsevier

such as economic values, are fundamentally *anthropocentric* in nature. Policies toward the environment will always tend to be based on a mix of intrinsic and instrumental value systems. In this paper, we deal with both.

Economic Concepts of Value

The history of economic thought is replete with struggles to establish the meaning of value; what is it and how is it measured. Aristotle first distinguished between value in use and value in exchange. The paradox of *use* versus *exchange* value remained unresolved until the 16th century (Schumpeter, 1978). The diamond-water paradox observed that while water has infinite or indefinite value, being necessary for life, its exchange value is low; yet unessential diamonds bear a high exchange value. Following this observation, there was widespread recognition of the distinction between exchange value and use value of goods. Galiani defined value to mean a relation of subjective equivalence between a quantity of one commodity and a quantity of another. He noted that this value depends on *Utility* and *Scarcity* (utilita et rarita) (Schumpeter, 1978). Two hundred years later, Adam Smith distinguished between exchange value and use value of goods by citing the diamond-water paradox, but used it to dismiss use value as a basis for exchange value. Smith formulated a cost of production theory of value, whereby wages, profit and rent are the three original sources of exchange value. In his famous beaver-deer example he suggested a labour theory of exchange value: if it takes twice the labour to kill a beaver than to kill a deer, one beaver will sell for as much as two deer. He also suggested a labour-disutility theory of exchange value, noting that goods exchange based upon the unpleasantness of the labour required to bring the goods to market. However, it is significant to note that Smith limited his labour theory to 'that early and rude state of society which precedes both the accumulation of stock and the appropriation of land'. In other words, when labour is the only scarce factor, goods will exchange based upon the ratio of labour use (Schumpeter, 1978).

In addition to formulating his hypothesis regarding the origins of exchange value, Smith sought to establish a unit of measure of value, or what he termed the real measure or real price of a good. He proposed that 'labour alone … never varying in its own value, is alone the ultimate and real standard' of the values of all commodities. Hence labour could be a numeraire, and it had special properties of invariant value (Schumpeter, 1978).

Ricardo also sought an invariant unit of measure for value. He felt that there was no commodity, including labour, whose exchange value could serve as an invariant standard to measure the variation in exchange values of other commodities. And it was not possible to add up commodities to measure national wealth or production with only exchange ratios. According to Ricardo, this measure must be invariant to changes in relative factor rewards, i.e. capital versus labour, and be a commodity whose capital and labour use did not vary over time, i.e. no technological change. He proposed that both wheat and gold possessed these properties (Blaug, 1968). While not creating value they could measure value.

While Ricardo had several followers, including J. S. Mill and Marx, labour theories of value and the pursuit of an invariant standard of value waned in the late 19th century.

This was partially in response to the logic of the utilitarians, such as Menger, Gossen, Jevons and Walras, who argued that exchange value was based on both utility and scarcity (Blaug, 1968). Sraffa, a noted Ricardian scholar, sought to resurrect the classical pursuit of a theory of value independent of demand or value in use. In his book, *Production of Commodities by Means of Commodities: Prelude to a Critique of Economic Theory,* Sraffa (1960) established conditions under which exchange ratios between commodities can be determined based on their use in production; i.e. a set of commodity prices that would exhaust the total product. These exchange ratios were not based on any optimality or marginality conditions. Instead, Sraffa divided commodities into basic (goods which entered into all production processes) and non-basic, and showed that an invariant standard of value would be a combination of basic commodities reflecting average input proportions in production. This contrived 'commodity' would then be usable as a measure of national wealth or income.[1]

The 'marginal' revolution in value theory originated with the confluence of several related streams of economic thought in the 20th century. Menger proposed there were different categories of wants or desires, such as food, shelter, clothing etc. that could be ordered in terms of their subjective importance. Within each category, there is an ordered sequence of desires for successive increments of each good. He postulated that the intensity of desire for one additional unit declines with successive units of the good (Blaug, 1968). Replacing the term 'desire for one additional unit' with the term 'Marginal Utility', we thus have the economic principle of diminishing marginal utility.

The idea that people have different, but ordered, categories of wants or desires raises the critical issue of whether trade-offs exist between categories. If individuals 'weight' categories, it implies a trade-off. At one extreme, categories may be lexicographically ordered, like words in a dictionary. One level of want must be satisfied before a lower level becomes relevant in the process of valuation. There are no trade-offs between levels of wants. For example, the need for caloric intake is likely superior to that of recreational pleasure – no number of recreational opportunities will likely substitute for an insufficient diet. In the lexicographic case, individuals would use their monetary resources hierarchically, satisfying higher order wants and needs first. When a higher order want or need is at risk, the individual would take resources away from lower level ones until higher level needs were satisfied. Lexicographic preferences do not mean monetary valuation is impossible, as individuals would still be able to state how much of their resources they would be willing to sacrifice for a good or service; but it may be all their resources if a high level need is at risk.

More problematic for valuation are instances where basic needs cannot be satisfied by the resources at an individual's disposal – i.e. time or money. Similar to Menger, Ekins and Max-Neef (1992) suggested the universality of basic human needs, including subsistence, affection, protection, understanding, leisure, identity and freedom. Although one can imagine needs like affection being 'purchasable' with money, or 'freedom' being purchasable by migration, many of these needs may not be satisfied by money or time because individuals simply may not consider them to be purchasable by money or time. Thus, not only is it possible that trade-offs between needs will not be possible, but some needs may not be reducible to money or time.

Lancaster (1971) introduced the concept of consumption technology, whereby consumers consider *characteristics* of goods. For example, food may be evaluated on caloric, protein or vitamin content. Different foods are substitutable depending on the composition of their characteristics. People allocate their budget across characteristics, purchasing goods that are efficient sources of desired characteristics. The technological inability to substitute characteristics may restrict the margins on which environmental goods and services can be valued. For example, while health may be valued, and individuals would be willing to pay for it, the proper mix of calories, protein and vitamins may make marginal increases or decrements in one of these characteristics either very highly valued or of very low value. Building on this insight, multiattribute utility theory formalizes the utility-generating technology by proposing that total utility is a function of the characteristics of goods or services. A simple example would be where utility, U, from food consumption is a linear function of the caloric, C, protein, P, and vitamin, V, content:

$$U = aC + bP + cV \tag{2.1}$$

Here, the parameters a, b, and c reflect the weighting of three factors in determining utility for food consumption. When utilities are measurable in monetary willingness to pay (WTP) or willingness to accept (WTA) compensation, these parameters represent the marginal *monetary* value of each characteristic. This logic forms the basis for hedonic pricing models of valuation, discussed below, whereby the value of market goods, say a house, depends upon the characteristics of the house and its location, as well as surrounding environmental amenities or disamenities.

Gossen proposed that in order to maximize satisfaction from a good, such as labour or money, an individual must allocate that good across different uses to equate their marginal utilities in each use (Blaug, 1968). Hence marginal utility would provide a basis for explaining exchange value. If we treat things such as iron, cement, fertilizer, natural agents and labour as incomplete consumable goods, the marginal utility of the goods they produce can be used to explain their exchange value. This logic established a full theory of value. It also demonstrated that exchange values could be based on use value. While the diamond-water paradox had been solved many times, the classical economists, such as Smith and Ricardo, could not resolve it using their labour theories of value. It was resolved only by recognizing the importance of utility and scarcity in determining exchange values, and the role of margins in value determination.

While the classical theorists sought a standard physical commodity unit for measuring exchange value, neoclassical theorists did not need such a commodity. As value was assumed to be determined by utility on the margin, and consumers were assumed to allocate money optimally across uses, the marginal utility of money was the same for an individual in all its uses. *Money* thus became the standard unit of measure.

The significance of the marginal utility theory of value to the evolving concept of ecosystem service valuation is that it can be used to measure use values, not just exchange values, in monetary units. The general optimization model of labour/leisure and consumption/saving given time and wealth constraints would yield equivalencies of goods for money, goods for time, and time for money. Time or money can thus be used as a standard of measure of use value; how much time or money will a person willingly sacrifice to obtain commodity X? In sum, as the pursuit of an economic theory of value traversed the broad metaphysical terrain of economic thought, the answer appears to have been found in the concept of value in use.[2]

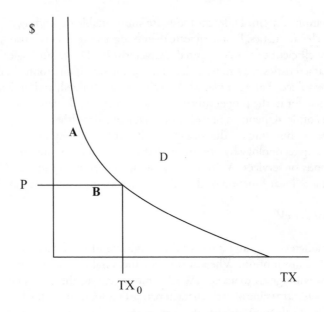

Figure 2.1 *Utility and exchange based values of goods and services*

The utility-based values of goods and services are reflected in people's WTP to attain them, or their WTA compensation to forgo them. WTP and WTA become measures of these values. They may be based on small marginal changes in the availability of these goods and services, or on larger changes including their complete absence or presence. These valuations are reflected in Figure 2.1. Let the curve D represent the WTP for each unit of the good or service, T, for an individual or group. This is a 'Marginal' WTP. The 'Total' WTP for T_0 units of T is the aggregated areas $A + B$. Area A may be very large for goods or services that have some utility threshold where the good becomes increasingly valuable as it becomes scarcer. This is true for many ecological goods and services, such as life support goods like oxygen and water; the 'Marginal' value is finite but the 'Total' value is indeterminate. This is the distinction that lies behind the diamond-water paradox noted above.

Exchange-based values are reflected in the prices, P, at which the goods or services are exchanged. When supply is T_0, and the item is sold competitively, a price P is determined which clears the market. These prices also reflect the 'Marginal' valuations placed on available quantities around T_0. So prices reflect 'Marginal' values when there are markets for the goods or services.[3] The 'Total' exchange value of T_0 is $P \times T_0$. This is an observable market value when there are markets to observe. But when there are no such markets, P must be determined indirectly, and $P \times T_0$ would represent a pseudo-market value. This would be the 'Total' exchange value of the good if there were a market with an available supply of T_0.

Measures of economic value are designed to reflect the difference that something makes to satisfaction of human preferences. If something is attainable only at a cost, then the difference it makes to satisfy preferences is the difference between its utility and the cost of attaining it. Formal concepts of Compensating and Equivalent Variations are used to reflect this difference (Varian, 1992). For example, suppose in Figure 2.1. that T_0 is available at a cost of P. Under these terms of availability, the welfare difference made by T_0 is area A. The 'Marginal' value that alterations in availability make to welfare would be reflected by changes in A. Using timber from trees as an example, suppose timber is harvested at a cost of P per unit of timber. The value of trees, per se, would be represented by area A, which is less than $A + B$.

Thus conceived, the basic notion of value that guides economic thought is inherently anthropocentric, or instrumental. While value can generally mean the contribution to a goal, objective, desired condition etc. the mental model used by economists is that value is based on want satisfaction, pleasure or utility goals. Things have value insofar as they propel individuals toward meeting pleasure and need objectives. Values of objects in the environment can be considered on the margin, as well as on the whole; i.e. the value of one additional tree versus the value of all trees. While value relates to the utility of a thing, the actual measurement of value requires some objective measure of the degree to which the thing improves pleasure, wellbeing and happiness.

In a finite world, the resources people have available to meet their personal objectives are limited. Economists have thus developed an extensive theory of how people behave in the presence of constraints on feasible activities (Varian, 1992). The working hypothesis is that people make decisions in order to optimize satisfaction, pleasure or utility. This optimization always takes place in the presence of constraints, such as income, wealth, time, resource supply etc. Optimization thus yields a deterministic set of possible decisions in most real-world situations – when constraints change, so do the decisions.

The essence of this perspective is that the economic world works largely deterministically, moving from one equilibrium to another in relatively stable fashion, and responds to changes in constraints in a predictable fashion. The determination of equilibrium is a resultant of conflicting forces, such as supply and demand, or unlimited wants and limited means. While there are instances of instability, disequilibria and indeterminism, these are treated as exceptions rather than the rule.

Since individuals can be observed making choices between objects in the marketplace while operating within the limits of income and time, economists have developed measures of value as imputations from these observed choices. While monetary measures of value are not the only possible yardstick, they are convenient since many choices involve the use of money. Hence, if you are observed to pay US$10 for a bottle of wine, the imputation is that you value wine to be at least US$10, and are willing to make a trade-off of US$10 worth of other things to obtain that bottle. The money itself has no intrinsic value, but represents other things you could have purchased. Time is often considered another yardstick of value; if you spend two hours golfing, the imputation is that you value the golf experience to be worth more than two hours spent in other activities. Value is thus a resultant of the expressed tastes and preferences of persons, and the limited means with which objects can be pursued. As a result, the scarcer the object of desire is, the greater its value will be on the margin.

Importantly, the 'technologies' of pleasure and production allow for some substitution between things. A variety of goods can induce pleasure and are thus treated conceptually as utility substitutes. A bear may substitute for an elk in consumption, hunting and in a wildlife viewing experience even though bears and elk are not substitutes in terms of ecosystem function. On the production side, inputs are also considered to be substitutable for one another. Machines and technology can substitute for people and natural inputs. Clearly, economists recognize that the relations between goods and services are often more complicated than this. For malnourished people, sugar is no technological substitute for protein, even though they both provide calories. As discussed earlier, preferences may be lexicographic – some things are more important than others, and cannot be substituted for lower level wants or needs. On the production side, no number of lumbermen is a substitute for timber when there is no timber. Production may require certain inputs, but at the same time there may be substitutability between others. As Krutilla (1967) suggests, there may be close substitutes for conventional natural resources, such as timber and coal, but not for natural ecological systems.

The neoclassical perspective also assumes that tastes and preferences are fixed and given, and that the fundamental economic 'problem' consists of optimally satisfying those preferences. Tastes and preferences usually do not change rapidly and, in the short run (i.e. 1–2 years), this basic economic assumption is probably not too bad. In the longer run, however, it does not make sense to assume tastes and preferences are fixed. People's preferences do change over longer time frames as the existence of a robust advertising industry attests. This observation is important because sustainability is an inherently long-run concept and ecosystem services are expected to continue into the far future. This fact is very disturbing for many economists because it takes away the easy definition of what is optimal. If tastes and preferences are fixed and given, then we can adopt a stance of 'consumer sovereignty' and just give people what they want. We do not have to know or care why they want it; we just have to satisfy their preferences efficiently.

However, if preferences change over time and under the influence of education, advertising, changing cultural assumptions, and variations in abundance and scarcity etc. we need a different criterion for what is 'optimal'. Moreover, we have to figure out how preferences change, how they relate to this new criterion, and how they can, or should, be changed to satisfy the new criterion (Norton et al, 1998). One alternative for the new criterion is sustainability itself, or more completely a set of criteria: sustainable scale (size of the economic subsystem), fair distribution, and efficient allocation (Daly, 1992). This set of criteria implies a two-tiered decision process (Page 1977; Daly and Cobb, 1989; Norton et al, 1998) of first coming to a social consensus on a sustainable scale and fair distribution and, second, using the marketplace and other social institutions like education and advertising to implement these decisions. This might be called 'community sovereignty' as opposed to 'consumer sovereignty'. It makes most economists very uncomfortable to stray from consumer sovereignty because it raises the question: if tastes and preferences can change, then who is going to decide how to change them? There is a real danger that a totalitarian government might be employed to manipulate preferences to conform to the desires of a select elite rather than the individuals in society.

Here, two points need to be kept in mind: (1) preferences are already being manipulated every day; and (2) we can just as easily apply open democratic principles to the problem as hidden or totalitarian principles in deciding how to manipulate preferences. Viewed in this light, the aforementioned question is transformed: do we want preferences to be manipulated unconsciously, either by a dictatorial government or by big business acting through advertising? Or do we want to formulate preferences consciously based on social dialogue and consensus with a higher goal in mind? Either way, we believe that this issue can no longer be avoided, and is one that will best be handled using open democratic principles and innovative thinking. Which leads us back to the role of individual preferences in determining value. If individual preferences change in response to education, advertising and peer pressure then value cannot solely originate with individual preferences. Values ultimately originate from within the constellation of shared goals to which a society aspires – value systems – as well as the availability of 'production technologies' that transform things into satisfaction of human needs.

In addition to income and education, time places constraints on value creation. Constraints of time and intertemporal substitutabilities create temporal implications for value. Economists presume that a present time preference exists due to limited time horizons and concerns for uncertainty in the future (Fisher, 1930). This means individuals will discount values of things in the future in comparison to the same things in the present. If I have an equal endowment of apples now and a year from now, I would place a greater value on having an apple now than on having an apple one year from now. The ability to convert things to money in the presence of positive financial interest rates will, therefore, result in the 'optimizing individual' discounting things in the future.

In contrast to economists' traditional assumptions of positive time preferences, or positive discount rates, psychologists suggest time preference is more complicated. For example, Loewenstein and Prelec (1991) find that in some circumstances people behave as if they have negative time preference, preferring more in the future to more now. The authors suggest this is due to dread, the anticipation of savouring better conditions in the future, and the aversion to loss. However, this negative time preference may not be operative when the time period is ambiguous. The implications of such experimental results for discounting in environmental policy settings are not clear, but they do raise serious questions about the standard practice of discounting future environmental benefits (Clark, 1973).

Ecological Concepts of Value

'Value' is a term that most ecologists and other natural scientists would prefer not to use at all, except perhaps in its common usage as a reference to the magnitude of a number – for example, 'the value of parameter b is 9.32'. Using the definition of value provided earlier, ecosystems and non-human species are presumed not to be pursuing any conscious goals, and, therefore, they do not have a 'value system'. Likewise, one cannot talk about 'value' as the degree to which an item contributes to achieving a goal in this context since there is no conscious goal being pursued. Nevertheless, some concepts of value are important in the natural sciences, and are in fact quite commonly used, and we try briefly to elucidate them here.

If one limits the concept of value to the degree to which an item contributes to an objective or condition in a system, then we can see how natural scientists use the concept of value all the time to talk about causal relationships between different parts of a system. For example, one could talk about the value of particular tree species in controlling soil erosion in a high slope area, or the value of fires in recycling nutrients in a forest.

There are other ways in which the concept of 'value' is used in the natural sciences. For example, a core organizing principle of biology is evolution by natural selection. Evolution in natural systems has three components: (1) generation of genetic variation by random mutations or sexual recombination; (2) natural selection by relative reproductive success; (3) transmission via information stored in the genes. While this process does not require conscious, goal-directed behaviour on the part of any of its participants, one can still think of the overall process as being 'goal-directed'. The 'goal' of 'survival' is embedded in the objective function of natural selection. While the process occurs without consciousness of this goal, species as a whole can be observed to behave 'as if' they were pursuing the goal of survival. Thus, one often hears evolutionary biologists talk about the 'survival value' of particular traits in organisms. Natural selection models, which maximize the fitness of species, are not only testable, they bear close similarities to economic utility maximization models (Low, 2000).

Beyond this, the idea of 'co-evolution' among a whole group of interacting species (Ehrlich and Raven, 1964) raises the possibility that one species is 'valuable' to the survival of another species. Extending this logic to the co-evolution of humans and other species, we can talk of the 'value' of natural ecosystems and their components in terms of their contribution to human survival.

Ecologists and physical scientists have also proposed an 'energy theory of value', either to complement or replace the standard neoclassical theory of value (Odum, 1971, 1983; Slesser, 1973; Gilliland, 1975; Costanza, 1980; Cleveland et al, 1984; Hall et al, 1992). It is based on thermodynamic principles where solar energy is considered to be the only primary input to the global ecosystem. This theory of value represents a return to the classical ideas of Ricardo and Sraffa (see above), but with some important distinctions. The classical economists recognized that if they could identify a 'primary' input to the production process then they could explain exchange values based on production relationships. The problem was that neither labour nor any other single commodity was really 'primary'.

The classical economists were writing before the physics of thermodynamics had been fully developed. Energy – or, more correctly, 'free' or 'available' energy – has special characteristics which satisfy the criteria for a 'primary' input: (1) Energy is ubiquitous. (2) It is a property of all of the commodities produced in economic and ecological systems. (3) While other commodities can provide alternative sources for the energy required to drive systems, the essential property of energy cannot be substituted for. Available energy is thus the only 'basic' commodity and is ultimately the only 'scarce' factor of production, thereby satisfying the criteria for a production-based theory that can explain exchange values.

Energy-based concepts of value must follow the basic principles of energy conversion. The first law of thermodynamics tells us that energy and matter are conserved. But, this law essentially refers to heat energy and mechanical work (*raw* energy or the bomb calorimeter energy). The ability to do work is related to the degree *of organization* or order of a thing relative to its environment, not its raw energy content. Heat must be organized as a temperature gradient between a high temperature source and a low temperature sink in order for useful work to be done. In a similar fashion, complex manufactured goods like cars have an ability to do work that is not related to their raw energy content. The second law of thermodynamics tells us that useful energy (organization) always dissipates (entropy or disorder always increases) within a closed system. In order to maintain organized structures (like an economy) one must constantly add organized, low entropy energy from outside the system.

Estimating total 'energy' consumption for an economy is not a straightforward matter because not all fuels are of the same quality – i.e. they vary in their available energy, degree of organization, or ability to do work. Electricity, for example, is more versatile and cleaner in end use than petroleum, and it also costs more energy to produce. In an oil-fired power plant it takes from 3–5 kcal of oil to produce each kcal of electricity. Thus, adding up the raw heat equivalents of the various forms of fuel consumed by an economy without accounting for fuel quality can radically distort the picture, especially if the mix of fuel types is changing over time.

An energy theory of value posits that, at least at the global scale, free or available energy from the sun (plus past solar energy stored as fossil fuels and residual heat from the earth's core) are the only 'primary' inputs to the system. Labour, manufactured capital and natural capital are 'intermediate inputs'. Thus, one could base a theory of value on the use in production of available energy that avoids the problems the classical economists encountered when trying to explain exchange values in economic systems. There have been a few attempts to empirically test this theory using both time-series data and cross-sectional data. Studies that have tried to adjust for fuel quality have shown a very close relationship between 'available energy' consumption and economic output. Cleveland et al (1984) and more recently Kaufmann (1992) have shown that almost all of the changes in E/GNP (or E/GDP) ratios in the US and OECD countries can be explained by changes in fuel quality and the percentage of personal consumption expenditures (PCE) spent directly on fuel. The latter effect is due to the fact that PCE is a component of GNP and spending more on fuel directly will raise GNP without changing real economic output. Figure 2.2 is an example of the explanatory power of this relationship for the US economy from 1932 to 1987. Much of the apparent gain in energy efficiency (decreasing E/GNP ratio) is due to shifts to higher quality fuels (like natural gas and primary electricity) from lower quality ones (like coal). Renewable energy sources are generally lower quality and shifts to them may cause significant increases in the E/GNP ratio.

Another way of looking at the relationship between available energy and economic output uses cross-sectional rather than time-series data. This avoids some of the problems associated with changes in fuel mix and distortions in GNP. For example, Costanza (1980), Costanza and Herendeen (1984) used an 87-sector input-output model of the US economy for 1963, 1967 and 1973, modified to include households and government as endogenous sectors (to include labour and government energy costs) to investigate the relationship between direct and indirect energy consumption (embodied energy) and dollar value of output. They found that dollar value of sector output was highly correlated (R^2 = 0.85–0.98) with embodied energy, though not with direct energy consumption or with embodied energy calculated excluding labour and government energy costs. Thus, if one makes some necessary adjustments to estimates of energy consumption in order to better assess 'available energy', it appears that the empirical link between available energy and economic value is rather strong.

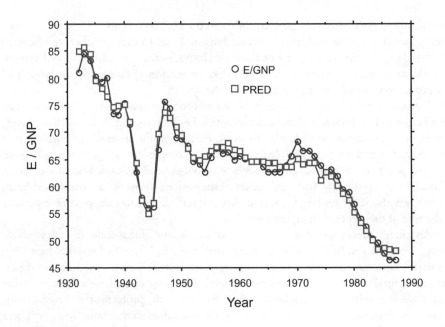

Note: From Cleveland et al (1984), Kaufmann (1992)

Figure 2.2 *The energy/GNP ratio for the US economy from 1932 to 1987.*
The predicted ratio (PRED) is based on a regression model with per cent of primary
energy from petroleum (%PET) from electricity (%ELEC) and per cent of personal
consumption expenditures spent on fuel (%PCE) as independent variables ($R^2 = 0.96$)

Some neoclassical economists have criticized the energy theory of value as an attempt to
define value independent of consumer preferences (see Heuttner, 1976). This criticism
is axiomatic as the stated purpose was to establish a biophysical theory of value *not* completely determined by social preferences. The energy theory of value overcomes some of
the problems with production-based theories of value encountered by the classical economists discussed earlier and does a reasonable job of explaining exchange values
empirically in the few cases where it has been tested. Despite the controversy and ongoing debate about the validity of an energy theory of value (Brown and Herendeen,
1996), it seems to be the only reasonably successful attempt to operationalize a general
biophysical theory of value.

Ecological Thresholds, Uncertainty and Economic Value

Ecosystems can be highly nonlinear within certain regions, and changes can be dramatic
or irreversible. The availability of ecosystem services may be dramatically altered at these
non-linear points for only minor changes in ecosystem conditions. A valuable service
provided to humans by naturally functioning ecosystems is their avoidance of adverse
threshold conditions, or what Ciriacy-Wantrup (1963) referred to as 'Critical Zones' for

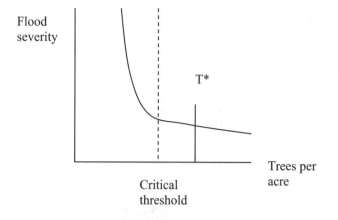

Figure 2.3 *The flood protection value of trees*

resource conservation. For example, trees in a forested ecosystem provide a hydrologic service of moderating water flows into streams during peak storm events. As Figure 2.3 above shows, let us suppose there is a relationship between the density of trees in a landscape and physical severity of downstream flooding. At tree densities exceeding the 'Critical Threshold', marginal changes in density can be evaluated using measures such as expected increases in flood damages. Under this marginal regime, there is a substitute for nature's services, flood protection or property replacement. Below the critical threshold, however, flood severity increases substantially as tree density diminishes. Economic values change substantially for slight alterations in ecosystem conditions because human lives and communities may be at substantial risk. Under these conditions, traditional monetary measures of value may not be able to adequately capture the impact of severe floods. Traditional valuation methods may not be acceptable as measures of the values of trees in proximity of the 'Critical Threshold'.

Due to the probabalistic nature of storm events, human society may wish to maintain tree densities well in excess of the critical threshold, say at T^*. There would be a welfare loss if tree densities fell below T^*, and this loss would be attributable to both the marginal increase in flood severity and to the fact that now the system is closer to a catastrophe. There would be an insurance premium that society would pay to avoid such a dramatic change in ecological states. Additional trees would have value both for their role in reducing expected flood damages, and as insurance for avoiding a natural catastrophe.

The example above illustrates that ecosystem service value has both efficiency and sustainability components. In the linear, marginal region, where the actual states of the economic and ecological systems are not dramatically altered, the values of changing tree densities are rationally based on efficiency goals; in this case avoiding having to repair flood damages. In the nonlinear, nonmarginal region, however, the value of trees is a sustainability value, as they protect the economic and ecological systems from collapse. Sustainability values may be more important than efficiency values around and below threshold limits. In short, sustainability values may be lexicographically superior to efficiency values.

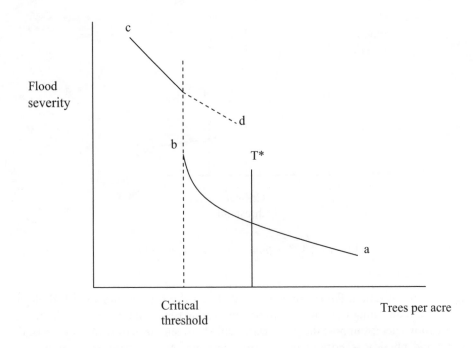

Figure 2.4 *Flood protection values of trees with ecosystem irreversibilities*

The example in Figure 2.3 has the property of reversibility. Even when tree densities fall below the Critical Threshold level and place society at high risk, planting more trees reverses the exposure to risk. This may not be the case with some ecosystem conditions. For example, reductions in tree densities below the Critical Threshold may alter landscape conditions for a long period of time even after tree densities have been increased to pre-threshold conditions.

In Figure 2.4 the ecological–economic system moves along path *cd* rather than *ba* once the threshold of irreversibility has been violated. This irreversibility would likely increase the value society would pay to avoid the threshold compared with conditions of relatively easy reversibility. The insurance value would include not only a premium to avoid a catastrophe, but an option value to avoid the irreversibility of flooding (Arrow and Fisher, 1974).

The recent wildfire in Los Alamos, New Mexico, in the summer of 2000, provides a dramatic, tragic example of the catastrophes and irreversibilities associated with being near critical thresholds. The fire was started as a controlled burn of several hundred acres by the US National Park Service. Years of improper forest management, such as natural fire suppression and grazing of understory vegetation created a circumstance in which a minor change, the small controlled burn, had disastrous consequences, destroying 300 homes and temporarily displacing 30,000 people. To make matters worse, the destruction of groundcover over nearly 50,000 acres will likely permanently alter soil conditions as erosion will be very severe. The former forest system may never be replicated. This situation is similar to conditions illustrated in Figure 2.4.

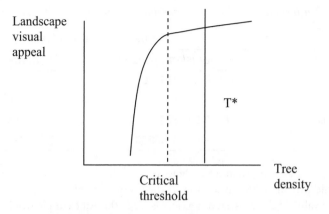

Figure 2.5 *The value of trees for visual appeal*

Another example may be the value of trees in a landscape. In Figure 2.5, alterations in tree densities above the Critical Threshold level only marginally change the visual appeal of the landscape. However, below this critical threshold the landscape is no longer a forest; the state of nature is altered substantially. Changes in tree densities above the critical threshold can be valued on the margin using traditional economic valuation techniques. However, suppose the forest is a critical visual element to a community, or the loss of forest has dire impacts on the state of the local economy or social fabric. Changes in tree densities below the critical threshold may not be meaningfully valued using traditional techniques. Furthermore, the same type of insurance value as in the case of flooding will give a premium to remaining above the critical threshold. Given there are probabalistic events such as storms and infestations, the community may wish to keep densities above T^*. Increases in density in the region around the critical threshold have value both for improving the visual appeal of the landscape as well as providing insurance that tree densities will not fall below this threshold.

In all of the above examples, critical thresholds in ecosystem structure or function do not necessarily imply economic thresholds for values. For example, if flooding impacts on communities were never severe or people were not highly dependent on the existence of a forest, marginal economic valuation methods would be appropriate across the whole range of tree densities. This is in spite of the fact that there may be thresholds of densities at which ecosystem structures and functions are substantially altered. The natural world may be in a nonlinear, nonmarginal condition, but the economic world remains a smooth one where substitutes readily mitigate significant ecosystem change. Of course, the opposite may be true also – i.e. gradual changes in natural conditions may lead to nonlinear changes in economic conditions. For example, water quality may gradually fall below certain standards and a lake is 'suddenly' closed to swimmers.

Critical thresholds where ecological conditions and dynamics are uncertain require valuation under uncertainty. Uncertainty may range from knowing the probabilities of conditions and their values, to only being able to identify the conditions but not their probabilities. There are several methods for dealing with such valuation dilemmas. For

Table 2.1 *Net income from coastal storm damages with and without barrier islands*

	Barrier island conditions	
	Barrier island present	No barrier island
Storm occurs	$I - C$ + US$200	$I - C$
No storm	I	I
Expected value	I + 0.5 (US$200 – C)	I + 0.5(– C)
Worst case	$I - C$ + US$200	$I - C$

example, suppose an ecosystem under State A would provide US$200 in services, but in State B would provide US$0 in services. If the probability of each state occurring is 0.5, the expected value of the ecosystem services is US$100. An example would be the storm protection value of an acre of coastal barrier islands under a hurricane (State A) or no hurricane (State B).

Under these conditions, the valuation of ecosystem services is not quite so simple. Individuals may be averse to risks and a loss may be weighted more heavily than a gain of comparable magnitude. Given this, what would be the WTP to preserve the barrier islands; what are they worth? The answer depends on whether the decision maker is risk averse. There are two uncontrollable states: *Storm* versus *No Storm,* each occurring with a 0.5 probability. There are two ecological conditions: *Barrier Island* and *No Barrier Island.* When base incomes are I and the base damages from a storm with no barrier protection are *C,* the matrix shown in Table 2.1 represents net income conditions under the storm and barrier island options.

Using expected values, the value of the barrier islands is US$100. However, the WTP to maintain the islands is given by:

$$0.5U(I - C + \text{US\$200} - \text{WTP}) + 0.5U(I - \text{WTP}) = 0.5U(I - C) + 0.5U(I) \quad (2.2)$$

or an amount such that the expected utility, net of WTP, of maintaining the barrier islands just equals the expected utility without the islands. It can be shown that under conditions of risk aversion, where the utility function is concave, WTP would be greater than the expected value of the loss, (US$100 in this case, but less than the full damage of US$200).[4] The excess of WTP over the expected value of the loss is the 'premium' that risk averters would pay rather than risk a full loss.

This example can be generalized in several ways. First, if the barrier islands have some additional value, such as recreational or aesthetic enjoyment, the value of the islands measured by WTP would be *additive* to the storm protection values. Second, when altering ecological conditions increases the probability that a loss will occur, risk averting individuals should be willing to pay something to avoid the increase in probability of loss. This WTP would reflect what the ecosystem is worth insofar as insuring against crossing thresholds and encountering adverse irreversible conditions.

When uncertainty consists of not knowing the probabilities of various ecological states, for example, of a hurricane, the above matrix can be used to illustrate valuation under this pure risk situation. If society is risk averse, a useful decision rule is to assume the worst will occur, and seek to minimize the worst-case scenario. For example, maintaining the barrier islands results in a worst-case scenario under a hurricane of $I - C +$ US\$200; while the worst case if islands are not maintained is $I - C$. The implied value of the barrier islands for planning purposes is US\$200 under this risk averse decision rule, as society would be willing to pay up to US\$200 to maintain these islands.

In this example, the ability to estimate storm damage cost savings provides guidance to valuing the resource as well as developing a decision rule. A simple decision rule would be to maintain and conserve an ecosystem service when the cost of doing so is not too great. This is the 'safe minimum standard' proposed by Ciriacy-Wantrup (1963), and elaborated on by others (Bishop, 1978). Under this standard, conservation practices avoid Ciriacy-Wantrup's 'Critical Zone' of dramatic, irreversible change in ecosystems. For example, soil conservation would avoid gulleys or maintain a maximum acceptable erosion rate; forest conservation would establish a maximum deforestation rate; rangelands conservation would maintain a minimum level of plant material after grazing; or species conservation would establish a minimum breeding stock or habitat condition. These standards are ecologically based, not economic; although violating them may be prudent if the economic costs are too high.

Conflicts between Economic and Ecological Values

We also recognize that economic and ecological measures of value may at times be at odds with one another. As humans are only one of many species in an ecosystem, the values they place on ecosystem functions, structures and processes may differ significantly from the values of those ecosystem characteristics to species or the maintenance (health) of the ecosystem itself. The intrinsic values of natural system features and processes within the natural system itself may possess different abundance and functional value properties than their corresponding economic values. Diminishing returns and utility would suggest some economic saturation in the demands for particular ecosystem services and conditions. For example, the marginal economic value for additional sunlight may be zero or possibly negative – skin cancer from excessive sunlight, excessive heat etc.

The differences between ecological and economic values relate to the relative abundance of ecosystem services within naturally functioning ecosystems and economies. Clearly, a service can be more abundant or scarce in one than another. While it is likely that specific ecosystem structures and processes have some functional role in an ecosystem, and, therefore, have 'value', they may not have direct or indirect value in market economies. There may be instances where an ecosystem is so isolated from human economic activity that what happens in it is irrelevant to human activity, even when all possible spatial and temporal connections are considered – i.e. only the intrinsic value remains. Of course, as humans continue to increasingly inhabit the planet, these instances become increasingly rare. As our understanding of connections between and within ecosystems expands, we find more and more instances of significant implications for human beings. These changing conditions in knowledge make it increasingly incumbent upon us to avoid the quick dismissal of isolated or presumably economically irrelevant ecosystems or their properties as irrelevant to human welfare.

Economic Valuation Methods

The exchange value of ecosystem services is the trading ratios for those services. When services are directly tradable in normal markets, the price is the exchange value. The exchange-based, welfare value of a natural good or service is its market price net of the cost of bringing that service to market. For example, the exchange-based value of timber to society is its 'stumpage rate', which is the market price of timber net of harvest and time allocated management costs. Exchange-based valuation is relatively simple, as trades exist from which to measure values.

Market prices reflect the valuation of goods and services, but only on the margin. For example, the price of a board foot of timber reflects what another board foot is worth to buyers. It does not reflect the whole value of all timber used by the buyers. You may pay only US$2 per board foot and that is all you would be willing to pay for the last of, say, the 5000 board feet you buy. But you may be willing to pay considerably more than US$10,000 for the opportunity to buy *all* 5000 board feet. Of course, the timber reflects only a portion of the full social value of a tree, which also provides an array of services such as soil amendment and stabilization, water storage and flood control, species habitat, aesthetics, climate control etc. In limited cases, markets for environmental services have been formed that tend to reflect the valuations of those services (Chichilnisky and Heal, 1998).

While exchange value requires markets or observable trades, the social value of services is much more broad and difficult to measure. These social values are what have captured the attention of environmental and resource economists. They have developed a number of techniques for valuing ecosystem services (Freeman, 1993; Kopp and Smith, 1993). The underlying concepts for social values that economists have developed are what a society would be willing and able to pay for a service, WTP, or what it would be willing to accept to forgo that service, WTA. The two valuation concepts may differ substantially in practice (Hannemann, 1991).

The economic valuation methodology essentially constructs WTP for a service; or constructs the adequate compensation for a service loss, representing WTA. Suppose the service is flood control provided by a wetland. Suppose damages from flooding were US$1 million. Society would then be willing to pay US$100,000 to reduce the probability of flooding by 10 per cent if the society, as a whole, is risk neutral. Suppose the wetlands reduce flooding probabilities by 20 per cent. When wetlands services are free, society receives US$200,000 million in services for nothing. In principle, the owner of a wetland providing such a service could capture up to this amount of social value if there was a capture mechanism. Markets for resource services provide capture mechanisms. They work relatively well for 'private' goods, where owners can deny access to the service if payments are not made and if making access available to one person essentially makes it unavailable to others. Raw materials and food production are good examples of these 'private' goods or services.

Many ecosystem services do not qualify for market trading because they are not 'private' in nature. For example, flood protection services of wetlands or trees, once made available to one person, may indirectly become available to all. Wetlands and forest owners could not capture all the potential social WTP for this service.

When there are no explicit markets for services, we must resort to more indirect means of assessing economic values. A variety of valuation techniques can be used to establish the WTP or WTA for these services. There are six major ecosystem service economic valuation techniques when market valuations do not adequately capture social value:

1 Avoided Cost (AC): services allow society to avoid costs that would have been incurred in the absence of those services; flood control avoids property damages or waste treatment by wetlands avoids health costs.
2 Replacement Cost (RC): services could be replaced with man-made systems; natural waste treatment can be replaced with costly treatment systems.
3 Factor Income (FI): services provide for the enhancement of incomes; water quality improvements increase commercial fisheries catch and incomes of fishermen.
4 Travel Cost (TC): service demand may require travel, whose costs can reflect the implied value of the service; recreation areas attract distant visitors whose value placed on that area must be at least what they were willing to pay to travel to it.
5 Hedonic Pricing (HP): service demand may be reflected in the prices people will pay for associated goods; housing prices at beaches exceed prices of inland homes.
6 Contingent Valuation (CV): service demand may be elicited by posing hypothetical scenarios that involve some valuation of alternatives; people would be willing to pay for increased fish catch or deer bag.

Each of these methods has its strengths and weaknesses. Also, each service has an appropriate set of valuation techniques. Some services may require that several techniques be used jointly. For example, the recreational value of an ecosystem will include not only the value that visiting recreationists place on the site (TC), but the increased incomes associated with site use (FI). Alexander et al (1998) have suggested an extreme FI for valuing global ecosystem services, measuring the rents that a hypothetical monopolistic owner of nature's services could charge the world's economy. For example, an extreme measure of rent from *all* natural system services would be the difference between global GDP and a global subsistence income. The paper by de Groot, Wilson and Boumans (2002) discusses the appropriate techniques for valuing different ecosystem services.

Some valuation techniques, while intuitively appealing, may misrepresent WTP or WTA valuation concepts in certain circumstances. This is especially a problem when using Replacement Cost (RC) methods. There may be circumstances when the social benefits that may be lost when ecosystem services are unavailable are less than the cost of replacement of those services; or when the benefits gained from enhanced services are less than alternative means of providing those services. For example, the Avoided Cost of illness under an ecosystem enhancement, such as wetlands treatment of waste, may be less than the cost of comparable waste treatment facilities. In this case, Avoided Cost is a more appropriate measure of value than Replacement Cost. The Replacement Cost measure of value of the world's coral reefs may far exceed the measure of benefits.

The Challenge of Aggregating Economic Values

The traditional procedure of economic valuation is to establish individual-based values using one of the methods described in the section on 'Conflicts between economic and ecological values' above. Isolated individual values are then aggregated to represent a socially-relevant unit – a community, a state, a nation or the entire planet. This is appropriate when the services provided are purely individually enjoyed, as is the case for 'private' goods and services that are not shared and where there are no substantial positive or negative (externality) impacts of one person's use on another. This is also the case for 'public' goods where enjoyment remains individual-based without externality impacts. An example would be the recreational enjoyment of an uncongested forest.

Isolated, individual-based valuation and aggregation are not appropriate, however, in instances where group values may hinge on group interactions, where preference formation is partially a social process, where shared knowledge is important, and where items valued have substantial interpersonal or social implications. Valuing a forest for timber, or even recreation, is appropriately an individual-based process. However, other values of the forest may be more communal, are not well-defined in preference functions, or have substantial interpersonal impacts. For example, the value of forests to a community whose social system, folklore etc. are intimately dependent on them is more than the sum of independent personal values.

One approach to ecosystem service valuation that has gained increasing recognition in the literature is small group deliberation (Jacobs, 1997; Coote and Lenaghan, 1997; James and Blarney, 1999). Derived from political theory, this evolving set of techniques is founded on principles of deliberative democracy and the assumption that public decision making should result, not from the aggregation of separately measured individual preferences, but from a process of open public debate (Dryzek, 1987; Fishkin, 1991; Habermas, 1984). Thus, the application of a participatory democracy approach to environmental issues establishes two validity criteria that set it apart from traditional nonmarket valuation approaches: decentralized forms of environmental policy formulation and the direct involvement of nonexperts in small decision making groups

The basic idea is that small groups of citizens can be brought together to deliberate about the social value of public goods and that the 'consensus' values derived in this open forum can then be used to guide environmental public policy (Jacobs, 1997). In this manner, discursive methods such as citizens' juries (Coote and Lenaghan, 1997), consensus conferences (James and Blamey, 1999), and deliberative CV techniques (Sagoff, 1998) have increasingly been proposed and used in North America, Europe and Australia to inform environmental decision making. One assumption common to all these techniques is that deliberative bodies of citizens can render informed judgements about environmental goods not simply in terms of their own personal utility, but also for society as a whole. The purpose of deliberation is to 'reach agreement on what should be done by or on the behalf of society as a whole' (Jacobs, 1997). In sum, open discourse is assumed to perform a 'corrective function' when each citizen alone has incomplete information, but acting together with others can piece together a more complete picture of true social value for ecosystem goods and services.

For example, we might consider the recently proposed deliberative, or 'group' CV technique (Jacobs, 1997; Sagoff, 1998). While there is a long tradition of group research in CV, the goal of such research has generally been to use focus groups to increase the content validity of hypothetical scenarios and diagnose potential problems that individual respondents may have with the payment vehicle (Mitchell and Carson, 1989). With a group CV, on the other hand, the explicit goal would be to derive a group-consensus value for the ecological good or service in question. The valuation exercise is, therefore, conducted in a manner similar to a conventional CV survey – using hypothetical scenarios and realistic payment vehicles – with the key difference being that value elicitation is not done through private questioning but through group discussion and consensus buildiing. Thus, the deliberative CV approach treats small group deliberation not as a diagnostic tool, but as an explicit mechanism for value elicitation.

Conclusions

The concepts of 'value', 'value system' and 'valuation' have many meanings and interpretations and a long history in several disciplines. We have provided a survey of some of these meanings as they relate to the issue of ecosystem service valuation. There is clearly not one 'correct' set of concepts or techniques to address this important issue. Rather, there is a need for conceptual pluralism and thinking 'outside the box'. After a long and interesting history, the issue of 'value' is now going through a period of development that should help us to make better, and more sustainable, decisions, not only as individuals, but also as groups, communities, and as stewards of the entire planet.

Acknowledgements

This work was conducted as part of the Working Group on the Value of the World's Ecosystem Services and Natural Capital; Toward a Dynamic, Integrated Approach, supported by the National Center for Ecological Analysis and Synthesis, a centre funded by NSF (Grant # DEB-0072909), the University of California, and the Santa Barbara campus. Additional support was also provided for the Postdoctoral Associate, Matthew A. Wilson, in the Group.

Notes

1   While accepting Sraffa's (1960) mathematical proof, some reviewers (Harrod, 1961; Reder, 1961) noted that the exchange values would not be independent of demand as Sraffa claimed. It was further noted that Sraffa's did not constitute a price theory in the sense of establishing the process of price determination.
2   Since the marginal utility of a good depends upon how much the person possesses, we would expect a difference depending upon whether the person is asked how

much they would sacrifice to obtain X or how much would they accept in compensation to forgo X (see Hicks, 1939).

3   Unfortunately, this is not the case for many unmarketed ecological goods and services – techniques that economists have developed for assessing the 'Marginal' values of goods are outlined in the section on 'Conflicts between economic and ecological values'.

4   When WTP = US$100, rearranging terms shows that $U(I - C + 100) - U(I - C) > U(I) - U(I - 100)$ for any concave utility function.

References

1   Alexander, A. List, J. A. Margolis, M. and d'Arge, R. C. (1998) 'A method for valuing global ecosystem services'. *Ecological Economics*, vol 27(2), pp161–170

2   Arrow, K. and Fisher, A. C, (1974) 'Environmental preservation, uncertainty and irreversibility'. *Quarterly Journal of Economics*, vol 88, pp312–319

3   Bishop, Richard G (1978) 'Endangered species and uncertainty: the economics of a safe minimum standard'. *American Journal of Agricultural Economics*, vol 60(1), pp10–18

4   Blamey, R. K. and Rosemary, F. J. (1999) 'Citizens' Juries – An Alternative or an Input to Environmental Cost–Benefit Analysis'. Conference of the Australian and New Zealand Society for Ecological Economics, Brisbane, Australia, 7 July, Griffith University

5   Blaug, M. (1968) *Economic Theory in Retrospect*. Irwin, Homewood, IL

6   Brown, M. T. and Herendeen, R. A. (1996) 'Embodied Energy Analysis and Energy Analysis: A Comparative View'. *Ecological Economics,* vol 19, pp219–235

7   Chichilnisky, G. and Heal, G. (1998) 'Economic returns from the biosphere'. *Nature*, vol 391(6668), pp629–630

8   Ciriacy-Wantrup, S. V. (1963) *Resource Conservation: Economics and Policies*. Division of Agricultural Sciences, University of California, University of California Press

9   Clark, C. W. (1973) 'The economics of overexploitation'. *Science,* vol 181, pp630–634

10   Cleveland, C. J., Costanza, R., Hall, C. A. S. and Kaufmann, R. (1984) 'Energy and the US economy: a biophysical perspective'. *Science*, vol 225, pp890–897

11   Coote, A. and Lenaghan, J. (1997) *Citizen Juries: Theory into Practice*. Institute for Public Policy Research, London

12   Costanza, R. (1980) 'Embodied energy and economic valuation'. *Science,* vol 210, pp1219–1224

13   Costanza, R. (2000) 'Social goals and the valuation of ecosystem services'. *Ecosystems*, vol 3, pp4–10

14   Costanza, R. and Herendeen, R. A. (1984) 'Embodied energy and economic value in the United States economy: 1963, 1967 and 1972'. *Resources and Energy*, vol 6, pp129–163

15   Daly, H. E. (1992) 'Allocation, distribution, and scale: towards an economics that is efficient, just, and sustainable'. *Ecological Economics,* vol 6, pp185–193

16   Daly, H. E. and Cobb, J.B. (1989) *For the Common Good: Redirecting the Economy Toward Community, the Environment and a Sustainable Future*. Beacon Press, Boston

17   de Groot, R. S., Wilsen, M. A. and Boumann, R. M. J. (2002) 'A typology for the classification, description and valuation of ecosystem functions, goods and services'. *Ecological Economics*, vol 41, pp 393–408

18   Dryzek John, S. (1987) *Rational Ecology: Environment and Political Economy*. Basil Blackwell, New York

19 Ehrlich, P. and Raven, P. (1964) 'Butterflies and plants: a study in coevolution'. *Evolution*, vol 8, pp586–608

20 Ekins, P. and Max-Neef, M. (eds) (1992) *Real-Life Economics*. Routledge, London

21 Fisher, Irving (1930) *The Theory of Interest*. Macmillan, New York

22 Fishkin, J. Y. S. (1991) *Democracy and Deliberation*. Yale University Press, New Haven

23 Freeman, M. (1993) *The Measurement of Environmental and Resource Values: Theory and Methods*. Resources for the Future, Washington, DC

24 Gilliland, M. W. (1975) 'Energy analysis and public policy'. *Science*, vol 189, pp1051–1056

25 Goulder, L. H. and Donald, K. (1997) 'Valuing ecosystem services: philosophical bases and empirical methods', in Daily, G. C. (ed) *Nature's Services: Societal Dependence on Natural Ecosystems*, Island Press, Washington, DC, pp23–48

26 Habermas, J. (1984) *The Theory of Communicative Action*. Beacon Press, Boston, MA

27 Hall, C. A. S. Cleveland, C. J. Kaufmann, K. (1992) *Energy and Resource Quality: The Ecology of the Economic Process*. University of Colorado Press, Colorado

28 Hanneman, M. (1991) 'Willingness to Pay and Willingness to Accept: How Much Can They Differ?' *American Economic Review*, vol 81(3), pp635–647

29 Harrod, R. (1961) Book review. The Economic Journal, vol 71, pp783–787

30 Heuttner, D. A. (1976) 'Net energy analysis: an economic assessment'. *Science*, vol 192, pp101–104

31 Hicks, J. R. (1939) *Value and Capital: An Inquiry Into Some Fundamental Principles of Economic Theory*. Oxford University Press, London

32 James, R. F. and Blamey, R. K. (1999) Citizen participation – some recent Australian developments. Pacific Science Conference, Sydney, Australia, 4 July

33 Jacobs, M. (1997) 'Environmental valuation, deliberative democracy and public decision-making', in Foster, J. (ed) *Valuing Nature: Economics, Ethics and Environment*, Routledge, London, UK, pp211–231

34 Kaufmann, R. K. (1992) 'A biophysical analysis of the energy/real GDP ratio: implications for substitution and technical change'. *Ecological Economics*, vol 6, pp35–56

35 Kopp, R. J. and Smith, V. K. (1993) *Valuing Natural Assets: The Economics of Natural Resource Damage Assessment*. Resources for the Future, Washington, DC

36 Krutilla, J. V. (1967) 'Conservation reconsidered'. *American Economic Review*, vol 57(4), pp777–786

37 Lancaster, K. (1971) *Consumer Demand: A New Approach*. Columbia University Press, New York

38 Leopold, A. (1949) *A Sand County Almanac*. Oxford University Press, NY

39 Loewenstein, G. Prelec, D. (1991) 'Negative time preference'. *American Economic Review*, vol 81(2), pp347–352

40 Low, B. S. (2000) *Why Sex Matters: A Darwinian Look at Human Behaviour*. Princeton University Press, Princeton, NJ

41 Mitchell, R. C. and Carson, R. T. (1989) *Using Surveys for Value Public Goods: The Contingent Valuation Method*. Resources for the Future, Washington, DC

42 Norton, B. and Costanza, R., Bishop, R. (1998) 'The evolution of preferences: why "sovereign" preferences may not lead to sustainable policies and what to do about it'. *Ecological Economics*, vol 24, pp193–211

43 Odum, H. T. (1971) *Environment, Power and Society*. Wiley, New York

44 Odum, H. T. (1983) *Systems Ecology: An Introduction*. Wiley, New York

45 Page, T. (1977) *Conservation and Economic Efficiency*. Johns Hopkins University Press, Baltimore

46 Reder, M. (1961) Book review. American Economic Review 51(4), pp688–725

47 Sagoff, M. (1998) 'Aggregation and deliberation in valuing environmental public goods: a look beyond contingent valuation'. *Ecological Economics*, vol 24, pp213–230

48 Schumpeter, Joseph, A. (1978) *History of Economic Analysis*. Oxford University Press, New York

49 Slesser, M. (1973) *Energy analysis in policy making. New Scientist*, vol 58, pp328–330.

50 Sraffa, P. (1960) *Production of Commodities by Means of Commodities: Prelude to a Critique of Economic Theory*. Cambridge University Press, Cambridge

51 Varian, H. R. (1992) *Microeconomic Analysis*. W.W. Norton, New York

3

The Development of Environmental Thinking in Economics

Clive L. Spash

Introduction

Neoclassical theorists, from the late Victorians to the present, have given economics the technocentric optimism which environmentalists fear has distracted from the need for fundamental changes in human behaviour. However, throughout this last century, there has been a subgroup of established economists concerned about resource conservation and systems limits. In the early 1900s such economists were largely practising agricultural economics, which became a distinct subdiscipline at this time. Following World War II, resource and then environmental economics also became established areas of study. However, the ability of these subdisciplines to explore environmental critiques was restricted because they remained within the neoclassical framework and therefore tended to defend that paradigm. The emphasis on a mono-disciplinary approach also discouraged pluralism. Ecological economics has therefore become the latest attempt to take seriously the concern that aspects of the world such as the diversity of life in the wild, ecosystems structure and functioning, and the resources humans build into their cultures are all something more than a useful component of a welfare-generating economic system.

A major concern behind this paper is the general lack of knowledge about these developments, and differences between and within schools of thought, amongst both those outside of economics concerned by economy–environment interactions, and those (natural and social scientists) applying economic analysis to the environment. In explaining how different economists view environmental analysis, associated professional societies and journals are identified. Individual economists can often be difficult to classify purely on the basis of their external association with a school of thought, and therefore some idea of underlying values needs to be probed. Thus, the aim here is to act as a guide by both identifying key individuals with their roles in forming and following different schools, and also by attempting to distil the essence of what is implied by various professional affiliations. A broad historical perspective is taken in tackling these tasks, although the general concern is to throw light on developments within economics in the

Note: Reprinted from Spash, C. (1999) 'The development of environmental thinking in economics'. *Environmental Values*, vol 8, pp413–435, copyright © (1999) with permission from The White Horse Press

latter part of this century. Those seeking detail about the ecological critique of economics between the 1860s and the 1940s should refer to the book by Juan Martinez-Alier (1990).

For many people ecological economics is indistinguishable from agricultural economics, resource economics or environmental economics. Yet, there are significant differences amongst which the most obvious is recognition of the need to fundamentally change the current approach to economic analysis. Mainstream economists regard subdisciplines which question the orthodoxy as inferior pursuits and have therefore resisted the message that environmental and natural systems are distinctive elements of human production and welfare. Ecological economics has grown, particularly in the last decade, for several reasons, including frustration with the subdisciplinary status of environmental economics, the apparent failure to impact legislation, and the disregard shown for natural science information on the environment by other economists. Thus, particularly in the US, ecological economics has been adopted by many as a revitalized environmental economics, while those avoiding it see the subject as at best a poor substitute for environmental economics and at worst bad economics by self-promoting natural scientists. However, the aspirations of ecological economics are far greater than merely providing a new lease of life for established disciplines and lie in the development of new ideas and an interdisciplinary research agenda to explore alternative paradigms.

Ecological economics in Europe has been able to develop more freely than in the US and has naturally evolved a socio-economic perspective, which in many ways reverts to a political economy of the past. Until recently, few economists in Europe chose to specialize by studying environmental issues and those that did lacked any specific training. Prior to the 1990s, in order to gain a higher degree in environmental and natural resource economics generally meant training in the US. Thus, no strong European schools developed in environmental economics and ecological economics was not seen as tied to a particular economic tradition. While the situation may now be changing, and there have always been exceptions on both sides of the Atlantic, the dominant lead in America has been preoccupied with linking standard economic and ecological models, rather than looking for a paradigm shift. This has encouraged researchers to subscribe to ecological economics while producing research results which would fit comfortably within neoclassical environmental economics. As a result, confusion has continued over defining what the subject involves, although, as this paper hopes to clarify, the progressive element in ecological economics is based upon fundamentally different values to those of the established schools and is trying to synthesize several different nonestablished perspectives.

From the Classical to the Neoclassical

Classical economists such as Adam Smith, the Reverend Malthus and David Ricardo were concerned with limits to growth but from a different perspective to the modern theories underlying the call for sustainable development. A key common aspect for these classical economists, in this regard, was human population growth. Once combined with the dependence of production upon labour and a scarcity of land, economic growth could only stagnate because profits for capital would decline relative to wages for labour.

The driving force was population growth operating economic consequences via a redistribution of returns. Absolute resource constraints were unnecessary for this theory.

John Stuart Mill, Stanley Jevons and Alfred Marshall departed from this model and moved economic theory into the modern era. Mill (1857) recognized the potential of nonrenewable resources to act as constraints on economic growth independent of population pressures. He is also noted for mentioning the threat of unrestrained economic growth for natural wilderness, self-determination in natural ecosystems, and the importance of natural beauty and grandeur. Mill argued that technology could postpone constraints imposed by resource scarcity, which he regarded as increasing relative prices rather than creating sudden catastrophe. In this regard, Jevons (1865) may be viewed as more pessimistic producing a treatise on the limits to growth in Britain due to coal depletion. The failure of his predicted disaster, due to the arrival of oil as a substitute and advances in technology, helped establish much of what remains in the mainstream economics argument against seeing resource depletion as problematic. Alfred Marshall, despite being one of several (e.g. Jevons, Menger and Walras), is often described as the father of modern neoclassical economics. His *Principles of Economics* encapsulated the central arguments, such as the use of marginal analysis (most commonly associated with supply and demand functions) and mathematical modelling, although this was relegated to footnotes throughout his own text (Marshall, 1890). Interestingly Marshall, like Adam Smith, has been selectively read by modern economists who have ignored the fact that his economics was intended to be integrated with ethics (Collison Black, 1990).

After the passing of these well-known Victorian economists, the tendency has been to regard the first part of this century as a period in which little or no concern for resource depletion or environmental issues was shown by economists (e.g. see comments by Heal, 1986). The standard exception is normally given as Hotelling (1931) and his theory of the mine describing optimal nonrenewable resource depletion. The earlier contribution of Gray (1914) has also been recognized, if less widely, and some have argued that he deserves more credit (see Crabbe, 1983). Gray may have been neglected because of his explicit recognition that the intergenerational allocation of resources was an ethical rather than efficiency issue. Other literature on the economics and management of mineral resources can also be found (e.g. Logan, 1930; Osgood, 1930; Wallace and Edminster, 1930; Tyron, 1932; Ciriacy-Wantrup, 1944). In addition, Martinez-Alier (1990) has documented some of the historical roots of thinking in the area of energy–economy interactions with respect to forgotten academic contributions between the time of Jevons and the 1940s. The economic theory of value is discussed with regard to resource depletion by Ise (1925) who also wrote on forestry.

In fact, several authors also addressed natural resource problems as conservation issues (e.g. van Hise, 1910; Gray, 1913; Hess, 1917; Hammar, 1942; Renner, 1942). Meanwhile the development of agricultural economics, which is now generally on the decline, produced work on soil conservation (Ciriacy-Wantrup, 1938; Bunce, 1942; Weitzell, 1943; Shepard, 1945). Also of note is the foundation of the journal *Land Economics* in 1925, originally as the *Journal of Land and Public Utility Economics*, now published quarterly by the University of Wisconsin Press with Daniel Bromley (an institutional economist) as editor. In recent times this journal's applied and policy concern has been related to land use and monetary valuation of the environment (e.g. the travel cost method and contingent valuation).

In general, the literature in the first part of this century can be regarded as developing concerns in economics about conservation issues (as wise use, not preservation) related to agriculture and forestry and establishing a theoretical approach to nonrenewable resource depletion which is still fundamental to resource economics. However, such topics were no longer the concern of central figures in economic philosophy but were already relegated to specialists in subdisciplines. Meanwhile, mainstream economics developed theories which by assumption implied economies could operate independently of either natural resource constraints or assimilative capacity and so further marginalized environmental issues.

Resource and Environmental Economics

The resource economists of the 1950s tended to build upon the conservation work just outlined. They regarded the environment as a source of materials which required some specialized management due to characteristics which differentiated them from manufactured goods. These economists can be viewed as within the neoclassical school and as having strong associations with agricultural economics. Resource economics is now generally based upon the study of abstract mathematical models describing the 'efficient' and 'optimal' use of fisheries, forests and minerals.

Ciriacy-Wantrup (1952) can be seen as stimulating the development of environmental economics. His work in the 1950s inspired many who would establish environmental economics as a distinct sub-discipline in the 1960s and 1970s (e.g. Krutilla, 1967). Among his contributions is the concept of a safe minimum standard which was later adopted and revitalised by Bishop (1978). This concept is now often cited as a rejection of the conventional treatment of risk under benefit–cost analysis and a recognition of the importance of uncertainty as a distinct type of unpredictability. Some argue the safe minimum standard provides a bridge between economists and ecologist (e.g. Tisdell, 1993, p148).

The work of Kapp (1950) should also be noted here as another significant contribution at this time, although largely outside the mainstream. His approach was based within institutional economics and was critical of some key aspects of what came to be environmental economics. For example, he attacked the portrayal of environmental problems as 'externalities' rather than pervasive social costs resulting from the structure and incentives under free markets. Kapp (1970) also opposed monetary valuation because power structures in actual markets distort prices which would then fail to reflect resource scarcity (e.g. markets are mostly oligopolistic rather than perfectly competitive). In addition, he noted that the consequences of environmental disruption and benefits from environmental improvement are highly heterogeneous and cannot be compared quantitatively with one another or with control costs. Hence, Kapp rejected even the principle that social costs and benefits were quantitatively comparable. Environmental protection would provide social benefits throughout society and for Kapp environmental policy formation was therefore a question of political economy rather than a technical issue to be decided by a tool such as benefit–cost analysis.

However, thought on environment–economy interactions within economics was moving in the opposite direction to Kapp. During the 1950s the US persisted with the worries of World War II about exhaustible resource depletion as evidenced by the Paley Report (Paley, 1952). This report helped lead to the foundation of Resources for the Future (RFF) which, among other activities, was responsible for promoting advances in environmental benefit–cost analysis, e.g. publishing early guides to the travel cost method (Clawson and Knetsch, 1966) and contingent valuation (Mitchell and Carson, 1989). RFF publishes a newsletter *Resources*, which covers US environmental policy from an economic perspective, but has on occasion included more critical authors such as Mark Sagoff. The institution remains a strong lobbying and research group favouring mainstream neoclassical resource and environmental economics and has supported key developments in this area.

During the 1960s, environmental economics appeared in the US as a distinct sub-discipline concerned with the growing pollution problems which were becoming evident to the general public. *Land Economics* refocused on environmental economics, and the *Natural Resource Journal*, with an environmental law perspective, developed concerns about the political economy of environmental issues. However, the subject began to expand more as the decade ended and novel influences were brought into the economic realm.

In the late 1960s and early 1970s, the laws of thermodynamics were rediscovered as concepts with considerable implications for economics. This led to the development of materials balance theory (Kneese, Ayres and d'Arge, 1972). Simultaneously, Georgescu-Roegen (1971) was developing an extensive critique of economics also based upon the laws of thermodynamics and in particular entropy; although, unlike materials balance theory, his work remained relatively unattractive to environmental economists. The implications of the materials balance work in conjunction with general equilibrium modelling is that all the prices in the economy are incorrect in terms of efficiency because everything has an associated environmental externality (Hunt and d'Arge, 1973). However, the widespread implications of this simple and intuitive point for economics and policy have never been fully realized.

Following trends in mainstream economics, mathematical modelling took on a powerful role in the development of theory and in particular optimal control theory was adopted to model fisheries, resource depletion and pollution control. This mathematical approach gave credibility to the new subdiscipline within mainstream economics but removed it further from the actual management of environmental issues of the day and may therefore have restricted its growth and wider appeal. Outside of North America, only a handful of academics can be regarded as even addressing the subject area at this time; for example, in the UK, E. J. Mishan and in Sweden, Karl-Göran Mäler and Peter Bohm.

Institutionally, the 1970s were a period of consolidation by those in the US. A major step in that regard was establishing the Association of Environmental and Resource Economists (AERE) which resulted from discussions amongst Larry Ruff, Terry Ferrar, John Cumberland, Alan Carlin, Ralph d'Arge and Kerry Smith. The *Journal of Environmental Economics and Management* (JEEM) had been established by Ralph d'Arge and Allen Kneese in May 1974 and AERE later became the organisation controlling the journal. William Baumol was the first President of AERE in 1978, followed the next year by Kneese. Also, in 1979, the association was formally incorporated as a non-profit organisation in Washington, DC under the leadership of John V. Krutilla. Initial funding was provided in 1980 by the Ford Foundation, the Alfred P. Sloan Foundation, RFF and the Resource and Environmental Economics Labouratory of the University of Wyoming.

This new association effectively united the discipline in the USA and has grown to a current [1999] membership of approximately 800. The core concerns can be assessed from the AERE newsletter, JEEM, the topics of annual workshops (established in 1986) and the sources funding the organization. The business office of AERE has always been located at RFF headquarters in Washington, DC, and been provided free of charge. The Secretary and Treasurer have always been professional staff members of RFF. Workshop funding is provided by the US Environmental Protection Agency, the National Oceanic and Atmospheric Administration (NOAA) and the Economic Research Service of the US Department of Agriculture. The controversy over the use of contingent valuation in the *Exxon Valdez* resource damage legal case led NOAA to establish a panel of experts which provided guidelines as to best practice. As this shows, certain branches of the US government have seemed interested in economic input on environmental issues, and this, increasingly, has meant the development of environmental benefit–cost analysis, although, as noted later, the failure of politicians to adopt economic prescriptions for the environment has been a continuing concern to environmental economists.

AERE and JEEM gave credibility to environmental economics and encouraged further specialization. Resource economists concentrated upon fisheries, forestry and mineral extraction, while environmental economists dealt with pollution control and benefit–cost analysis. Together, resource and environmental economics explained how neoclassical models were flawed in their neglect of the resource base and waste sinks. They generally claimed corrections to markets could be made to avoid these problems and achieve efficiency gains. While popular environmentalism of the time was arguing in favour of legal restrictions and zero pollution, these economists favoured market-based instruments and optimal pollution levels determined by taking costs and benefits into account.

As the first dedicated publication in the area, JEEM held high hopes for constructive progress. However, the practical policy content originally proposed for JEEM was lost amongst mathematical models and theoretical expositions which, while winning the journal respect amongst mainstream economists, did little to address issues in practical environmental management. In general, JEEM developed into the theoretical journal of environmental economics, although in recent years some more critical articles, addressing wider concerns, have appeared, e.g. Vatn and Bromley (1994). The influence of JEEM on the subdiscipline was very strong for many years because few academic peer reviewed journals provided an outlet for those specializing in the economics of the environment. In terms of the mainstream economics journals, environmental economics was excluded with only rare exceptions. Not until the early 1990s was there a rapid growth of journals addressing economy–environment interactions and room for the expression of alternative approaches. As environmental problems became increasingly of political significance at this time, even the mainstream journals occasionally felt the need to address the subject, although usually restricting attention to specific topics dealt with by invited authors in special issues with no replies or comments allowed. Thus, despite the efforts made in establishing a distinct subdiscipline, environmental economics has remained a marginal pursuit within mainstream economics.

After the popular revival of environmentalism in the late 1980s, Europe started to follow in the footsteps of the North Americans. As environmental concern among the general public seemed to subside in the late 1970s and early 1980s so had the chance of adopting a more progressive attitude to these issues in economics departments around Europe. Not until 1991 was a European Association of Environmental and Resource Economists (EAERE) finally established. Straight away an associated journal published by Kluwer Academic, *Environmental and Resource Economics* (ERE), was started. The EAERE is a separate organization from the US AERE, with independent activities, although closer links are now being forged. The organization and journal have been strongly connected with academics in the Netherlands and Italy. The presidents have been Henk Folmer, Rudiger Pethig, Domenico Sinescalco and Aart de Zeeuw. The society has emphasized within its statutes the view of environmental and resource economics as a science, and this has been reflected in mathematical modelling and following the trends set by mainstream economics.

For many, this more formal spread of an apparent environmental concern within economic circles in Europe was welcomed as another opportunity to get the message across to politicians and fellow economists that the environment and economy interact in fundamental ways. However, neither have seemed particularly moved by what environmental economists have been saying. The main response to this neglect, apparent within environmental economics for sometime, has been to regard politicians and the political process as barriers to rational policy development. A general bewilderment has been expressed at the disregard shown by politicians for the message of even basic textbooks in environmental economics. Articles on this theme have appeared regularly in the academic literature (e.g. why have so few pollution taxes been adopted while legal restrictions seem to proliferate?, why are pollution standards set without regard to costs and benefits?); for a recent example see Shogren (1998).

At the same time, in areas where environmental economics has been regarded as susceptible to criticism for failing to address certain issues, the models have been extended. For example, environmental valuation methods have moved far from their original concentration on the direct use values of mainstream microeconomics into areas where questions relating to future generations and the existence of species are discussed. Those versed in the theoretical limits of neoclassical models have tended to regard these extensions into foreign territory as ill-advised and beyond the proper remit of economists. Thus, contingent valuation studies are attacked from within environmental economics as failing to conform to the assumption of the free market (e.g. no arbitrage) and being based upon stated, as opposed to revealed, preferences. Yet, by persisting within the relatively secure confines of mainstream neoclassical theory, environmental economics must then confine the terms of debate and so remain largely unable to adequately address or even consider central issues of concern for environmental policy. For example, concerns over the long-term impact of environmental pollution are inadequately addressed as technical issues about the appropriate discount rate, while the assumption that intergenerational equity can be captured within a specific model of preference utilitarianism precludes central aspects of the ethical debate (see Spash, 1993). Thus, the requirements of neoclassical theory come into conflict with the concerns raised by environmental issues.

In order for environmental economics to maintain a position of good standing within economics requires recruiting those with strong mathematical skills and a theoretical mindset. Those concerned with practical conservation and ecosystems management who lack that theoretical interest will therefore be discouraged from pursuing environmental economics as a method to advance their understanding of economy–environment inter-actions, and are likely to seek more direct routes to pursue their environmental concerns. For example, one of the latest trends in economics has been for game theoretic approaches which emphasize mathematical skills. Game theory applications to environ-mental issues seem to have been boosted by the availability of arms negotiations models developed during the cold war and have spread to other environmental subjects such as international relations (see Patterson, 1996). While perhaps academically satisfying, this preoccupation seems no more likely to help reduce environmental problems than it did bring about the demolition of the Berlin wall. For those concerned with achieving envi-ronmental policy changes, environmental economics therefore often appears to follow the wrong pursuits. This is unproblematic insofar as different disciplines allow speciali-zation and alternative disciplines exist for individuals to pursue their interests. However, for economists wishing to study the environment the choice has been absent and the approach in environmental economics often intolerant of open debate. Thus, several factors have led to discontent within environmental economics including the rather poor record of achieving policy change, the subdisciplinary status and, perhaps most importantly, tensions between conforming to and wishing to change the mainstream economic approach.

Ecological Economics

A tradition of thought which can be classified as ecological economics can be traced back at least to the middle of the last century (Martinez-Alier, 1990). However, the cur-rent movement is founded upon the concerns of the 1960s and early 1970s for limits to growth (e.g. Boulding, 1966; Meadows et al, 1972) and the study of the flow of energy and materials in the economy based upon the work of Georgescu-Roegen (1971). In addition, the management of environmental externalities as pervasive social costs and the resulting restrictions on the applicability of benefit–cost analysis reflect the studies of Kapp (1950). However, past writers expressing such an ecological critique of econom-ics failed to find a collective institutionalized academic niche which would establish a discipline or new paradigm. The more formal establishment of associations and journals only occurred in the late 1980s.

In Barcelona in 1987, at a meeting hosted by Juan Martinez-Alier, the International Society for Ecological Economics (ISEE) was born. European researchers played a key role in the formal creation of the movement, voting in Barcelona for the name Ecologi-cal Economics while placing an American ecologist, Bob Costanza, at the head. Among the 30 people present at this meeting were Malte Faber, Silvio Functowiz, Mario Giampietro, Ann-Marie Jansson, Martin O'Connor, John Proops, Jerry Ravetz and Mathias Ruth. The society was formally established in the USA in 1988 and has expanded from there to include branches in Australia/New Zealand, Brazil, Canada and Europe, chapters in India and Russia, an affiliated society in China and proposed chap-ters in Africa and across South America. The ISEE now has almost 2000 members in 81 countries. The society journal, *Ecological Economics,* is published 12 times per year by Elsevier Science Publishers and a quarterly bulletin is sent to members. The current structure (under reform) has a Board of Directors which consists of Bob Costanza, Herman Daly, Ann-Marie Jansson, John Peet and Juan Martinez-Alier, while the society President is Richard Norgaard.

The ISEE headquarters are currently based at the University of Maryland's Institute for Ecological Economics (IEE) which was itself founded in 1991 by grants from The Ford Foundation and the John D. and Catherine T. MacArthur Foundation. Full-time IEE faculty include the Director Bob Costanza, Associate Director Herman Daly and Senior Fellow John Cumberland (who was involved in the early development of the AERE). Costanza has exerted a strong influence over the society, as both chairman of the Board and president for the first decade and editor of the society journal. As the society has expanded, the need for a regionally representative, democratic structure has grown and a move away from the dominant US base seems inevitable.

Ecological economics as an international society was founded around the idea of uniting two groups of academics coming from narrow methodological backgrounds, ecologists trained in natural science falsificationist methodology and neoclassical economists trained in logical positivism. Indeed, in the introduction to the first issue of the journal *Ecological Economics*, Bob Costanza stated that the subject would extend the overlap between neoclassical environmental economics and ecological impact studies and encourage new ways of thinking about linkages between ecological and economic systems. Neoclassical economics was to be included as a subset of the new discipline; something of a surprise for many environmental economists no doubt. However, a more open model of pluralism was probably intended where different approaches to the same issue are compared and contrasted rather than subsumed under a new overarching structure. More importantly, excessive concentration on the 'improved linkage' approach detracted from the search for and adoption of a new paradigm.

In this latter regard, the methodology of ecological economics is still refreshingly open. For example, at the risk of generalizing, the European branch tends more to socio-economics and political economy while the Americans lean towards a scientific approach. The European Society for Ecological Economics (ESEE) was formally established as a charity in France in 1996 with the election of the officers of the Society held during a European Conference at the University of Versailles; Sylvie Faucheux was re-elected in 1998 to a second term as president. The movement in Europe has aims quite distinct from environmental economics societies such as the EAERE or AERE. As in the ISEE, the central objectives are to combine knowledge across the specialist areas of ecology and economics and see that policy advice on environmental problems be formulated on this basis. In addition, the ESEE encourages analysis of the social aspects of environmental policy and wider consideration of the place of humans within the environment. This implies a different methodology from mainstream economics while allowing for a discourse on the development of a socio-economic and ecological discipline. A series of books on ecological economics is to be published by the ESEE through Edward Elgar Publishers in order to help synthesize new ideas. A distinguishing feature of the European movement is the search for cooperation with philosophers, sociologists and psychologists to explore ethical, social and behavioural fundamentals of human wellbeing.

While the pluralism expounded by this approach is refreshing, the apparent expansion of economics may worry some that colonization of ideas is all that is intended.

Previous extensions of neoclassical economics (e.g. crime, health, environment) seem to have reassured the economics profession of the universality of their approach while allowing outside critiques to be regarded as largely irrelevant. For example, the concept of total economic value has been used by some to claim all environmental values can be adequately addressed in benefit–cost analysis. Unfortunately, some research along these lines has indeed appeared under the guise of ecological economics and, despite being technically deficient even within the neoclassical paradigm, has been widely publicized, for example, attempting to value the world's ecosystems in monetary terms. However, such work clearly deviates from what is progressive in ecological economics and also corrupts the meaning and content of concepts in both ecology (e.g. ecosystems functions) and economics (e.g. marginal valuation under *ceteris paribus*).

The potential of ecological economics to develop new paradigms has attracted a variety of those more critical of established approaches. The disparate positions held by this group of individuals is unified by the common belief that effective environmental policy formation requires linking natural and social sciences. That is, studying environmental problems without regard to economics is viewed as misguided in the same way as the economic approach has been misguided by excluding the natural science perspective. The work of environmental economists is then commended for identifying problems in the efficient allocation of resources and exposing the fallacy of economic analysis independent of the biosphere. However, this same work leads these critics to the conclusion that much of neoclassical economics is an impediment to further advancement. Yet, the pluralism preached by ecological economics encourages the continued participation of and reluctance to move beyond mainstream economic approaches.

Thus, a tension has remained within ecological economics. A crude characterization of this situation might be that there are two possible directions for ecological economics: either accept neoclassical theory as basically sound and aim to develop mathematical models linking it with ecology or, learning from past experience, accept that how economic systems interact with nature means moving away from old approaches and developing new paradigms. The first path has in principle been trodden by resource and then environmental economics for several decades, although without specific emphasis on ecology and with wavering enthusiasm by the late 1980s. While neoclassical economics offers a type of theoretical rigour attractive to scientifically trained academics, this same rigour reduces environmental problems to narrow technical issues and deliberately excludes a range of potential options and an interdisciplinary approach. Given the critique of economics that underlies the historical writings in the area, and that drove the formation of ecological economics, the second approach seems the only sensible alternative.

Whether all those currently subscribing to the movement will follow the developing path is unclear but unlikely. Currently, there are several contending themes which might define the core of ecological economics and pulling these together without alienating certain factions will be difficult. In a past edition of *Environmental Values*, Giuseppe Munda (1997) outlined his opinion of what form some of the key concepts. These were that ecological economics is concerned about the policy consequences of its arguments, openly claims ethical positions rather than neutrality, accepts that values can be disputed and incommensurable, recognizes distributional issues as a primary concern and sees the ecological concept of scale as limiting material growth. In addition, he proposed the co-evolutionary paradigm as described by Norgaard (1988; 1994) as a potential unifying theme. Evolutionary dynamics are an important aspect of ecological economics which emphasize that economic and environmental systems are interacting and changing, often unpredictably, rather than static, and this implies analysing non-deterministic processes rather than optimal paths to static equilibria. However, the particular interpretation via the coevolutionary paradigm remains a topic for open debate within ecological economics. Thus, while the subject remains open, and is for this reason attractive to many struggling to develop a comprehensive understanding of environmental values, Munda describes what is progressive in ecological economics and shows how it is moving distinctively away from mainstream economics.

As new concepts are developed within ecological economics, the 'improved linkage' route of combining existing economic approaches with natural science information seems too limiting. The themes of the developing subject area no longer sit comfortably in the mechanistic framework of environmental and resource economics and as a result the divide between the two seems set to grow. In this regard, the reader should note that the neoclassical approach is but one type of economics which has been operating within ecological economics. Institutional economics has been exerting its influence and may offer a forum for open debate more amenable to many (for a review see Spash and Villena, 1998). Marxism and socialism have also been entering the debate with authors considering how the environment should be included in their more traditional analyses; one result has been the development of political ecology, (see, for example, O'Connor, 1994; Keil et al, 1998). In addition, rethinking the role of science in society along the lines proposed by Funtowicz and Ravetz (1992; 1993) will change the perception of ecologists and economists as to their role in environmental policy formation.

Defining Values of Ecological Economics

Ecological economics is currently more of a movement than a discipline because the interdisciplinary requirements make a core methodology hard to define. One approach to trying to probe the values which underlie the subject is to look at what ecological economists do. This requires identifying those who ascribe to the discipline and studying their work. However, as noted, an initial policy in the ISEE was to gain wide support from established academics prepared to sign up to the general concept of studying economy–environment interactions. Environmental economists interested in how ecology might contribute to economics joined, while continuing their work as before, and only some of these had a view to developing new approaches. This has resulted in the names of individuals long associated with a narrow neoclassical environmental economics approach appearing under the banner of ecological economics.

Others, trying to draw together ecology and neoclassical environmental and resource economics, see no contradiction in being on the governing council of neoclassical associations, such as EAERE or AERE, while assuming the mantle of ecological economics. The potential contradiction is avoided for them because they study 'ecology and economies' and in doing so regard each as distinct subject areas with specific types of narrowly defined interactions. For example, Turner, Perrings and Folke (1997) 'do not see ecological economics as an alternative paradigm' (p27), refer to it as being closer to renewable resource economics than environmental economics, and reduce all concerns to side constraints on economic activities (convenient for the optimal control modelling favoured by resource economists).

This perception of the movement as 'ecology and economies' can be associated with the expression of a particular set of values and concentration upon the science approach to both subjects. An individual trained in mathematics or physics who has switched into economics (not uncommon) and who is concerned about the environment might prefer the greater degree of linkage between natural science and economics emphasised by ecological economics. Similarly, an ecologist might feel their interest in economic interactions with the environment is best served by adopting neoclassical models from environmental economics and assume this is the only aim of ecological economics. These people might also satisfy their core concern, to extend the scientific approach by linking models, through association with environmental economics where a logical positivist methodology is still common and the emphasis is upon technical competence and mathematical model-building skills. Technical competence is of course important to avoid misleading use of current economic tools, but extending technical competence across disciplines is a relatively limited (although often challenging) educational goal. However, what such individuals do not require is a new discipline called ecological economics because for them there is only a combined science of 'ecology and economies' based upon the two established disciplines.

Ecological economics consists of more than linking economic market models with ecological production function analysis and providing 'robust' numbers. Otherwise it would indeed merely be environmental economics renamed and could employ the same methods and methodology. As the history of environmental economics has shown, the emphasis on being a part of the mainstream school of economics has meant pushing to one side problems which fail to conform to theoretical expectations. Examples of such problems are Georgescu-Roegen's work on entropy, Ciriacy-Wantrup's concerns about the epistemology of uncertainty, Kapp's critiques of valuation, and the general inadequacies of the underlying behavioural model as noted, for example, by Knetsch (1994). Furthermore, while environmental and resource economics has been restricted to microeconomics, ecological economics has been progressive at both microeconomic (e.g. household consumption) and macroeconomic (economic growth and sustainability) levels.

Consideration of ecology also presents fundamental insights into economics rather than a few extra constraints. Holling et al (1995) suspect many economists ignore ecological information despite the accumulated body of evidence from natural, disturbed and managed ecosystems. In particular, they identify four key features common to the function and structure of many ecosystems which economists should bring into their subject. A précis of their points is as follows:

1   Ecosystem change is episodic rather than continuous and gradual. For example, uncommon events, such as hurricanes, can unpredictably reshape structure at critical times or in vulnerable locations.
2   Scaling up from small to large is a nonlinear process. Thus, spatial attributes vary with scale rather than being uniform.

3 Ecosystems exhibit multiple equilibria, an absence of equilibria and are destabilized by forces far from equilibria. The movement between such states maintains structure and diversity. This contrasts with the conception of ecosystems as single equilibrium systems with functions operating to maintain the stable state.
4 Recognizing that ecosystems have multiple features, which are uncertain and unpredictable, requires management and policies to be flexible, adaptive and experimental at scales compatible with those of critical ecosystem functions.

Besides learning from ecology the movement has begun to look across other divides such as ethics, psychology and politics, and to recognize the importance of methodological and value issues. For example, debates over the motives behind natural capital maintenance are poorly reflected by reduction purely to the degree to which people believe inputs are substitutable, a very mechanistic reductionism; driving issues concern ignorance being epistemologically different from risk (Faber, Manstetten and Proops, 1996) and the recognition of nonhuman values (Spash and Clayton, 1997). Other ethical considerations relate to the moral standing of unborn future generations and the inadequacy of debates upon appropriate interest rate derivation to even address the issue (Spash, 1993). A defining aspect of commitment to ecological economics is then the extent to which concepts, such as discounting, are seen as problematic in themselves, the issues they raise are debated and the search initiated for alternative approaches. For some economists even questioning the orthodoxy is heretical, and values and information which it excludes must therefore be irrelevant to economics. The socio-economic approach to ecological economics accepts the need for future generations of humans to have a voice and that both intra- and inter-generational distribution are issues the current economic and political system fails to adequately address.

This concern for disenfranchised humans and the importance given to distributional issues is common amongst ecological economists. Social and community values are recognized as key to improving human wellbeing and therefore part of the consideration in addressing environmental problems. Appealing to a theory of human motivation based solely upon individual preferences, even when altruistic, is then somewhat contradictory. Much of environmentalism is concerned with a sense of community across space and time. An opinion shared with socialist critiques is that free market systems educate individuals to act as selfish hedonists and create self-perpetuating power structures which reinforce inequity. Thus, ecological economics is also interested in exploring alternative institutions and processes. Such an institutional approach needs to consider how a variety of values can be expressed and how to prevent the loss of values which occurs when they are squeezed to fit within the free market paradigm. The aim for ecological economics must be to develop new ways of thinking about the world around us and approaches for resolving (not necessarily solving) environmental conflicts.

More controversial is the extent to which ecological economists accept that moral standing be given to nonhuman entities. Proops (1989, pp62, 72) has identified questions over rights for animal species, plants and depletable resources as part of the research agenda on ethical values required in ecological economics. While Costanza and Daly (1987, p4) have noted the ability of humans to misperceive the value of natural resources which leads them to state that: 'Some notion of intrinsic value must therefore be introduced as a check on human perceptions and to allow us to study the economies of nature which do not include humans'. Unfortunately, they fail to expand upon their conception of intrinsic value. One possible expression of this concern might be in the development by ecologists and social scientists of the concept of ecosystem health which seems to equate ecosystems to people in that ecosystems are more than an aggregation of component species and the implication is that as entities they can be harmed, i.e. be given poor health (Costanza, 1992, pp240–241). There also seems to be a key underlying concern in the concept of natural capital maintenance that goes beyond preservation of useful engineering features, and this might also be described as value within ecosystems themselves. Although, naming nature as capital is a mechanistic approach which reduces the meaning of the underlying concept, similar in effect to 'commodification' of wildlife. Thus, for ecologists studying ecosystems health and economists discussing natural capital, ecosystems are in fact often regarded as purely functional production systems serving human ends. In fact there appears to be a concentration upon aspects of value which contribute either directly or indirectly to human wellbeing. Indeed, while discussions on the basis for sustainability have brought the land ethic of Aldo Leopold (1987) into play, the values expressed are mostly couched in terms of poverty alleviation and intergenerational equity (see Spash and Villena, 1998). Thus, recognition that nonhuman entities have value beyond reduction to individual human preferences, expressed either in the market place or political arena, remains an issue for open debate in ecological economics. Any debate which does ensue will undoubtedly reflect different cultural values which themselves require greater acceptance within economics.

Neoclassical economists traditionally withdraw from such debates, claiming these matters are noneconomic. They may therefore reject the results which indicate that people hold values diverging from theoretically accepted expectations, e.g. claiming studies have been poorly or unscientifically conducted. Ethical debates in benefit–cost analysis have resulted in open attacks on even the idea of studying environmental ethics (Pearce, 1996). Methods, such as contingent valuation, may be rejected completely rather than asking what they actually indicate when unexpected results arise. Others try to extend the model to include any occurrence of wider concepts of value in a comprehensive benefit–cost analysis. When confronted by the possibility that nonhuman existence may have some value in and of itself, some environmental economists have claimed this is approximated by human willingness to pay for a poorly defined concept of another entity's existence. However, methods such as contingent valuation can be used to show the presence of rights-based positions which can be consistent with rejecting this interpretation (Spash, 1998). The point here is that, in making values fit the a priori model, the concepts missing from economic theory or which fall outside the market are perverted, e.g. equating intrinsic value to existence value (Pearce, Markandya and Barbier, 1990), reducing ignorance to probabilities (Chichilnisky and Heal, 1993).

This process of narrowing down the room for debate is standard practice within mainstream economics. In a presidential address for the ISEE, Richard Norgaard (1998, p7) briefly discussed a challenge he repeatedly faces, often from fellow economists (from both the political right and left), that 'hurting peasants to save forests is immoral'. He states that:

...the dilemma is symptomatic of a larger problem, how economics and public discourse have coevolved in a particularly dishonest and morally vacuous way. Now I ask why the choice is between the peasant and the forest that our descendants might need? Where are the people driving the BMWs today, or even those driving Fords, in this myth? Why is it that we have these debates between rich environmentalists and rich developmentalists over moral dilemmas where the rich themselves are absent?

He goes on to locate the cause of such myths within the historical development of welfare economics as a method for removing any apparent need for moral discourse or politics from the agenda of the economic policy adviser.

As Norgaard notes, such mythical dilemmas are used to defend the status quo. This can be seen in other areas such as the perpetuation of the myth of the 'tragedy of the commons' (Hardin, 1968), which has been used to deride communitarian values and promote private ownership. The historical tragedy has been the destruction by private profiteers of customs and cultures which managed resources in common and prevented over-exploitation. However, the myth of common ownership being a tragedy is far more useful for those who favour the spread of private property rights and the rule of the market. A whole set of issues about institutional arrangements, political structures and cultural relationships with nonhuman entities is then neatly reduced to the efficiency of private markets.

This is part of a more general methodological problem in economics where, of the two roots of economics, the engineering aspect has become dominant while the ethical approach is ridiculed as unscientific. Sen (1987) has argued that the ethical approach to economics is traceable to Aristotle and the engineering one to Kautilya, a 4th-century adviser to the Indian emperor. In reintroducing the ethical element as an integral part of economics, and recognizing the narrowness of reducing such issues to an engineering equation, ecological economics is taking a distinct and neglected path to economic policy.

Conclusions

Environmental concerns have been relatively unimportant for established economists during the past century but have in recent decades become politically (and therefore economically) relevant. Mono-disciplinary approaches to environment–economy interactions have been recognized by many to be inadequate. Figure 3.1 summarizes the process of development which thinking about the role of the environment has undergone this century within economics. In this process, ecological economics is an important departure because it attempts to integrate and synthesize many different disciplinary perspectives. In order to achieve social and environmental sustainability, there is a belief in the need to understand current approaches to economics and ecology but most importantly to develop a new paradigm.

The review here shows that ecological economics has been viewed by some as merely linking environmental economics with ecology. However, this is inconsistent with the ecological and environmental critique of economics which resource and environmental economists have been unable to address. The argument has been put forward

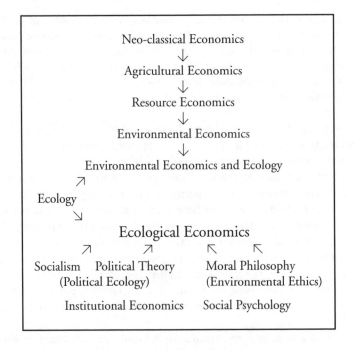

Figure 3.1 *Economic perspectives on the environment*

that in Europe a socio-economic approach has been developing while in North America the dominant trend has been to favour an objective science viewpoint. This latter view was termed the 'improved linkage' approach and defines a group of scholars working under 'ecology and economies'. Rather confusingly for the external observer, this approach has encouraged neoclassical economists to present their work under the title of ecological economics. However, ecological economics is moving beyond these disciplines; for example, by placing importance upon the open discussion of ethical issues, rather than assuming resource and environmental problems can be meaningfully analysed from the ethically neutral perspective of an objective science. Ecological economics is synthesizing different perspectives and is raising issues which environmental economics has been unable to address. For example, the psychological model of individual behaviour underlying microeconomics is unable to account for such fundamental concepts as social context, environmental attitudes and ethical beliefs. When it tries to do so the theoretical anomalies either cause a rapid retreat or dramatic perversion of the original concept.

A central part of defining ecological economics as a distinct new subject rotates around the importance of incorporating moral values and being prepared to openly debate difficult issues, such as the set of morally considerable entities, the rights of future generations and treatment of the poor. The socio-economic approach to ecological economics recognizes a failure to account for issues of equity and culture and rejects the dominance of efficiency in economics. Some consensus exists around the key aspects of any new paradigm, which will need to include the recognition of ecosystems constraints, a concern for equity, fairness, effectiveness and efficiency in economic systems, and a regard for the moral standing of others both within current and across future generations of humans. The independent value of nonhuman entities remains more controversial. In order to address these issues, the subject is moving towards a new political economy. However, whereas one individual might in the past have aspired to master the sum of human knowledge in such a subject, this no longer seems possible. More feasible and necessary is an open mind working with others from different disciplinary backgrounds but with similarly open minds.

An interdisciplinary approach to the environment can only be achieved by individuals being prepared to cross disciplinary boundaries and learn the language of other academic disciplines. This is where ecological economics holds out the greatest hope. In the past, much emphasis in environmental work has been placed upon rhetorical reference to interdisciplinary research but in fact this has meant producing reports which are merely a combination of chapters written by mono-disciplinary groups and bound together without regard to the inconsistencies. Open debate and synthesis are essential to allow academics the potential to understand why their work is seen as incorrect, or even on occasion offensive, to those with other perspectives. At the same time, this must be achieved without making individuals paranoid or feeling they must be defensive and withdraw behind their disciplinary boundaries. A central aim of this type of pluralism is to create the academic freedom to address environmental problems. Ecological economics offers the potential for individuals to be specialists in one area while being mindful of other perspectives.

As ecological economics moves away from the engineering approach to the ethical side of economics there will be a transition in which some of the methods, if not the methodology, of environmental and resource economics remain of practical use. However, as shown in Figure 3.1, ecological economics as the study of wellbeing in society is open to influences from several disciplines as well as attracting economists of various persuasions (e.g. socialist, institutional, environmental). The point of ecological economics is to recognize the environment as a complex collection of ethical and evaluative considerations. While many environmental economists would accept the relevance of considerations outside their analysis, they claim to leave these to the mythical 'decision maker'. The potential of ecological economics is to include these as essential aspects of analysis. Thus, for example, the goals of traditional 'development' and 'growth' can be recognized as being excessively materialistic on social, ethical and environmental grounds. In this way, ecological economics is now facing the challenge of exploring how to go beyond the limits of the disciplines it combines and develop a political economy of Nature.

References

1   Bishop, R. C. (1978) 'Endangered species and uncertainty: the economics of a safe minimum standard'. *American Journal of Agricultural Economics,* vol 60, pp10–18
2   Boulding, K. E. (1966) 'The economics of the coming Spaceship Earth', in H. Jarrett (ed) *Environmental Quality in a Growing Economy: Essays from the Sixth RFF Forum.* Johns Hopkins University Press, Baltimore, pp3–14

3   Bunce, A. C. (1942) *The Economics of Soil Conservation*. Iowa State College Press, Ames, IA

4   Chichilnisky, G. and Heal, G. (1993) 'Global environmental risks'. *Journal of Economic Perspectives,* vol 7(4), pp65–86

5   Ciriacy-Wantrup, S. (1938) 'Soil conservation in European farm management'. *Journal of Farm Economics,* vol 20(February)

6   Ciriacy-Wantrup, S. (1944) 'Taxation and the conservation of resources'. *Quarterly Journal of Economics,* vol 58(February)

7   Ciriacy-Wantrup, S. (1952) *Resource Conservation: Economics and Policies*. University of California Press, Berkeley

8   Clawson, M. and Knetsch, J. L. (1966) *Economics of Outdoor Recreation*. Johns Hopkins University Press, Baltimore and London

9   Collison Black, R. D. (1990) 'Jevons, Marshall and the utilitarian tradition'. *Scottish Journal of Political Economy,* vol 37(February), pp5–17

10   Costanza, R. (1992) 'Toward an operational definition of ecosystem health', in R. Costanza, B. G. Norton and B. D. Haskell (eds) *Ecosystem Health: New Goals for Environmental Managment*. Island Press, Washington, DC, pp239–256

11   Costanza, R. and Daly, H. E. (1987) 'Toward an ecological economics'. *Ecological Modelling,* vol 38, pp1–7

12   Crabbe, P. J. (1983) 'The contribution of L. C. Gray to the economic theory of exhaustible resources'. *Journal of Environmental Economics and Management,* vol 10, pp195–220

13   Faber, M., Manstetten, R. and Proops, J. (1996) *Ecological Economics: Concepts and Methods*. Edward Elgar, Cheltenham, England

14   Funtowicz, S. O. and (1992) 'The good, the true and the postmodern'. *Futures,* vol 24(10), pp963–976

15   Funtowicz, S. O. and Ravetz, J. R. (1993) 'Science for the post-normal age'. *Futures,* vol 25(7), pp739–755

16   Georgescu-Roegen, N. (1971) *The Entropy Law and the Economic Process*. Harvard University Press Cambridge, MA

17   Gray, L. C. (1913) 'The economic possibilities of conservation'. *Quarterly Journal of Economics,* vol 27, pp515–519.

18   Gray, L. C. (1914) 'Rent under the assumption of exhaustibility'. *Quarterly Journal of Economics,* vol 28 pp466–489

19   Hammar, C. H. (1942) 'Society and conservation'. *Journal of Farm Economics* vol 24(February), pp109–123

20   Hardin, G. (1968) 'The tragedy of the commons'. *Science,* vol 162(13 December 1968), pp1243–1248

21   Heal, G. (1986) 'The intertemporal problem', in D. W. Bromley (ed.) *Natural Resource Economics Policy Problems and Contemporary Analysis*. Kluwer Nijhoff Publishing, Boston, pp1–36

22   Hess, R. H. (1917) 'Conservation and economic evolution', in Ely et al, (eds) *The Foundations of Natural Prosperity*. Macmillan, New York

23   Holling, C. S. Schindler, D. W. Walker, B. W. and Roughgarden, J. (1995) 'Biodiversity in the functioning of ecosystems: An ecological synthesis', in Perrings, C., Mäler, K.-G., Folke, C., Holling, C. S. and Jansson, B.-O. (eds) *Biodiversity Loss: Economics and Ecological Issues*. Cambridge University Press, Cambridge, England

24   Hotelling, H. (1931) 'The economics of exhaustible resources'. *The Journal of Political Economy,* vol 39(2), pp137–175

25   Hunt, E. K. and d'Arge, R. C. (1973) On lemmings and other acquisitive animals: Propositions on consumption. *Journal of Economic Issues,* vol 7(June), pp337–353

26   Ise, J. (1925) 'The theory of value as applied to natural resources'. *American Economic Review,* vol 15, pp284–291.

27 Jevons, W. S. (1865) *The Coal Question: An Inquiry Concerning the Progress of the Nation and the Probable Exhaustion of our Coal-mines.* Macmillan, London

28 Kapp, K. W. (1950) *The Social Costs of Private Enterprise.* Shocken, New York

29 Kapp, K. W. (1970) 'Environmental disruptions and social costs: A challenge to economists'. *Kyklos,* vol 23, pp833–847.

30 Keil, R., Bell, D. V. J., Penz, P. and Fawcett, L. (eds) (1998) *Political Ecology: Global and Local.* Routledge, London

31 Kneese, A. V., Ayres, R. U. and d'Arge, R. C. (1972) *Economics and the Environment: A Materials Balance Approach.* Resources for the Future, Washington, DC

32 Knetsch, J. L. (1994) 'Environmental valuation: Some problems of wrong questions and misleading answers'. *Environmental Values,* vol 3(4), pp351–368

33 Krutilla, J. V. (1967) 'Conservation reconsidered'. *American Economic Review,* (September): pp777–786

34 Leopold, A. (1987) *A Sand County Almanac and Sketches Here and There.* Oxford University Press, Oxford, England

35 Logan, L. M. (1930) *Stabilization of the Petroleum Industry.* University of Oklahoma Press, Norman

36 Marshall, A. (1890) *Principles of Economics.* Macmillan, London

37 Martinez-Alier, J. (1990) *Ecological Economics: Energy, Environment and Society.* Basil Blackwell, Oxford, England

38 Meadows, D. H., Meadows, D. L., Randers, J. and Behrens III, W. W. (1972) *The Limits to Growth.* Universe Books, New York

39 Mill, J. S. (1857) *Principles of Political Economy.* Parker, London

40 Mitchell, R. C. and Carson, R. T. (1989) *Using Surveys to Value Public Goods: The Contingent Valuation Method.* Resources for the Future, Washington, DC

41 Munda, G. (1997) 'Environmental economics, ecological economics, and the concept of sustainable development'. *Environmental Values,* vol 6(2), pp213–233

42 Norgaard, R. B. (1988) 'Sustainable development: A co-evolutionary view'. *Futures,* December, pp606–662

43 Norgaard, R. B. (1994) *Development Betrayed: The End of Progress and a Coevolutionary Revisioning of the Future.* Routledge, London

44 Norgaard, R. B. (1998) *Beyond Growth and Globalization.* 10th V. T. Krishnamachari Lecture, Institute of Economic Growth, Delhi, India

45 O'Connor, M. (ed) (1994) *Is Capitalism Sustainable? Political Economy and the Politics of Ecology.* Guilford Press, New York

46 Osgood, W. (1930) *Increasing the Recovery of Petroleum.* McGraw-Hill, New York

47 Paley, W. S. (1952) *Resources for Freedom: Report of the President's Materials Policy Commission.* Washington, DC, Government Printing Office

48 Patterson, M. (1996) *Global Warming and Global Politics.* Routledge Ltd. London

49 Pearce, D. (1996) *Valuing the environment: The perspective of ecological economics.* Valuing the Environment Lecture Series, University of Cambridge, England

50 Pearce, D. Markandya, A. and Barbier, E. B. (1990) *Blueprint for a Green Economy.* Earthscan, London

51 Proops, J. (1989) 'Ecological economics: Rationale and problem areas'. *Ecological Economics,* vol 1(1), pp59–76

52 Renner, G. T. (1942) *Conservation of Natural Resources.* Wiley, New York

53 Sen, A. K. (1987) *On Ethics and Economics.* Basil Blackwell, Oxford, England

54 Shepard, W. (1945) *Food of Famine: The Challenge of Erosion.* Macmillan, New York

55 Shogren, J. F. (1998) 'A political economy in an ecological web'. *Environmental and Resource Economics,* vol 11(3–4), pp557–570

56 Spash, C. L. (1993) 'Economics, ethics, and long-term environmental damages'. *Environmental Ethics,* vol 15(2), pp117–132

57 Spash, C. L. (1998) 'Investigating individual motives for environmental action: Lexicographic preferences, beliefs and attitudes', in Lemons, J., Westra, L. and Goodland, R. (eds) *Ecological Sustainability and Integrity: Concepts and Approaches.* Kluwer Academic Publishers, Dordrecht, The Netherlands, vol 13, pp46–62

58 Spash, C. L. and Clayton, A. M. H. (1997) 'The maintenance of natural capital: Motivations and methods'. *Philosophy and Geography (Space, place and environmental ethics),* pp143–173

59 Spash, C. L. and Villena, M. (1998) *Investigating an institutional approach to the environment: socio-ecological economics.* International Society for Ecological Economics 5th Biennial Conference, Santiago, Chile

60 Tisdell, C. (1993) *Environmental Economics: Policies for Environmental Management and Sustainable Development.* Edward Elgar, Aldershot, England

61 Turner, K., Perrings, C. and Folke, C. (1997) in van den Bergh, J. C. J. M. and van der Straaten, J. (eds) *Economy and Ecosystems in Change.* Cheltenham: Edward Elgar, pp25–49

62 Tyron, F. G. (1932) *Mineral Economics.* McGraw-Hill, New York

63 van Hise, C. R. (1910) *The Conservation of Natural Resources in the US.* Macmillan, NY

64 Vatn, A. and Bromley, D. W. (1994) Choices without prices without apologies. *Journal of Environmental Economics and Management,* vol 26, pp129–148

65 Wallace, B. and Edminster, L. R. (1930) *International Control of Raw Materials.* Brookings Institute, Washington DC

66 Weitzell, E. C. (1943) 'Economics of soil conservation'. *Land Economics,* vol 19(August), pp339–353

Part 2

Philosophical and Ethical Themes in Environmental Values

Introduction

Philosophers have long been interested in nature and environmental issues – Plato has been described (although not without criticism) as an environmentalist, Aristotle wrote essays that justified the domination of humans over nature and argued for the taming and preservation of wild animals, and Descartes drew an impermeable line between rational culture and irrational nature positing that animals were mechanistic clock-like bodies devoid of all consciousness and unable to feel pleasure or pain. As a subfield of philosophy, environmental ethics continues to inquire about our moral relationship with nature and animals, but from a position of immediacy and crisis. The entire planet is faced with widespread environmental degradation and environmentally linked diseases that threaten both human and other animal populations. Beginning with the writings in the first half of the 20th century by John Muir and Aldo Leopold, and gaining wide currency in the 1960s with the rising concern about species extinction and population growth, environmental ethics focuses on the philosophical question of our *moral obligations* to the environment, such as what *ought we value* in nature and animals and whether nature and animals have value above and beyond their usefulness for humans.

While there are many different approaches to answering questions of morality and value, the five papers in Part 2 discuss some of the key philosophical and ethical themes in environmental values. The first two papers describe the strengths and weaknesses of anthropocentric (human-centred) value theory (which gives intrinsic value to humans and denies such value status to all others, both living and nonliving) and non-anthropocentric value theory (which gives intrinsic value to at least some living organisms). The next three papers focus on the tenets of one of the most influential Western conservation environmental philosophies of the 20th century, deep ecology (which holds that all living things are alike in having value in their own right over and above their use for humans, and that humans have no right to reduce the diversity of life forms except to satisfy vital needs) and its connection to different social, political and economic contexts. The last paper addresses the biological basis of environmental ethics.

In the first paper, J. Baird Callicott argues that the development of a *non-anthropocentric value theory* is the most important philosophical work to be done in the field of environmental ethics. He considers environmental ethics a major paradigm shift in moral philosophy because it provides the theoretical framework for the *moral standing* or *moral considerability* of things natural and not human (such as natural entities, natural communities or nature as a whole). Worried that without a basis in non-anthropocentric thinking, environmental ethics would never be revolutionary, Callicott examines numerous non-anthropocentric value theories for their potential in meeting the challenge. He discards as inadequate both 'ethical hedonism' (since it limits moral standing to only sentient beings, or those capable of experiencing pleasure and pain) and 'ethical conativism' (since moral standing is given to both plants and animals, rigorous conativists would be required to starve themselves to death). Better alternatives, but still inadequate, are 'theistic axiology' (all aspects of the natural world are good and have intrinsic value, or the 'stewardship view' in which humans are obligated to protect and take care of nature as a biospheric community) and 'holistic rationalism' (all good things are intrinsically good or valuable to the degree of their 'goodness'). From his review of the alternatives, Callicott establishes four essential elements of an appropriate value theory for environmental ethics: (1) both individual organisms and 'superorganismic entities' (such as populations or entire species) must be seen as having intrinsic value; (2) a provision must be made for the differential value of wild and domestic organisms (since we tend to value individual domestic animals, such as a companion dog, differently than individual wild animals, such as reindeer); (3) the theory must be consistent with current evolutionary and ecological biology; and (4) the theory must give intrinsic value to all of the parts and species in our present ecosystem, not equal value for just any ecosystem. Callicott concludes that a genuine non-anthropocentric environmental ethic is a sentiment of *biophilia*, which recognizes that all individuals are members of a community of interdependent parts, including soil, water, plant, animals, the land, and each individual extends sympathy and concern to all members of the biotic community though different in species.

Bryan Norton argues against the assertion that environmental ethics must be based upon a non-anthropocentric value theory. Drawing a distinction between weak and strong anthropocentrism, Norton suggests that the concept of value should be pragmatic not intrinsic, and a *weak anthropocentric* position provides the best basis for an environmental ethic. In strong anthropocentrism, all sanctioned values are *felt preferences* of humans, or any human desire or need that can at least be temporarily sated by some specifiable individual experience. Weak anthropocentrism, on the other hand, recognizes *considered preferences*, or any human desire or need expressed after careful thought and deliberation. Thus, weak anthropocentrism provides the framework to criticize human preferences that exploit nature but without attributing intrinsic value to the natural world. Norton also argues that, since most Western ethical theory is individualistic (behaviour that harms other individuals unjustifiably is prohibited), ethical guidance concerning all current environmental issues must be non-individualistic. Concluding that an adequate environmental ethic need not be non-anthropocentric and must not be limited to individual interests, Norton speculates that over time a weak anthropocentric environmental ethic will promote a sense of harmony with nature and an adjustment in our felt preferences, without having to resort to the assumption that nonhuman others have intrinsic value.

Arne Naess responds to a critique of 'anti-anthropocentric biocentrism' (a concept developed in a previously published article by Richard A. Watson) by arguing in favour of *deep ecology*, a non-anthropocentric value theory that maintains the *intrinsic value of all beings* (human and nonhuman) and the intrinsic value of the diversity in life forms. The implication of these principles is the belief that humans do not have the right to take nonhuman lives, except in cases where it is necessary to satisfy *vital needs*. Naess argues that the qualification that nonhuman lives may be sacrificed to satisfy vital needs has been overlooked in characterizing the traditional position of deep ecologists. He proposes that the oversight of this important qualification is the result of a failure by some to distinguish between the deep ecology social movement and the philosophical or academic iterations of deep ecology. Naess argues instead that supporters of deep ecology should be engaged in examining what vital needs entail in practice and insisting on the intrinsic value of all life on Earth.

Ramachandra Guha offers a critique of deep ecology from the perspective of the developing world in his argument that the anthropocentric/non-anthropocentric dichotomy is itself problematic in the context of developing nations. Guha frames his discussion around the assertion that the non-anthropocentric position is biocentric (in biocentrism the biosphere comes first, and in anthropocentrism, humans come first). He takes issue with the assertion that all human intervention in nature must be to 'preserve biotic integrity' and not for the sake of human interests. He contends that the two main environmental problems in the world are overconsumption in industrialized nations and increasing militarization, and that the anthropocentric/biocentric (or non-anthropocentric) dichotomy does little to inform these issues. Instead, he points to *economic and political structures* and individual *consumption* patterns as the likely causes of environmental problems. Guha argues that these causes of environmental degradation are not only unrelated to anthropocentrism but that if humans were acting in a truly anthropocentric way (putting human needs above all else), overconsumption and militarization would not be problems since in the end they endanger human life. The Western version of the *value of wilderness* is also problematic for Guha. He argues that an emphasis on wilderness protection has been imposed upon developing world countries, with negative effects on the indigenous population. Guha's conception of an appropriate environmental ethic would attend to both environmental and social justice concerns, critique the consumer society mentality in the industrial world that grounds many environmental problems, and provide an appropriate framework for a global environmental movement.

Ariel Salleh also critiques deep ecologists and their version of biocentrism. Drawing on the insights of *ecofeminism* (a combination of environmental advocacy and feminist analysis), Salleh argues that in their quest to critique anthropocentrism and promote a biocentric perspective, deep ecologists have neglected issues of *social inequalities*. She contends that the deep ecology perspective is grounded in the perspectives and values of privileged white men, which is linked to why they have failed to attend to social inequalities and the perspectives of others. She asks how a value theory derived from women's perspectives would be different from one derived from the perspective of men, and she draws numerous distinctions between the deep ecology and the ecofeminist perspectives, such as the tendency for ecofeminists to draw attention to women's *reproductive labour* and the ways in which reproductive labour fosters a close relationship between women and nature. Further, Salleh argues that deep ecology is grounded in paid professionalism, whereas ecofeminism is rooted in praxis that is tied to '*life needs*' (which is related to women's reproductive labour), and that deep ecology has not systematically attended to the multinational-corporate industrial society and its effects, both on the environment and on women. Salleh concludes that deep ecology has been constructed by men who are advantaged by patriarchal and capitalist institutions and that the movement ignores the place of labour in the maintenance of human life and in the exchange between culture and nature.

In the last article, Stephen Kellert explores the notion that all humans have an *innate biological need* to affiliate with and value the natural environment (E. O. Wilson's *biophilia hypothesis*). Kellert argues that human *dependence on nature* for survival and personal fulfillment is expressed by nine values that show a human affinity for the natural world: utilitarian (values nature for the goods and services that can be derived from it), naturalistic (values are related to direct contact with nature), ecologistic-scientific (values nature for the knowledge that can be derived from it), aesthetic (values the physical beauty of nature), symbolic (values are related to the use of language about nature used to communicate to others), humanistic (values are based on emotional attachment), moralistic (value is one of a spiritual connection with nature), dominionistic (value is based upon the domination of nature) and negativistic (value is related to a fear of and alienation from nature). Kellert argues that each value type not only represents an evolutionary advantage by contributing to a more fulfilling experience for humans, but is also indicative of how the conservation of nature is driven by self-interest and biological need. He concludes that the ethical responsibility for conserving nature is rooted in the biological pursuit of self-interest rather than in altruism or compassion.

Linda Kalof and Terre Satterfield

4

Non-Anthropocentric Value Theory and Environmental Ethics

J. Baird Callicott

Over the last decade, environmental ethics has emerged as a new subdiscipline of moral philosophy. As with anything new in philosophy or the sciences, there has been some controversy, not only about its legitimacy, but about its very identity or definition. The question of legitimacy has been settled more or less by default: professional philosophical interest in environmental philosophy seems to be growing as, certainly, work in the field proliferates. The question of identity – just what is environmental ethics? – has not been so ingenuous.

Environmental ethics may be understood to be but one among several new sorts of applied philosophies, the others of which also arose during the 1970s. That is, it may be understood to be an *application* of well-established conventional philosophical categories to emergent practical environmental problems. On the other hand, it may be understood to be an *exploration* of alternative moral and even metaphysical principles, forced upon philosophy by the magnitude and recalcitrance of these problems.[1] If defined in the former way, then the work of environmental ethics is that of a philosophical yeoman or underlabourer (to employ Locke's self appraisal); if defined in the latter way, it is that of a theoretician or philosophical architect (as in Descartes' self-image). If interpreted as an essentially theoretical, not applied discipline, the most important philosophical task for environmental ethics is the development of a non-anthropocentric value theory.[2] Indeed, as the discussion which follows will make clear, without a non-anthropocentric axiology the revolutionary aspirations of theoretical environmental ethics would be betrayed and the whole enterprise would collapse into its more workaday, applied counterpart.

The subject of this paper, accordingly, is a synoptic and critical review of various preferred candidates for a non-anthropocentric value theory for environmental ethics. Ethical hedonism and conativism are treated as theoretically inadequate non-anthropocentric extensions of the prevailing anthropocentric paradigm. Theism, holism and sentimentalism are then discussed, in turn, as possible models. A modified and modernized form of the last of these is recommended as the best alternative.

An anthropocentric value theory (or axiology), by common consensus, confers intrinsic value on human beings and regards all other things, including other forms of life, as being only instrumentally valuable, i.e. valuable only to the extent that they are

Note: Reprinted from *American Philosophical Quarterly*, vol 21, Callicott, J. B., 'Non-anthropocentric value theory and environmental ethics', pp299–309, copyright © (1984), with permission from University of Illinois Press

means or instruments which may serve human beings. A non-anthropocentric value theory (or axiology), on the other hand, would confer intrinsic value on some non-human beings.

In general, the recently developed kinds of applied ethics apply normal ethics ('normal' as in 'normal science') to novel moral problems (for example, how to treat 'neomorts' or dispose of 'radwastes') generated by novel technologies. In environmental ethics, if so construed, one would need only carefully consider the effects of our environmental actions, the pollution people create, the resources they consume etc. on other people.[3] It may then be decided what the right thing to do is by, say, a standard utilitarian calculus, limited by considerations of human justice, human rights, human duties and human liberties. Since normal ethical theory is conventionally anthropocentric, no critical *theoretical* thinking needs to be done. Environmental ethics is thus reduced more or less to benefit–cost analyses and public policy considerations.[4] Such benefit–cost/public policy exercises are environmental because the arena or theatre of action and decision making is the natural environment and they are ethical because all interested (human) parties are considered equally and the limitations on acceptable courses of action, however economically efficient, current in the political culture are respected.

When pursued from a more speculative or theoretical orientation, the focus of attention of environmental ethics shifts from the *application* of normal ethical theory to the *criticism* of normal ethical theory. Environmental ethics so construed is environmental because it concerns nonhuman natural entities, natural communities or nature as a whole, and ethical because it attempts to provide theoretical grounds for the *moral standing* or *moral considerability* of nonhuman natural entities, natural communities or nature as a whole.[5] So construed, environmental ethics is not an applied ethics similar to biomedical or business ethics; it constitutes, rather, nothing less than an incipient paradigm shift in moral philosophy.[6]

Like revolutionary moments in the sciences, the present demand for a paradigm shift in ethics is stimulated in part by certain experiential moral problems which evade satisfactory resolution by means of an uncritical application of normal ethical theory.[7] Examples of such intractable environmental moral problems are the progressive deterioration and destruction of biocoenoses, massive anthropogenic local extirpation and total global extinction of species, and global biological simplification, homogenization and impoverishment.[8] There is something clearly morally wrong about this human assault on nonhuman forms of life and natural systems. Normal (anthropocentric) moral theory, however, can only explicate this intuitively felt wrongness in terms of actual and potential losses of natural resources (either material or spiritual) and disruption of natural services.[9] But there seems to be something wrong about the radical destruction of nonhuman life on Earth and/or the ubiquitous replacement by human beings and human symbionts of nonhuman forms of life that goes beyond the diminishment of natural aesthetic amenities, or the loss of medical or other resources, or even the destabilization of the human life support system, 'Spaceship Earth' (as sometimes it is called from a subconscious anthropocentric point of view).

The most conservative and, probably because it is the most conservative, by far the most fully developed and discussed attempt to provide a non-anthropocentric axiology for environmental ethics is popularly known as 'animal liberation'.[10] It is the most conservative because it requires the least change in the reigning anthropocentric, utilitarian normal ethical paradigm. In fact, it insists less on a change in the axiology of utilitarian moral theory than on its rigorous and consistent implementation.

The axiology of classical utilitarianism is hedonic. Good and evil are defined in terms of pleasure and pain, respectively. And since utilitarianism is an *ethical* hedonism, moral agents, when morally evaluating courses of action, are required to be strictly impartial between the experiential loci of pleasure and pain. Conventionally such impartial or equal consideration has been limited to the pleasure and pain of human beings. But such a limitation is, theoretically speaking, ad hoc; it is not derivable from the first principles of the theory itself, as Bentham, its architect, clearly recognized.[11] Hence, classical utilitarianism, consistently implemented, is non-anthropocentric.

Since it provides for the direct moral standing of at least some non-human natural entities classical hedonic utilitarianism strictly interpreted, with no ad hoc limitations, might, prima facie, serve as the axiological basis for a non-anthropocentric environmental ethic. If so, it should be preferred to all theoretical alternatives since it least departs from normal ethics.

Ethical hedonism, however, is, upon a moment's reflection, an obviously inadequate axiological basis for a comprehensive environmental ethic since it limits moral considerability to only those beings capable of experiencing pleasure and pain, 'sentient' beings in the jargon of animal liberation. While it may include most complex animal organisms within its purview, it clearly excludes all plants. Thus, other things being equal, it would permit the destruction of a Sequoia grove to provide pasture for a liberated and exponentially increasing population of feral cattle. And it has other, less obvious, drawbacks. For example, it makes no distinction between wild and domestic organisms. A Pekinese lap dog and a 'bobby calf' have the same moral status as a wild timber wolf and a wild otter. Further, it fails to articulate our considered moral intuitions respecting collective or holistic entities – species, biocoenoses, biomes and the biosphere itself – since none of these collective entities is any more sentient than a plant.[12]

A more inclusive non-anthropocentric axiology, structurally similar in basic logical form to ethical hedonism, has no generally recognized rubric, but may be descriptively named 'ethical conativism'. It is the axiological foundation of the popular Schweitzerian reverence-for-life ethic and its more analytic, academic equivalent, the Feinberg-Goodpaster life-principle ethic. Conativism defines interests in terms of conations (hypostatized as the will-to-live in Schweitzer) and intrinsic value in terms of interests.[13] Something is intrinsically valuable and owed moral consideration if interests, construed in the broadest possible sense, may be intelligibly assigned it. Plants have interests, so construed, though they may not be conscious of them. Hence, conativism opens the community of morally considerable beings to plants as well as animals; it provides, thus, moral status for all living things.

Ethical conativism is not a normal moral theory because it is non-anthropocentric. Indeed, it is biocentric in the literal sense of the term – life-centred.[14] Nevertheless, it is clearly an extension, a stretching, of normal moral theory so as to embrace with the least theoretical restructuring living, nonhuman natural entities. Like both the utilitarian and deontological variations of normal ethics, it assigns intrinsic value to *discrete individuals,* indeed, first and foremost to oneself. It then moves from egoism to biocentric egalitarianism by a process of generalization, elegantly described by Goodpaster, typical of prevailing ethical theory.[15]

Hence, as a theoretical basis for a non-anthropocentric environmental ethic, ethical conativism shares many of the inadequacies of ethical hedonism. Indeed, the only *practical* difference is that plants, as well as animals, are members of the moral club and thus must be extended moral consideration or moral standing. Like ethical hedonism, no theoretical justification is provided for differential treatment of wild and domestic organisms, nor for the moral considerability of superorganismic entities. Further, even its proponents frankly admit that it is, if taken seriously, impossible to live by as it would imply a quietism so absolute as to be suicidal.[16]

This last observation hints at the deeper cognitive dissonance between normal ethical theory and the theoretical requirements of non-anthropocentric environmental ethics. Stretching normal ethical theory to its limits, first to provide moral standing for sentient, then conative entities ironically results in a life-denying, rather than life-affirming, moral philosophy. Not only would conativism's rigorous adherents be required to starve *themselves* to death, nature itself mocks and defies the intractable moral atomism which hedonism and conativism uncritically appropriate from the normal ethical paradigms. Nature notoriously appears indifferent to individual life and/or individual suffering. Struggle and death lie at the very heart of natural biotic processes, both ecological and evolutionary. An adequate biocentric axiology for environmental ethics could hardly morally condemn the very processes which it is intended to foster and protect.[17] More particularly – and for the same reason, its atomistic presuppositions – neither can ethical conativism, any better than ethical hedonism, adequately address what is emerging as the most pressing of all contemporary environmental problems, 'the silent crisis of our time', threatened massive species extinction and the consequent biotic impoverishment of the Earth.[18]

However, a new, revolutionary moral paradigm is no more created *ex nihilo* than a new, revolutionary scientific paradigm. Without some historical continuity, a new theory, natural or moral, could not be recognized as such. Copernicus, for example, having pressed the Ptolemaic model to its limits, did not abandon altogether mathematical astronomy as hopeless and take up, say, a mystical approach. Rather, he turned to the history of his science and searched among his predecessors for helpful ideas, cast aside or neglected along the way. And what he found in the astronomy of the Pythagoreans and Aristarchus was a bold insight which he successfully developed and applied to the experiential problems at hand.[19]

Neither should we turn away from moral philosophy as such and retreat to some sort of moral mysticism. In the historical backwaters of moral philosophy, similarly, there may repose some helpful insights which may be developed and tried against contemporary experiential environmental problems which elude solution by normal ethical theory even when stretched to its logical limits. In the tradition there appear three prima facie attractive alternatives, one of which seems the best.

Historically the first and theoretically the most obvious possibility is theistic axiology. If God is posited as the arbiter of value, anthropocentrism is immediately and directly overcome. If God, moreover, is conceived as in the Judaeo-Christian tradition to be the creator of the natural world, and to have declared His creation to be *good*, then the creation as a whole, including, as its centrepiece, the biosphere, and the components of the creation, species prominently among them, have, by immediate inference, intrinsic value.

The same tradition of thought, however, provides for a unique place for man among creatures.[20] Man is said to be created in the 'image of God' and given 'dominion' over the creation. But this could be interpreted as conferring a special responsibility, not a special privilege, on humanity. Indeed, it could be employed to obviate the problem for non-anthropocentric environmental ethics posed by the absence of moral reciprocity alleged by some critics to be the Achilles heel of the entire enterprise.[21] The human role in nature may, thus, not be to conquer and master it, but to be God's steward and benign viceroy. The stewardship interpretation is hard to reconcile with God's charge to man to 'subdue' the creation, but the conqueror interpretation is no less hard to reconcile with God's later charge to man to 'dress the garden and keep it'.[22]

The stewardship interpretation, all things considered, seems to have the most textual support and to be the most plausible. Most appealingly, from the point of view of the theoretical requirements of non-anthropocentric environmental ethics, the theistic axiology of the Judaeo-Christian tradition provides intrinsic value less for individuals than for the more permanent and persistent *forms* of nature and for the natural world *as a whole*. It is clear, for example, when God is creating plants and animals, that He is establishing species, and it is understood that individuals naturally come and go. Thus in fulfilling our role as stewards, i.e. in dressing the garden and keeping it, our task is not primarily one of preventing individual animal suffering or looking out for the interests of individual plants and animals, but of preserving species, maintaining the integrity of natural communities and ensuring the healthy functioning of the biosphere, the garden, as the whole.[23]

In Genesis there is even the tantalizing suggestion that man's original sin was environmental, not sexual as usually supposed. Upon eating the fruit of the tree of the knowledge of good and evil, the first noetic revelation was self-consciousness: Adam and Eve became aware that they were naked. This unique human self-awareness is logically necessary for deliberate human self-centredness, i.e. for anthropocentrism. Thus, anthropocentrism, far from being a natural and divinely sanctioned value orientation is, upon this interpretation of Biblical theism, the original source of all evil in the world. Other elements of the myth, the curses, banishment and so on, are not only consistent with this interpretation, they seem actually to reinforce it.

This theistic axiology has one main drawback as a non-anthropocentric value theory for environmental ethics. It is primitive, essentially mythic, ambiguous and inconsistent with modern science, and more especially with modern ecological, evolutionary biology. It is therefore metaphysically discordant with the worldview in which environmental problems are perceived as fundamentally important and morally charged in the first place.

A second alternative may be called, for reasons which should be evident in a moment, holistic rationalism. Some ancient philosophers, Plato most notably, and some early modern philosophers, especially Leibniz, posited the existence of an objective, impersonal Good from which value flowed. Things, or more generally and abstractly, phenomena, accordingly, are intrinsically good or valuable to the degree that they exemplify the characteristics of the Good. Clearly, this is not an anthropocentric axiology since value is not determined in terms either of human nature or of human interests. A development and application of this originally Platonic axiological approach might provide a suitable non-anthropocentric axiology for environmental ethics.

The nature of the Good in Plato's dialogues is very elusive. Recent scholarship inclines to the view that by 'the Good' Plato understood a formal *principle of order* of the highest degree of generality, and by 'order' he more definitely meant formal logico-mathematical design.[24] A good house or ship is one that is well-ordered, i.e. its parts are measured, proportioned and fitted together according to a rational design; the goodness of body (health), of soul (virtue) or society (justice) and of the cosmos as a whole is similarly defined.[25] Likewise, Leibniz believed that this was the best of all possible worlds because it exhibits, 'the greatest possible variety, together with the greatest *order* that may be; that is to say the greatest possible perfection'.[26] The most perfect possible world is 'the one which is at the same time the simplest in hypotheses and the richest in phenomena'.[27]

In contemporary conservation literature one sometimes finds *biological* systemic diversity and/or complexity apparently posited as a good in itself.[28] This usually undefended intuition seems best theoretically articulated by the axiological strand of thought about value notably represented by Plato and Leibniz. The most well-known and oft-quoted adaptation to ecological conservation of the general theory that the formal properties of natural systems – order, parsimony, harmony, complexity and variety – are objective, intrinsic values is the summary maxim of Aldo Leopold's 'land ethic': 'A thing [i.e. an action] is right when it tends to preserve the integrity, stability, and beauty of the biotic community. It is wrong when it tends otherwise'.[29]

Though Leopold's land ethic is (with all its charm and simplicity) conceptually and logically more well-grounded than it may at first appear, Leopold makes no deliberate effort specifically to explain or defend the necessity of this, his cardinal moral precept. A more recent, philosophically self-conscious, development of Leopold's conception of the intrinsic value of diverse, complex and integrated ecosystems has been attempted by Peter Miller.[30] Miller posits 'richness' as an irreducible, objective, intrinsic value. While Miller very fully characterizes or *describes* 'richness' ('the richness of natural systems [consists of] their inner and outer profusion, unity', etc.) he does not adequately *explain* why richness should be valued *for the sake of itself*, or, more concretely, why a rich (viz, diverse, complex and stable) biota is *intrinsically* better than a simple, impoverished or catastrophic one. The value of 'richness', so described, is certainly explicable instrumentally: a biologically rich world is aesthetically and epistemically more satisfying and it is materially more secure than an impoverished or 'poor' world, but these are clearly anthropocentric concerns.

From the classical rationalistic axiological perspective, the *system itself*, classically the cosmos and its various microcosmic subsystems, often including human society, was considered valuable per se or at least to exemplify or instantiate 'the Good'. In its present adaptation to non-anthropocentric environmental ethics, rational holism would consider the *biosphere* as a whole and its several subsystems – biomes, biocoenoses and micro-ecosystems, species and their populations – to be valuable. It thus clearly avoids the fundamental theoretical inadequacy for a non-anthropocentric environmental ethic of the hedonic and conative extensions of normal ethics, namely, an intractable atomistic or individualistic bias. Indeed, it has the opposite drawback, a detached indifference to individual welfare.

The axiological orientation of classical rationalism has, in fact, been, in theory at least, so detached, general and abstract that its conscription in service of non-anthropocentric environmental ethics could easily boomerang in another way. One may morally decry the very real and imminent prospect of an abrupt, massive reduction of biotic diversity to be succeeded by a 'mono-culture' consisting of tens of billions of human beings, their habitations, their economic cultivars (and the pests thereof), human transportation, distribution, and communication networks, and little else. However, if one forthrightly and articulately defends one's considered intuition that this process of anthropogenic biological impoverishment is objectively morally wrong by positing organic 'richness' (biotic diversity, complexity and harmony) as objectively and impersonally good, one might well be accused of temporal parochialism. Considering our time as but an infinitesimal moment in the three and a half billion year tenure of life on planet Earth, the present tendency of man to extirpate and eventually extinguish other species and take over their habitats for himself and his domesticated symbionts might be viewed quite disinterestedly as but a brief transitional stage in the Earth's evolutionary odyssey. Nonhuman life will go on even under the worst possible anthropogenic destructive scenario presently conceivable, nuclear holocaust, and in time speciation will occur, novel species will radiate anew, and novel ecosystems will mature. The new Age (of Insects, perhaps) will eventually be just as diverse, orderly, harmonious and stable, and thus no less good than our current ecosystem with its present complement of species.

The deeply felt and widely shared moral intuition that *extant* nonhuman species and the biosphere in its *current* state have intrinsic value, therefore, does not seem adequately articulated by holistic rationalism. There is something valuable, it seems intuitively certain, about *our* world (with us in it!) which nevertheless resists reduction to our *interests* or to our *tastes*. For its articulation and explanation this intuition, if it is to withstand critical examination, will require a moral theory that is at once humanistic, but not anthropocentric.

From this brief review and critique of candidates for an axiology for non-anthropocentric environmental ethics, a number of criteria which an adequate axiology must meet have emerged. An adequate value theory for non-anthropocentric environmental ethics must provide for the intrinsic value of both individual organisms and a hierarchy of superorganismic entities – populations, species, biocoenoses, biomes and the biosphere. It should provide differential intrinsic value for wild and domestic organisms and species. It must be conceptually concordant with modern evolutionary and ecological biology. And it must provide for the intrinsic value of *our present* ecosystem, its component parts and complement of species, not equal value for any ecosystem.

The historical philosophical theory of value most concordant with modern biology is David Hume's, to take up the penultimate criterion first. In fact, so concordant is it that Hume's analysis of value allowing for divergencies of detail has been long absorbed into the *biological* explanation of moral and moral-like animal behaviour.[31]

According to Hume all behaviour is motivated by passion, emotion, feeling or sentiment.[32] For purposes of moral theory, the passions may be divided into two classes, the self-oriented (e.g. fear, jealousy, animal appetites) and the other-oriented (e.g. love, sympathy, charity). The other-oriented passions are not derivative of the self-oriented ones. They are equally primitive and autochthonous. Thus, the moral standing of beings other than oneself is *not* reached by the process of generalization described by Goodpaster, characteristic of normal ethical theory.[33]

For Hume, the existence of these 'moral sentiments' was a fundamental psychological fact, the origins of which he could not and did not attempt to explain. Darwin in the next century undertook to explain them 'exclusively from the side of natural history'.[34] The very existence of morals presents an evolutionary paradox. Given the mechanics of natural selection, we should expect human (and all other animal behaviour, for that matter) to become ever more competitive, hostile, rapacious and violent instead of ever more cooperative, deferential, genteel and caring. Darwin assumed Hume's moral psychology, rather than Kant's or any other philosophical account, since emotion or passion is a more primitive and universal animal capacity than reason or any other supposed wellspring of moral behaviour.

Darwin supposed that the most rudimentary other-oriented sentiments were the parental–filial affections. They facilitated, especially among mammals, reproductive success and, hence, would be conserved by natural selection. For those species which survived better in social aggregates than as solitaries slight variations of the parental–filial affections, for example, affection and sympathy for other kin, would be conserved as such affections would facilitate social integration and expansion and, in turn, survival and successful reproduction. As the relationship between social evolution and the evolution of the other-oriented or moral sentiments is one of positive feedback, ethics evolved correlatively to social evolution. As proto-human and eventually human societies grew larger and more complex the moral sentiments grew correlatively more widely cast and delicate and moral behaviour became more generally directed and refined. Finally, Darwin imagined 'as man advanced in civilization, and small tribes are united into larger communities, the simplest reason would tell each individual that he ought to extend his social instincts and sympathies to all the members of the same nation though personally unknown to him'.[35]

Darwin's hypothetical and sometimes speculative account of the origins of morals has recently been supplanted by more scientifically rigorous work.[36] Nevertheless, Darwin's fundamental approach, rudimentary insights and Humean foundations have been retained in contemporary biosocial thought.

Aldo Leopold incorporated Darwin's theory of the origins of ethics (and therefore its Humean foundations) in his celebrated 'land ethic', the seminal and by now classical attempt to provide a non-anthropocentric environmental ethic.[37] Leopold, indeed, represented the 'land ethic' as the next 'step' in the ongoing process of social-ethical evolution. 'All ethics', he wrote, 'rest upon a single premise: that the individual is a member of a community of interdependent parts'. This is Darwin's explanation of moral evolution in a nutshell. 'The land ethic simply enlarges the boundaries of the community to include soils, waters, plants, and animals, or collectively: the land'.[38] Leopold, in effect, simply pointed out that ecology represents plants, animals (including human beings), soils and waters as members of one humming 'biotic community'. When this essentially ecological idea becomes a general and settled habit of thought and perception, then, to paraphrase Darwin, the simplest reason would tell each individual that he ought to extend his social instincts and sympathies to all the members of the same (biotic) community though differing from him in species.

Hume, Darwin and Leopold all recognize in addition to social sympathies and affections for fellow *members* of society, whether tribal, national or biotic, special social sentiments the object of which is society itself.[39] Patriotism is the name of the social sentiment directed to the nation as a superorganismic entity. Presently there is no name for the emergent feeling, the object of which is the biosphere per se and its several superorganismic subsystems. We could, perhaps, call it biophilia.

Value, according to Hume, is subjective and affective. Therefore, it may seem that though Hume's theory of value is concordant with evolutionary and ecological biology, it fails one basic requirement of an adequate axiology for non-anthropocentric environmental ethics: it is not non-anthropocentric. Value depends upon human sentiments; according to Hume, 'you never can find it, till you turn your reflection into your own breast...'[40] Granted. But a crucial distinction remains to be drawn. Value may be grounded in human feelings, but neither the feelings themselves nor, necessarily, the breast or self in which they reside are their natural objects.[41] The *moral* sentiments are, by definition, other-oriented. And they are intentional, that is, they are not valued themselves, or even experienced apart from some object which excites them and onto which they are, as it were, projected.[42] Their natural objects are not limited, except by convention, to other human beings. They are, rather, naturally excited by fellow social members (and by society itself) which may include, as in both contemporary ecological thought and tribal representation, nonhuman beings and a larger than human social order.[43]

Therefore, the Darwin–Leopold environmental ethic, grounded in the axiology of Hume, is genuinely and straightforwardly non-anthropocentric, since it provides for the *intrinsic* value of nonhuman natural entities. It is also, nonetheless, humanistic since intrinsic value ultimately depends upon human valuers. It provides both for the intrinsic value of nonhuman individual organisms and for superorganismic entities – populations, species, biocoenoses, biomes and the biosphere. Other individual organisms are, as it were, fellow-members of the biotic community and the biosphere is, as it were, our tribe or nation, with smaller collective entities, like species, actuating the moral sentiments once actuated by so many totemic clans.

Contemporary human beings are genetically endowed with the affective capacity to value unselfishly evolved by our tribal ancestors. Who or what is valued for the sake of itself, however, is determined as much by culture as by genes. We now perceive the Earth to be a small, precious oasis in a hostile desert of largely cold, empty space. The Earth is our cosy home. We now perceive other living things as literally kindred beings, coevolved ultimately from one ancestral cell. We value the Earth and 'our fellow-voyagers ... in the odyssey of evolution', not only for what they can do for us, but for themselves, just as, when our cultural horizons were less expansive, we valued quite selflessly our children, other relatives, local neighbours and the tribal whole to which we belonged.[44, 45]

Notes

1   Among the first academic philosophical discussions to suggest the need for newly constructed moral and metaphysical principles to deal with emergent environmental problems is Richard Routley's, 'Is there a need for a new, an environmental ethic?', *Proceedings of the Fifteenth World Congress of Philosophy*, vol 1 (1973), pp205–210, simultaneously Arne Naess; 'The shallow and deep, long range ecol-

ogy movement', *Inquiry*, vol 16 (1973), pp95–100, distinguished between essentially applied and critical-theoretical approaches to environmental philosophy. Subsequently, a critical-theoretical approach to environmental philosophy has been sometimes referred to as 'deep ecology'.

2   A clear and original statement of the centrality of the conceptual problem of a non-anthropocentric axiology for environmental ethics may be found in Holmes Rolston, III, 'Is there an ecological ethic?', *Ethics*, vol 85 (1975), pp93–109.

3   Tom Regan, 'The nature and possibility of an environmental ethic', *Environmental Ethics*, vol 3 (1981) denies that an anthropocentric environmental ethic is an environmental ethic at all. He prefers to call an anthropocentric environmental ethic 'a management ethic', 'an ethic *for the use* of the environment' as opposed to a genuine environmental ethic which is 'an ethic *of* the environment' (p20).

4   Kristin Shrader-Frechette's approach to environmental ethics in *Environmental Ethics* (Pacific Grove, Boxwood Press, 1981) is a recent example. She writes, 'What I have shown is that there is a strong rational foundation for using existing utilitarian and egalitarian ethical theories to safeguard the environment. Utilitarian doctrines clearly protect the interests of future generations and egalitarian schemes prohibit any environmental hazards against which persons cannot be assured equal protections' (p23). William Frankena, 'Ethics and the environment', in K. Goodpaster and K. Sayre, eds, *Ethics and Problems of the 21st Century* (Notre Dame, University of Notre Dame Press, 1979) appears to support such an approach. He writes, 'We have had a number of calls for a "new ethics" in recent times, and today we are again told that we need a new one for dealing with the environment. Actually, however, ... our old ethics, or at least its best parts, are entirely satisfactory as a basis for our lives in the world. The trouble being only that not enough of us live by it enough of the time...' (p3). See also W. H. Murdy, 'Anthropocentrism: A modern version', *Science*, vol 187 (1975), pp1168–1172.

5   The phrase 'moral considerability' was introduced into the literature of environmental ethics by Kenneth Goodpaster, 'On being morally considerable', *Journal of Philosophy*, vol 75 (1978), pp306–25.

6   Bill Devall, 'The deep ecology movement', *Natural Resources Journal*, vol 20 (1980), pp299–322, to some extent anticipates this judgement. Devall, however, is talking about *social* 'paradigms' and *movements* while this discussion is more narrowly confined to moral *theories* and draws attention to an analogy between normal and revolutionary *scientific theory* and normal and revolutionary *moral theory*. John Rodman, 'Paradigm change in political science', *American Behavioural Scientist*, vol 24 (1980), pp49–78, employs the Kuhnian concept of 'paradigm change' more as it is employed herein since Rodman is concerned with theory construction in a discipline of social science and less with a movement and its various proponents and programmes. An application of this concept to metaphysics has been provided by Alan R. Drengson, 'Shifting paradigms: From the technocratic to the person-planetary', *Environmental Ethics*, vol 2 (1980), pp221–240.

7   See Richard Routley, 'Is there a need for a new, an environmental ethic?' More recently, Tom Regan, 'On the nature and possibility of an environmental ethic', has insisted upon the need for a new non-anthropocentric moral paradigm, set out certain requirements it must satisfy, but finally is skeptical that any theory may succeed.

Very recently, Evelyn B. Pluhar, 'Justification of an environmental ethic', *Environmental Ethics*, vol 5 (1983), pp47–61, reiterated the need for a non-anthropocentric environmental ethic and has taken up with more hope of success Regan's axiological criteria. Pluhar recommends a theory of intrinsic value similar, though expressed in different terms, to the one recommended below.

8   For a convenient summary see Norman Myers, *The Sinking Ark, A New Look at the Problem of Disappearing Species* (New York, Pergamon Press, 1979). Myers predicts that 'if present average patterns of exploitation persist' one million species, one third to one tenth the Earth's present complement of species, may become extinct by the end of the 20th century (p4).

9   The concept of considered or reflective intuition and its role in critical moral thought has been very recently and clearly discussed by Tom Regan, *The Case for Animal Rights*, unpublished manuscript, pp4,17–19. He there distinguished considered or reflective intuition from a 'gut-reaction' first impression and from the more technical metaethical concept of intuition tied to Moorean non-natural properties.

10 Both the term and the classic work on the subject are Peter Singer's. See Peter Singer, *Animal Liberation* (New York, New York Review, 1975). For a guide to the literature, see Charles R. Magel, *A Bibliography of Animal Rights and Related Matters* (Washington, University Press of America, 1981).

11 The famous passage, routinely quoted by animal liberationists, is Jeremy Bentham, *Principles of Morals and Legislation*, New Edition (Oxford, Oxford University Press, 1823), ch XVII, sec 1.

12 For a full discussion of these and other inadequacies (so far as a non-anthropocentric axiology for environmental ethics is concerned) of classical utilitarianism with an animal liberation twist see J. Baird Callicott, 'Animal liberation: A triangular affair', *Environmental Ethics*, vol 2 (1980), pp311–338.

13 See Albert Schweitzer, *Civilization and Ethics*, ed by John Naish, partially reprinted in Regan and Singer, eds, *Animal Rights and Human Obligations* (Englewood Cliffs, Prentice Hall, 1976), pp133–138; and Kenneth Goodpaster, 'On being morally considerable'. Joel Feinberg, 'The rights of animals and unborn generations', in Wm. T. Blackstone, ed, *Philosophy and Environmental Crisis* (Athens, University of Georgia Press, 1974), provides the clearest possible statement:

> A mere thing, however valuable to others, has no good of its own. The explanation of that fact, I suspect, is that mere things have no conative life: no conscious wishes, desires, and hopes; or urges and impulses; or unconscious drives, aims, goals; or latent tendencies, directions or growth, and natural fulfillments. Interests must be compounded somehow out of conations;…(pp. 49–50)

Though Feinberg himself did not draw the inference, Goodpaster points out that this statement, by implication, would commit Feinberg to moral standing for plants as well as animals. Hence, one may refer to the Feinberg-Goodpaster life-principle ethic, though Feinberg is something of a silent partner.

14 The phrases coined by Naess in 'The shallow and deep, long range ecology movement', (and picked up as slogans of the deep ecology movement), 'biocentric

egalitarianism in principle' and 'the right to live and blossom' appear to have a conative basis.

15 See Kenneth Goodpaster, 'From egoism to environmentalism' in *Ethics and Problems of the 21st Century*, pp21–35.

16 Goodpaster, 'On being morally considerable' writes, 'the clearest and most decisive refutation of the principle of respect for life is that one cannot *live* according to it, ... we must eat, experiment to gain knowledge, protect ourselves from predation, ... to take seriously the criterion of considerability being defended, all these things must be seen as somehow morally wrong' (p324). Schweitzer, in *Civilization and Ethics* writes, 'it remains a painful enigma how I am to live by the rule of reverence for life in a world ruled by creative will which is at the same time destructive will' (p136).

17 For an elaboration of these points see J. Baird Callicott, 'Animal liberation: A triangular affair'; John Rodman, 'The liberation of nature', *Inquiry*, vol 20 (1977), pp83–131; and Paul Shepard, 'Animal rights and human rites', *North American Review*, winter 1974, pp35–41.

18 The quoted phrase is from Thomas Eisner et al, 'Conservation of Tropical Forests', *Science*, vol 213 (1981), p1314.

19 See Thomas Kuhn, *The Copernican Revolution* (Cambridge, Harvard University Press, 1957).

20 The term 'man' is used here not without sensitivity to the issue of gender bias in language. It is, however, a term so grafted to the conceptual complex under consideration that the distinctive flavour of that complex would be lost without it. Hence, it is used, but used apologetically. Let a similar caveat be registered here also in respect to the capitalized masculine pronoun used to refer to God.

21 See, for example, Michael Fox, 'Animal liberation: A critique', *Ethics*, vol 88 (1978), p112; and John Passmore, *Man's Responsibility for Nature: Ecological Problems and Western Traditions* (New York, Charles Schribner's Sons, 1974), p116.

22 Later in the order of the text, but not later in temporal order of composition: see Arthur Weiser, *The Old Testament: Its Formation and Development*, trans by D. Barton (New York, Association Press, 1961).

23 A recent application to environmental conservation of this interpretation of the Judeao-Christian theistic axiology may be found in David Ehrenfeld, 'The conservation of non-resources', *American Scientist* vol 64 (1976), pp648–655.

24 'The Tübingen school', most notably, H. J. Kramer, *Arete bei Platan and Aristotles: zum Wesen und zur Geschichte der platonischen Ontologie* (Heidelberg, Heidelberger Akademie, 1959). English readers may consult J. N. Findlay, *Plato: The Written and Unwritten Doctrines* (London, Routledge and Kegan Paul, 1974).

25 Plato's most explicit and clear statement of the nature of goodness is *Gorgias*, 503c–508c.

26 G.W. Leibniz, 'Monadology', no 58 in G. R. Mongomery, trans *Leibniz* (LaSalle, IL, Open Court, 1962), p263.

27 G.W. Leibniz, 'Discourse on metaphysics', sec. 6 in *Leibniz*, p11.

28 See, for example, Noel J. Brown, 'Biological diversity: The global challenge' in *Proceedings of the US Strategy Conference on Biological Diversity, Nov 16–18, 1981* (Washington, Department of State Publication 9263, 1982), pp22–27.

29 Aldo Leopold, *A Sand County Almanac* (New York, Oxford University Press, 1949), p224.

30 Peter Miller, 'Value as richness: Toward a value theory for an expanded naturalism in environmental ethics', *Environmental Ethics,* vol 4 (1982), pp101–114. Miller's theory as any naturalistic theory of value falls to Moore's open question as it is directly pointed out.

31 This is not surprising. According to a new study of Hume by J. L. Mackie, *Hume's Moral Theory* (London, Routledge and Kegan Paul, 1980), Hume's interest in ethics, 'is a demand for an explanation of the sort typically given by the empirical sciences: "Here is a curious phenomenon, human morality ... why is it there and how did it develop?"' (p6).

32 See David Hume, *Treatise of Human Nature,* Book III, Part I.

33 Goodpaster, 'From egoism to environmentalism' identifies Hume along with Kant as one of the progenitors of contemporary normal ethical theory, a fundamental feature of which is the identification of a psychological property upon which one's own value (for oneself) rests and then the generalization of this property so as to include as equally valuable a limited set of psychologically similar 'others'. Thus one moves from egoism to limited altruism. This is a mistake. Goodpaster quite correctly describes the moral logic of contemporary normal ethical theory, but he wrongly attributes it originally to Hume as well as to Kant. The actual historical forebear of the paradigm Goodpaster calls the H-family of moral theory (after Hume) is Bentham (and thus it should have been called the B-family).

34 Charles Darwin, *The Descent of Man and Selection in Relation to Sex,* second edition (New York, J. A. Hill, 1904), p97.

35 *Ibid,* p124. For Darwin's full account, summarized in this paragraph, see *Descent,* ch4.

36 Most notably by W. D. Hamilton, 'The genetical theory of social behaviour', *Journal of Theoretical Biology,* vol 7 (1964), pp1–32; R. L. Trivers, 'The evolution of reciprocal altruism', *Quarterly Review of Biology,* vol 46 (1971), pp35–57; Edward O. Wilson, *Sociobiology: The New Synthesis* (Cambridge, Belknap Press, 1975).

37 For a more detailed study of the relationship of the moral analyses of Hume and Darwin to Aldo Leopold's land ethic, see J. Baird Callicott, 'Elements of an environmental ethic: Moral considerability and the biotic community', *Environmental Ethics,* vol 1 (1979), pp71–81 and 'Hume's is/ought dichotomy and the relation of ecology to leopold's land ethic', *Environmental Ethics,* vol 4 (1982), pp163–174.

38 Leopold, *Sand County,* pp203–204.

39 See Hume, *Treatise,* pp484–485; Darwin, *Descent,* p122; and Leopold, *Sand County,* p204.

40 Hume, *Treatise,* pp468–469.

41 A formal distinction related to this one is fully developed by Richard and Val Routley, 'Against the inevitability of human chauvinism' *in Ethics and Problems of the 21st Century,* pp36–59, and 'Human chauvinism and environmental ethics' in Mannison, McRobbie and Routley, eds, *Environmental Philosophy* (Canberra, Australian National University, 1980), pp96–189.

42 The idea that the moral sentiments are 'projected' or 'objectified' is regarded by Mackie in *Hume's Moral Theory,* ch v, as the best interpretation of Hume's sentimentalism. With an approach like this one, according to Pluhar, 'The justification

of an environmental ethic', though we fail to establish purely objective intrinsic value, we avoid the following dilemma for a non-anthropocentric environmental ethic: 'either leave the ethic unjustified and beg the question by affirming it ... or leave it unjustified and be skeptical about it' (p60).

43 For the social representation of nature by tribal peoples and its relationship to tribal environmental ethics see Thomas W. Overholt and J. Baird Callicott, *Clothed-in-Fur and Other Tales: An Introduction to an Ojibwa World View* (Washington, University Press of America, 1982) and J. Baird Callicott, 'Traditional American Indian and Western European attitudes toward nature: An overview', *Environmental Ethics*, vol 4 (1982), pp293–318.

44 The quoted phrase is from Leopold, *Sand County,* p109.

45 This is a revised version of a paper read to the invited symposium on anthropocentrism and environmental ethics at the 57th annual meeting of the American Philosophical Association–Pacific Divison, 24–26 March, 1983, Berkeley, California. Research for this paper was assisted by the University of Maryland Center for Philosophy and Public Policy's Working Group on Species Preservation, directed by Bryan Norton and Henry Shue.

5

Environmental Ethics and Weak Anthropocentrism

Bryan G. Norton

Introduction

In two essays already published in this journal, I have argued that an environmental ethic cannot be derived, first, from rights or interests of nonhumans and, second, from rights or interests of future generations of humans.[1] Those negative conclusions pave the way for a more positive discussion of the nature and shape of environmental ethics and, in the present paper, I undertake that task. In particular, I address the question of whether there must be a distinctively environmental ethic.

Discussions of this question in the literature have equated a negative answer with the belief that the standard categories of rights, interests and duties of individual human beings are adequate to furnish ethical guidance in environmental decision making. A positive answer is equated with the suggestion that nature has, in some sense, intrinsic value. In other words, the question of whether environmental ethics is distinctive is taken as equivalent to the question of whether an environmental ethic must reject anthropocentrism, the view that only humans are loci of fundamental value.[2] Environmental ethics is seen as distinctive vis-à-vis standard ethics if and only if environmental ethics can be founded upon principles which assert or presuppose that nonhuman natural entities have value independent of human value.

I argue that this equivalence is mistaken by showing that the anthropocentrism/nonanthropocentrism debate is far less important than is usually assumed. Once an ambiguity is noted in its central terms, it becomes clear that nonanthropocentrism is not the only adequate basis for a truly environmental ethic.[3] I then argue that another dichotomy, that of individualism versus nonindividualism, should be seen as crucial to the distinctiveness of environmental ethics and that a successful environmental ethic cannot be individualistic in the way that standard contemporary ethical systems are. Finally, I examine the consequences of these conclusions for the nature and shape of an environmental ethic.

Before beginning these arguments, I need to clarify how I propose to test an adequate environmental ethic. I begin by assuming that all environmentally sensitive individuals believe that there is a set of human behaviours which do or would damage

Note: Reprinted from *Environmental Ethics*, vol 6, Norton, B. G., 'Environmental ethics and weak anthropocentrism', pp131–148, copyright © (1984), with permission from author

the environment. Further, I assume that there is considerable agreement among such individuals about what behaviours are included in that set. Most would decry, for example, careless storage of toxic wastes, grossly overpopulating the world with humans, wanton destruction of other species, air and water pollution, and so forth. There are other behaviours which would be more controversial, but I take the initial task of constructing an adequate environmental ethic to be the statement of some set of principles from which rules can be derived proscribing the behaviours included in the set which virtually all environmentally sensitive individuals agree are environmentally destructive. The further task of refining an environmental ethic then involves moving back and forth between the basic principles and the more or less controversial behaviours, adjusting principles and/or rejecting intuitions until the best possible fit between principles and sets of proscribed behaviours is obtained for the whole environmental community. In the present paper I address the prior question of basic principles. I am here only seeking to clarify which principles do (and which do not) support the large set of relatively uncontroversial cases of behaviours damaging to the environment. An ethic will be adequate, on this approach, if its principles are sufficient to entail rules proscribing the behaviours involved in the noncontroversial set. My arguments, then, are not directed at determining which principles are *true,* but which are *adequate* to uphold certain shared intuitions. Questions concerning the truth of such principles must be left for another occasion.

Anthropocentrism and Nonanthropocentrism

I suggest that the distinction between anthropocentrism and nonanthropocentrism has been given more importance in discussions of the foundations of environmental ethics than it warrants because a crucial ambiguity in the term *anthropocentrism* has gone unnoticed.[4] Writers on both sides of the controversy apply this term to positions which treat humans as the only loci of intrinsic value.[5] Anthropocentrists are therefore taken to believe that every instance of value originates in a contribution to human values and that all elements of nature can, at most, have value instrumental to the satisfaction of human interests.[6] Note that anthropocentrism is defined by reference to the position taken on *loci* of value. Some nonanthropocentrists say that human beings are the *source* of all values, but that they can designate nonhuman objects as loci of fundamental value.[7]

It has also become common to explain and test views on this point by reference to 'last man examples' which are formulated as follows.[8] Assume that a human being, *S,* is the last living member of *Homo sapiens* and that *S* faces imminent death. Would *S* do wrong to wantonly destroy some object *X*? A positive answer to this question with regard to any nonhuman *X* is taken to entail nonanthropocentrism. If the variable *X* refers to some natural object, a species, an ecosystem, a geological formation etc., then it is thought that positions on such questions determine whether a person is an anthropocentrist or not, because the action in question cannot conceivably harm any human individual. If it is wrong to destroy *X,* the wrongness must derive from harm to *X* or to some other natural object. But one can harm something only if it is a good in its own right in the sense of being a locus of fundamental value.

Or so the story goes. I am unconvinced because not nearly enough has been said about what counts as a human interest. In order to explore this difficult area, I introduce two useful definitions. A *felt preference* is any desire or need of a human individual that can at least temporarily be sated by some specifiable experience of that individual. A *considered preference* is any desire or need that a human individual would express after careful deliberation, including a judgement that the desire or need is consistent with a rationally adopted worldview – a worldview which includes fully supported scientific theories and a metaphysical framework interpreting those theories, as well as a set of rationally supported aesthetic and moral ideals.

When interests are assumed to be constructed merely from felt preferences, they are thereby insulated from any criticism or objection. Economic approaches to decision making often adopt this approach because it eschews 'value judgements' – decision makers need only ask people what they want, perhaps correct these preferences for intensity, compute the preferences satisfied by the various possible courses of action, and let the resulting ordinal ranking imply a decision.

A considered preference, on the other hand, is an idealization in the sense that it can only be adopted after a person has rationally accepted an entire worldview and, further, has succeeded in altering his felt preferences so that they are consonant with that worldview. Since this is a process no one has ever completed, references to considered preferences are hypothetical – they refer to preferences the individual would have if certain contrary-to-fact conditions were fulfilled. Nonetheless, references to considered preferences remain useful because it is possible to distinguish felt preferences from considered preferences when there are convincing arguments that felt preferences are not consistent with some element of a worldview that appears worthy of rational support.

It is now possible to define two forms of anthropocentrism. A value theory is *strongly anthropocentric* if all value countenanced by it is explained by reference to satisfactions of felt preferences of human individuals. A value theory is *weakly anthropocentric* if all value countenanced by it is explained by reference to satisfaction of some felt preference of a human individual or by reference to its bearing upon the ideals which exist as elements in a worldview essential to determinations of considered preferences.

Strong anthropocentrism, as here defined, takes unquestioned felt preferences of human individuals as determining value. Consequently, if humans have a strongly consumptive value system, then their 'interests' (which are taken merely to be their felt preferences) dictate that nature will be used in an exploitative manner. Since there is no check upon the felt preferences of individuals in the value system of strong anthropocentrism, there exists no means to criticize the behaviour of individuals who use nature merely as a storehouse of raw materials to be extracted and used for products serving human preferences.

Weak anthropocentrism, on the other hand, recognizes that felt preferences can be either rational or not (in the sense that they can be judged not consonant with a rational worldview). Hence, weak anthropocentrism provides a basis for criticism of value systems which are purely exploitative of nature. In this way, weak anthropocentrism makes available two ethical resources of crucial importance to environmentalists. First, to the extent that environmental ethicists can make a case for a worldview that emphasizes the close relationship between the human species and other living species, they can also make a case for ideals of human behaviour extolling harmony with nature. These ideals are then available as a basis for criticizing preferences that merely exploit nature.

Second, weak anthropocentrism as here defined also places value on human experiences that provide the basis for value formation. Because weak anthropocentrism places value not only on felt preferences, but also on the process of value formation embodied in the criticism and replacement of felt preferences with more rational ones, it makes possible appeals to the value of experiences of natural objects and undisturbed places in human value formation. To the extent that environmentalists can show that values are formed and informed by contact with nature, nature takes on value as a teacher of human values. Nature need no longer be seen as a mere satisfier of fixed and often consumptive values – it also becomes an important source of inspiration in value formation.[9]

In the final section of this paper I develop these two sources of value in nature more fully. Even there my goal is not to defend these two bases for environmental protection as embodying true claims about the value of nature – that, as I said at the outset is a larger and later task. My point is only that, within the limits set by weak anthropocentrism as here defined, there exists a framework for developing powerful reasons for protecting nature. Further, these reasons do not resemble the extractive and exploitative reasons normally associated with strong anthropocentrism.

And they do not differ from strongly anthropocentric reasons in merely theoretical ways. Weakly anthropocentric reasoning can affect behaviour as can be seen by applying it to last man situations. Suppose that human beings choose, for rational or religious reasons, to live according to an ideal of maximum harmony with nature. Suppose also that this ideal is taken seriously and that anyone who impairs that harmony (by destroying another species, by polluting air and water etc.) would be judged harshly. But such an ideal need not attribute intrinsic value to natural objects, nor need the prohibitions implied by it be justified with nonanthropocentric reasoning attributing intrinsic value to nonhuman natural objects. Rather, they can be justified as being implied by the ideal of harmony with nature. This ideal, in turn, can be justified either on religious grounds referring to human spiritual development or as being a fitting part of a rationally defensible worldview.

Indeed, there exist examples of well developed worldviews that exhibit these characteristics. The Hindus and Jains, in proscribing the killing of insects etc., show concern for their own spiritual development rather than for the actual lives of those insects. Likewise, Henry David Thoreau is careful not to attribute independent, intrinsic value to nature. Rather he believes that nature expresses a deeper spiritual reality and that humans can learn spiritual values from it.[10] Nor should it be inferred that only spiritually oriented positions can uphold weakly anthropocentric reasons. In a post-Darwinian world, one could give rational and scientific support for a worldview that includes ideals of living in harmony with nature, but which involve no attributions of intrinsic value to nature.

Views such as those just described are weakly anthropocentric because they refer only to human values, but they are not strongly so because human behaviour is limited by concerns other than those derivable from prohibitions against interfering with the satisfaction of human felt preferences. And practically speaking, the difference in behaviour between strong anthropocentrists and weak anthropocentrists of the sort just described and exemplified is very great. In particular, the reaction of these weak anthropocentrists to last man situations is undoubtedly more similar to that of non-anthropocentrists than to that of strong anthropocentrists. Ideals such as that of living in harmony with nature imply rules proscribing the wanton destruction of other species or ecosystems even if the human species faces imminent extinction.

But it might be objected that positions such as those here sketched only appear to avoid attributions of intrinsic value to nature and natural objects. For example, Tom Regan has argued that a position similar to them makes covert appeal to the intrinsic value of nonhuman objects and hence fails to embody a purely anthropocentric argument for the preservation of nature. He writes:

> If we are told that treating the environment in certain ways offends against an ideal of human conduct, we are not being given a position that is an alternative to, or inconsistent with, the view that nonconscious objects have a value of their own. The fatal objection which the offense against an ideal argument encounters, is that, rather than offering an alternative to the view that some nonconscious objects have inherent value, it presupposes that they do.[11]

Prior to this conclusion, Regan states three propositions which are intended to support it:

> The fitting way to act in regard to *X* clearly involves a commitment to regarding *X* as having value … An ideal which enjoins us not to act toward *X* in a certain way but which denies that *X* has any value is either unintelligible or pointless. Ideals, in short, involve the recognition of the value of *that toward which* one acts.[12]

Regan's three propositions, however, are either false or they fail to support his conclusion. If the value they refer to is inclusive of intrinsic and instrumental value, the propositions are true but do not support the conclusion that all ideals of human conduct imply intrinsic value of the object protected by the ideal. Ideals regarding the treatment of my neighbour's horse (viewed as a piece of private property) imply only that the horse has instrumental, not intrinsic, value. If, on the other hand, Regan intends the references to value in the three propositions to refer to *intrinsic* value exclusively, then all three propositions are clearly false. I can accept that there is a fitting way to act in regard to my neighbour's horse, without thereby accepting any commitment to accord intrinsic value to it. Nor am I thereby committed to anything either unintelligible or pointless. I need not recognize the intrinsic value of the horse; I can, alternatively, recognize the intrinsic value of my neighbour and her preference that the horse not be harmed.

The example of the horse provides a counterexample to Regan's argument, thereby showing that the argument is unsound. It does so, admittedly, by appealing to the instrumental value of the horse for human preference satisfaction. It does not, therefore, directly address the question of whether there are ideals of environmental protection supportable on weakly anthropocentric grounds, but which imply no intrinsic value for the protected objects. The examples mentioned earlier, however, fulfil this function. If the Hindu, the Jainist or the follower of Thoreau appeals to ideals designed to improve humans spiritually, then they can justify those ideals without attributing intrinsic value to the objects protected. Nor are the spiritual aspects of these examples essential. If ideals of human behaviour are justified as fitting parts of a worldview which can be rationally supported from a human perspective, then these ideals, too, escape Regan's argument – they might support protection of nature as a fitting thing for humans to strive toward, without attributing intrinsic value to nature.

Nor need weak anthropocentrism collapse into strong anthropocentrism. It would do so if the dichotomy between preferences and ideals were indefensible. If all values can, ultimately, be interpreted as satisfactions of preferences, then ideals are simply human preferences. The controversy here is reminiscent of that discussed by early utilitarians. John Stuart Mill, for example, argued that because higher pleasures ultimately can be seen to provide greater satisfactions, there is thus only a single scale of values – preference satisfaction.[13] It is true that weak anthropocentrists must deny that preference satisfaction is the only measure of human value. They must take human ideals seriously enough so that they can be set against preference satisfactions as a limit upon them. It is therefore no surprise that weak anthropocentrists reject the reductionistic position popular among utilitarians. Indeed, it is precisely the rejection of that reductionism that allows them to steer their way between strong anthropocentrism and nonanthropocentrism. The rejection of this reduction is, of course, a commitment that weak anthropocentrists share with nonanthropocentrists. Both believe there are values distinct from human preference satisfaction, rejecting the reduction of ideals to preferences. They differ not on this point, but on whether the justification of those ideals must appeal to the intrinsic value of nonhuman objects.

Weak anthropocentrism is, therefore, an attractive position for environmentalists. It requires no radical, difficult-to-justify claims about the intrinsic value of nonhuman objects and, at the same time, it provides a framework for stating obligations that goes beyond concern for satisfying human preferences. It, rather, allows the development of arguments to the effect that current, largely consumptive attitudes toward nature are indefensible, because they do not fit into a worldview that is rationally defensible in terms not implying intrinsic value for nonhumans. It can also emphasize the value of nature in forming, rather than in satisfying, human preferences, as preferences can be modified in the process of striving toward a consistent and rationally defensible worldview.

Individualism and Nonindividualism

The distinctions and arguments presented above convince me that, while the development of a nonanthropocentric axiology committed to intrinsic value for nonhuman natural entities remains an interesting philosophical enterprise, the dichotomy on which it is based has less importance for the nature of environmental ethics than is usually thought. In particular, I see no reason to think that, if environmental ethics is distinctive, its distinctiveness derives from the necessity of appeals to the intrinsic value of nonhuman natural objects. Once two forms of anthropocentrism are distinguished, it appears that from one, weak anthropocentrism, an adequate environmental ethic can be derived. If that is true, authors who equate the question of the distinctiveness of an adequate environmental ethic with the claim that nature or natural objects have intrinsic value are mistaken.

There is, nevertheless, reason to believe that an adequate environmental ethic is distinctive. In this section, I argue that no successful environmental ethic can be derived from an individualistic basis, whether the individuals in question are human or nonhuman. Since most contemporary ethical systems are essentially individualistic, an adequate environmental ethic is distinctive, not by being necessarily nonanthropocentric as many environmental ethicists have argued or assumed, but, rather, by being nonindividualistic.

Standard contemporary ethical theories, at least in the US and Western Europe are essentially individualistic. By this I mean that the behavioural prohibitions embodied in them derive from the principle that actions ought not to harm other individuals unjustifiably. Utilitarians derive ethical rules from the general principle that all actions should promote the greatest possible happiness for the greatest possible number of individuals. This means that actions (or rules) are judged to be legitimate or not according to whether more good (and less harm) for individuals will result from the action than from any alternative. On this view, the satisfaction of each individual interest is afforded an initial prima facie value. Some such interests are not to be satisfied because the information available indicates that if they are, some greater interest or sets of interests of some individuals cannot be satisfied concurrently with them. The utilitarian principle, supplemented by empirical predictions about the consequences of actions for individuals, filters happiness-maximizing actions from others that do not maximize happiness. For present purposes, the important point is that the satisfaction of individual interests is the basic unit of value for utilitarians, and in this sense, utilitarianism (either of the act or rule variety) is essentially individualistic.[14]

Contemporary deontologists derive ethical prohibitions from individual rights and obligations to protect those rights.[15] Individuals make claims, and when these claims conflict with claims made by other individuals, they are judged to be legitimate or illegitimate according to a set of ethical rules designed to make such decisions. Although these rules, in essence, are the embodiment of a system of justice and fairness, the rules adjudicate between claims of individuals, and consequently modern deontology is essentially individualistic.[16] Therefore, both utilitarianism and modern deontology are essentially individualistic in the sense that the basic units of ethical concern are interests or claims of individuals.

It is characteristic of the rules of environmental ethics that they must prohibit current behaviours that have effects upon the long-range future as well as the present. For example, storage of radioactive wastes with a half-life of thousands of years in containers that will deteriorate in a few centuries must be prohibited by an adequate environmental ethic, even if such actions, on the whole, provide the most benefits and no harms to currently living individuals. Likewise, human demographic growth, if subsequent generations continue that policy, will create severe overpopulation, a behaviour negatively affecting the future of the environment, and hence human reproductive behaviour must be governed by an adequate environmental ethic. An adequate environmental ethic must therefore prohibit current activities generally agreed to have negative effects on the environment of the future.

I have argued at length elsewhere that a paradox, due to Derek Parfit, effectively precludes systems of ethics which are individualistic in the sense defined above from governing current decisions by reference to their effects on future individuals.[17] To summarize that argument briefly, it exploits the insight that no system of ethics built exclusively upon adjudications of interests of present and future individuals can govern current decisions and their effects on future individuals because current environmental decisions determine what individuals will exist in the future. Parfit's argument notes that current decisions regarding consumption determine how many individuals and which individuals will be born in the future. On a policy of fast demographic growth and high consumption, different individuals will exist a century from now than would exist if the current generation adopts a policy of low growth and moderate consumption. Assume, as most environmentalists do, that a policy of high growth and immoderate consumption will leave the future with a lower quality of life than more moderate growth policies would. The individuals who are, in fact, born as a result of the immoderate growth policies cannot complain that they would have been better off had the policies been different – for they would not even have existed had moderate policies been adopted. That is, Parfit's paradox shows that current policy cannot be governed by reference to harms to the interests of future individuals, because those policies determine who those individuals will be and what interests they will have. Attempts to govern behaviours affecting the distant future cannot, therefore, be governed by appeal to individual interests of future persons, since the very existence of such individuals hangs in the balance until all relevant decisions are made.

Since the ethical intuitions shared by all environmentally sensitive individuals include prohibitions against behaviours which may have negative effects only in the long-term future (and not in the present), the rules of environmental ethics cannot be derived from the usual, individualistic systems of ethics currently in vogue. Note, also, that my argument concerning individualism makes no assumption that only human individuals make claims or have interests and rights. Future nonhuman individuals are, likewise, affected by human policies regarding consumption and reproduction. Consequently, expansion of the loss of individual rights holders, or preference havers to include nonhumans in no way affects the argument. No ethical system which is essentially individualistic, regardless of how broadly the reference category of individuals is construed, can offer ethical guidance concerning current environmental policy in all cases.

A Proposal for an Adequate
Anthropocentric Environmental Ethic

The arguments of the last section are surprisingly simple and general, but if they are sound, they explain the fairly general intuition that environmental ethics must be distinctive in some sense, although not in the sense usually assumed. So far my conclusions have all been negative – I have argued that an adequate environmental ethic *need not* be nonanthropocentric and that an adequate environmental ethic *must not* be limited to considerations of individual interests. From these conclusions a new direction for environmental ethics emerges which is weakly anthropocentric – it finds all value in human loci – and which is also nonindividualistic in the sense that value is not restricted to satisfactions of felt preferences of human individuals. In other words, the arguments of the first two sections of the paper (1) positively define a space by establishing the possibility of a weakly, but not strongly, anthropocentric environmental ethic and (2) negatively constrain that ethic by eliminating the possibility that it be purely individualistic.

My purpose now is not to demonstrate that the ethical principles I have set out are definitely correct or that they are the only adequate principles available. My goal, rather, is to present a valid alternative for environmental ethics that is adequate in a manner that no purely individualistic, strongly anthropocentric ethic can be, while avoiding difficult-to-defend references to the intrinsic value of nonhuman natural objects.

I begin my explication with an analogy. Suppose an extremely wealthy individual, through a will, sets up a very large trust fund 'to be managed for the economic well-being of my descendants'. Over the years, descendants will be born and die, and the class of beneficiaries will change through time. Suppose, also, that the family drifts apart emotionally and becomes highly contentious. I suggest that two sorts of controversies, each with its own distinctive logic, could arise concerning the fund. First, there may be issues about the *fair distribution* of proceeds of the trust. Some descendants might claim that other descendants are not entitled to full shares, because they are, or are descended from, an illegitimate offspring of a member of the family. Or it might be disputed whether adopted children of descendants are included in the terms of the will.

Second, there may well be disputes about the *management* of the trust. Here, there may be questions concerning what sorts of investments are 'good investments'. Should all investments be safe ones, thereby insuring a continued, although smaller income? Might the principle of the trust be invaded in years where the income from investments is unusually low? Might one generation simply spend the principle, dividing it fairly among themselves, showing no concern for future descendants?

To apply this analogy in obvious ways, ethical questions about the environment can be divided into ones concerning distributional fairness within generations and others concerning longer-term, cross-generational issues. If the arguments in the third section are correct, then the latter are not reducible to the former; nor do they have the same logic. It can be assumed that many environmental concerns, as well as nonenvironmental ones, can be resolved as issues of distributional fairness. If a property owner pollutes a stream running through his property, this action raises a question of fairness between him and his downstream neighbours.[18] These moral issues are, presumably, as amenable to resolution using the categories and rules of standard, individualistic ethics as are non-environmental ones.

But there are also many questions in environmental ethics that are analogous to questions of management of a trust across time. Soil, water, forests, coal, oil etc. are analogous to the principle of the trust. If they are used up, destroyed or degraded, they no longer provide benefits. The income from the trust provides an analogy for renewable resources. As long as the productive resource (analogous to the principle of the trust) is intact, one can expect a steady flow of benefits.

One feature that makes environmental ethics distinctive is concern for protection of the resource base through indefinite time. Parfit's paradox shows that these concerns cannot be accounted for by reference to concerns for individuals and to the obligation not to harm other individuals unjustifiably. The obligations are analogous to those accepted by an individual who is appointed executor of the trust fund. Although decisions made by the executor affect individuals and their wellbeing, the obligation is to the integrity of the trust, not to those individuals. While one might be tempted to say that the obligation of the executor is to future individuals who will be born, but who are at this time unknown, this conceptualization also involves a failure to perceive the profundity of Parfit's paradox. Suppose all of the members of a given generation of the family in question sign an agreement not to have offspring and thereby convince the executor to disburse the principle of the trust equally among current beneficiaries. Perhaps this is consistent with the terms of the trust, but it shows that the current choices of the executor cannot be guided by abstract conceptions of 'future individuals'. When current decisions about management are interlocked with not-yet-decided questions affecting the future existence of individuals, it is impossible to refer to those individuals as the basis of guidance in making current management decisions.

Suppose a generation of the entire human species freely decided to sterilize itself, thereby freeing itself to consume without fear of harming future individuals. Would they do wrong? Yes.[19] The perpetuation of the human species is a good thing because a universe containing human consciousness is preferable to one without it.[20] This value claim implies that current generations must show concern for future generations. They must take steps to avoid the extinction of the species and they must provide a reasonably stable resource base so that future generations will not suffer great deprivation. These are the bases of rules of management analogous to the rules for administering a trust fund. They do not have individuals or individual interests as their reference point, but they do govern behaviour that will affect future individuals.

It is now possible to outline a weakly anthropocentric, nonindividualistic environmental ethic. Such an ethic has two levels. The distributional level has as its principle that one ought not to harm other human individuals unjustifiably. This principle rests upon the assumption that felt preferences, desires that occur within individual human consciousness, have equal prima facie value. Rules for the fair treatment of individuals are derived from the principle of no harm and prescribe fair treatment of individuals, whether regarding benefits derived from the environment or from other sources. Since there is nothing distinctive about the environmental prescriptions and proscriptions that occur on this level – they do not differ in nature from other issues of individual fairness – I do not discuss them further.

Decisions on the second level of environmental ethics, which I call the level of 'allocation', cannot, however, be based upon individual considerations. The central value placed on human consciousness is not a result of aggregating the value of individual consciousnesses, because the value of ongoing consciousness cannot be derived from the value of individual consciousnesses – they cannot be identified or counted prior to the making of decisions on resource allocation.[21] Therefore, obligations on this level are owed to no individual and can be called 'generalized obligations'. They are obligations of the current generation to maintain a stable flow of resources into the indefinite future and, consequently, they are stated vis-à-vis resources necessary for ongoing human life, not vis-à-vis individual requirements. Resources represent the means for supporting life looked at from a nonindividual perspective. The individual perspective determines needs and wants and then seeks means to fulfil them. Concern for the continued flow of resources ensures that sources of goods and services such as ecosystems, soil, forests etc. remain 'healthy' and are not deteriorating. In this way, options are held open and reasonable needs of individuals for whatever goods and services can be fulfilled with reasonable labour, technology and ingenuity. The emphasis of this concern, however, is not individualistic since it is not focused on the fulfilment of specifiable needs, but rather on the integrity and health of ongoing ecosystems as holistic entities.

While the long-term nature of the concern implies that the stability of the resource base must be protected, this stability is not the same thing as ecological stability. It is an open (and controversial) question as to what the stability of ecosystems means. Further, there are controversies concerning the extent to which there are scientifically support-able generalizations about what is necessary to protect ecological stability. For example, it is highly controversial whether diversity, in general, promotes and/or is necessary for ecological stability.[22] These controversies are too complex to enter into here, but they are relevant. To the extent that scientists know what is necessary to protect the resource base, there is an obligation to act upon it. Even if there are few sweeping generalizations such as those concerning diversity and stability, there are a wide variety of less general rules that are well supported and are being systematically ignored in environmental pol-icy. Ecologists and resource managers know that clear-cutting tropical forests on steep slopes causes disastrous erosion, that intensely tilling monocultures causes loss of top-soil, and that overexploitation of fisheries can cause new and far less productive species compositions. Further, there is an obligation, where knowledge is lacking, to seek that knowledge in order to avoid unintentional destruction.

An ethic of resource allocation should apply to nonrenewable resources as well as to renewable ones and should also imply a population policy. The general injunction to maintain the stability of the resource base across generations follows from the value of human consciousness. It implies that, with respect to renewable or interest-bearing resources, present generations should not harvest more than the maximum sustainable yield of the resource. But what does stability imply with respect to nonrenewable resources? Although at first glance it would seem to suggest that a stable supply can only be sustained if no utilization takes place, this reasoning is based on a confusion – it is not the case that there is an obligation to have a certain, fixed amount of goods in sup-ply, but rather there is an obligation to maintain a stable level of goods *available for use*. The ethical principle, in other words, is directed at maintaining the possibility of human consciousness which requires resource use. What is required, then, is a constant supply of resources available for utilization by succeeding generations. Once the problem is framed in this manner, human technology and the phenomenon of substitutability of products become relevant. Present humans may use up nonrenewable resources, pro-vided they take steps to provide suitable substitutes. If, for example, the present generation uses up a major portion of the accumulated fossil fuels available, they will have done nothing wrong if they leave the next generation with a technology capable of deriving energy from renewable sources such as the sun, wind or ocean currents.[23] There are significant trade-offs available back and forth between renewable and nonrenewable resources.

Note also that this system implies a population principle – the level of population in any given generation should be determined by the requirements for the stability of the resource flow. Such a determination would be based on an assessment of (a) how many people are consistent with the maximal sustainable yield of renewable resources and (b) how many people are consistent with a level of use for nonrenewable resources which does not outstrip the ability of the existing technology to produce suitable substi-tutes. A population principle follows, in turn, from this stability principle. One need not identify future individuals or worry about utilities of possible individuals on this approach. The obligation is to maintain maximum sustainable yield consistent with the stability of the resource flow. The population principle sets a population policy for a generation as a whole based on the carrying capacity of the environment. Questions about who, in a given generation, should have children and how many each individual can have, may be treated as questions of interpersonal equity among the existing individuals of any given generation. The ethical obligations constituting an ethic of allocation are quite simple as they derive from a single value – that of ongoing human consciousness. In general form, however, they do not state specifically what to do; they only require actions necessary to retain a stable resource base through indefinite time. Scientific knowledge can, in principle, nevertheless, indicate specific actions necessary in order to fulfil that obligation. Scientific evidence is sufficient to imply that many currently widespread practices violate those obligations either directly or cumulatively and are, in terms of this system, immoral. There are also areas where scientific knowledge is insufficient to decide whether and how certain practices are destructive. Here, the obligation is to be cautious and to proceed to obtain the information necessary.

While science plays a crucial role in this system, the system is not naturalistic. It does not derive moral obligations from purely scientific statements. Central to all obligations of present individuals to the future is an obligation to perpetuate the value of human consciousness. Science elucidates and makes concrete the specific obligations flowing from that central obligation but does not support it.

Relating the Two Levels

The ethic proposed has two levels – one has the prima facie equality of felt preferences of individual humans as its central value principle; the other has the value of ongoing human life and consciousness as its central value principle. Rules and behaviours justified on these two levels can, of course, conflict. If felt preferences are overly consumptive, then the future of human life may be threatened. Conversely, one can imagine situations where concern for the future of the human species might lead to draconian measures threatening the life or livelihood of current individuals by limiting the satisfaction of felt preferences. Weak anthropocentrism, nevertheless, because it recognizes the important difference between felt and considered preferences, can adjudicate these disputes.

The most common conflict, the one many environmentalists fear we now face, exists when overly consumptive felt preferences cause serious overexploitation of nature and thereby threaten the resource base necessary for continued human life. This conflict can be resolved by taking human ideals into consideration. If, for example, one's total worldview contains as an ideal the continuation of human life and consciousness, then the felt preferences in question are irrational – they are inconsistent with an important ethical ideal. Similarly, if a rational worldview recognizing that the human species evolved from other life forms includes an ideal calling for harmony with nature, this ideal, likewise, can function to criticize and alter felt preferences. By building ecological principles and ideals regarding the proper human treatment of nature into a rationally supported worldview, weak anthropocentrists can develop vast resources for criticizing felt preferences of human individuals which threaten environmental stability and harmony.

It can be argued that experiences of nature are essential in constructing a rational worldview. Likewise, scientific understanding of nature seems essential for the construction of such a worldview. Nor would it be very surprising if it turned out that analogies, symbols, and metaphors drawn from nature provided an essential source of guidance in choosing ethical and aesthetic ideals as well.[24] Other species and unspoiled places would thereby have great value to humans, not only for the way in which they satisfy human felt preferences, but also for the way they serve to enlighten those preferences. Once one recognizes the distinction between felt preferences and considered preferences, nature assumes a crucial role in informing values by contributing to the formation of a rational worldview, the criterion by which felt preferences are criticized.

Environmental Ethics and Intrinsic Value

The conflicts that exist between the levels of distributive fairness and allocation require thoughtful discussion and debate, but that discussion and debate can take place without appeal to the intrinsic value of nonhuman natural objects. The value of ongoing human consciousness and the rules it implies for resource allocation can serve as a basis for criticism of consumptive and exploitative felt preferences. Further, ideas such as that of human harmony with nature and the human species' evolutionary affinity to other species, can serve to strengthen and add flesh to the worldview available for the critique of current environmentally destructive behaviours.

When I refer to an environmental ethic, then, I refer, first of all, to the rules of distributive fairness guiding behaviours affecting other human beings' use of the environment. Second, I refer to the rules of allocation affecting the long-term health of the biosphere as a functioning, organic unit. An environmental ethic, nevertheless, is more than these rules: it also encompasses the ideals, values and principles that constitute a rational worldview regarding the human species' relationship to nature. In these sources are bases for evaluating the rules of right action and for criticizing currently felt preferences. Aesthetic experience of nature is an essential part of the process of forming and applying these ideals and, hence, is also a central part of the environmental ethic here described.

Some nonanthropocentrists, such as J. Baird Callicott, have developed in more detail such ideas as the human affinity to other species and have concluded that it is rational for humans to 'attribute' intrinsic value to other species on the basis of affective feelings toward them,[25] but if, as I have argued, a sense of harmony with nature can, once it becomes an entrenched part of our worldview, serve to correct felt preferences, then it can also serve to bring felt preferences more in line with the requirements of resource allocation without any talk about intrinsic value. Of course, since human beings, as highly evolved animals, share many needs for clean air, clean water, ecosystem services etc. in the long term with other species it would not be surprising that *speaking as if* nature has intrinsic value could provide useful guidance in adjusting human felt preferences. And since these preferences are now far too exploitative and too consumptive for the good of our own species, showing concern for other species that share our long-term needs for survival might be one useful tool in a very large kit.

The point of this essay, however, has been to show that one need not make the questionable ontological commitments involved in attributing intrinsic value to nature, since weak anthropocentrism provides a framework adequate to criticize current destructive practices, to incorporate concepts of human affinity to nature, and to account for the distinctive nature of environmental ethics. All of these are essential elements in an ethic that recognizes the distinction between felt and considered preferences and includes important aesthetic and ethical ideals. These ideals, which can be derived from spiritual sources or from a rationally constructed worldview, can be based on and find their locus in human values. And yet they are sufficient to provide the basis of criticism of currently overconsumptive felt preferences. As such they adjudicate between ethical concerns for distributional fairness in the present and concerns of allocation which have reference to the long-term future. Essential to this adjudication is the development of principles of conduct that respect the ongoing integrity of functioning ecosystems seen as wholes. In this way they transcend concern for individualistically expressed felt preferences and focus attention on the stable functioning of ongoing systems. If all of this is true, Occam's razor surely provides a basis for favouring weak anthropocentrism over nonanthropocentrism.

Notes

1   Bryan G. Norton, 'Environmental ethics and nonhuman rights', *Environmental Ethics*, vol 4 (1982), pp17–36, and 'Environmental ethics and the rights of future generations', *Environmental Ethics*, vol 4 (1982), pp319–337.

2   See, for example, Richard Routley, 'Is there a need for a new, an environmental ethic?' *Proceedings of the XV World Congress of Philosophy*, vol 1 (1973), pp205–210; Holmes Rolston, III, 'Is there an ecological ethic?' *Ethics*, vol 85 (1975), pp93–109; Tom Regan, 'The nature and possibility of an environmental ethic', *Environmental Ethics*, vol 3 (1981), pp19–34; and Evelyn B. Pluhar, 'The justification of an environmental ethic', *Environmental Ethics*, vol 4 (1982), pp319–337.

3   See Regan, 'The nature and possibility of an environmental ethic', who distinguishes 'an ethic of the environment' from 'an ethic for the use of the environment' (p20), where the former, but not the latter, recognizes the intrinsic (inherent) value of nonhuman elements of nature. If the arguments of this paper are persuasive, Regan's distinction will lose interest.

4   My thoughts on this subject have been deeply affected by discussions of the work of Donald Regan and J. Baird Callicott. See Donald Regan, 'Duties of preservation', and J. Baird Callicott, 'On the intrinsic value of nonhuman species', in *The Preservation of Species*, edited by Bryan G. Norton (Princeton University Press, 1986).

5   I borrow this phrase from Donald Scherer, 'Anthropocentrism, atomism, and environmental ethics', *Environmental Ethics*, vol 4 (1982), pp115–123.

6　I take anthropocentrism to be interchangeable with homocentrism. See R. and V. Routley, 'Against the inevitability of human chauvinism', in *Ethics and Problems of the 21st Century*, edited by K. E. Goodpaster and K. M. Sayre (Notre Dame, University of Notre Dame Press, 1979), pp56–57. Routley and Routley show that 'human chauvinism' (anthropocentrism, homocentrism) are equivalent to the thesis of man's 'dominion', which they describe as 'the view that the earth and all its nonhuman contents exist or are available for man's benefit and to serve his interests'.

7　See J. Baird Callicott, 'On the intrinsic value of nonhuman species', in Norton, *The Preservation of Species* (Princeton University Press, 1986), and Pluhar, 'The justification of an environmental ethic'.

8　See, for example, Richard Routley, 'Is there a need for a new, an environmental ethic?' p207; Routley and Routley, 'Human chauvinism and environmental ethics', in *Environmental Philosophy*, edited by D. S. Mannison, M. A. McRobbie and R. Routley (Canberra, Australian National University, Department of Philosophy, 1980), p121; and Donald Regan, 'Duties of preservation,' in Norton, *The Preservation of Species*.

9　For fuller discussions of this point, see Mark Sagoff, 'On preserving the natural environment', *Yale Law Journal*, vol 84 (1974), pp205–67; Holmes Rolston, III, 'Can and ought we to follow nature?' *Environmental Ethics*, vol 1 (1979), pp7–21; and Bryan G. Norton, *The Spice of Life* (in preparation) [1984].

10　See Henry David Thoreau, *Walden* (New York, Harper and Row, 1958). Note page 64, for example, where Thoreau writes: 'One value of even the smallest well is, that when you look into it you see that earth is not continent but insular. This is as important as that it keeps butter cool.'

11　Regan, 'The nature and possibility of an environmental ethic', pp25–26. It involves no distortion, I think, to equate Regan's use of *inherent* with mine of *intrinsic*.

12　Ibid, p25.

13　John Stuart Mill, *Utilitarianism*, ch 2.

14　1 do not intend to imply here that utilitarians are limited to treating human interests as felt preferences. Utilitarians adopt varied interpretations of interests in relation to happiness. My point is only that human individual interests, however determined, are the basis of their moral calculus.

15　I qualify the position here discussed as 'contemporary' deontology because there is a strain of thought in Kant which emphasizes that the imperatives are abstract principles. Modern neo-Kantians such as Rawls, however, emphasize the more individualistic strains in Kant, placing him more in the contractarian tradition. Contractarian deontologists – those that fit clearly into the liberal tradition – are my concern here. (I am indebted to Douglas Berggren for clarifying this point.)

16　For a clear explanation of how rights function to adjudicate individual claims, see Joel Feinberg, 'The nature and value of rights', *Journal of Value Inquiry*, vol 4 (1970), pp243–257. While not all writers agree that rights originate in claims, the disputes are immaterial here. For example, McCloskey's linkage of rights to 'entitlements' is not inconsistent with my point. H. J. McCloskey, 'Rights', *Philosophical Quarterly*, vol 15 (1965), pp115–127.

17　See, 'Energy and the further future', in *Energy and the Future*, edited by Douglas MacLean and Peter G. Brown (Totowa, NJ, Rowman and Littlefield, 1983). I apply Parfit's 'paradox' to environmental ethics in 'Environmental ethics and the rights of future generations', *Environmental Ethics*, vol 4 (1982), p321. See that essay for a more detailed discussion.

18 This is not to suggest, of course, that such action could not also have more long-term effects raising issues of the second sort as well.

19 This answer implies a disanalogy with the trust fund situation, provided one accepts the judgement that no wrong would be committed if a generation of the family chose not to reproduce. I think there is a disanalogy here, as different reproductive obligations would arise if the future of the human species were at stake. Suppose one answers this question negatively regarding the future of humankind and then considers the possibility that the last human individual might wantonly destroy other species, natural places etc. I would still reject such wanton acts as inconsistent with good human behaviour, relying upon weakly anthropocentric arguments as described above.

20 I willingly accept the implication of this value claim that, in a situation of severely contracting human population, some or all individuals would have an obligation to reproduce, but I will not defend this central claim here. Although I believe it can be defended, I am more interested in integrating it into a coherent ethical system than in defending it.

21 On a closely related point, see Brian Barry, 'Circumstances of justice and future generations', in Sikora and Barry, eds, *Obligations to Future Generations* (Philadelphia, Temple University Press, 1978).

22 See Norton, *The Spice of Life*.

23 I am, for the sake of the example, ignoring other long-term effects of the use of fossil fuels. Problems due to the greenhouse effect would, of course, also have to be solved.

24 See references in note 9 above.

25 Callicott, 'On the intrinsic value of nonhuman species'. Also see Pluhar, 'The Justification of an environmental ethic' for a somewhat different approach to attribution of intrinsic value.

6

A Defence of the Deep Ecology Movement

Arne Naess

In a recent article Richard A. Watson criticizes a position he calls 'anti-anthropocentric biocentrism'.[1] He also attacks what he considers to be misplaced mysticism and religion. According to Watson, man should learn to behave in an ecologically sound manner simply because this is necessary for human survival. To touch deeper issues is unwarranted. The value of human survival he (implicitly) takes to be an intrinsic value – and I agree. But those who have dedicated, and wish to dedicate, much of their life and energy to protecting nature against destruction have had this planet with all its life forms in mind. *In order to be heard* they have had to argue almost exclusively in terms of human health and wellbeing, even though their motivation has been both broader and deeper.

Very few, and probably none, of the pioneers in the fight against the destructive activity of human beings on our planet in this century have envisaged that this activity would or could lead to the extinction of the human species. The possibility that there would be *no* areas where a sufficient number of humans could survive is one that has not concerned them.

Consider a recent example. A handful of wolves in southern Norway kill sheep and frighten parents who imagine that the wolves will attack their children on their way to school. Parents should be able to feel that their children are safe, all agree, but it costs a lot of money to hire 'shepherds' for the children. Conclusion: kill the wolves. Professional hunters try hard to do this, but Norwegian wolves know too much about hunters and how to avoid them.

Those who might argue that man should not try to kill the wolves, since they are good for human survival, are unlikely to stop the hunters. Human survival is a weak argument not only from the point of view of parents, sheep owners and hunters, but also from that of politicians.

The strong opposition to killing the wolves stems from people who (1) consider these animals to have intrinsic value, every one of them, and maintain that in principle each of them has the same right to live and blossom as we and our children have and (2) consider it the duty of a rich industrial nation to safeguard both sheep and wolves. We *cannot* send sheep, who are rendered helpless through thousands of years of human manipulation, into wolf territory without a shepherd, if at all. The opponents also dig

Note: Reprinted from *Environmental Ethics*, vol 6, Naess, A., 'A defence of the deep ecology movement', pp265–270, copyright © (1984), with permission from author

into cultural history explaining how wolves came to have a worse public image than bears, for instance, and how this bad public image has been exploited by great authors like the brothers Grimm, resulting in baseless fears that children may be attacked on their way to school. Last but not least they work out proposals on how to solve the economic problems involved, for instance, the payment of shepherds.

Abstract reasons about living in harmony with the natural order, about the possible medical and scientific value of every species, are important, but man has a heart, not only a brain. Strong philosophical or religious views are required. Among nonacademics they are mostly unarticulated, but are influential if they are appealed to.

Watson argues against the views of those he calls the 'ecosophers'. From the names he mentions it is more appropriate to consider his argument to be against the members of the deep ecology movement. The tenets of this movement may perhaps be roughly formulated as follows: (1) The wellbeing of nonhuman life on Earth has value in itself. This value is independent of any instrumental usefulness for limited human purposes. (2) Richness and diversity in life forms contribute to this value and are a further value in themselves. (3) Humans have no right to interfere destructively with nonhuman life except for purposes of satisfying vital needs. (4) Present interference is excessive and detrimental. (5) Present policies must therefore be changed. (6) The necessary policy changes affect basic economic and ideological structures and will be the more drastic the longer it takes before significant change is started. (7) The ideological change is mainly that of appreciating life quality (focusing on situations involving inherent value) rather than enjoying a high standard of life (measured in terms of available means). (8) Those who subscribe to the foregoing points have an obligation directly or indirectly to try to implement the necessary changes.

As exponents of anti-anthropocentric biocentrism Watson mentions George Sessions, myself and some others, but I do not know anybody who fits the description he offers. Although Watson concludes that the position is internally contradictory, a 'position' with the vagueness and ambiguity of anti-anthropocentric biocentrism can scarcely aspire to be contradictory. That would demand a minimum of preciseness.

The absence of anti-anthropocentric biocentrists does not, in my mind, make the article of Watson uninteresting or unimportant. Let me try to substantiate this, but at the same time try to eliminate some misunderstandings.

The term *ecosopher*, which he uses, usually refers to a philosopher whose total view is inspired by ecology and the deep ecology movement. Both Sessions and myself are supporters of the movement and we are also ecosophers, but the great majority of the supporters have not developed any ecosophy. Moreover, the important groups of Christian supporters tend to repudiate the term because they find their total view is primarily inspired by the Bible. In what follows I write as if Watson had used the term 'supporter of the deep ecological movement' rather than the term *ecosopher*.

Watson is right if he is of the opinion that supporters of the deep ecology movement sometimes write or talk *as if* human needs, goals or desires should *under no circumstances* 'be taken as privileged or overriding' in considering 'the needs, desires, interests, and goals' of a nonhuman living beings (p245). Such a norm, if followed uncritically, would, of course, make humans into a strange kind of proletarian and would result in their extinction. Rather, what engages the supporters of the deep ecological movement is the question 'under *what* circumstances...' This question is not capable of any precise, general answer.[2] A short formula runs as follows: 'A vital need of the nonhuman living being *A* overrides a peripheral interest of the human being *B*'. There is substantial support of this vague sentence among large groups of people as long as the set of *A*'s is restricted to the set of those mammals and birds which are not used for food. Supporters of the deep ecology movement are in favour of a much wider set of beings under a wider set of circumstances, but there are of course large individual and cultural differences. It is undesirable to try to establish complete conformity.

The sentence expressing Watson's definition of anti-anthropocentric biocentrism (p245) might conceivably be *interpreted* in such a way that some supporters of the movement might find it suitable as an expression of their position. The same holds true of many other sentences in his article, but rarely have I found semantical considerations as relevant as when I try to understand a colleague in environmental debates! For example, the second of five alleged principles of the 'movement' – and here (p251) Watson uses the term *movement* – runs as follows: 'The human species should not change the ecology of the planet'. Inevitably, humans change and will change the ecology of the Earth, if *ecology* here implies 'at least one of the ecosystems'. This holds even if the human population mercifully is reduced to one tenth of the present population, and even if the 'ecological consciousness' (Sessions) deepens considerably. But Watson may interpret his sentence differently. Anyway, many of us subscribe to the maxim of Barry Commoner: '...any major man-made change in a natural system is likely to be *detrimental* to that system'. This is a typical *maxim* of a movement, not a proposition in an ecosophy, a systematic philosophy. It has a comparable rhetorical function to Commoner's fourth 'law': 'There is no such thing as a free lunch' and to the maxim 'Nature knows best'. Confusion increases when the rhetorics of a movement is treated like seminar exercises in university philosophy.

According to Watson, he has exposed 'five principles' of anti-anthropocentric biocentrism. I have already commented on number two. Number one is similar to a part of Watson's proposed definition: 'The needs, desires, interests, and goals of humans are not privileged.' For some interpretations ('not' = 'not in every case') the formulation of the 'principle' is acceptable; however, if 'not privileged' is interpreted in the direction of 'never privileged', it is obviously unacceptable, whatever the plausible interpretation of *privileged*.

The third principle runs as follows: 'The world ecological system is too complex for human beings ever to understand.' It seems that this formulation is an absolutistic modification of Aldo Leopold's expression '...may never be fully understood' (quoted by Watson on p246). If there is a question of understanding *fully* what goes on in one gram of soil when a thousandth part of a milligram of a certain poison is administered, we must answer, I think, in the negative. We would have to understand countless millions of living beings in their close interaction. But if only general notions about what happens on our planet are implied, some humans, including Watson, already understand quite a lot. Again vagueness and ambiguity render it difficult to be for or against the 'position'.

The fourth principle, according to Watson, is that 'the ultimate goal, good, and joy of humankind is contemplative understanding of Nature'. This principle apparently has something to do with a misunderstood interpretation of Spinoza and has little to do with the deep ecology movement. Activeness is a basic concept in Spinoza and active life in nature is a goal of most participants in the movement.

The more complex fifth principle (see p251) may sound adequate to many deep ecologists, but some of the terms such as *harmonious* and *equilibrium,* which were highly valued as key terms in the 1960s, are, I think, less adequate today. Every species in the long run alters ecosystems and mankind cannot be an exception. It is the kind of alteration that matters. Humans have special responsibilities because of their capacity at least to pose the problem of long-term consequences of their behaviour.

Watson does contribute effectively to the fight against superficial views about diversity, complexity and ecological balance:

> Another obvious anthropocentric element in ecosophic thinking is the predilection for ecological communities of great internal variety and complexity. But the barren limestone plateaus that surround the Mediterranean now are just as much in ecological balance as were the forests that grew there before man cut them down. And 'dead' Lake Erie is just as much in ecological balance with the life on the land that surrounds it as it was in pre-Columbian times. (p254)

The 'maximum diversity and complexity' *norms* of ecosophy cannot be derived from the *science* of ecology. Often supporters of the movement write as if they believed in such a derivation. In part it is due to broad, normative usages of the term *ecology,* including much that cannot be part of a science. But the term *ecosophy* – eco-wisdom – was introduced in order to contrast normative, philosophical views from facts and theories within the science of ecology. It was also introduced to stress the necessity of clarifying the relation between abstract principles and concrete decisions. Wisdom, not science, implies such a relation.

Neither giraffes nor crocodiles have developed any ecosophical norms or theories of gravitational waves. These are specific human products. I do not see, however, why ecosophy or theory of gravitational waves should therefore be classed as 'anthropocentric'. Human 'predilections' are human. Thus far I agree with Watson.

Watson mentions a 'hands-off-nature' position and shows convincingly that it implies 'setting man apart'. Excellent. The supporters of the movement are, in my view, intensively active in their relation to nature, but not in the sense of large-scale digging, cutting and altering ecosystems. However, are they mainly meditating? Life in and with Nature may or may not involve contemplation.[3]

Nils Faarlund has introduced the potent slogan 'traceless *ferd* [movement and conduct] in nature' as a main slogan for his international school of outdoor life. Cross-country skiing? Yes. Vast machinery of slalom centres? No. As other valuable slogans of the movement, they are useless or false when interpreted in an absolutist way. (Traceless? Impossible!) As objects of analysis they are in my view indispensable in philosophical seminars at universities, but not as concepts and propositions.

Wilderness experience often includes meditation in certain senses, but it also includes the active *use* of natural resources. Heidegger, I suppose, does not contrast use of tools, for instance, the use of an axe, with 'letting beings be'. Zimmerman says only that Heidegger is against treating beings 'merely as objects *for* the all-powerful Subject'. We may be active in relation to a flower without touching it. We may be passive when trampling on a flower. But in springtime in deserts you cannot walk without trampling on tiny flowers almost every step. That is not a sufficient reason not to live in deserts after rain falls. There is no general norm in ecosophy against our full life in nature, and this implies acceptance of hurting and killing. Ecosophy, as I conceive it, *says yes to the fullest self-realization of man.*

Tom Regan's 'preservation principle' (quoted on p246) is a slogan that lends itself to passivist, Utopian interpretations, especially out of context, but it is also capable of reasonable applications in everyday life, for instance, in the offices of regional planners: when interfering with this river, are we just meddling, or are we doing something necessary in order to satisfy basic needs of humans? Are we destroying this forest or are we merely changing it in a nondestructive way?

In conclusion, I think it may be appropriate to note that in Protagoras' statement about *homo mensura* nothing is said about what is measured. Man may be the measure of all things in the sense that only a human being has a measuring *rod*, but what he measures he may find to be greater than himself and his survival.

Notes

1   Richard A. Watson, 'A critique of anti-anthropocentric biocentrism', *Environmental Ethics*, vol 5(1983), pp245–256.
2   Paul W. Taylor, 'In defense of biocentrism', *Environmental Ethics*, vol 5 (1983), pp237–243.
3   This reference of Sessions to perennial philosophy, quoted by Watson on p246, is misleading. I do not think that Sessions insists that meditation is a central feature of man/nature relations. Nor does he think that this is so for Spinoza.

7

Radical American Environmentalism and 'Wilderness' Preservation: A Third World Critique

Ramachandra Guha

Even God dare not appear to the poor man except in the form of bread.

Mahatma Gandhi

Introduction

The respected radical journalist Kirkpatrick Sale recently celebrated 'the passion of a new and growing movement that has become disenchanted with the environmental establishment and has in recent years mounted a serious and sweeping attack on it – style, substance, systems, sensibilities and all'.[1] The vision of those whom Sale calls the 'New Ecologists' – and what I refer to in this article as deep ecology – is a compelling one. Decrying the narrowly economic goals of mainstream environmentalism, this new movement aims at nothing less than a philosophical and cultural revolution in human attitudes toward nature. In contrast to the conventional lobbying efforts of environmental professionals based in Washington, it proposes a militant defence of 'Mother Earth', an unflinching opposition to human attacks on undisturbed wilderness. With their goals ranging from the spiritual to the political, the adherents of deep ecology span a wide spectrum of the American environmental movement. As Sale correctly notes, this emerging strand has in a matter of a few years made its presence felt in a number of fields: from academic philosophy (as in the journal *Environmental Ethics*) to popular environmentalism (for example, the group Earth First!).

In this article I develop a critique of deep ecology from the perspective of a sympathetic outsider. I critique deep ecology not as a general (or even a foot soldier) in the continuing struggle between the ghosts of Gifford Pinchot and John Muir over control of the US environmental movement, but as an outsider to these battles. I speak admittedly as a partisan, but of the environmental movement in India, a country with an ecological diversity comparable to the US but with a radically dissimilar cultural and social history.

Note: Reprinted from *Environmental Ethics*, vol 11, Guha, R., 'Radical American environmentalism and "wilderness" preservation: A third world critique', pp71–83, copyright © (1989), with permission from author

My treatment of deep ecology is primarily historical and sociological, rather than philosophical, in nature. Specifically, I examine the cultural rootedness of a philosophy that likes to present itself in universalistic terms. I make two main arguments: first, that deep ecology is uniquely American, and despite superficial similarities in rhetorical style, the social and political goals of radical environmentalism in other cultural contexts (for example, West Germany and India) are quite different; second, that the social consequences of putting deep ecology into practice on a worldwide basis (what its practitioners are aiming for) are very grave indeed.

The Tenets of Deep Ecology

While I am aware that the term *deep ecology* was coined by the Norwegian philosopher Arne Naess, this article refers specifically to the American variant.[2] Adherents of the deep ecological perspective in this country, while arguing intensely among themselves over its political and philosophical implications, share some fundamental premises about human-nature interactions. As I see it, the defining characteristics of deep ecology are fourfold:

First, deep ecology argues that the environmental movement must shift from an 'anthropocentric' to a 'biocentric' perspective. In many respects, an acceptance of the primacy of this distinction constitutes the litmus test of deep ecology. A considerable effort is expended by deep ecologists in showing that the dominant motif in Western philosophy has been anthropocentric – i.e. the belief that man and his works are the centre of the universe – and conversely, in identifying those lonely thinkers (Leopold, Thoreau, Muir, Aldous Huxley, Santayana etc.) who, in assigning man a more humble place in the natural order, anticipated deep ecological thinking. In the political realm, meanwhile, establishment environmentalism (shallow ecology) is chided for casting its arguments in human-centred terms. Preserving nature, the deep ecologists say, has an intrinsic worth quite apart from any benefits preservation may convey to future human generations. The anthropocentric-biocentric distinction is accepted as axiomatic by deep ecologists, it structures their discourse, and much of the present discussion remains mired within it.

The second characteristic of deep ecology is its focus on the preservation of unspoilt wilderness – and the restoration of degraded areas to a more pristine condition – to the relative (and sometimes absolute) neglect of other issues on the environmental agenda. I later identify the cultural roots and portentous consequences of this obsession with wilderness. For the moment, let me indicate three distinct sources from which it springs. Historically, it represents a playing out of the preservationist (read *radical*) and utilitarian (read *reformist*) dichotomy that has plagued American environmentalism since the turn of the century. Morally, it is an imperative that follows from the biocentric perspective; other species of plants and animals, and nature itself, have an intrinsic right to exist. And finally, the preservation of wilderness also turns on a scientific argument – viz. the value of biological diversity in stabilizing ecological regimes and in retaining a gene pool for future generations. Truly radical policy proposals have been put forward by deep ecologists on the basis of these arguments. The influential poet Gary Snyder, for example, would like to see a 90 per cent reduction in human populations to allow a restoration of pristine environments, while others have argued forcefully that a large portion of the globe must be immediately cordoned off from human beings.[3]

Third, there is a widespread invocation of Eastern spiritual traditions as forerunners of deep ecology. Deep ecology, it is suggested, was practiced both by major religious traditions and at a more popular level by 'primal' peoples in non-Western settings. This complements the search for an authentic lineage in Western thought. At one level, the task is to recover those dissenting voices within the Judaeo-Christian tradition; at another, to suggest that religious traditions in other cultures are, in contrast, dominantly if not exclusively 'biocentric' in their orientation. This coupling of (ancient) Eastern and (modern) ecological wisdom seemingly helps consolidate the claim that deep ecology is a philosophy of universal significance.

Fourth, deep ecologists, whatever their internal differences, share the belief that they are the 'leading edge' of the environmental movement. As the polarity of the shallow/deep and anthropocentric/biocentric distinctions makes clear, they see themselves as the spiritual, philosophical and political vanguard of American and world environmentalism.

Towards a Critique

Although I analyse each of these tenets independently, it is important to recognize, as deep ecologists are fond of remarking in reference to nature, the interconnectedness and unity of these individual themes.

(1) Insofar as it has begun to act as a check on man's arrogance and ecological hubris, the transition from an anthropocentric (human-centred) to a biocentric (humans as only one element in the ecosystem) view in both religious and scientific traditions is only to be welcomed.[4] What are unacceptable are the radical conclusions drawn by deep ecology, in particular, that intervention in nature should be guided primarily by the need to preserve biotic integrity rather than by the needs of humans. The latter for deep ecologists is anthropocentric, the former biocentric. This dichotomy is, however, of very little use in understanding the dynamics of environmental degradation. The two fundamental ecological problems facing the globe are (i) overconsumption by the industrialized world and by urban elites in the Third World and (ii) growing militarization, both in a short-term sense (i.e. ongoing regional wars) and in a long-term sense (i.e. the arms race and the prospect of nuclear annihilation). Neither of these problems has any tangible connection to the anthropocentric-biocentric distinction. Indeed, the agents of these processes would barely comprehend this philosophical dichotomy. The proximate causes of the ecologically wasteful characteristics of industrial society and of militarization are far more mundane: at an aggregate level, the dialectic of economic and political structures, and at a microlevel, the lifestyle choices of individuals. These causes cannot be reduced, whatever the level of analysis, to a deeper anthropocentric attitude toward nature; on the contrary, by constituting a grave threat to human survival, the ecological degradation they cause does not even serve the best interests of human beings! If my identification of the major dangers to the integrity of

the natural world is correct, invoking the bogy of anthropocentricism is at best irrelevant and at worst a dangerous obfuscation.

(2) If the above dichotomy is irrelevant, the emphasis on wilderness is positively harmful when applied to the Third World. If in the US the preservationist/utilitarian division is seen as mirroring the conflict between 'people' and 'interests', in countries such as India the situation is very nearly the reverse. Because India is a long settled and densely populated country in which agrarian populations have a finely balanced relationship with nature, the setting aside of wilderness areas has resulted in a direct transfer of resources from the poor to the rich. Thus, Project Tiger, a network of parks hailed by the international conservation community as an outstanding success, sharply posits the interests of the tiger against those of poor peasants living in and around the reserve. The designation of tiger reserves was made possible only by the physical displacement of existing villages and their inhabitants; their management requires the continuing exclusion of peasants and livestock. The initial impetus for setting up parks for the tiger and other large mammals such as the rhinoceros and elephant came from two social groups, first, a class of ex-hunters turned conservationists belonging mostly to the declining Indian feudal elite and second, representatives of international agencies, such as the World Wildlife Fund (WWF) and the International Union for the Conservation of Nature and Natural Resources (IUCN), seeking to transplant the American system of national parks onto Indian soil. In no case have the needs of the local population been taken into account, and as in many parts of Africa, the designated wildlands are managed primarily for the benefit of rich tourists. Until very recently, wildlands preservation has been identified with environmentalism by the state and the conservation elite; in consequence, environmental problems that impinge far more directly on the lives of the poor – for example, fuel, fodder, water shortages, soil erosion and air and water pollution – have not been adequately addressed.[5]

Deep ecology provides, perhaps unwittingly, a justification for the continuation of such narrow and inequitable conservation practices under a newly acquired radical guise. Increasingly, the international conservation elite is using the philosophical, moral and scientific arguments used by deep ecologists in advancing their wilderness crusade. A striking but by no means atypical example is the recent plea by a prominent American biologist for the takeover of large portions of the globe by the author and his scientific colleagues. Writing in a prestigous scientific forum, the *Annual Review of Ecology and Systematics*, Daniel Janzen argues that only biologists have the competence to decide how the tropical landscape should be used. As 'the representatives of the natural world', biologists are 'in charge of the future of tropical ecology', and only they have the expertise and mandate to 'determine whether the tropical agroscape is to be populated only by humans, their mutualists, commensals, and parasites, or whether it will also contain some islands of the greater nature – the nature that spawned humans, yet has been vanquished by them'. Janzen exhorts his colleagues to advance their territorial claims on the tropical world more forcefully, warning that the very existence of these areas is at stake: 'if biologists want a tropics in which to biologize, they are going to have to buy it with care, energy, effort, strategy, tactics, time, and cash'.[6]

This frankly imperialist manifesto highlights the multiple dangers of the preoccupation with wilderness preservation that is characteristic of deep ecology. As I have suggested, it seriously compounds the neglect by the American movement of far more

pressing environmental problems within the Third World. But perhaps more importantly, and in a more insidious fashion, it also provides an impetus to the imperialist
yearning of Western biologists and their financial sponsors, organizations such as the
WWF and IUCN. The wholesale transfer of a movement culturally rooted in American
conservation history can only result in the social uprooting of human populations in
other parts of the globe.

(3) I come now to the persistent invocation of Eastern philosophies as antecedent in
point of time but convergent in their structure with deep ecology. Complex and internally differentiated religious traditions – Hinduism, Buddhism and Taoism – are
lumped together as holding a view of nature believed to be quintessentially biocentric.
Individual philosophers such as the Taoist Lao Tzu are identified as being forerunners of
deep ecology. Even an intensely political, pragmatic and Christian influenced thinker
such as Gandhi has been accorded a wholly undeserved place in the deep ecological pantheon. Thus the Zen teacher Robert Aitken Roshi makes the strange claim that Gandhi's
thought was not human-centred and that he practiced an embryonic form of deep ecology which is 'traditionally Eastern and is found with differing emphasis in Hinduism,
Taoism and in Theravada and Mahayana Buddhism'.[7] Moving away from the realm of
high philosophy and scriptural religion, deep ecologists make the further claim that at
the level of material and spiritual practice 'primal' peoples subordinated themselves to
the integrity of the biotic universe they inhabited.

I have indicated that this appropriation of Eastern traditions is in part dictated by
the need to construct an authentic lineage and in part by a desire to present deep ecology
as a universalistic philosophy. Indeed, in his substantial and quixotic biography of John
Muir, Michael Cohen goes so far as to suggest that Muir was the 'Taoist of the [Ameri-
can] West'.[8] This reading of Eastern traditions is selective and does not bother to
differentiate between alternate (and changing) religious and cultural traditions; as it
stands, it does considerable violence to the historical record. Throughout most recorded
history the characteristic form of human activity in the 'East' has been a finely tuned but
nonetheless conscious and dynamic manipulation of nature. Although mystics such as
Lao Tzu did reflect on the spiritual essence of human relations with nature, it must be
recognized that such ascetics and their reflections were supported by a society of cultiva-
tors whose relationship with nature was a far more active one. Many agricultural
communities do have a sophisticated knowledge of the natural environment that may
equal (and sometimes surpass) codified 'scientific' knowledge; yet, the elaboration of
such traditional ecological knowledge (in both material and spiritual contexts) can
hardly be said to rest on a mystical affinity with nature of a deep ecological kind. Nor is
such knowledge infallible; as the archaeological record powerfully suggests, modern
Western man has no monopoly on ecological disasters.

In a brilliant article, the Chicago historian Ronald Inden points out that this
romantic and essentially positive view of the East is a mirror image of the scientific and
essentially pejorative view normally upheld by Western scholars of the Orient. In either
case, the East constitutes the Other, a body wholly separate and alien from the West; it
is defined by a uniquely spiritual and nonrational 'essence', even if this essence is valor-
ized quite differently by the two schools. Eastern man exhibits a spiritual dependence
with respect to nature – on the one hand, this is symptomatic of his prescientific and
backward self; on the other, of his ecological wisdom and deep ecological consciousness.

Both views are monolithic, simplistic and have the characteristic effect – intended in one case, perhaps unintended in the other – of denying agency and reason to the East and making it the privileged orbit of Western thinkers.

The two apparently opposed perspectives have then a common underlying structure of discourse in which the East merely serves as a vehicle for Western projections. Varying images of the East are raw material for political and cultural battles being played out in the West; they tell us far more about the Western commentator and his desires than about the 'East'. Inden's remarks apply not merely to Western scholarship on India, but to Orientalist constructions of China and Japan as well:

> Although these two views appear to be strongly opposed, they often combine together. Both have a similar interest in sustaining the Otherness of India. The holders of the dominant view, best exemplified in the past in imperial administrative discourse (and today probably by that of 'development economies'), would place a traditional, super-stition-ridden India in a position of perpetual tutelage to a modern, rational West. The adherents of the romantic view, best exemplified academically in the discourses of Christian liberalism and analytic psychology, concede the realm of the public and impersonal to the positivist. Taking their succour not from governments and big busi-ness, but from a plethora of religious foundations and self-help institutes, and from allies in the 'consciousness industry', not to mention the important industry of tour-ism, the romantics insist that India embodies a private realm of the imagination and the religious which modern, Western man lacks but needs. They, therefore, like the positivists, but for just the opposite reason, have a vested interest in seeing that the Ori-entalist view of India as 'spiritual', 'mysterious', and 'exotic' is perpetuated.[9]

(4) How radical, finally, are the deep ecologists? Notwithstanding their self-image and strident rhetoric (in which the label 'shallow ecology' has an opprobrium similar to that reserved for 'social democratic' by Marxist-Leninists), even within the American context their radicalism is limited and it manifests itself quite differently elsewhere.

To my mind, deep ecology is best viewed as a radical trend within the wilderness preservation movement. Although advancing philosophical rather than aesthetic argu-ments and encouraging political militancy rather than negotiation, its practical emphasis – viz, preservation of unspoilt natures – is virtually identical. For the main-stream movement, the function of wilderness is to provide a temporary antidote to modem civilization. As a special institution within an industrialized society, the national park 'provides an opportunity for respite, contrast, contemplation, and affirmation of values for those who live most of their lives in the workaday world'.[10] Indeed, the rapid increase in visitations to the national parks in postwar America is a direct consequence of economic expansion. The emergence of a popular interest in wilderness sites, the his-torian Samuel Hays points out, was 'not a throwback to the primitive, but an integral part of the modern standard of living as people sought to add new "amenity" and "aes-thetic" goals and desires to their earlier preoccupation with necessities and conveniences'.[11]

Here, the enjoyment of nature is an integral part of the consumer society. The pri-vate automobile (and the lifestyle it has spawned) is in many respects the ultimate ecological villain, and an untouched wilderness the prototype of ecological harmony;

yet, for most Americans it is perfectly consistent to drive a thousand miles to spend a holiday in a national park. They possess a vast, beautiful and sparsely populated continent and are also able to draw upon the natural resources of large portions of the globe by virtue of their economic and political dominance. In consequence, America can simultaneously enjoy the material benefits of an expanding economy and the aesthetic benefits of unspoilt nature. The two poles of 'wilderness' and 'civilization' mutually coexist in an internally coherent whole, and philosophers of both poles are assigned a prominent place in this culture. Paradoxically as it may seem, it is no accident that Star Wars technology and deep ecology both find their fullest expression in that leading sector of Western civilization, California.

Deep ecology runs parallel to the consumer society without seriously questioning its ecological and socio-political basis. In its celebration of American wilderness, it also displays an uncomfortable convergence with the prevailing climate of nationalism in the American wilderness movement. For spokesmen such as the historian Roderick Nash, the national park system is America's distinctive cultural contribution to the world, reflective not merely of its economic but of its philosophical and ecological maturity as well. In what Walter Lippman called the American century, the 'American invention of national parks' must be exported worldwide. Betraying an economic determinism that would make even a Marxist shudder, Nash believes that environmental preservation is a 'full stomach' phenomenon that is confined to the rich, urban and sophisticated. Nonetheless, he hopes that 'the less developed nations may eventually evolve economically and intellectually to the point where nature preservation is more than a business'.[12]

The error which Nash makes (and which deep ecology in some respects encourages) is to equate environmental protection with the protection of wilderness. This is a distinctively American notion, borne out of a unique social and environmental history. The archetypal concerns of radical environmentalists in other cultural contexts are in fact quite different. The German Greens, for example, have elaborated a devastating critique of industrial society which turns on the acceptance of environmental limits to growth. Pointing to the intimate links between industrialization, militarization and conquest, the Greens argue that economic growth in the West has historically rested on the economic and ecological exploitation of the Third World. Rudolf Bahro is characteristically blunt:

> The working class here [in the West] is the richest lower class in the world. And if I look at the problem from the point of view of the whole of humanity, not just from that of Europe, then I must say that the metropolitan working class is the worst exploiting class in history... What made poverty bearable in eighteenth or nineteenth-century Europe was the prospect of escaping it through exploitation of the periphery. But this is no longer a possibility, and continued industrialism in the Third World will mean poverty for whole generations and hunger for millions.[13]

Here the roots of global ecological problems lie in the disproportionate share of resources consumed by the industrialized countries as a whole *and* the urban elite within the Third World. Since it is impossible to reproduce an industrial monoculture worldwide, the ecological movement in the West must begin by cleaning up its own act. The Greens advocate the creation of a 'no growth' economy, to be achieved by scaling down current (and clearly unsustainable) consumption levels.[14] This radical shift in consumption and production patterns requires the creation of alternate economic and political structures – smaller in scale and more amenable to social participation – but it rests equally on a shift in cultural values. The expansionist character of modern Western man will have to give way to an ethic of renunciation and self-limitation, in which spiritual and communal values play an increasing role in sustaining social life. This revolution in cultural values, however, has as its point of departure an understanding of environmental processes quite different from deep ecology.

Many elements of the Green programme find a strong resonance in countries such as India, where a history of Western colonialism and industrial development has benefited only a tiny elite while exacting tremendous social and environmental costs. The ecological battles presently being fought in India have as their epicentre the conflict over nature between the subsistence and largely rural sector and the vastly more powerful commercial-industrial sector. Perhaps the most celebrated of these battles concerns the Chipko (Hug the Tree) movement, a peasant movement against deforestation in the Himalayan foothills. Chipko is only one of several movements that have sharply questioned the nonsustainable demand being placed on the land and vegetative base by urban centres and industry. These include opposition to large dams by displaced peasants, the conflict between small artisan fishing and large-scale trawler fishing for export, the countrywide movements against commercial forest operations, and opposition to industrial pollution among downstream agricultural and fishing communities.[15]

Two features distinguish these environmental movements from their Western counterparts. First, for the sections of society most critically affected by environmental degradation – poor and landless peasants, women and tribals – it is a question of sheer survival, not of enhancing the quality of life. Second, and as a consequence, the environmental solutions they articulate deeply involve questions of equity as well as economic and political redistribution. Highlighting these differences, a leading Indian environmentalist stresses that 'environmental protection per se is of least concern to most of these groups. Their main concern is about the use of the environment and who should benefit from it'.[16] They seek to wrest control of nature away from the state and the industrial sector and place it in the hands of rural communities who live within that environment but are increasingly denied access to it. These communities have far more basic needs, their demands on the environment are far less intense, and they can draw upon a reservoir of cooperative social institutions and local ecological knowledge in managing the 'commons' – forests, grasslands and the waters – on a sustainable basis. If colonial and capitalist expansion has both accentuated social inequalities and signalled a precipitous fall in ecological wisdom, an alternate ecology must rest on an alternate society and polity as well.

This brief overview of German and Indian environmentalism has some major implications for deep ecology. Both German and Indian environmental traditions allow for a greater integration of ecological concerns with livelihood and work. They also place a greater emphasis on equity and social justice (both within individual countries and on a global scale) on the grounds that in the absence of social regeneration environmental regeneration has very little chance of succeeding. Finally, and perhaps most significantly, they have escaped the preoccupation with wilderness perservation so characteristic of American cultural and environmental history.[17]

A Homily

In 1958, the economist J. K. Galbraith referred to overconsumption as the unasked question of the American conservation movement. There is a marked selectivity, he wrote, 'in the conservationist's approach to materials consumption. If we are concerned about our great appetite for materials, it is plausible to seek to increase the supply, to decrease waste, to make better use of the stocks available, and to develop substitutes. But what of the appetite itself? Surely this is the ultimate source of the problem. If it continues its geometric course, will it not one day have to be restrained? Yet in the literature of the resource problem this is the forbidden question. Over it hangs a nearly total silence'.[18]

The consumer economy and society have expanded tremendously in the three decades since Galbraith penned these words; yet his criticisms are nearly as valid today. I have said 'nearly', for there are some hopeful signs. Within the environmental movement several dispersed groups are working to develop ecologically benign technologies and to encourage less wasteful lifestyles. Moreover, outside the self-defined boundaries of American environmentalism, opposition to the permanent war economy is being carried on by a peace movement that has a distinguished history and impeccable moral and political credentials.

It is precisely these (to my mind, most hopeful) components of the American social scene that are missing from deep ecology. In their widely noticed book, Bill Devall and George Sessions make no mention of militarization or the movements for peace, while activists whose practical focus is on developing ecologically responsible lifestyles (e.g. Wendell Berry) are derided as 'falling short of deep ecological awareness'.[19] A truly radical ecology in the American context ought to work toward a synthesis of the appropriate technology, alternate lifestyle and peace movements.[20] By making the (largely spurious) anthropocentric-biocentric distinction cental to the debate, deep ecologists may have appropriated the moral high ground, but they are at the same time doing a serious disservice to American and global environmentalism.[21]

Notes

1   Kirkpatrick Sale, 'The forest for the trees: Can today's environmentalists tell the difference?' *Mother Jones*, vol 11, no 8 (November 1986), p26.
2   One of the major criticisms I make in this essay concerns deep ecology's lack of concern with inequalities *within* human society. In the article in which he coined the term *deep ecology*, Naess himself expresses concerns about inequalities between and within nations. However, his concern with social cleavages and their impact on resource utilization patterns and ecological destruction is not very visible in the later writings of deep ecologists. See Arne Naess, 'The shallow and the deep, long-range ecology movement: A summary', *Inquiry*, vol 16 (1973), p96; (I am grateful to Tom Birch for this reference).
3   Gary Snyder, quoted in Sale, 'The forest for the trees', p32. See also Dave Foreman, 'A modest proposal for a wilderness system', *Whole Earth Review*, no 53 (Winter 1986–1987), pp42–45.

4   See, for example, Donald Worster, *Nature's Economy: The Roots of Ecology* (San Francisco, Sierra Club Books, 1977).

5   See Centre for Science and Environment, *India: The State of the Environment 1982: A Citizens Report* (New Delhi, Centre for Science and Environment, 1982); R. Sukumar, 'Elephant-man conflict in Karnataka', in Cecil Saldanha, ed, *The State of Karnataka's Environment* (Bangalore, Centre for Taxonomic Studies, 1985). For Africa, see the brilliant analysis by Helge Kjekshus, *Ecology Control and Economic Development in East African History* (Berkeley, University of California Press, 1977).

6   Daniel Janzen, 'The future of tropical ecology', *Annual Review of Ecology and Systematic*, vol 17 (1986), pp305–306; emphasis added.

7   Robert Aitken Roshi, 'Gandhi, dogen, and deep ecology', reprinted as appendix C in Bill Devall and George Sessions, *Deep Ecology: Living as if Nature Mattered* (Salt Lake City, Peregrine Smith Books, 1985). For Gandhi's own views on social reconstruction, see the excellent three-volume collection edited by Raghavan Iyer, *The Moral and Political Writings of Mahatma Gandhi* (Oxford, Clarendon Press, 1986–1987).

8   Michael Cohen, *The Pathless Way* (Madison, University of Wisconsin Press, 1984), p120.

9   Ronald Inden, 'Orientalist constructions of india', *Modern Asian Studies*, vol 20 (1986), p442. Inden draws inspiration from Edward Said's forceful polemic, *Orientalism* (New York, Basic Books, 1980). It must be noted, however, that there is a salient difference between Western perceptions of Middle Eastern and Far Eastern cultures, respectively. Due perhaps to the long history of Christian conflict with Islam, Middle Eastern cultures (as Said documents) are consistently presented in pejorative terms. The juxtaposition of hostile and worshipping attitudes that Inden talks of applies only to Western attitudes toward Buddhist and Hindu societies.

10 Joseph Sax, *Mountains Without Handrails: Reflections on the National Parks* (Ann Arbor, University of Michigan Press, 1980), p42. See also Peter Schmitt, *Back to Nature: The Arcadian Myth in Urban America* (New York, Oxford University Press, 1969), and Alfred Runte, *National Parks: The American Experience* (Lincoln, University of Nebraska Press, 1979).

11 Samuel Hays, 'From conservation to environment: Environmental politics in the United States since World War Two', *Environmental Review*, vol 6 (1982), p21. See also the same author's book entitled *Beauty, Health and Permanence: Environmental Politics in the United States, 1955–85* (New York, Cambridge University Press, 1987).

12 Roderick Nash, *Wilderness and the American Mind,* 3rd ed (New Haven, Yale University Press, 1982).

13 Rudolf Bahro, *From Red to Green* (London, Verso Books, 1984).

14 From time to time, American scholars have themselves criticized these imbalances in consumption patterns. In the 1950s, William Vogt made the charge that the United States, with one sixteenth of the world's population, was utilizing one third of the globe's resources. (Vogt, cited in E. F. Murphy, *Nature, Bureaucracy and the Risk of Property* [Amsterdam, North Holland, 1977, p. 29]). More recently, Zero Population Growth has estimated that each American consumes 39 times as many resources as an Indian. See *Christian Science Monitor,* 2 March 1987.

15 For an excellent review, see Anil Agarwal and Sunita Narain, eds, *India: The State of*.
   the Environment 1984–85: A Citizens Report (New Delhi, Centre for Science and
   Environment, 1985). See also Ramachandra Guha, *The Unquiet Woods: Ecological
   Change and Peasant Resistance in the Indian Himalaya* (Berkeley, University of California Press, 1989, expanded edition 2000).

16 Anil Agarwal, 'Human-nature interactions in a third world country', *The Environmentalist*, vol 6 no 3 (1986), p167.

17 One strand in radical American environmentalism, the bioregional movement, by
   emphasizing a greater involvement with the bioregion people inhabit, does indirectly challenge consumerism. However, as yet bioregionalism has hardly raised the
   questions of equity and social justice (international, intranational and intergenerational) which I argue must be a central plank of radical environmentalism.
   Moreover, its stress on (individual) *experience* as the key to involvement with nature
   is also somewhat at odds with the integration of nature with livelihood and work
   that I talk of in this paper. See Kirkpatrick Sale, *Dwellers in the Land: The Bioregional Vision* (San Francisco, Sierra Club Books, 1985).

18 John Kenneth Galbraith, 'How much should a country consume?' in Henry Jarrett,
   ed, *Perspectives on Conservation* (Baltimore, Johns Hopkins Press, 1958), pp91–92.

19 Devall and Sessions, *Deep Ecology*, p122. For Wendell Berry's own assessment of
   deep ecology, see his 'Amplictions: Preserving wildness', *Wilderness*, vol 50 (Spring
   1987), pp39–40,50–54.

20 See the interesting recent contribution by one of the most influential spokesmen of
   appropriate technology – Barry Commoner, 'A reporter at large: The environment',
   New Yorker 15 June 1987. While Commoner makes a forceful plea for the convergence of the environmental movement (viewed by him primarily as the opposition
   to air and water pollution and to the institutions that generate such pollution) and
   the peace movement, he significantly does not mention consumption patterns,
   implying that 'limits to growth' do not exist.

21 In this sense, my critique of deep ecology, although that of an outsider, may facilitate the reassertion of those elements in the American environmental tradition for
   which there is a profound sympathy in other parts of the globe. A global perspective may also lead to a critical reassessment of figures such as Aldo Leopold and
   John Muir, the two patron saints of deep ecology. As Donald Worster has pointed
   out, the message of Muir (and, I would argue, of Leopold as well) makes sense only
   in an American context; be has very little to say to other cultures. See Worster's
   review of Stephen Fox's *John Muir and His Legacy*, in *Environmental Ethics*, vol 5
   (1983), pp277–281.

8

Class, Race and Gender Discourse in the Ecofeminism/Deep Ecology Debate

Ariel Salleh

Liberal Patriarchalism and the Serviced Society

The separation of humanity and nature is the lynch pin of patriarchal ideology, and both deep ecology and ecofeminism share a desire to dislodge that pin. For deep ecologists, overcoming the division between humanity and nature promises a release from alienation. For ecofeminists, it promises release from a complex set of exploitations based on patriarchal identification of femaleness with the order of nature. Perhaps because most deep ecologists happen to have been men, and middle class, their environmental ethic has had difficulty in moving beyond psychological and metaphysical concerns to a political analysis of the 'materiality' of women's oppression. Building on earlier exchanges between ecofeminism and deep ecology, in particular, 'The Ecofeminism/Deep Ecology Debate: A Reply to Patriarchal Reason', amplifies the claim that deep ecology is held back from maturation as a Green philosophy by its lack of a fully rounded political critique.[1] To this end, I urge adherents of deep ecology to become more reflexively aware of the socio-historical grounding of their discourse.

Although there are different emphases among women's groupings internationally, a growing number of ecofeminists now address capitalist patriarchy as an oppressive system of global power relations.[2] They situate both environmentalism and women's struggle against the instrumental rationality and dehumanizing commodity culture that comes with industrial production. Accordingly, ecofeminists of a socialist persuasion are disturbed to hear the father of deep ecology, Arne Naess, claim that 'total egalitarianism is impossible', that some human exploitation will always be 'necessary'.[3] Women's complex treatment as a sexual, reproductive and labour 'resource' is glossed over in the deep ecological agenda. Yet there are, and have always been, people who cultivate and prepare food, build shelter, carry loads, labour to give birth, wash and tend the young, maintain dwellings, feed workers and mend their clothes. Whether in the First World or the Third World (which is two-thirds of the global population), women's labour 'mediation of nature' serves as the infrastructure to what is identified as men's 'productive economic' role. This subsumption of women's energies, most often by means of the

Note: Reprinted from *Environmental Ethics*, vol 15, Salleh, A., 'Class, race and gender discourse in the ecofeminism/deep ecology debate', pp225–244, copyright © (1993), with permission from author

institution of the family, is homologous to exploitative class relations under the capitalist system. The family is integrally connected with and makes industrial production possible by 'reproducing' the labour force, in the several senses of that word. However, as productivism intensifies with new technologies and the promise of ever greater profits, labour becomes increasingly removed from the satisfaction of basic needs. As a result, under the guise of 'development', a new dimension is added to the women's role constellation – that of conspicuous consumer. Moreover, as the economic fetish penetrates personal culture, even sexual relations between men and women come to resemble relations between things, thereby deepening women's exploitation even further.[4]

Deep ecologists do not recognize that women have not been consulted about their interests in this system of social relations. Just as the environment is damaged by 'development', women's lives are vitiated by men's systematic appropriation of their energies and time. Writing by Brinda Rao in India, Berit As in Norway, and Barbara Ehrenreich in the United States provides ample documentation of this appropriation.[5] The work of developing world peasant women is fairly obviously tied to 'natural' functions and material labour. These women grow most of the world's food and care for their families with a minimum of disruption to the environment and with minimum reliance on a cash economy. They labour with independence, dignity and grace – and those of us looking for sustainable models may soon want to take advice from such women. In contrast, in supposedly advanced industrial nations, women's maintenance work as housewives or imported guest workers is made dependent on and largely mystified by 'labour-saving devices', such as dishwashing machines, blenders and the like. Nevertheless, cultural assumptions concerning women's apparently universal role of mediating nature still hold. It is for this reason that reproductive rights remain contentious in the United States. Ecofeminists join Dave Foreman's cry to 'free shackled river', but more than rivers remain shackled!

Deep ecologist Warwick Fox, who has wondered why ecofeminists have not discussed the class basis of deep ecology, has failed to note that my early ecofeminist criticism in ' Deeper than Deep Ecology' refers repeatedly to women's labour as validation of their perspectives.[6] As the sociology of knowledge teaches us, people's perception is shaped by their place in the system of productive relations. Nevertheless, the gulf between manual or sustaining productive labour and mental or conceptualizing work is especially profound in industrialized societies. A whole gamut of questions surrounding labour relations is ideologically suppressed, and in the US it is clouded by the question of race as well. In late capitalism, the middle class, including academics, are 'serviced' in their daily needs by hidden workers. Not surprisingly, deep ecology reflects the idealism and individualism of such a privileged group, its preoccupation being 'cultural issues' such as meaning, the psychological and 'rights'. However, even more invisible as labour and not even recognized by a wage are the domestic services of women. Michael Zimmerman's typically middle-class and white articulation of women's lot – he sees them enjoying 'the advantages' of a consumer society – illustrates this standard oversight, though the fault is not entirely his, since it largely reflects the liberal feminist attitude he relies on to make his case against ecofeminism.[7] It is not only women's socialization, the various belief systems which shape 'the feminine role', but also the very practical nature of the labour which most women do that gives them a different orientation to the world around them and, therefore, different insights into its problems. In both North and

South, this labour may include the physicality of birthing, suckling and subsequent household chores, but is not restricted to such activities. Even in the public work force, women's employment is more often than not found in maintenance jobs – reflecting cultural attitudes to women as 'carers'.[8]

Radical feminist analyses of the psychodynamic underlying patriarchal social relations, again and again, return to the symbolic killing of mother/nature/woman as the root cause of the 'masculine' will to objectify and control other forms of being. Zimmerman's writing is fairly symptomatic in this respect. Although ten or more pages of his 'Feminism, Deep Ecology, and Environmental Ethics' are generously given to exposition of the feminist literature, and a concluding paragraph endorses its findings, his article is still querulous. The same observation applies to Fox's response to ecofeminist criticisms of deep ecology. While both Zimmerman and Fox cast doubt on the reality of patriarchal power, Zimmerman's ambivalent article also contains information about how ideology works to protect men from seeing the actual nature of social relations under patriarchy. He quotes the following remark of Naomi Scheman: 'Men have been free to imagine themselves as self-defining only because women held the intimate social world together by their caring labours'.[9] Similarly, we know that the capitalist entrepreneur sees himself as a man of high achievement, blind to the fact that the wage labourer is responsible for the generation of his surplus. In the patriarchal perspective, self appears to be independent; yet, to quote Jim Cheney, 'The atomistically defined self acts as a sponge, absorbing the gift of the other, turning it into capital'. Cheney goes on: 'This is one way of understanding the frequent feminist claim that males in patriarchy feed on female energy'.[10] Capital can be psychological and sexual as much as economic. On the positive side, the actuality of caring for the concrete needs of others gives rise to a morality of relatedness among ordinary women, and this sense of kinship seems to extend to the natural world as well. Consider the reasoning of an Indian peasant woman whose drinking water has been spoiled by village men moving across to a pumped supply for status reasons, or the sensibility of a woman who watches a tree grow over the grave of a child she has suckled. These understandings engraved in suffering make sharp contrast to the abstract philosophical formulations of deep ecology. For ecofeminism, the body is indeed an instrument of our knowledge of the world.[11]

Professional versus grassroots base

As I put it in an earlier critique, '…what is the organic basis of [the deep ecological] paradigm shift? … Is deep ecology a sociologically coherent position?'[12] One of the most distressing things about the field of environmental ethics is the extent to which it has been taken over by paid professional specialists. What gives authenticity, validity and 'depth' to ecofeminism, in contrast, is that it is implicitly tied to a praxis rooted in life needs and the survival of habitat. Deep ecology is primarily concerned with identification, or rather, re-identification of the so-called 'human' ego with nature. For deep ecologists, however, the recommended route for recovering this connected sensuous self is meditation or leisure activities, such as backpacking. How does such activity compare as an integrating biocentric experience with the hands-on involvement of the African subsistence farmer who tends her field with an astonishing knowledge of seeds, water habits and insect catalysts – and whose land is the continuing staff of the children she has borne out of her body? There is surely a large portion of illusion and self-indulgence in the North's comfortable middle-class pursuit of the cosmic 'transpersonal Self'. Despite Naess' careful reformulations, in an age of 'me now', the deep ecologists' striving for 'Self-realization' demands close scrutiny.

Many deep ecological difficulties in coming to terms with ecofeminism can be traced to the socio-political grounding of the deep ecology movement in bourgeois liberalism. Hence, it is probably no surprise that even as deep ecologists put forward their key concept of 'ecocentrism' as 'the way out' of our environmental holocaust, an implicit endorsement of the Enlightenment rationalist notion of ever upward progress threatens to collide with the principle. For instance, some deep ecologists believe that 'anthropocentric' political critiques, such as socialism and feminism, can, in principle, be taken care of by the wider framework of ecocentrism. Fox writes, 'Supporters of deep ecology hold that their concerns well and truly *subsume* the concerns of those movements that have restricted their focus to a more egalitarian human society'.[13] Not only is Fox's ambitious totalizing programme spoiled by the serious gaps in deep ecology's theorization, it is also out of sync with his pluralist claim to respect the unfolding of 'other voices' in the universe: the words of women, among others. Fox's attraction to 'transpersonal psychology' hangs on the self-actualizing logic of middle-class individualism. Similarly, his assertion that self-interest is fused with that of Gaia as a whole, strikingly resembles the guiding hand behind Adam Smith's libertarian political economy, or Rawls' theory of justice. Despite a will to transcendence, there is an implicit positivism or naive realism in these formulations.[14] Deep ecology has no sense of itself as spoken by a particular group lodged in history. Oblivious to its own cultural context, the deep ecological voice rings out as a disembodied absolute.

Abstract essences versus reflexivity

According to Rosemary Ruether, women throughout history have not been particularly concerned to create transcendent, overarching, all-powerful entities, or like classical Greek Platonism and its leisured misogynist mood, to project a pristine world of abstract essences.[15] Women's spirituality has focused on the immanent and intricate ties among nature, body and personal intuition. The revival of the goddess, for example, is a celebration of these material bonds. Ecofeminist pleas that men, formed under patriarchal relations, look inside themselves first before constructing new cosmologies have been dismissed, for example, by Fox, in 'The Deep Ecology: Ecofeminism Debate and its Parallels', as a recipe for inward-looking possessive parochialism and, hence, ultimately war![16] But that would surely only be the case if deep ecologists failed to shrug off their conditioning as white-Anglo-Saxon-Protestant-professional property holders, which they assure us, they are very keen to do. Interestingly, the universalizing, cosmopolitan stance of this particular protest by Fox is somewhat at loggerheads with the deep ecologists' own professed commitment to bioregionalism. In the name of 'theoretical adequacy', Fox's article disregards history. Consequently, his prose blurs who has done what to whom, over the centuries and on into the present. To quote:

[Certain] classes of social actors have … habitually assumed themselves to be *more fully human* than others, such as women ('the weaker vessel'), the 'lower' classes, blacks, and non-Westerners ('savages', 'primitives', 'heathens')…

That anthropocentrism has served as the most fundamental kind of legitimation employed by *whatever* powerful class of social actors one wishes to focus on can also be seen by considering the fundamental kind of legitimation that has habitually been employed with regard to large-scale or high-cost social enterprises such as war, scientific and technological development, or environmental exploitation. Such enterprises have habitually been undertaken not simply in the name of men, capitalists, whites or Westerners, for example, but in the name of God (and thus our essential humanity…) …

(This applies, notwithstanding the often sexist expression of these sentiments in terms of 'man', 'mankind', and so on, and notwithstanding the fact that certain classes of social actors benefit disproportionately from these enterprises.)[17]

This passage is a sample of liberal-pluralist mystification in its most blatant form. Its author next goes on to mention Bacon and the rise of science, but without touching on the corresponding elimination of one class of social actors, namely, the six million women who perished as witches for their scientific wisdom. Fox believes that all modern liberation movements have had recourse to the same legitimating device – 'humanity'. Apparently, a belief that this label is available for the use of everyone is the reason why deep ecologists still use the term *man* so persistently.

Zimmerman, in turn, entirely misses the point of ecofeminism by portraying it as an argument about women being 'better than men'.[18] Ecofeminism does not set up a static ontological prioritization of 'woman'. Instead, it is a strategy for social action. Equally, men in the Green and the ecosocialist movements, by examining the parallel exploitation of nature and women, are entering into a process of praxis, the results of which will unfold over time. Fox, in his own way, shelves the question of our political responsibility as historical agents by insisting that all people need to understand is that 'evolutionary outcomes' simply represent 'the way things happen to have turned out', nothing more. For someone concerned with 'simplistic' and 'facile' political theorization, his familiar charge against ecofeminism beats the lot. Notwithstanding earlier posturing about the 'errors of essentialism' in ecofeminist thought, Fox soon emerges as a kind of Spencerian sociobiologist. In fact, the deep ecologists, for all their anxieties about 'genetic doctrines' in feminism, seem to be strongly inclined this way. George Sessions too speaks favourably about 'the recent studies in ethology and genetics which posit a basic human and primate nature'.[19] Is this the old double standard again?

Technology-productive and reproductive relations

When it comes to the question of technology, Zimmerman's text becomes as rudderless as the modern industrial apparatus itself. He notes that some feminists – 'essentialists' he calls them, though they remain unnamed – are critical of science and technology, while other feminists, also unspecified, argue that it is not 'intrinsically evil'.[20] There are, indeed, differences among feminists on technology. Liberal feminists, like their brothers, the reform environmentalists, imagine that solutions to social and ecological problems can be found within 'the advanced industrial technostructure'. Liberal feminism should not be grouped with ecofeminism, however, any more than resource environmentalism should be grouped with deep ecology. Ecofeminists go further than both liberal feminists, who see technology as emancipatory, and Marxist feminists who argue that technology is neutral and that it is all a matter of who controls it. Ecofeminists observe that the instrumental-rational mode of production inevitably trickles over into the sphere of consciousness and social relations. As a Heideggerian, Zimmerman should know that there are ample reasons for dismantling the technomonster, given its far-reaching impact into human phenomenology. Yet, he still seems to hold a neutralist thesis, claiming that 'Modern science and technology are potentially liberating…' Further, he asks: 'While benefiting from the material well-being and technological progress made possible by masculinist science and industry, do women rid themselves of responsibility…?'[21] It is hard to believe that this 'growth'-oriented statement should be made in defense of deep ecology. Perhaps Zimmerman genuinely does believe that societies accrue benefit from 'advanced' technologies. Perhaps they do for the middle-class men who designed and sold them; nevertheless, the young Korean micro-chip worker steadily going blind at her bench and the California aerospace worker coming down with immune deficiencies have not experienced such wellbeing. The problem is, and this is a point well made in Don Davis' article, that deep ecology as a movement has no systematic analysis of multinational-corporate industrial society and its effects.[22]

Equally innocent of the force of contemporary instrumentalism, Wittbecker writes that 'human populations are plastic and could probably be decreased without fascism, by economic, religious, or cultural means'. Deep ecologist Bill Devall's tone is similarly managerial, preoccupied as he is with population control.[23] The phenomenon of 'overpopulation' does need to be seriously examined. However, given the ethical issues of eugenics-genocide and of a woman's right over her own body, the targeting of 'population control' by white male environmentalists in the North has both racist and sexist dimensions. Observe how many Americans opposed to abortion in the US endorse population control programmes in Asia and South America. Even as a matter of social equity, where children provide supplementary farm labour for overworked mothers in the South, it is inappropriate for grey-suited international policy advisers to demand population control. Such programmes originated in a post-World War II middle-class urban desire to protect the quality of life – that is, high levels of consumerism. These days the argument for population control is formulated more prudently in terms of protecting the Earth's 'scarce' resources. Even this injunction, however, as it is applied to the Third World exclusively, is patently hypocritical. Each infant born into the so-called advanced societies uses about 15 times more global resources during his or her lifetime than a person born in the Third World. Population restraint may well be called for in the North, hopefully complemented by a scaling back of high technology excess. On the other hand, subsistence dwellers in the South are producers as much as consumers: as 'prosumers' they are practical examples of human autonomy in a nonexploitative relation to the land. What much of this talk about population control may express is a projection and displacement of guilt experienced by those who continue to live comfortably off the invisible backs of working women in the Third World. Even deeper, the constant focus on population control may reflect some profound psychosexual fear of that 'different' voice.[24]

With regard to biotechnology, Fox agrees with the ecofeminist position that deep ecologists should oppose it; nevertheless, given deep ecology's lack of attention to industrialism and technological rationality, it is not consistently opposed by most deep ecologists. Sessions has said that he believes there 'might be a point one day down the road when we can handle genetic engineering'. Naess has also defended its use. For example, he has proposed that a genetically engineered microorganism be released in order to counter a mite infecting the eyes of African children.[25] This proposal is a very anthropocentric focus for an ecocentric theory, and it matches oddly with earlier claims by Naess and Sessions that it is better not to approach the nonhuman world reductionistically in terms of its usefulness to humans. Devall's fine tenet that 'there is wisdom in the stability of natural processes' is violated here, as is Devall's and Sessions' 'refusal to acknowledge that some life forms have greater or better intrinsic value than others'. Concern about the unintended consequences of human 'hubris' is one level of argument. Feminist critiques of patriarchal science are another. It might be also added, following the logic of Frances Moore Lappé, that if the standard of living – the 'vital needs' – of African villages were not decimated by pressures from a predatory white-male dominated international economic order, such children might not succumb to malnutrition and disease in the first place. Given this line of reasoning, genetic engineering can scarcely be justified as a 'vital need'. In fact, there can be no emergence from this exploitative system as long as humans pursue expensive technological-fix panaceas, such as genetic engineering. Even so, according to Devall and Sessions, 'cultural diversity today requires advanced technology, that is, techniques that advance the goals of each culture'.[26] Is this why John Seed from the Council of All Beings can be seen travelling with a lap-top computer? What some deep ecologists seem to forget when it comes to the question of technology is that there is no such thing as a free lunch. While Devall condemns 'false consciousness' in New Age advocates of genetic engineering and computer technology, one looks in vain for a clear deep ecological praxis on these matters. His discussion of genetic engineering remains descriptive and agnostic in tone, eventually sliding off into renewed denunciation of human overpopulation as the most important 'agent of extinction'. In other words, women workers in the South can pick up the tab for ecological crisis.

Patriarchal Postures and Discursive Strategies

Another metalevel of the debate between ecofeminism and deep ecology is the psychosexual dynamic that runs through it. As with the class and ethnic grounding of deep ecology, gender politics also shapes the context in which philosophical judgements are made. Without an awareness of this fact, the Green, deep ecological, and socialist movements lose reflexivity and run the risk of being partial, single issue, and reformist in focus. Sadly, the deep ecologists' reception of ecofeminist views has been marked by resistance. Perhaps this resistance should be no surprise, since their spokespeople have been men, and the psychological literature suggests that masculine identity is defined by separation rather than closeness. There is certainly nothing uniquely deep ecological in their responses; the strategies used to shore up their standpoints are quite familiar to the experience of women working in male-dominated institutions. As Karen Warren reminds us, 'Ecofeminists take as their central project the unpacking of connections between the twin oppressions of women and nature. Central to this project is a critique of the sort of thinking which sanctions that oppression.'[27] Elizabeth Dodson Gray and many others have exposed the pervasiveness of the androcentric conceptual frame. Yet, it is not only the epistemology itself that women must attend to, but an armoury of discursive techniques that back up and protect the bastion of masculine meaning. Among these, the index to Dale Spender's bibliographic history of feminism names the following common patriarchal procedures for dealing with intellectual and political challenges by women: ageism, appropriation, burial (of contribution), contempt (sexual), character assassination, the double bind, the double standard, harassment, isolation, charges of man hating, masculine mind, misrepresentation, namelessness, scapegoating and witch hunting.[28] Note that while these postures have no substantive value, they are readily insinuated into the context of evaluation. As late 20th-century politics moves toward a holistic agenda, it becomes crucial for activist men to be able to identify when they are falling back on these time-honoured discursive practices.

Denial and omission

Spender's catalogue is not exhaustive, as we shall see. Fox, a deep ecologist who wants to dissolve 'ontological divisions', adds to Spender's list by creating a disposable hierarchy of ecofeminisms. What makes for a 'better' ecofeminism? Apparently, it is the work of women building on the theoretical foundations of Buddhism, Taoism, Spinoza, Heidegger and systems theory![29] Fox's androcentrism is so strong that he remains unembarrassed by the implications of this legitimation device. Because the entire history of patriarchy is an exercise in suppressing the wisdom of women's experiences, deep ecologists would do well to bear this ancient agenda in mind. A related example occurs in the book by Devall and Sessions, whose text echoes snippets of my ecofeminist 'Deeper than Deep Ecology' critique, while denying its existence by omitting documentation. Published two years after that unacknowledged essay, the authors respond to the prod with a three-page acknowledgement of women's contributions to ecology. Yet, there is no sign of any effort to integrate ecofeminism within the book's conceptualization as a whole. Chapter one, which reviews environmentalist scenarios – reformist, New Age, libertarian – fails to mention the ecofeminist approach. Chapter two, which reviews 'the minority tradition', including nameless native Americans and 'primal peoples', gives eight lines to the 'Women's Movement'. These remarks mislead because of their brevity, moreover, and risk confusing not only sex and gender stereotypes, but also paradigmatic differences within feminism itself. There is also a short 'appendix' on ecology and domestic organization by Carolyn Merchant, whose other published work on patriarchal reason would have resounding epistemological implications for deep ecologists, if they absorbed it.[30] Concerning Devall's later book, Greta Gaard has observed that it 'gives the section on Eros, Gender and Ecological Self less than five pages ... he devotes an entire paragraph [to] citing a series of feminist analyses, but does not even paraphrase or address their objections to deep ecology...'[31]

In addition to the documentation of ecofeminist literature being flimsy, the deep ecologists' preparation for debate and grasp of feminist thought is also lacking in respect. Devall and Sessions cite Dorothy Dinnerstein, Susan Griffin and Jessie Bernard purportedly on how 'our culture inhibits the development of psychological maturity in women'. In fact, each of these feminist authors discusses the inhibition of 'masculine' psychic maturity under patriarchy. Only Griffin is referenced, however, and Bernard's name is given the masculine spelling 'Jesse'. This lack of respect strongly suggests that the material has been consulted very indifferently, if at all, by the deep ecologists.[32] Failing to recognize that women's perspectives are materially grounded in their working lives as carers, Fox and Zimmerman lean heavily on arguments about *essentialism*. No one who responded to 'Deeper than Deep Ecology' follows up footnote citations offering a dialectical refutation of the essentialism question. Again, although Fox cites Janet Biehl's critique of deep ecology, he never grapples with it.[33] Given that they are happy enough to set up a normative taxonomy of women's writing, it is remarkable that defenders of deep ecology have read so little ecofeminist literature. Their discussions focus on the writings of a handful of North American authors and myself. No European or Third World material is acknowledged, let alone examined. Perhaps the most damaging instance of denial used by deep ecologists is their disregard of my original ecofeminist endorsement of their ideals. To repeat, '*The appropriateness of attitudes expressed in Naess and Devall's seminal papers is indisputable.*'[34] This lapse has deflected the focus of subsequent exchanges between ecofeminism and deep ecology away from constructive mutuality.

Projection and personalization

Bolstered by adjectives like 'simplistic' and 'facile' – three or four times on one page in connection with social ecology and what are to him the less acceptable species of ecofeminism – Fox says that ecofeminism's simplistic analyses are overinclusive and that they target all men, capitalists, whites, indiscriminately as 'scapegoats' for what is wrong with the world.[35] His personalization here mirrors the form of those arguments that produce the example of Margaret Thatcher as proof that feminism is wrong. Individual women can be powerful, wealthy or racist, but their circumstances have no bearing on the structural oppression of the female sex. Conversely, while a class of men may be preserved by entrenched structural privilege, specific individuals may still commit themselves against their class interest. In my discussion of Australian politics in 'A Green Party: Can the Boys Do without One?' I talk, for example, about men working together with women in dismantling patriarchy, and about the potential of conservative churchgoers and corporate wives as catalysts in social change.[36] Fox's tactic of personalization is one to guard against, for it is invariably resorted to by those whose class has a vested interest in ignoring what a structural analysis tells them.

On the same page, Fox claims that 'simplistic' ecofeminist analyses are 'inauthentic' because they lead to 'a complete denial of responsibility' on the part of those who theorize. Because the ecofeminist literature presents an interdisciplinary synthesis of epistemological, political, economic, cultural, psychodynamic and ecological insights, it can scarcely wear the label 'oversimplified'. The term *essentialism* is also plainly misapplied for the same reason. As for avoiding responsibility, most ecofeminist writers, North and South, have practical experience of movement activism, and that is what stimulates their insights. Women in the thousands have taken up campaigns over toxics, wilderness and peace, not only in autonomous separatist groupings, but in mainstream environmental organizations where they make up two-thirds of the labour force. Women are certainly embracing ecological responsibility, so much so that it has even been remarked that it looks like they are being used all over again in their traditional house-keeping role as unpaid keepers of *oikos* at large.[37] Since women actually receive less than ten per cent of the world's wage, why should they want to maintain this destructive global economy? As women around the world make the connection between sustainability and equality, they are doing just what Fox's either/or logic claims they cannot do. They are becoming 'a class in themselves'.

When will men lay down their arms? Zimmerman takes up the offensive on behalf of deep ecology with a proposition that perhaps women really accrue benefit from patriarchy:

> ...feminists try to temper [their] portrayal by saying that *individual* men are not to blame, since they have been socialized... What traits, then, are women projecting on to men? And what benefits accrue to women through projecting such traits? Do women split off from themselves and project onto men violence, aggressiveness, selfishness, greed, anger, hostility, death hating, nature fearing, individuality, and responsibility? And as a result of bearing the projected traits, do men behave much more violently, selfishly, etc., than they would if these traits were withdrawn by women?[38]

I have commented in relation to Fox's work that personalization is invariably used by those who have difficulty thinking about people in groups or classes. Here it is Zimmerman who loses grasp of the structural level of analysis. If women do simply 'project characteristics' onto men, that is, if they are ideas only in women's heads, then why do patriarchal statistics corroborate that ninety per cent of violent crimes are committed by men? Indeed, are men 'responsible' at all for their behaviour? What of the wholesale abandonment of 150,000 women and children in the US each year? What about responsibility in the nuclear industry? What has gone wrong with women's self-fulfilling projection there? According to Zimmerman's 'critique of feminism', feminists must realize that men, too, are victims of patriarchy. Of course, I made this point myself in 'Deeper than Deep Ecology' with the allusion to masculine self-estrangement. Hilkka Pietila also picks up on it when she writes: 'A long process of male liberation is needed ... in order to meet feminine culture without prejudice... Salleh *still anticipates* a new ally within the personality of men, and it is ... the feminine aspects of men's own constitution...'[39] Nevertheless, women have all but given up trying to get their brothers into self-discovery through mutually supportive consciousness-raising groups as pioneered by radical feminism in the 1970s. Zimmerman, in contrast, is confident that it is feminism itself which must engage in searching self-criticism. Surely, the emergence of five or six feminist paradigms in the space of two decades already demonstrates the women's movements' vitality and openness to renewal. Where is the men's movement and its political, as opposed to psychological, analysis?

Women were early to point out how the personal and political intermesh, and hence how 19th century moralizers like 'blame' and 'accuse', are not apt in a postmodern reflexive culture where people strive to understand their own class implications in repressive social structures. Instead, Zimmerman ponders whether patricentric attitudes become more or less entrenched with 'education'. As we can see from the present exchange, education as such is no panacea. Unless people learn how to recognize the social/personal infrastructure of labour that sustains them daily, a paradigm shift is not likely. Zimmerman is almost there when he remarks that 'we are making use of norms and following cultural practices that threaten the future of life on Earth'. But who is this 'we'? Women's and men's 'roles' and values are not everywhere the same. He knows this. After all, he takes hope from the 'global awakening of the quest for the feminine voice that can temper the one-sidedness of the masculine voice'.[40] Although ecofeminists share this hope, they also want it known that as far as any 'quest' goes, a majority of the world's population, North and South, are already 'speaking the feminine'. The problem is: do they have standing? What is called for now is a move beyond tokenism, an admission of all women into the ranks of humanity.[41]

Caricature and trivialization

The quest for the 'feminine voice' is a recurrent theme in late 20th-century philosophy, as recent French poststructuralist writing reveals. Alice Jardine's extensive research into this trend suggests, however, that gynesis, or speaking like a woman, is somewhat suspect when it is fashionably pursued by affluent Parisian homosexual *litterateurs*.[42] It deteriorates into parody, and beyond that into an upmarket semi-academic export commodity. A revolution in gender relations cannot go anywhere at the level of ideas, language or ritual alone; it needs an objective 'material base'. Such professional philosophers as Zimmerman, however, are far removed from this perception. His class-based idealism brings him to conclude that it is 'epistemology, metaphysics, and ethics' that have 'led to the present exploitation'.[43] From an ecofeminist perspective, change demands that relationships of production and reproduction be equably rearranged between men and women and nature – in such a way that freedom and necessity are identically experienced. Equality and sustainability are closely interlinked.

The philosophy of 'difference', so poorly served by the deep ecologists' cheap paraphrase of ecofeminism – 'that women are better than men' – has been widely debated over the past decade among liberal, Marxist, poststructuralist and ecofeminists. The exploration of this theme marks an important phase in women's political consciousness. It converges both with men's personal efforts to escape the strictures of patriarchy and with new epistemological directions in science.[44] It is true that some men may still 'think the feminine' in an unreconstructed way. Look at Wittbecker's attempt to dispose of my own critique in the traditional manner: 'Hysterical hyperbolism is a perilous path to consciousness...'[45] Consider, too, the uncritical use of woman/nature imagery by some early Earth First! deep ecologists, whose lurid metaphors of familial rape are meant to highlight their manly self-sacrifice in protecting 'Mother Earth' and her 'virgin forests'. The thought style of monkey-wrench politics has tended to reinforce the intrinsic psychosexual dynamic lying beneath the exploitation of nature, women, and less privileged peoples. Other men defensively subvert any notion of 'difference' by using it to set up a double bind, affirming 'what they knew all along about women'. Zimmerman himself professes concern that arguments based on gender types 'run the risk of simply reaffirming traditional views that women are "feelers", while men are "thinkers."'[46] If nothing else, the ecofeminism/deep ecology debate should put an end to this assumption.

Fox is especially given to caricature of those he wants to debate, even when he is not fully cognizant of his terms. While no doubt endorsing wolves' rights to be wolves, he takes my rhetorical line about women being allowed to 'love themselves' entirely out of its context in cultural politics. His next gambit relies on Wittbecker's poorly reasoned charge that I treat 'the sexes as if they were two species'. This alleged dualism is cobbled together with the playful Irigarayan title 'A Green Party: Can the Boys Do without One?' in order to illustrate an 'oppositional' approach.[47] As Adorno would say, a totalitarian culture knows no irony. In a related vein, Fox has claimed that 'The extent to which people in general are ready to equate opposition to human centeredness with opposition to humans per se can be viewed as a function of the dominance of the anthropocentric frame of reference in our society.'[48] Fox does not see that the extent to which deep ecologists equate opposition to patriarchy with opposition to men per se can be viewed as a function of the dominance of their own androcentric frame of reference.

Discredit and invalidation

It is easier to think through an issue if there is a clear distinction between 'them and us', self and other; hence, Fox 'weighs up' the 'relative merits' of deep ecology and ecofeminism. Having polarized the two, he casts doubt over the value of ecofeminist 'anthropocentrics' by means of a footnote reference to racism at Greenham Common in 1987.[49] In fact, the racism in question was felt to be displayed by socialist women from the Campaign for Nuclear Disarmament toward Wilmette Brown, an Afro-American legal aid adviser to ecofeminist activists and a well-known advocate in the wages-for-housework campaign. As those familiar with ideological crosscurrents within feminism know, many leftists are antagonistic to the wages-for-housework campaign, which cuts right across their ideal of socialized domestic production. The confrontation was thus an ideological one, but exacerbated in that a black activist stood at the centre of it. Greenham ecofeminists, sensitive to the interconnectedness of all forms of domination – classism, racism, sexism and speciesism – took all facets of the problem in hand and tried to work them out. Carrying this 'inclusiveness' further, an April 1989 meeting of the Woman Earth Peace Institute in San Francisco pioneered an effective model for ensuring racial parity at ecofeminist gatherings.[50] Fox's divisive approach is a dubious one for a radical thinking man in the late 20th century to engage in. Which brings up another question: where are the Afro-American or Third World 'spokespeople' for the deep ecology movement?

Zimmerman writes that 'Critics of feminism' – though, since these are not referenced, one must infer it is the author himself speaking – 'regard as disingenuous the claim that the real motive of feminism is to liberate *all* people. Such critics contend that feminists have their own power agenda.'[51] Obviously, feminists have a power agenda; they are involved in a political struggle designed to redress an inequitable system. Or, if Zimmerman means that individual feminist women are on a 'power trip', then there is a margin of truth in that as well, inasmuch as women attempting to achieve equality alongside male peers have to compete harder to arrive at the same result because of structural discrimination and harassment along the way. However, if he is implying that women only want power, then that is silly. The personal costs of being a feminist in both career and domestic terms are enormous. Nobody would bother with the struggle unless she were committed to the vision of a just society. It may be at least several generations before the community at large even begins to digest what feminists are talking about.

Current statistics, for example, indicate that 25 per cent of Australian men still believe that it is all right for a man to hit 'his' wife. In the US, a woman is battered every 18 seconds. In the meantime, there are few benefits for feminists, or even their daughters in the foreseeable future. Ecofeminism is directed toward a long-term transvaluation of values. Women working to this end certainly glean no rewards from the system that they are trying to deconstruct. In a way, deep ecology's 'critique of feminism' itself reflects why the ecofeminist sensibility came forward in the first place. In Charlene Spretnak's words, 'Ecofeminism addresses the terror of nature and of female power, and the ways out of this mesmerizing condition...'[52]

Ambivalence and appropriation

While Zimmerman and Cheney, each from their different viewpoints, have observed that convergencies between ecofeminism and deep ecology exist only 'at first glance' or 'on the face of it', a fraction of the deep ecological mindset still hopes for some sort of I/ thou accommodation between the movements. Fox talks about a synthesis and, astonishingly, turns to Cheney's critique and Zimmerman's 'evenhanded' examination in defence of his own claim that there is 'no real incompatibility'.[53] The logic of Fox's turn is incredible, first, in light of Zimmerman's highly ambivalent attitude toward feminism, and second, given Cheney's sceptical thesis that deep ecology may be symptomatic of an inability to identify realistically with others, a manifestation of the patriarchal vacillation between 'selfish appetite' and 'oceanic fusion'.[54] Ecofeminists certainly resist a patronizing subsumption of women's thoughtful labours under the deep ecological umbrella, just as much as they find it offensive to see men raiding and colonizing feminist ideas in order to modernize male dominance. Nevertheless, ignoring our disquiet over the deep ecologists' lack of regard for the environmental consequences of technology, economics, race and gender relations, Fox recommends that inasmuch as ecofeminists 'extend' their concerns to the ecological, then there is no 'significant difference'. He calls for an alliance with Patsy Hallen, in terms of her paper, subtitled 'Why Ecology Needs Feminism', and with Marti Kheel, despite the latter's uncompromising exposé of patriarchal thinking in environmental ethics. On the next page, and relaxing back into the authoritative white, male, academic register, he announces 'major problems associated with Kheel's critique'.[55] In one important concession, he writes, 'Deep ecologists completely agree with ecofeminists that men have been far more implicated in the history of environmental destruction than women.'[56] This assertion more or less unhinges Fox's efforts to generate a coherent stand, providing a good example of what liberal pluralism looks like in practice.[57]

Zimmerman also arrives at a point where he is keen 'to unite' and finds 'no real disagreement on basics', etc., and he adopts the ecofeminist analysis that

> So long as patriarchally raised men fear and hate women, and so long as men conceive of nature as female, men will continue in their attempts to deny what they consider to be the feminine/natural within themselves and to control what they regard as the feminine/natural outside themselves.[58]

Does he really believe this statement? It seems doubtful, for with the next breath, he writes, 'Salleh's critique is, in my opinion, only partly accurate...'[59] This opinion, however, is never demonstrated, for he does not say which 'part' he has in mind, or whether the 'parts' represent a reader divided within his intellectual/emotional growth. Although intellectual capacities recognize what is true in ecofeminism, emotionally the reader is unsettled by the feminine voice. After all, Zimmerman reads the 'Deeper than Deep Ecology' critique as 'accusatory', rather than, say, 'challenging' or 'confronting'.[60] Thus, the question is: since ultimately he endorses ecofeminist conclusions, what is Zimmerman defending at such length?

Ambivalence also marks Devall's work. He is happy to take on board the odd ecofeminist insight – for example, Starhawk's revisioning of power, the heroic example of India's Chipko women, or Sarah Ebenreck's farm ethic. He has even come to agree with the ecofeminist premise that 'the ecological crisis has complex psychosexual roots'. Yet, like other deep ecologists, Devall is anxious to move quickly beyond that messy problem 'to explore the ecological self'. The emphasis on gender difference runs the risk of 'divisiveness', he claims, and 'distracts us from the real work'. This 'after the Revolution' line is a familiar one to feminists who took their first steps hand in hand with brother Marxists. The language is identical, in fact, for what speaks here is the voice of patriarchy. Of course, many men want to avoid doing their personal/political homework; doing so could well upset their comfortable status quo. Nevertheless, humans cannot simply pass over their psychosexual conditioning in this way, as the present textual analysis demonstrates. In Devall's own words, 'Healing requires bringing forth that which is suppressed in culture' and levelling with it, however painful and confusing this experience may be. As every deep ecologist knows, band-aid solutions do not work.[61]

Conclusion

Richard Ohmann is not himself a deep ecologist, but a man sensitive to the terrain of gender politics that now underlies both daily routine and theoretical work. He approaches our dilemma in this way:

> ... progressive male intellectuals and professionals have arrived at feminism by an inexorable development and by a moral logic that flows from our strongest allegiances... If we are 'in' feminism at all, we are dragged into it kicking and screaming, and now that we're there, we should think of ourselves as on extended probation, still learning. What we do there with our experience, our competence, and our gender and class confidence, is a matter to be negotiated with caution, flexibility, improvisation, listening, and often doubtless through a strategic fade into the wallpaper. But I don't see drawing back from the knowledge that feminism is our fight, too.[62]

Clearly there is a long way yet to go. In terms of a Green or ecosocialist political practice, the new politics will demand of men and women more than just rational understanding of their respective positions as bearers of class, race and gender domination, if they are to recover their shared human complementarity. Men, moreover, whose history has taken them on such a destructive path, will need to open up to a deep therapeutic acceptance of the process of mother/nature/woman killing in the making of their own identities. Although the personal and the transpersonal are intermeshed, as far as deep ecology goes, this inner movement has been lacking. Constructed by a class of men that is serviced by both patriarchal and capitalist institutions, deep ecology with its valuable move to 'ecocentrism' remains out of touch with the material source of its continuing existence. Significantly, its theorization ignores the place of labour in the creation and sustenance of human life and its pivotal role in our human exchanges with nature. In short, as it is presently formulated, deep ecology reflects the disembodied conditions of its own production. This situation is, and should be, a matter for concern, if not despair, among committed environmental radicals, ecosocialists, and ecofeminists.

Notes

1   Ariel Salleh 'The ecofeminism/deep ecology debate: A reply to patriarchal reason'. *Environmental Ethics*, vol 14 (1992), pp195–216

2   For discussion of the international status of ecofeminism and its regional variations, see Ariel Salleh, 'From centre to margin', *Hypatia*, vol 6 (1991), pp206–214.

3   Arne Naess, 'The shallow and the deep, long range ecology movement', *Inquiry*, vol 16 (1973), pp95–100. A qualification of Naess' views appears in *Ecology, Community and Life Style: Outline of an Ecosophy*, trans David Rothenberg (New York, Cambridge University Press, 1989). Here, the impact of culture and personal experience on ethical intuition is acknowledged in a way that could serve as a model for other deep ecologists.

4   Ariel Salleh, 'Epistemology and the metaphors of production', *Studies in the Humanities*, vol 15 (1988), p136.

5   Brinda Rao, 'Gender and ecology in India', *Capitalism, Nature, Socialism*, vol 2 (1989), pp65–82; Berit As, 'A five dimensional model for change', *Women's Studies International Quarterly*, vol 4 (1980); Barbara Ehrenreich, *The Hearts of Men* (New York, Anchor, 1983).

6   Warwick Fox, 'The deep ecology-ecofeminism debate and its parallels', *Environmental Ethics*, vol 11 (1989), p14. Compare Ariel Salleh, 'Deeper than deep ecology: The ecofeminist connection', *Environmental Ethics*, vol 6 (1984), pp335–341, especially points 3 and 4.

7   Michael Zimmerman, 'Feminism, deep ecology, and environmental ethics', *Environmental Ethics*, vol 9 (1987), pp21–44.

8   For an early ecofeminist ethic based on 'caring', see Marti Kheel, 'The liberation of nature: A circular affair', *Environmental Ethics*, vol 7 (1985), pp135–149. The analysis of caring has since become a veritable growth area for professional philosophers, thus neutralizing the radical feminist impulse which originally politicized it.

9   Zimmerman, 'Feminism, deep ecology, and environmental ethics', p31. The reference is to Naomi Scheman, 'Individualism and the objects of psychology' in S. Harding and M. Hintikka, eds *Discovering Reality* (Boston, Reidel, 1983), p234.

10 Jim Cheney, 'Ecofeminism and deep ecology', *Environmental Ethics*, vol 9 (1987), p124.

11 Vandana Shiva, *Staying Alive* (London, Zed, 1989) conveys the voice of Indian women farmers to a Western educated readership. Alternatively, an academic feminist argument connecting pain with political insight is made in Ariel Salleh, 'On the dialectics of signifying practice', *Thesis Eleven*, vols 5/6 (1982), pp72–84.

12 Salleh, 'Deeper than Deep Ecology', p339.

13 Fox, 'Deep ecology-ecofeminism debate', p9 (emphasis added). Since writing this piece, I have discovered that Jim Cheney explicates the totalizing implications of Fox's stand powerfully and eloquently in 'The neo-stoicism of radical environmentalism', *Environmental Ethics,* vol 11 (1989), pp293–325.

14 Unfortunately, Robyn Eckersley's recent book *Environmentalism and Political Theory: Toward an Ecocentric Approach* (New York University at Stonybrook Press, 1992) perpetuates Fox's naive realism.

15 Rosemary Ruether, *New Woman, New Earth* (New York, Seabury, 1975).

16 Fox, 'Deep Ecology-Ecofeminism Debate', p12.

17 Ibid, pp22–23.

18 Zimmerman, 'Feminism, deep ecology, and environmental ethics', p34.

19 Bill Devall and George Sessions, *Deep Ecology: Living as if Nature Mattered* (Salt Lake City, Peregrene Smith, 1985), p225. On *essentialism* as red herring, see Salleh, 'The ecofeminism/deep ecology debate', and 'Essentialism and ecofeminism', *Arena*, vol 94 (1991), pp167–173.

20 Zimmerman, 'Feminism, deep ecology, and environmental ethics', p40.

21 Ibid, pp40,41–42.

22 Don Davis, 'The seduction of Sophia', *Environmental Ethics*, vol 8 (1986), pp151–162.

23 Alan Wittbecker, 'Deep anthropology, ecology and human order', *Environmental Ethics*, vol 8 (1986), p269; and Bill Devall, *Simple in Means, Rich in Ends* (Salt Lake City, Peregrene Smith, 1988).

24 This paragraph is adapted from Ariel Salleh, 'Living with nature: Reciprocity or control', in R. and J. Engel, eds, *Ethics of Environment and Development* (London, Pinter/University of Arizona Press, 1990), p251.

25 George Sessions, personal communication, Los Angeles, March 1987; Arne Naess, personal communication, Oslo, August 1987.

26 See Bill Devall and George Sessions, *Deep Ecology*, pp71–73.

27 Karen Warren, 'Feminism and ecology: Making connections', *Environmental Ethics*, vol 9 (1987), p6.

28 Dale Spender, *Women of Ideas and What Men Have Done to Them* (London, Routledge, 1982). See also Margo Adair and Sharon Howell, *The Subjective Side of Politics* (San Francisco, Tools for Change, 1988).

29 Fox, 'The Deep Ecology-Ecofeminism Debate', p13, n20.

30 Bill Devall and George Sessions, *Deep Ecology*; compare Carolyn Merchant *The Death of Nature* (San Francisco, Harper and Row, 1980).

31 Greta Gaard, 'Feminists, animals, and the environment', paper presented at the annual convention of the National Women's Studies Association, Baltimore, 1989, p10.

32 Devall and Sessions, *Deep Ecology*, p180; p221, n2. The missing references are Dorothy Dinnerstein, *The Mermaid and the Minataur* (New York, Harper and Row, 1976) and Jessie Bernard, *The Future of Marriage* (New York, World Publications, 1972).

33 Janet Biehl's article 'It's deep but is it broad?' appeared in *Kick It Over*, Winter 1987, pp2A–4A, at a time when she identified herself with social ecofeminism.

34 Salleh, 'Deeper than deep ecology', p339 (emphasis added).

35 Fox, 'The deep ecology-ecofeminism debate', p16.

36 Ariel Salleh, 'A green party: Can the boys do without one?' in Drew Button, ed, *Green Politics in Australia* (Sydney, Angus and Robertson, 1987), p88.

37 See the special women's issue of *Environmental Review*, vol 8 (1984); and Ariel Salleh, 'The growth of ecofeminism', *Chain Reaction*, vol 36 (1984), pp26–28.

38 Zimmerman, 'Feminism, ecology, and environmental ethics', p41.

39 Hilkka Pietila, 'Daughters of mother earth', in Engel and Engel, *Ethics of Environment and Development*, p243 (emphasis added).

40 Zimmerman, 'Feminism, ecology, and environmental ethics', p41.

41 The participation of women from all continents in the 1992 United Nations Conference on Environment and Development is a case in point. Even so, at one point. developing world government negotiators were prepared to 'trade off' women's rights, if the United States would concede its high level of resource depletion by leaving references to 'overconsumption' in Agenda 21 texts!

42 Alice Jardine, *Gynesis* (Cambridge, MA. Harvard University Press, 1985).

43 Zimmerman, 'Feminism, ecology, and environmental ethics', p44. The same tendency is manifest in his book *Heidegger's Confrontation with Modernity* (Indiana University Press, 1990), even while a 'feminist perspective' is incorporated into the last five pages of text.

44 See Benjamin Lichtenstein, 'Feminist epistemology', *Thesis Eleven*, vol 21 (1988).

45 Wittbecker, 'Deep anthropology and human order', p265, n18.

46 Zimmerman, 'Feminism, Ecology, and Environmental Ethics', p34.

47 Fox, 'The deep ecology-ecofeminism debate', pp17–18. As well as being poorly informed, notes 33 and 41 of this article are classic examples of misrepresentation by trivialization.

48 Ibid, p20.

49 Ibid, p14, n24.

50 Jacinta McCoy, personal communication, Eugene, Oregon, June 1989.

51 Zimmerman, 'Feminism, ecology, and environmental ethics', p41.

52 Charlene Spretnak, Address to the First International Ecofeminist Conference, University of Southern California, Los Angeles, March 1987.

53 Fox, 'The deep ecology-ecofeminism debate,' p9, n7.

54 Cheney follows Carol Gilligan, *In a Different Voice* (Cambridge, MA. Harvard University Press, 1982).

55 Fox, 'The deep ecology-ecofeminism debate', p9, n7; p10, n11. Patsy Hallen, 'Making peace with nature: Why ecology needs feminism', *The Trumpeter*, vol 4, no 3 (1987), pp3–14; Marti Kheel, 'The liberation of nature'.

56 Fox, 'The deep ecology-ecofeminism debate', p14.

57 In tandem with Fox, Eckersley, in *Environmentalism and Political Theory*, also tries to appropriate ecofeminism for deep ecology. In quite uncritical language, she describes ecofeminist theory as 'nesting within' ecocentrism and as an 'essential tributary'. Moreover, focusing exclusively on the world of ideas, Eckersley sees ecocentrism as waiting to be 'fleshed out in a political and economic direction'.

Women's ongoing political/economic resistance, North and South, remains invisible to her.

58 Zimmerman, 'Feminism, ecology, and environmental ethics', p24.
59 Ibid, p39.
60 Devall, *Simple in Means, Rich in Ends,* pp56–57.
61 Richard Ohmann, 'In, with', in A. Jardine and P. Smith, eds, *Men in Feminism* (New York, Methuen 1987) p187.

9

The Biological Basis for Human Values of Nature

Stephen R. Kellert

The biophilia hypothesis boldly asserts the existence of a biologically based, inherent human need to affiliate with life and lifelike processes (Wilson, 1984). This proposition suggests that human identity and personal fulfilment somehow depend on our relationship to nature. The human need for nature is linked not just to the material exploitation of the environment but also to the influence of the natural world on our emotional, cognitive, aesthetic and even spiritual development. Even the tendency to avoid, reject and, at times, destroy elements of the natural world can be viewed as an extension of an innate need to relate deeply and intimately with the vast spectrum of life about us.

The hypothesis suggests that the widest valuational affiliation with life and lifelike processes (ecological functions and structures, for example) has conferred distinctive advantages in the human evolutionary struggle to adapt, persist and thrive as individuals and as a species. Conversely, this notion intimates that the degradation of this human dependence on nature brings the increased likelihood of a deprived and diminished existence – again, not just materially, but also in a wide variety of affective, cognitive and evaluative respects. The biophilia notion, therefore, powerfully asserts that much of the human search for a coherent and fulfilling existence is intimately dependent upon our relationship to nature. This hypothesized link between personal identity and nature is reminiscent of Aldo Leopold's alteration (1966, p240) of Descartes' dictum of selfhood from 'I think, therefore I am' (an anthropocentric conception of human identity) to 'as a land-user thinketh, so is he' (a biocentric view of selfhood, recognizing Leopold's concept of land as a metaphor for ecological process).

This chapter explores the biophilia notion by examining nine fundamental aspects of our species' presumably biological basis for valuing and affiliating with the natural world. These hypothesized expressions of the biophilia tendency (regarded not as an instinct but as a cluster of learning rules) are referred to as the utilitarian, naturalistic, ecologistic-scientific, aesthetic, symbolic, humanistic, moralistic, dominionistic and negativistic valuations of nature.

Before commencing the description of these basic values, it might be worth explaining briefly how these hypothesized categories of the basic human relationship to nature evolved in my work. This digression proceeds less from any personal indulgence than

Note: Reprinted from *Biophilia Hypothesis* by Stephen R. Kellert and Edward O. Wilson, eds, copyright © (1993) by Island Press. Reproduced with permission of Island Press, Washington, DC

from a desire to indicate how the dimensions of the biophilia tendency became apparent as possibly universal expressions of the human dependence on nature.

A limited version of the typology of nine perspectives of nature was developed in the late 1970s as a way of describing basic perceptions of animals (Kellert, 1976). This typology was employed in a study of nearly 4000 randomly distributed Americans residing in the 48 contiguous states and Alaska (Kellert, 1979, 1980, 1981). Expanded versions of the typology were subsequently used in researching human perceptions of varying taxa including wolves (Kellert, 1986d, 1991a), marine mammals (Kellert, 1986b, 1991b), diverse endangered species (Kellert, 1986c), invertebrates (Kellert, 1986a, 1992) and bears (Kellert, 1993a); in analysing the nature-related perspectives of diverse human groups such as hunters (Kellert, 1978), birders (Kellert, 1985b), farmers (Kellert, 1984a) and the general public distinguished by age (Kellert, 1985a), gender (Kellert, 1987), socio-economic status (Kellert, 1983), and place of residence (Kellert, 1981, 1984b); in exploring cross-cultural perspectives of nature and animals in Japan (Kellert, 1991c), Germany (Schulz, 1986; Kellert, 1993b), and Botswana (Mordi, 1991); and in examining historical shifts in perceptions of animals in Western society (Kellert, 1985c).

The point of this digression is to note that in each study the value dimensions were revealed although they might vary, often greatly, in content and intensity. What began as merely the objective of describing variations in people's perceptions of animals gradually emerged as the possibility of universal expressions of basic human affinities for the natural world. The typology may be simply a convenient shorthand for describing varying perspectives of nature. Its occurrence, however, in a wide variety of taxonomic, behavioural, demographic, historic and cultural contexts suggests the distinct possibility that these categories might very well be reflections of universal and functional expressions of our species' dependence on the natural world.

Classification of Values

The task of this chapter is to describe each of these categories as indicative of the human evolutionary dependence on nature as a basis for survival and personal fulfilment. As suggested, nine hypothesized dimensions of the biophilia tendency – the utilitarian, naturalistic, ecologistic-scientific, aesthetic, symbolic, humanistic, moralistic, dominionistic and negativistic – are described here. This description is followed by a discussion of how this deep dependence on nature may constitute the basis for a meaningful and fulfilling human existence – that is, how the pursuit of self-interest may constitute the most compelling argument for a powerful conservation ethic.

Utilitarian

The utilitarian dependence on nature is both something of a misnomer and at the same time manifest. The possible inappropriateness of the term stems from the presumption that *all* the biophilia tendencies possess utilitarian value in the sense of conferring a measure of evolutionary advantage. The use of the utilitarian term here is restricted to the conventional notion of material value: the physical benefits derived from nature as a fundamental basis for human sustenance, protection and security.

It has long been apparent that a biological advantage exists for humans in exploiting nature's vast cornucopia of food, medicines, clothing, tools and other material benefits. What may constitute a major conservation development in recent years is the increasing recognition and detailed delineation of the potential and often unrealized material value of various genetic, biochemical and physical properties of diverse plant and animal species (Myers, 1978; Prescott-Allen, 1986). Of particular significance has been the expanding realization of the 'hidden' material value in nature represented by obscure species and unimpaired ecosystems, such as undiscovered organisms of the tropical rain forests, as potential repositories of material benefit as human knowledge expands to exploit the earth's vast genetic resource base (Eisner, 1991).

Naturalistic

The naturalistic tendency may simplistically be regarded as the satisfaction derived from direct contact with nature. At a more complex and profound level, the naturalistic value encompasses a sense of fascination, wonder and awe derived from an intimate experience of nature's diversity and complexity. The mental and physical appreciation associated with this heightened awareness and contact with nature may be among the most ancient motive forces in the human relationship to the natural world, although its recreational importance appears to have increased significantly in modern industrial society.

The naturalistic tendency involves an intense curiosity and urge for exploration of the natural world. This interest in direct experience of living diversity, and its possible evolutionary roots, is suggested by Wilson (1984, pp10, 76):

> Because species diversity was created prior to humanity, and because we evolved within it, we have never fathomed its limits… The living world is the natural domain of the more restless and paradoxical part of the human spirit. Our sense of wonder grows exponentially; the greater the knowledge, the deeper the mystery and the more we seek knowledge to create new mystery… Our intrinsic emotions drive us to search for new habitats, to cross unexplored terrain, but we still crave this sense of a mysterious world stretching infinitely beyond.

Discovery and exploration of living diversity undoubtedly facilitated the acquisition of increased knowledge and understanding of the natural world, and such information almost certainly conferred distinctive advantages in the course of human evolution. As Seielstad has remarked (1989, p285): 'The surest way to enrich the knowledge pool that will keep the flywheel of cultural evolution turning is to nourish the human spirit of curiosity'. A genetic basis for this naturalistic tendency is suggested by Iltis (1980:3): 'Involvement with nature … may be in part genetically determined; human needs for natural diversity … must be inherent. Man's love for natural colours, patterns and harmonies … must be the result … of … natural selection through eons of mammalian and anthropoid evolution'.

The naturalistic tendency has been cited as providing an important basis for physical fitness and the acquisition of various 'outdoor skills' such as climbing, hiking, tracking and orienteering. The possession of these skills and associated states of mental and physical wellbeing have been empirically described for a variety of contemporary outdoor activities with a strong emphasis on the naturalistic experience (Driver and Brown, 1983; Kaplan, 1992). The mental benefits of these activities have been related to tension release, relaxation, peace of mind and enhanced creativity derived from the observation of diversity in nature. The psychological value of the outdoor recreational experience is noted by Ulrich et al (1991, p203) in a review of the scientific literature: 'A consistent finding in well over 100 studies of recreation experiences in wilderness and urban nature areas has been that stress mitigation is one of the most important verbally expressed perceived benefits'. Kaplan (1983, p155), drawing on extensive research of the naturalistic experience, concluded in a rather more subjective vein: 'Nature matters to people. Big trees and small trees, glistening water, chirping birds, budding bushes, colourful flowers – these are important ingredients in a good life'.

Ecologistic-Scientific

While important differences distinguish the scientific from the ecologistic relationship to nature, both perspectives similarly reflect the motivational urge for precise study and systematic inquiry of the natural world and the related belief that nature can be understood through empirical study. The ecologistic experience may be regarded as more integrative and less reductionist than the scientific, involving an emphasis on interconnection and interdependence in nature as well as a related stress on integral connections between biotic and abiotic elements manifest in the flow of energy and materials within a system.

The concept of ecology is, of course, a modern scientific formulation: Leopold (1966, p176) proclaimed it 'the outstanding scientific discovery of the twentieth century'. Still, the notion of ecology encompasses far more than the conventional and narrow expression of scientific inquiry. Leopold, despite the previous assertion, recognized this possibility and remarked (1966, p266): 'Let no man jump to the conclusion that Babbitt must take his PhD in ecology before he can "see" his country. On the contrary, the PhD may become as callous as an undertaker to the mysteries at which he officiates'.

Still, the ecologistic experience of nature often involves a recognition of organizational structure and complexity barely discernible to the average person. This difficulty of perspective reflects the fact that most important ecological processes are prominently manifest at the bottom of biological food chains and energy pyramids often associated with the activities of invertebrate and microbial organisms. As invertebrates represent more than 90 per cent of the planet's biological diversity, they perform most of the critical ecological functions of pollination, seed dispersal, parasitism, predation, decomposition, energy and nutrient transfer, the provision of edible materials for adjacent trophic levels, and the maintenance of biotic communities through mutualism, host-restricted food webs and a variety of other functions and processes. Most people hardly recognize these ecological tendencies, let alone the species integral to their performance, preferring to direct their emotional and conscious awareness of nature to larger vertebrates and prominent natural features.

The human understanding of ecological function is thus at its initial stages of articulation and recognition through systematic inquiry and careful investigation. Nonetheless, the broad realization of ecological process has probably always been intuitively and empirically apparent to the astute human observer. An understanding of organismic and habitat interdependence has likely been the mark of certain figures throughout human history. Moreover, this ecological insight has probably conferred distinctive advantages in the meeting and mastering of life's physical and mental requirements – including increased knowledge, the honing of observational and recording skills, and the recognition of potential material uses of nature through direct exploitation and mimicry. The sense of nature's functional and structural interconnectedness may have further instilled in the prudent observer a cautious respect for nature likely to temper tendencies toward overexploitation and abuse of natural processes and species.

The scientific experience of nature, in contrast to the ecologistic, involves a greater emphasis on the physical and mechanical functioning of biophysical entities as well as a related stress on issues of morphology, taxonomy and physiological process. The scientific perspective, as previously suggested, tends to be reductionistic: it focuses on constituent elements of nature often independent of the understanding of entire organisms or their relations to other species and natural habitats. Despite this restricted emphasis, often divorced from direct experiential contact with nature, the scientific outlook shares with the ecologistic an intense curiosity and fascination with the systematic study of life and lifelike processes. The depth and intensity of this pursuit of knowledge can often lead to a profound appreciation of nature's wonder and complexity. A sense of this wonder can be discerned in Scott McVay's description of such scientists as Wilson, Vishniac and von Frisch (1987, pp5–6):

> I start with wonder, awe and amazement of the profusion of life... E. O. Wilson ... wrote that a genetic description of a mouse would fill every page of the Encyclopedia Britannica in every edition starting with the first printing in the 1750s to the present day... Roman Vishniac [found] more wonder in a drop of pond water than in travelling to the most remote places on the planet... Karl von Frisch ... said that there was miracle enough in a single species to provide a life's work.

Such reflections suggest a derivative satisfaction from experiencing the complexity of natural process quite apart from its apparent utility or evolutionary advantage. Yet the actual and potential benefits of such awareness are also quite evident. One can imagine the value of vastly enhanced knowledge and understanding of nature conferred upon those who developed the capacities for precise observation, analysis and detailed study of even a fraction of life's extraordinary diversity.

Aesthetic

The physical beauty of nature is certainly among its most powerful appeals to the human animal. The complexity of the aesthetic response is suggested by its wide-ranging expression from the contours of a mountain landscape to the ambient colours of a setting sun to the fleeting vitality of a breaching whale. Each exerts a powerful aesthetic impact on most people, often accompanied by feelings of awe at the extraordinary physical appeal and beauty of the natural world.

The human need for an aesthetic experience of nature has been suggested by the apparent inadequacy of artificial or human-made substitutes when people are exposed to them. This preference for natural design and pattern has been revealed in a variety of studies as Ulrich has noted (1983, p109): 'One of the most clear-cut findings in the ... literature ... is the consistent tendency to prefer natural scenes over built views, especially when the latter lack vegetation or water features. Several studies have [shown] that even unspectacular or subpar natural views elicit higher aesthetic preference ... than do all but a very small percentage of urban views'. Additional research suggests that this aesthetic preference for nature may be universally expressed across human cultures (Ulrich 1983, p110): 'Although far from conclusive, these findings ... cast some doubt on the position that [aesthetic] preferences vary fundamentally as a function of culture'.

Living organisms often function as the centrally valued element in people's aesthetic experience of nature. Unlike the previously described ecologistic-scientific emphasis on relatively obscure organisms, the aesthetic response is typically directed at larger, charismatic megavertebrate species. The basis for this aesthetic focus on relatively large animals is elusive yet, in all likelihood, critical to the understanding of the human attraction to and dependence on nature. Leopold (1966, pp137,129–130) powerfully describes this aesthetic significance in alluding to the presence and absence of wildlife in the natural landscape:

> The physics of beauty is one department of natural science still in the Dark Ages... Everybody knows, for example, that the autumn landscape in the north woods is the land, plus a red maple, plus a ruffed grouse. In terms of conventional physics, the grouse represents only a millionth of either the mass or energy of an acre. Yet subtract the grouse and the whole thing is dead. An enormous amount of some kind of motive power has been lost... My own conviction on this score dates from the day I saw a wolf die... We reached the old wolf in time to watch a fierce green fire dying in her eyes. I realized then, and have known ever since, that there was something new to me in those eyes – something known only to her and to the mountain.

Leopold referred to this central aesthetic of animals in the landscape as its 'numenon', its focus of meaning, in contrast to merely the 'phenomenon' of a static and lifeless environment. This essential aesthetic is perhaps what George Schaller (1982) recognized in his reference to the Himalayas as 'stones of silence' upon discovering the near extirpation of its endemic caprine fauna – in contrast to Leopold's revelation of the wolf's role in the landscape as requiring one to 'think like a mountain'. The animal in its contextual environment appears to confer upon its habitat vitality and animation, what Rolston (1986a) has called the essential wildlife aesthetic of 'spontaneity in motion'.

The biological advantage of the aesthetic experience of nature is difficult to discern, yet, as Wilson suggests (1984, p104), 'with aesthetics we return to the central issue of biophilia'. The aesthetic response could reflect a human intuitive recognition or reaching for the ideal in nature: its harmony, symmetry and order as a model of human experience and behaviour. The adaptational value of the aesthetic experience of nature could further be associated with derivative feelings of tranquillity, peace of mind and a related sense of psychological wellbeing and self-confidence. The aesthetic response to varying landscapes and species may also reflect an intuitive recognition of the greater likelihood of food, safety and security associated with human evolutionary experience. Kaplan and Kaplan suggest, for example (1989, p10): 'Aesthetic reactions [to nature] ...

reflect neither a casual nor a trivial aspect of the human makeup. Rather, they appear to constitute a guide to human behaviour that is both ancient and far-reaching. Underlying such reactions is an assessment of the environment in terms of its compatibility with human needs and purposes'. Iltis has further argued for a genetic component in the human aesthetic response to nature (1973, p5): 'Human genetic needs for natural pattern, for natural beauty, for natural harmony, [are] all the results of natural selection over the illimitable vistas of evolutionary time'. A more empirical delineation of this aesthetic preference for certain landscapes and species as a possible function of human evolutionary experience, associated with the likelihood of encountering food, safety and security, is offered by Heerwagen and Orians. (See Chapter 4 in Kellert and Wilson, 1993, and Orians, 1980.)

Symbolic

The symbolic experience of nature reflects the human use of nature as a means of facilitating communication and thought (Lévi-Strauss, 1970; Shepard, 1978). The use of nature as symbol is perhaps most critically reflected in the development of human language and the complexity and communication of ideas fostered by this symbolic methodology. The acquisition of language appears to be enhanced by the engendering of refined distinctions and categorizations. Nature, as a rich taxonomy of species and forms, provides a vast metaphorical tapestry for the creation of diverse and complex differentiations. As Lawrence suggests (see Chapter 10 in Kellert and Wilson, 1993) with reference to animals, though the notion can be more broadly extended to other categories of nature, 'it is remarkable to contemplate the paucity of other categories for conceptual frames of reference, so preeminent, widespread, and enduring is the habit of symbolizing in terms of animals'. Shepard further emphasizes the importance of animate nature as a facilitator of human language and thought (1978, pp249, 2):

> Human intelligence is bound to the presence of animals. They are the means by which cognition takes its first shape and they are the instruments for imagining abstract ideas and qualities...They are the code images by which language retrieves ideas ... and traits... Animals are used in the growth and development of the human person, in those most priceless qualities we lump together as 'mind'... Animals ... are basic to the development of speech and thought.

A limited indication of the symbolic function is reflected in the finding (Kellert, 1983) that animals constitute more than 90 per cent of the characters employed in language acquisition and counting in children's preschool books. Studies by Shepard (1978), Bettelheim (1977), Campbell (1973), Jung (1959) and others indicate the significance of natural symbols in myth, fairy tale, story and legend as an important means for confronting the developmental problems of selfhood, identity, expressive thought and abstraction.

An enduring question of modern life is the degree to which the human capacity for technological fabrication has provided an effective substitute for traditional natural symbols as the primary means of communication and thought. The unlikelihood of this possibility is suggested by the evolutionarily very short time period of modern industrial life relative to the long course of human evolution during which nature constituted the sole environment for our species' language development (Shepard 1978). More important, the dependence of the human psyche on highly varied and refined distinctions seems to be matched only by the extraordinary diversity, complexity and vividness of the natural world as an extremely rich and textured system. Plastic trees, stuffed animals and their fabricated kin seem but a meagre substitute more likely to result in a stunted capacity for symbolic expression, metaphor and communication.

Humanistic

The humanistic experience of nature reflects feelings of deep emotional attachment to individual elements of the natural environment. This focus, like the aesthetic, is usually directed at sentient matter, typically the larger vertebrates, although humanistic feelings can be extended to natural objects lacking the capacity for reciprocity such as trees and certain landscapes or geological forms.

The humanistic experience of strong affection for individual elements of nature can even be expressed as a feeling of 'love' for nature, although this sentiment is usually directed at domesticated animals. Companion animals are especially given to the process of 'humanization' of nature in the sense of achieving a relational status not unlike other humans might assume, even family members. The therapeutic mental and physical benefits of the companion animal have been documented in various studies, at times even resulting in significant healing benefits (Katcher and Beck, 1983; Anderson et al, 1984; Rowan, 1989; Chapters 3 and 5 in Kellert and Wilson, 1993).

The humanistic experience of nature can result in strong tendencies toward care and nurturance for individual elements of nature. From an adaptational viewpoint, the human animal as a social species, dependent on extensive cooperative and affiliational ties, may especially benefit from the interactive opportunities fostered by a humanistic experience of nature. An enhanced capacity for bonding, altruism and sharing may be important character traits enhanced by this tendency. The use of companion animals for a variety of functional tasks, such as hunting and protection, may also contribute to evolutionary fitness through the acquisition of diverse skills and understandings of nature. This knowledge born of intimate human interaction with a nonhuman species is conveyed in Barry Lopez' description of semidomesticated wolves (1978, p282):

> The wolves moved deftly and silently in the woods and in trying to imitate them I came to walk more quietly and to freeze at the sign of slight movement. At first this imitation gave me no advantage, but after several weeks I realized I was becoming far more attuned to the environment we moved through. I heard more ... and my senses now constantly alert, I occasionally saw a deer mouse or a grouse before they did... I took from them the confidence to believe I could attune myself better to the woods by behaving as they did – minutely inspecting things, seeking vantage points, always sniffing at the air. I did, and felt vigorous, charged with alertness.

Moralistic

The moralistic experience of nature encompasses strong feelings of affinity, ethical responsibility and even reverence for the natural world. This perspective often reflects the conviction of a fundamental spiritual meaning, order and harmony in nature. Such sentiments of ethical and spiritual connectedness have traditionally been articulated in poetry, religion and philosophy, but today they can even be discerned in the modern discourse of scientific language, as suggested by Leopold's remarks (1966, pp222, 231):

> Land is not merely soil; it is a fountain of energy flowing through a circuit of soils, plants, and animals... A thing is right when it tends to preserve the integrity, stability, and beauty of the biotic community. It is wrong when it tends otherwise.

The moralistic perspective has often been associated with the views of indigenous peoples (see Chapter 6 in Kellert and Wilson, 1993). Booth, Booth and Jacobs (1990) describe important elements in the moralistic experience of nature among indigenous North Americans prior to European acculturation. They emphasize a fundamental belief in the natural world as a living and vital being, a conviction of the continuous reciprocity between humans and nature, and the certainty of an inextricable link between human identity and the natural landscape. This outlook is powerfully reflected in the words of Luther Standing Bear (1933, p45):

> We are of the soil and the soil is of us. We love the birds and beasts that grew with us on this soil. They drank the same water as we did and breathed the same air. We are all one in nature. Believing so, there was in our hearts a great peace and a willing kindness for all living, growing things.

A more Western articulation of this moralistic identification with nature, somewhat rationalized by the language of modern science, is offered by Loren Eiseley (1946, pp209–210):

> It is said by men ... that the smallest living cell probably contains over a quarter of a million protein molecules engaged in the multitudinous coordinated activities which make up the phenomenon of life. At the instant of death, whether of man or microbe, that ordered, incredible spinning passes away in an almost furious haste... I do not think, if someone finally twists the key successfully in the tiniest and most humble house of life, that many of these questions will be answered, or that the dark forces which create lights in the deep sea and living batteries in the waters of tropical swamps, or the dread cycles of parasites, or the most noble workings of the human brain, will be much if at all revealed. Rather, I would say that if 'dead' matter has reared up this curious landscape of fiddling crickets, song sparrows, and wondering men, it must be plain even to the most devoted materialist that the matter of which he speaks contains amazing, if not dreadful powers, and may not impossibly be, as Hardy has suggested, 'but one mask of many worn by the Great Face behind'.

From the perspective of this inquiry, the vexing question is the possible biological significance of a moralistic experience of nature. It might be supposed that a moralistic outlook articulated in a group context fostered feelings of kinship, affiliation and loyalty leading to cooperative, altruistic and helping behaviour. Strong moralistic affinities for nature may also produce the desire to protect and conserve nature imbued with spiritual significance, as Gadgil (1990) has described for the nearly 6 per cent of historic India regarded as sacred groves. It may be sufficient to suggest that a biological advantage is conferred on those who experience a profound sense of psychological wellbeing, identity and self-confidence produced by the conviction of an ultimate order and meaning in life. The expression of this insight and its possibly pervasive significance is eloquently expressed by John Steinbeck (1941, p93):

> It seems apparent that species are only commas in a sentence, that each species is at once the point and the base of a pyramid, that all life is related... And then not only the meaning but the feeling about species grows misty. One merges into another, groups melt into ecological groups until the time when what we know as life meets and enters what we think of as non-life: barnacle and rock, rock and earth, earth and tree, tree and rain and air. And the units nestle into the whole and are inseparable from it... And it is a strange thing that most of the feeling we call religious, most of the mystical outcrying which is one of the most prized and used and desired reactions of our species, is really the understanding and the attempt to say that man is related to the whole thing, related inextricably to all reality, known and unknowable. This is a simple thing to say, but a profound feeling of it made a Jesus, a St Augustine, a Roger Bacon, a Charles Darwin, an Einstein. Each of them in his own tempo and with his own voice discovered and reaffirmed with astonishment the knowledge that all things are one thing and that one thing is all things – a plankton, a shimmering phosphorescence on the sea and the spinning planets and an expanding universe, all bound together by the elastic string of time.

Dominionistic

The dominionistic experience of nature reflects the desire to master the natural world. This perspective may have been more frequently manifest during earlier periods of human evolution; its occurrence today is often associated with destructive tendencies, profligate waste and despoliation of the natural world. Yet this view may be too narrow and associated with exaggerated dominionistic tendencies. Life, even in the modern era, may be regarded as a tenuous enterprise, with the struggle to survive necessitating some measure of the proficiency to subdue, the capacity to dominate, and the skills and physical prowess honed by an occasionally adversarial relationship to nature. Rolston's insight (1986b, p88) is helpful:

> The pioneer, pilgrim, explorer, and settler loved the frontier for the challenge and discipline... One reason we lament the passing of wilderness is that we do not want entirely to tame this aboriginal element... Half the beauty of life comes out of it... The cougar's fang sharpens the deer's sight, the deer's fleet-footedness shapes a more supple lioness... None of life's heroic quality is possible without this dialectical stress.

Beyond an enhanced capacity to subjugate nature, the dominionistic experience may foster increased knowledge of the natural world. As Rolston's remarks intimate, the predator understands and even appreciates its prey to a degree no mere external observer can attain, and this perspective may be as true for the human hunter of deer or mushrooms as it is for the wolf stalking its moose or the deer its browse. While the survival value of the dominionistic experience may be less evident today than in the evolutionary past, one suspects a false arrogance in the denial of the human inclination to master nature in favour of strong emotional bonds of affection or kinship for life. The dominionistic experience of nature, like all expressions of the biophilia tendency, possesses both the capacity for functional advantage as well as exaggerated distortion and self-defeating manifestation.

Negativistic

The negativistic experience of nature is characterized by sentiments of fear, aversion and antipathy toward various aspects of the natural world. Most advocates of conservation regard fear and alienation from the natural world as inappropriate and often leading to unwarranted harm and destruction. The potential biological advantage of avoiding, isolating and even occasionally harming presumably threatening aspects of nature can, however, be recognized. (See Chapter 3 in Kellert and Wilson, 1993.) The disposition to fear and reject threatening aspects of nature has been cited as one of the most basic motive forces in the animal world. As Öhman suggests (1986, p128): 'Behaviours that can be associated with fear are pervasive in the animal kingdom. Indeed, one could argue that systems for active escape and avoidance must have been among the first functional behaviour systems that evolved'.

The human inclination to fear and avoid threatening aspects of nature has been particularly associated with reptiles such as snakes and arthropods such as spiders and various biting and stinging invertebrates. A predisposition to fear and avoid such creatures and other harmful elements of nature may have conferred some advantage during the course of human evolution resulting in its statistically greater prevalence. This potential has been described by Ulrich et al in a review of the scientific literature (1991, p206): 'Conditioning studies have shown that nature settings containing snakes or spiders can elicit pronounced autonomic responses ... even when presented subliminally'. Schneirla (1965) further notes that the occurrence of 'ugly, slimy, erratic' moving animals, such as certain snakes and invertebrates, provokes withdrawal responses among vertebrate neonates in the absence of overt or obvious threat.

Studies of human attitudes toward invertebrates (Kellert, 1993c), as well as related research by Hardy (1988) and Hillman (1991), have discovered a variety of motivational factors in the human tendency to dislike and fear arthropods. First, many humans are alienated by the vastly different ecological survival strategies, spatially and temporally, of most invertebrates in comparison to humans. Second, the extraordinary 'multiplicity' of the invertebrate world seems to threaten the human concern for individual identity and selfhood. Third, invertebrate shapes and forms appear 'monstrous' to many people. Fourth, invertebrates are often associated with notions of mindlessness and an absence of feeling – the link between insects or spiders and madness has been a common metaphor in human discourse and imagination. Fifth, many people appear challenged by the radical 'autonomy' of invertebrates from human will and control.

These sentiments of fear and alienation from nature can foster unreasonable human tendencies and the infliction of excessive harm and even cruel behaviour on animals and other elements of nature. Singer (1977) has referred to this tendency as 'specicide' – reflecting the willingness to pursue the destruction of an entire species, such as Lopez (1978) has described for the wolf in North America or might exist towards certain rodent, insect and spider species. Hillman ruefully remarked in this regard (1991): 'What we call the progress of Western Civilization from the ant's eye level is but the forward stride of the great exterminator'.

Negativistic tendencies toward nature, given our modern technical prowess, have often resulted in the massive destruction of elements of the natural world. Yet the extent of today's onslaught on nature should not preclude one from recognizing its possible evolutionary origin or its continued biological advantage expressed at a more modest and even 'rational' level. Fear of injury or even violent death in nature will continue to be an integral part of the human repertoire of responses to the natural world, and a realistic tension with threat and danger in nature is part of the challenge of survival. It might even be suggested that some measure of fear of the natural world is essential for the human capacity to experience a sense of nature's magnificence and sublimeness. The power of pristine nature to inspire and challenge human physical and mental development in all likelihood requires considerable elements of fear and danger.

Exploration

The presentation of nine, presumably biologically based, human valuations of nature represents an exploratory effort at supporting the biophilia hypothesis. While these descriptions certainly do not constitute 'proof' of the biophilia complex, the typology may provide a heuristic approach for systematically examining the evolutionary basis of each of the suggested values. Each category of the typology is thought to represent a basic human relationship and dependence on nature indicating some measure of adaptational value in the struggle to survive and, perhaps more important, to thrive and attain individual fulfilment. A summary of the biophilia values is presented in Table 9.1.

This chapter has relied on conceptual and descriptive analysis for delineating basic elements of the biophilia hypothesis. As suggested earlier, a limited empirical corroboration of the typology has been provided by the results of various studies, conducted by the author and others, of diverse cultures and demographic groups, human perceptions of varying taxa, and historical shifts in perspectives of nature. Although methodological problems preclude the assertion of this evidence as proof, these findings offer restricted support of the typology's occurrence. And although these results do not constitute a sufficient validation of the categories as biologically based expressions of human dependence on nature, their widespread empirical expression suggests the possibility that they may represent universal human characteristics. What appears to be relative is not the occurrence of the value types across cultures, taxa and time but the content and intensity of this expression and its adaptational importance.

It has been argued in this chapter that each value type is indicative of our species' dependence on the natural world and represents a potential evolutionary advantage. It follows that their cumulative, interactive and synergistic impact may contribute to the possibility of a more fulfilling personal existence. The effective expression of the biophilia need may constitute an important basis for a meaningful experience of self.

The conservation of nature is rationalized, from this perspective, not just in terms of its material and commodity benefits but, far more significantly, for the increased

Table 9.1 *A typology of biophilia values*

Term	Definition	Function
Utilitarian	Practical and material exploitation of nature	Physical sustenance/security
Naturalistic	Satisfaction from direct experience/contact with nature	Curiosity, outdoor skills, mental/physical development
Ecologistic-Scientific	Systematic study of structure, function and relationship in nature	Knowledge, understanding, observational skills
Aesthetic	Physical appeal and beauty of nature	Inspiration, harmony, peace, security
Symbolic	Use of nature for metaphorical expression, language, expressive thought	Communication, mental development
Humanistic	Strong affection, emotional attachment, 'love' for nature	Group bonding, sharing, cooperation, companionship
Moralistic	Strong affinity, spiritual reverence, ethical concern for nature	Order and meaning in life, kinship and affiliational ties
Dominionistic	Mastery, physical control, dominance of nature	Mechanical skills, physical prowess, ability to subdue
Negativistic	Fear, aversion, alienation from nature	Security, protection, safety

likelihood of fulfilling a variety of emotional, cognitive and spiritual needs in the human animal. An ethical responsibility for conserving nature stems, therefore, from more than altruistic sympathy or compassionate concern: it is driven by a profound sense of self-interest and biological imperative. As Wilson suggests (1984, p131): 'We need to apply the first law of human altruism, ably put by Garrett Hardin: never ask people to do anything they consider contrary to their own best interests'. Nature's diversity and healthy functioning are worthy of maintenance because they represent the best chance for people to experience a satisfying and meaningful existence. The pursuit of the 'good life' is through our broadest valuational experience of nature. This deeper foundation for a conservation ethic is reflected in the words of René Dubos (1969, p129):

> Conservation is based on human value systems; its deepest significance is the human situation and the human heart... The cult of wilderness is not a luxury; it is a necessity for the preservation of mental health... Above and beyond the economic ... reasons for conservation, there are aesthetic and moral ones which are even more compelling... We are shaped by the earth. The characteristics of the environment in which we develop condition our biological and mental being and the quality of our life. Were it only for selfish reasons, therefore, we must maintain variety and harmony in nature.

The converse of this perspective is the notion that a degraded relationship to nature increases the likelihood of a diminished material, social and psychological existence. This chapter has intimated several possibilities in this regard, and it may be relevant to note the finding that significant abusers of nature, particularly those who inflict in childhood wilful harm on animals, are far more likely in adulthood to reveal repeated patterns of violence and aggressive behaviour toward other people (Kellert and Felthous, 1985; Felthous and Kellert, 1987). Indeed, presumably socially acceptable forms of destructive conduct toward nature may in retrospect come to be regarded as false and short-term benefits, as Leopold's lament of the last of the passenger pigeons suggests (1966, p109):

> We grieve because no living man will see again the onrushing phalanx of victorious birds sweeping a path for spring across the March skies, chasing the defeated winter from all the woods and prairies... Our grandfathers were less well-housed, well-fed, well-clothed than we are. The strivings by which they bettered their lot are also those which deprived us of pigeons. Perhaps we now grieve because we are not sure, in our hearts, that we have gained by the exchange. The gadgets of industry bring us more comforts than the pigeons did, but do they add as much to the glory of the spring?

A sceptical response to the assertion of the biophilia tendency as a biologically based human need to affiliate with nature is the view that this hypothesis is an expression of cultural and class bias. This view suggests that the assertions trumpeted here are but a romantic ideology of nature, paraded in the guise of biology, promoted for essentially elitist political and social reasons. Such a critique may claim that the biophilia hypothesis condemns, by implication, all those mired in poverty and trapped within urban walls to another stereotype of a less fulfilling human existence.

Abraham Maslow's (1954) notion of a hierarchy of needs may offer one response to this critique – implying the pursuit of self-realization through a broad valuational experience of nature as a higher order of human functioning. In other words, the biophilia tendency might become manifest once the basic human needs for survival, protection and security have been realized. This argument, while superficially appealing, probably reflects a naive assumption of human functioning. People are typically inclined to pursue concurrently a wide range of simple to complex needs if they are not overwhelmed by the sheer necessity of confronting the material basis for survival (a relatively rare condition).

Any presumption of the relative unimportance of the biophilia tendency among persons of lower socio-economic status or urban residence may, in itself, be an elitist and arrogant characterization. Nature's potential for providing a more satisfying existence may be less obvious and apparent among the poor and urban than the rich and rural, but this deprivation represents more a challenge of design and opportunity than any fundamental irrelevance of the natural world for a class of people. As Leopold noted (1966, p266): 'The weeds in a city lot convey the same lesson as the redwoods... Perception ... cannot be purchased with either learned degrees or dollars; it grows at home as well as abroad, and he who has a little may use it to as good advantage as he who has much'. The capacity of nature to enrich and enlarge the human experience is a potential inherent in all but the most deprived and encapsulated within concrete walls. Society's obligation is not to bemoan the seeming 'absence' of nature in the inner city or among the poor but to render its possibility more readily available. The presumption that only the materially advantaged and conveniently located can realize nature's value represents an arrogant characterization.

A more fundamental question is the recognition in modern society of the human need to affiliate deeply and positively with life's diversity. This is a complex issue too difficult to address here in detail. A partial response, however, may be provided by the results of the previously cited studies conducted in the US and Japan. While these studies explore the biophilia hypothesis only indirectly, they offer circumstantial information regarding the modern relationship to the natural world among persons living in highly urban, technologically oriented industrial societies. Insufficient space precludes all but a very brief summarization of these results, although more detailed information regarding the studies can be found elsewhere (Kellert, 1979, 1981, 1983, 1991c, 1993b).

Both the US and Japan have been described as nations with a pronounced appreciation for the natural world. Americans, for example, are known to be especially supportive of nature conservation: nearly 10 per cent of the American public is formally affiliated with at least one environmental organization (Dunlap, 1978), and American environmental legislation is recognized as among the most comprehensive and protective in the world (Bean, 1983). Extensive outdoor recreational activity among Americans is reflected in nearly 300 million annual visits to national parks, and three-fourths of the public participates in some form of wildlife-related outdoor recreational activity (Foresta, 1984; USFWS, 1990).

Japanese culture too has been characterized as encouraging a strong appreciation for nature (Minami, 1970; Watanabe, 1974; Higuchi, 1979; Murota, 1986). Often cited expressions of this interest include the practices of Shintoism, flower arranging, plant cultivation (such as bonsai), the tea ceremony, certain poetry forms, rock gardening and various celebrations of the seasons. Higuchi (1979, p19) has described a Japanese view of nature 'based on a feeling of awe and respect', while Watanabe (1974, p280) has remarked on a Japanese 'love of nature ... resulting in a refined appreciation of the beauty of nature'. Murota (1986, p105) suggests: 'The Japanese nature is an all-pervasive force... Nature is at once a blessing and friend to the Japanese people'.

Despite these assertions of an especially refined appreciation for nature in the US and Japan, our research has revealed only limited concern for the natural world among the general public in both countries. Citizens of the US and Japan typically expressed strong interest in nature only in relation to a small number of species and landscapes characterized by especially prominent aesthetic, cultural and historic features. Furthermore, most Americans and Japanese expressed strong inclinations to exploit nature for various practical purposes despite the likelihood of inflicting considerable environmental damage. Most respondents revealed, especially in Japan, indifference toward elements of the natural world lacking any aesthetic or cultural value. Very limited knowledge and understanding of nature was found, particularly in Japan.

Japanese appreciation of nature was especially marked by a restricted focus on a small number of species and natural objects – often admired in a context emphasizing control, manipulation and contrivance. This affinity for nature was typically an idealistic rendering of valued aspects of the natural environment, usually lacking an ecological or ethical orientation. This appreciation was described by one Japanese respondent as 'a love of seminature', representing a largely emotional and aesthetic interest in using 'the materials of seminature to express human feelings'. Other respondents described it as a perspective of nature dominated by a preference for the artificial, abstract and symbolic rather than any realistic experience of the natural world; a motivation to 'touch' nature from a controlled and safe distance; an adherence to strict rules of seeing and experiencing nature intended to express only the centrally valued aspect; a desire to isolate favoured aspects of nature in order to 'freeze and put walls around it'. Environmental features falling outside the valued aesthetic and symbolic boundaries tended to be ignored, dismissed or judged unappealing (Saito, 1983).

American respondents revealed a somewhat more generalized interest and concern for nature, especially among highly educated and younger Americans in comparison to similar demographic groups in Japan. On the other hand, nature appreciation among most Americans was largely restricted to particularly valued species and landscapes, while other aspects of the natural world were typically subordinated to strong utilitarian concerns. The great majority of Americans revealed little appreciation of 'lower' life-forms, tending to restrict their appreciation to the large vertebrates.

In conclusion, most Americans and Japanese expressed a pronounced concern for only a limited number of species and natural objects. The biophilia tendency, as described here, was broadly evident only among a small segment of the population in both countries, most prominently the better educated and the young in the US.

A New Basis for Conservation?

A largely conceptual argument has been offered here in support of the biophilia hypothesis. It appears that a variety of basic valuations of nature are consistent with the possibility of increased evolutionary fitness at both the individual and species levels. Each expression of the biophilia tendency – the aesthetic, dominionistic, ecologistic-scientific, humanistic, moralistic, naturalistic, symbolic, utilitarian and even negativistic – has been depicted as potentially enhancing the basis for a profound development of self. A range of adaptational advantages has been cited as resulting from these basic experiences of nature – enhanced physical skills and material benefits, greater awareness, increased protection and security, opportunities for emotional gratification, expanded kinship and affiliational ties, improved knowledge and cognitive capacities, greater communication and expressive skills, and others.

A conservation ethic of care, respect and concern for nature was regarded as more likely to emanate from the conviction that in our relationship to the natural world exists the likelihood of achieving a more personally rewarding existence. As Iltis has suggested (1980, pp3, 5), our mental and physical wellbeing may represent a far more compelling basis for nature conservation than the mere rationalization of enhanced material benefit:

> Here, finally, is an argument for nature preservation free of purely [material] utilitarian considerations; not just clean air because polluted air gives cancer; not just pure water

because polluted water kills the fish we might like to catch; … but preservation of the natural ecosystem to give body and soul a chance to function in the way they were selected to function in their original phylogenetic home… Could it be that the stimuli of non-human living diversity makes the difference between sanity and madness ?

Iltis's question intimates the still tenuous state of our understanding of the biophilia phenomenon. The sophistication and depth of future inquiry may prove the measure of Iltis's response to his own question (1973, p7):

We may expect that science will [someday] furnish the objective proofs of suppositions about man's needs for a living environment which we, at present, can only guess at through timid intuition; that one of these days we shall find the intricate neurological bases of why a leaf or a lovely flower affects us so very differently than a broken beer bottle.

The importance of this recognition of our basic human dependence on nature is suggested by the meager appreciation of the natural world evinced among the general public in modern Japan and the United States. The great majority of people in these two leading economic nations recognized to only a limited extent the value of nature in fostering human physical, cognitive, emotional, and spiritual development. Most Americans and Japanese expressed an aloofness from the biological matrix of life, restricting their interest to a narrow segment of the biotic and natural community. This narrow emphasis on certain species and landscapes is clearly an insufficient basis for a fundamental shift in global consciousness – one capable of countering the contemporary drift toward massive biological impoverishment and environmental destruction.

References

1 Anderson, R., Hart, B. and Hart, L. (1984) *The Pet Connection.* University of Minnesota Press, Minneapolis
2 Bean, M. (1983) *The Evolution of National Wildlife Law.* Praeger, NY
3 Bettelheim, B. (1977) *The Uses of Enchantment.* Vintage Books, NY
4 Booth, A., Booth, H. and Jacobs, H. M. (1990) 'Ties that bind: Native American beliefs as a foundation for environmental consciousness'. *Environmental Ethics*, vol 12, pp27–43
5 Campbell, J. (1973) *Myths to Live By.* Viking Press, NY
6 Driver, B. and Brown, P. (1983) 'Contributions of behavioural scientists to recreation resource management', in Altman, I. and Wohlwill, J. (eds), *Behaviour and the Natural Environment*, Plenum Press, NY
7 Dubos, R. (1969) *Ecology and Religion in History.* Oxford University Press, NY
8 Dunlap, R. (1978) *Environmental Concern.* Vance Bibliographies, Monticello, III
9 Eiseley, L. (1946) *The Immense Journey.* Random House, NY
10 Eisner, T. (1991) 'Chemical prospecting: a proposal for action', in Bormann, H. and Kellert, S. (eds), *Ecology, Economics, Ethics: The Broken Circle,* Yale University Press, New Haven
11 Felthous, A. and Kellert, S. (1987) 'Childhood cruelty to animals and later aggression against people'. *American Journal of Psychiatry*, vol 144, pp710–717
12 Foresta, R. (1984) *America's National Parks and Their Keepers*, Johns Hopkins University Press, Baltimore

13 Gadgil, M. (1990) 'India's deforestation: Patterns and processes'. *Society and Natural Resources*, vol 3, pp131–143.

14 Hardy, T. (1988) 'Entomophobia: The case for Miss Muffet'. *Bulletin of the Entomological Society of America*, vol 34, pp64–69.

15 Higuchi, K. (1979) *Nature and the Japanese*, Kodansha International, Tokyo

16 Hillman, J. (1991) *Going Bugs*, Spring Audio, Cassettes, NY

17 Iltis, H. (1973) 'Can one love a plastic tree?' *Bulletin of the Ecological Society. America*, vol 54, pp5–7, 19.

18 Iltis, H. (1980) 'Keynote address'. trans *Symp.: The Urban Setting: Man's Need for Open Space.* Connecticut College, New London

19 Jung, C. (1959) *The Archetype and the Collective Unconscious*, Pantheon Books, New York

20 Kaplan, R. (1983) 'The role of nature in the urban context', in Altman, I. and Wohlwill, J. (eds), *Behaviour and the Natural Environment*, Plenum Press, New York

21 Kaplan, S. (1992) 'The restorative environment: Nature and human experience'. In D. Relf (ed.), *The Role of Horticulture in Human Wellbeing and Social Development.* Timber Press, Portland, OR

22 Kaplan, R. and Kaplan, S. (1989) *The Experience of Nature: A Psychological Perspective.* Cambridge University Press, Cambridge

23 Katcher, A. and Beck, A. (1983) *New Perspectives on Our Lives with Companion Animals.* University of Pennsylvania Press, Philadelphia

24 Kellert, S. (1976) 'Perceptions of animals in American society'. *Transactions of the North American Wildlife and Natural Resources Conference,* vol 41, pp533–546.

25 Kellert, S. (1978) 'Characteristics and attitudes of hunters and anti-hunters'. *Transactions of the North American Wildlife and Natural Resources Conference,* vol 43, pp412–423.

26 Kellert, S. (1979) *Public Attitudes Toward Critical Wildlife and Natural Habitat Issues.* US Government Printing Office, Washington

27 Kellert, S. (1980) *Activities of the American Public Relating to Animals.* US Government Printing Office, Washington

28 Kellert, S. (1981) *Knowledge, Affection and Basic Attitudes Toward Animals in American Society.* US Government Printing Office, Washington

29 Kellert, S. (1983) 'Affective, evaluative and cognitive perceptions of animals' in Altman, I. and Wohlwill, J. (eds), *Behaviour and the Natural Environment.* Plenum Press, NY

30 Kellert, S. (1984a) 'Public attitudes toward mitigating energy development impacts on western mineral lands'. *Proceeding Issues and Technical Management Impacted Western Wildlife.* Thorne Ecological Institute, Boulder

31 Kellert, S. (1984b) 'Urban American perceptions and uses of animals and the natural environment'. *Urban Ecology,* vol 8, pp209–228.

32 Kellert, S. (1985a) 'Attitudes toward animals: Age-related development among children'. *Journal of Environmental Education,* vol 16, pp29–39.

33 Kellert, S. (1985b) 'Birdwatching in American society'. *Letters in Science,* vol 7, pp343–360.

34 Kellert, S. (1985c) 'Historical trends in perceptions and uses of animals in 20th century America'. *Environmental Review,* vol 9, pp34–53.

35 Kellert, S. (1986a) 'The contributions of wildlife to human quality of life', in Decker, D. and Goff, G. (eds) *Economic and Social Values of Wildlife.* Westview Press, Boulder

36 Kellert, S. (1986b) 'Marine mammals, endangered species, and intergovernmental relations', in Silva, M. (ed.) *Intergovernmental Relations and Ocean Resources.* Westview Press, Boulder

37 Kellert, S. (1986c) 'Social and perceptual factors in the preservation of animal species', in Norton, B. (ed) *The Preservation of Species.* Princeton University Press, Princeton

38 Kellert, S. (1986d) 'The public and the timber wolf in Minnesota'. *Transactions of the North American Wildlife and Natural Resources Conference*, vol 51, pp193–200.

39 Kellert, S. (1987) 'Attitudes, knowledge, and behaviours toward wildlife as affected by gender'. *Bulletin of the Wilderness Society*, vol 15, pp363–371.

40 Kellert, S. (1991a) 'Public views of wolf restoration in Michigan'. *Transactions of the North American Wildlife and Natural Resources Conference*, vol 56, pp152–161.

41 Kellert, S. (1991b) 'Public views of marine mammal conservation and management in the northwest Atlantic'. *International Marine Mammals Association Technical Report*. Guelph, Ontario, pp91–104

42 Kellert, S. (1991c) 'Japanese perceptions of wildlife'. *Conservation Biology*, vol 5, pp297–308.

43 Kellert, S. (1993a) 'Public attitudes toward bears and their conservation', in Servheen, C. (ed) *Proceeding of the 9th International Bear Conference*, US Fish and Wildlife and Forest Services, Missoula

44 Kellert, S. (1993b) 'Attitudes toward wildlife among the industrial superpowers: United States, Japan, and Germany'. *Journal of Social Issues*, vol 49, pp53–69.

45 Kellert, S. (1993c) 'Values and perceptions of invertebrates'. Submitted to *Conservation Biology*

46 Kellert, S. and Felthous, A. (1985) Childhood cruelty toward animals among criminals and noncriminals. *Human Relations,* vol 38, pp1113–1129.

47 Leopold, A. (1966) *A Sand County Almanac.* Oxford University Press, New York

48 Lévi-Strauss, C. (1970) *The Raw and the Cooked.* Harper and Row, New York

49 Lopez, B. (1978) *Of Wolves and Men.* Scribner's, New York

50 Luther Standing Bear. (1933) *Land of the Spotted Eagle.* University of Nebraska Press, Lincoln

51 Maslow, A. (1954) *Motivation and Personality.* Harper and Row, New York

52 McVay, S. (1987) 'A regard for life: Getting through to the casual visitor'. *Philosophical Zoo Review*, vol 3, pp4–6.

53 Minami, H. (1970) *Psychology of the Japanese People.* East-West Center, Honolulu

54 Mordi, R. (1991) *Attitudes Toward Wildlife in Botswana.* Garland Publishing, New York

55 Murota, Y. (1986) 'Culture and the environment in Japan'. *Environmental Management*, vol 9, pp105–112.

56 Myers, N. (1978) *The Sinking Ark.* Pergamon Press, New York

57 Öhman, A. (1986) 'Face the beast and fear the face: Animal and social fears as prototypes for evolutionary analyses of emotion'. *Psychophysiology*, vol 23, pp123–145.

58 Orians, G. (1980) 'Habitat selection: General theory and applications to human behaviour', in Lockard, J. (ed) *The Evolution of Human Social Behaviour.* Elsevier, New York

59 Prescott-Allen, C and Prescott-Allen, R. (1986) *The First Resource.* Yale University Press, New Haven

60 Rolston, H. (1986a) 'Beauty and the beast: Aesthetic experience of wildlife', in Decker, D. and Goff, G. (eds) *Economic and Social Values of Wildlife.* Westview Press, Boulder

61 Rolston, H. (1986b) *Philosophy Gone Wild.* Prometheus Books, Buffalo

62 Rowan, A. (1989) *Animals and People Sharing the World.* University Press of New England, Hanover, NH

63 Saito, Y. (1983) 'The aesthetic appreciation of nature: Western and Japanese perspectives and their ethical implications'. Doctoral thesis, University of Michigan. University Microfilms, Ann Arbor

64 Schaller, G. (1982) *Stones of Silence.* Viking Press, NY

65 Schneirla, T. (1965) *Principles of Animal Psychology.* Prentice-Hall, Englewood Cliffs, NJ

66 Schulz, W. (1986) 'Attitudes toward wildlife in West Germany', in Decker, D. and Goff, G. (eds) *Economic and Social Values of Wildlife.* Westview Press, Boulder

67 Seielstad, G. (1989) *At the Heart of the Web.* Harcourt Brace Jovanovich, Orlando

68 Shepard, P. (1978) *Thinking Animals: Animals and the Development of Human Intelligence.* Viking Press, NY

69 Singer, P. (1977) *Animal Liberation.* Avon Books, NY

70 Steinbeck, J. (1941) *Log from the Sea of Cortez.* P. P. Appel, Mamaroneck, NY

71 Ulrich, R. (1983) 'Aesthetic and affective response to natural environment', in Altman, I. and Wohlwill, J. (eds) *Behaviour and the Natural Environment.* Plenum Press, New York

72 Ulrich, R. et al (1991) 'Stress recovery during exposure to natural and urban environments'. *J. Env. Psych*, vol 11, pp201–230.

73 US Fish and Wildlife Service (USFWS) (1990) *1990 National Survey of Hunting, Fishing and Wildlife-Associated Recreation.* Department of the Interior, Washington

74 Watanabe, H. (1974) 'The conception of nature in Japanese culture'. *Science*, vol 183, pp279–282.

75 Wilson, E. O. (1984) *Biophilia: The Human Bond with Other Species.* Harvard University Press, Cambridge

Part 3

Anthropological and Sociological Themes in Environmental Values

Introduction

Since the publication of Rachel Carson's *Silent Spring* more than 40 years ago there has been widespread acknowledgement that human action can and does adversely affect the environment. Much work has been done to understand how humans come to value the environment and how values come to change. Anthropologists and sociologists have made important contributions to the study of environmental values by drawing attention to how values are framed by social institutions and cultural practices. The papers in this section explore key socio-cultural links with environmental values, including social sources of values (religion, gender and geography) and general environmental beliefs (such as shared beliefs about how the world works and endorsement of an ecological worldview).

In the first paper, Eckberg and Blocker examine the connection between *religion* and environmentalism (pro-environmental attitudes and behaviour), in a test of the theory that Christians are predisposed (through Biblical teachings) to have dominion over nature and value the environment only for its usefulness to humans. This theory is called the *Lynn White Thesis* after the author of a much-cited but controversial essay, 'The Historical Roots of Our Ecological Crisis' (1967). Using survey data, they found that people who were religious sectarians (primarily conservative Protestants) do not adhere to a green lifestyle (such as eating organic or vegetarian or restricting automobile use), and do not participate in environmental actions (such as recycling). However, people who are religiously active (regular church attendance and strong identification with church) do recycle and tend to live a green lifestyle. Finally, they find that environmental issues are not at all important to those belonging to the 'common religiosity' category (Christians who believe in God and an afterlife). Together these findings lead the reader to conclude that the *influence of religion on environmentalism is complex*: while religious fundamentalism (sectarianism) decreases environmentalism, religious participation increases personal environmental action and the tendency to live a green lifestyle.

Dunlap, Van Liere, Mertig and Jones use 15 statements about nature and the relationship between humans and the natural world to measure endorsement of an *ecological worldview* (the New Ecological Paradigm). Using survey data to examine the social characteristics that are linked to a pro-ecological orientation, they reveal a set of robust and consistent patterns: Political liberals adhere to an ecological worldview, Democrats are the most pro-ecological; endorsement of an ecological worldview decreases with age and increases with levels of education. The authors conclude that adherence to a *New Ecological Paradigm* reflects a tendency to see the world ecologically, which in turn is related to pro-environmentalism. Also, the NEP is valuable in its responsiveness to experience with, and new information about, environmental problems.

Stern, Dietz and Kalof also examine environmentalism as a new worldview, but they employ a *social psychological* way of thinking about environmental problems. They argue that there are three *value orientations* towards the environment: *social-altruistic* (people value the welfare of others and will take action to prevent harm to others); *egoistic or self-interest* (people value the environment for economic or biological reasons); and *biospheric* (people value both human and nonhuman beings and the diversity of all forms of life). Using social psychology and feminist theory, they develop a model that presumes that people will be motivated to take action if they believe that things they value will be harmed by environmental conditions. Survey data are used to examine the links between beliefs about the *consequences for self, others* and the *biosphere* (the three value orientations) of environmental conditions (pollution and environmental protection laws) and environmental behaviours (political action and willingness to pay for an improved environment). Also, because of the theory that women are socialized to care about others and thus are more altruistic than men, they examine *gender differences* in value orientations, beliefs about the consequences of particular environmental conditions, and environmental behaviour. The authors find that, while people are willing to take political action regardless of their value orientations, only those who believe in consequences for self (the egoistic or self-interest value orientation) are willing to pay higher taxes for improved environmental quality (a biospheric value oriented person would be willing to pay an increased income tax, but not an increased gas tax). Finally, the authors find that women are more likely than men to believe that environmental conditions have consequences for self, others and the biosphere. However, there is no gender difference in value importance or the strength of the belief in consequences. The authors conclude that, while men and women may hold similar values, women are more attentive than men to the connection between environmental conditions and things they value.

Norton and Hannon propose that environmental values are derived from a local *commitment to place* in which people strive to protect their natural and cultural heritage. Noting that people want to be near 'good' things, such as schools and churches, and away from 'bad' things, such as sewage treatment plants and prisons, they argue that the strength of opposition to unpopular industries or support for desirable land uses will be determined by the distance of the activity from one's own geographic place. The authors use the concepts *place* and *space* to explain the source of environmental values. They argue that environmental values are connected to time, the biogeography of place, the surrounding space around place (which shapes our perception of self) and to a sense of scale for interpreting events that influence our experiences. The authors propose a theory of *place-relative value formation*: sense-of-place values are expressed in the models we use to think about environmental problems, which involve choosing what to see and what to protect. Thus, environmental values are formed subjectively in the space around a place. Further, individuals think about environmental decisions in a specific cultural context and from a specific geographical orientation with a sense of place and layers (or scales) of different values. They use *hierarchy theory* to understand how communities make moral and evaluative decisions: an individual has a particular perspective from which she observes and acts, and this perspective is embedded in a larger conceptualization of the space around the individual's place. Norton and Hannon define a *triscaler system* as one that includes three basic values that orient from a sense of place: locally developed value scale (preferences of individuals); larger community-oriented value scale oriented toward protecting and contributing to the community (including the ecological community); and a global value scale that is concerned that our species will survive and thrive. They discuss the triscaler system and the possibility of locally based environmental management using four examples that illustrate the interaction between place-based and centralized decision making processes. The authors determine that centralism and top-down authority force values downward because of constraints from above, while localism and resistance to enforcement of centralized authority force values up through the hierarchy. The multiscalar theory also shows that creative, diverse and sustainable decisions come from forcing values up the hierarchy.

Linda Kalof and Terre Satterfield

References

1   Carson, R. (1962) *Silent Spring*. Houghton Mifflin, Boston
2   White, L. Jr (1967) 'The historical roots of our ecological crisis'. *Science*, vol 155, pp1203–1207

10

Christianity, Environmentalism and the Theoretical Problem of Fundamentalism

Douglas Lee Eckberg and T. Jean Blocker

Introduction

Recent years have witnessed considerable discussion of possible relationships between religion and environmental attitudes, much of it centring on Lynn White's (1967) controversial argument that Christian beliefs carry an anti-nature bias.[1] The evidence brought to the topic has tended to support the argument, though not unanimously or unambiguously, and researchers do not agree on its interpretation. Further, the studies have a number of different methodological limitations, and it is quite possible that differences in findings stem from these. In this paper we will review findings and limitations of several major studies on the topic. We will then address the topic, using data from the 1993 General Social Survey that should overcome some of those problems.

Survey Research and the Lynn White Thesis

White's well-known essay does not need much introduction. Briefly, he proposed that the desacralization of nature in Genesis 1 predisposes Christians to regard the environment as having value primarily through its use by humans, and as falling properly under human dominion. People living in such a culture could be expected to be unconcerned about the general state of nature insofar as they would be oriented primarily toward its exploitation.

Social scientists have engaged in an extended discussion of the argument on three interrelated topics. The first of these concerns evidence of the relationship between Christian beliefs and environmental attitudes. The second concerns White's theological astuteness, whether the creation stories in Genesis actually support dominion over nature. Several scholars have argued that a proper interpretation of Genesis leaves room for a nurturant 'stewardship' element that is present in Genesis 2 (e.g. Shaiko, 1987). This then leads to the third issue, that of evidence for such a stewardship effect.

Note: Reprinted from *Journal for the Scientific Study of Religion*, vol 35, Eckberg, D. L. and Blocker, T. J., 'Christianity, environmentalism and the theoretical problem of fundamentalism', pp343–355, copyright © (1996), with permission from the Society for the Scientific Study of Religion

We believe that a strictly theological consideration of this matter is unwise. There are many conflicting Christian theologies. To postulate one or another as correct is to involve one in debates that lie outside the scope of social science expertise. Further, as a practical matter, White could be 'correct' even if his theology is faulty, or wrong even if correct theologically. It is possible that the presence of 'dominion' statements about nature in the introductory chapter of Genesis, under an interpretation that at one time was culturally dominant, could have real effects even if the actual theological situation were more balanced. On the other hand, the Genesis 2 stewardship account might orient Christians toward something of a nurturant stance on nature even if its author(s) actually leaned more toward mastery. We will, therefore, not engage in extended hermeneutics, but we will begin with the *nominal* expectation that there exists a dominion effect. We base this on the facts that the dominion account is earlier and more straightforward than the stewardship account, and even the latter is oriented toward manipulation of the land.

White's essay treated the dominion ethic as a macrolevel social fact with macro-level effects, but research on it relies extensively on surveys that implicitly treat it as an issue of the perceptions of *individuals*. This substitution causes difficulties. To follow Peter Berger's usage, culture is external to us as well as internal. Even if a dominion ethic is part of Christian culture, as White suggests, it might not manifest itself as an association among cognitions within individuals, especially not among members of the general public, whose level of theoretical interest is low (see Berger, 1967, pp30–32). A statistical link between scripture and an individual's social cognitions requires that two conditions be met. First, scriptural statements must have meaning for the individual. That is, they must be well known and be interpreted as having important explanatory or directive force. They must be more than just recited words. Second, the individual must be motivated to maintain consistency among cognitions.

In survey research on this topic, researchers have looked for associations between individual belief in the Bible, membership in an appropriate church, or belief in some relevant elements of theology, on the one hand, and environmental attitudes or (seldom) actions on the other. If either of the above conditions fails to hold, a statistical association will be attenuated. On the other hand, an association might exist for reasons *besides* the authority of the Bible on environmental issues. The researcher is not usually in a position to trace the exact lines of influence. Therefore, one must go beyond simple associations and generate hypotheses that are precisely related to the issue – and even then the matter may be subject to reasonable disagreement.

While survey researchers have not fully explored the ramifications of the problem, many have explored the topic. Available studies do find substantial, though not unequivocal, evidence for a scripture-dominion relationship. Hand and Van Liere (1984) found in a Washington State sample that Christians were less concerned about environmental issues than were others, and more likely to believe that humans should have mastery over nature. Among those in conservative Protestant and sectarian denominations, 'mastery over nature' was positively predicted by attendance, and this was independent of effects of several social background measures (see also Van Liere and Dunlap, 1980). In a test of Biblical effects, Eckberg and Blocker (1989) found direct effects of belief in the Bible on several indexes of environmental concerns in a sample from Tulsa, Oklahoma. Biblical belief suppressed environmental concern, though not greatly, on four different factor-based indexes.

Others have found at least some similar evidence, but not in all situations or not unambiguously. Woodrum and Hoban (1994) found no independent effects of religiosity measures on environmental concerns with a North Carolina sample. Shaiko (1987), Kanagy and Willits (1989), Guth et al (1993, 1995) and Greeley (1993) all found environmental effects in the postulated direction, but their results were complex, and they have offered different explanations of them.

Shaiko (1987), for example, found that Christian members of environmental organizations (as opposed to Jews and other non-Christians) more often expressed a mastery-over-nature orientation. On three of four measures of specific environmental concerns, he found some evidence of independent 'Christianity' effects that supports a dominion argument. However, he argued that the variety of findings pointed toward a stewardship effect as well.

Using General Social Survey data, Greeley (1993) found that an effect of Biblical belief on support of environmental spending could be attenuated by controlling other religious measures and a measure of political orientation. He argued that any Biblical 'effect' is simply spurious, stemming not from the Bible's treatment of nature but from 'a harsher system of narrative symbols' among fundamentalists – which he operationalized as the degree of 'graciousness' of the image of God – along with political conservatism and rigid morality (Greeley 1993, p20). However, Greeley demonstrated no effects of religious graciousness, and we see no a priori reason why religious harshness would be associated with a lack of concern about nature. Harshness could equally well be expressed as hostility toward polluters and despoilers.

His account of a role for political attitudes strikes us as plausible. He holds that since fundamentalists are disproportionately conservative politically they may be 'anti-green' because they see environmentalism as 'liberal'. Guth et al (1995) also discuss the interplay of religion and green politics, and we believe it is worthwhile to investigate the possible association.

Using a sizable Pennsylvania sample, Kanagy and Willits (1993) generally replicated the findings of the previous studies but discovered a unique *behavioural* effect of church attendance, namely, a slight, and independent, *positive* effect of church attendance on 'reported environmental behaviours'. Like Shaiko, they interpreted these mixed findings as evidence of *both* stewardship and dominion attitudes. However, as the modest effect of attendance was independent of effects of beliefs, its meaning is unclear. Derkson and Gartell (1993) found that simple 'easy access to a structured recycling programme' is generally more important than attitudes in predicting recycling activities. With this in mind, it is at least possible that there exists an attendance-access relationship in the Pennsylvania sample. It could also be the case that attendance and recycling are both measures of general activity in voluntary associations. In either case the relationship *might* be spurious.

Using a very large sample of members of diverse religious social action organizations, Guth and his colleagues (Guth, Kellstedt, Smidt and Green 1993; also see Guth, Green, Kellstedt and Smidt, 1995), have found substantial religious effects in directions predicted by White's thesis, effects that greatly outweigh those of standard social background measures. Ultimately, they conclude that there is a 'fundamentalism' effect on environmental attitudes that stems partly from Biblical literalism, but also from 'dispensationalist emphases on separation of Christians from the world and the proximity of End Times' (Guth et al, 1993, p381). This fundamentalism effect is similar to Greeley's

(1993) 'harshness' effect except that their data appear to document theological effects independently of general political orientation.

Concerning the attendance-recycling association mentioned above, Guth's team (1995) found a positive, independent effect of religious salience on policy-oriented environmental indexes in two of seven samples they employed. In their other paper (1993), they found a slight positive independent effect of 'revivalism', an index that includes a measure of attendance. These were not the major foci of the papers but they are nonetheless intriguing.

Limitations of Previous Research

White's essay did not deal with all aspects of Christian religiosity or all attitudes toward the environment, but was limited to creation theology and humanity's relationship to nature. Strictly speaking, the thesis would only lead us to expect direct relationships between measures of orthodoxy of beliefs and measures of dominion-like beliefs and on actions. One would *not* expect noncognitive measures of religiosity, for example religious attendance, to have effects independently of beliefs. Further, only *dominion* beliefs should be readily predicted by theological orthodoxy; nothing about White's essay would lead one to argue, for example, that orthodox Christians would be less concerned about environmental *hazards* than would others.

None of these studies has been able to address the issue fully. Hand and Van Liere, Shaiko, and Kanagy and Willits, for example, have no measures of religious beliefs at all. Shaiko's and some of Guth's samples come from action groups rather than the general population, raising the question of generalizability (but having the advantage of focusing on those who are most likely to seek theoretical consistency in their legitimations). Eckberg's and Blocker's indexes do not clearly measure dominion beliefs, but rather environmental concerns. Both Guth et al papers have limited measures of environmental attitudes and none of dominion attitudes. Greeley is limited to a single, three-option attitude item that confounds environmental 'concern' with attitudes toward governmental spending. Only Kanagy and Willits employ clear measures of behaviour or reported behaviour.

The 1993 General Social Survey as a Data Source

There now exists a data set that can overcome most of these problems, the 1993 General Social Survey (GSS). As is well known, the GSS is a national probability survey of non-institutionalized adults, administered most years since 1972 by the National Opinion Research Center (Davis and Smith, 1993). In 1993, for the first time, it included a battery of questions on environmental knowledge, beliefs and actions. Even if we exclude a series of questions that specifically tap knowledge of environmental matters (but include an environmental spending question that comes from outside the battery) the survey has 42 such items. This is a far larger number of environmental items than in any of the above studies, and it includes measures of dominion-like beliefs, environmental fears, policy orientations and reported actions.

The GSS has regularly included a number of questions on religious matters. The 1993 GSS is not as detailed in this area as in the past, and many religion items on the survey were asked of only about two-thirds of the sample. However, it does include several measures of religious belief (including Bible beliefs), action and affiliation. In addition, the GSS regularly includes measures of socio-economic status, of family background and so forth, that can be used to test the spuriousness or directness of effects. We therefore are in the position of being able to investigate effects of a variety of elements of religiosity on various environmental beliefs and reported actions. First, however, we must simplify our data set.

Environmental attitude and action indexes

In order to reduce the number of environmental items to a reasonable number we created indexes based on item wording and scoring. We employed only those items that obtained reasonable correlations with their fellows, and used principal components analysis with Varimax rotation to confirm the factorial nature of the indexes. In all, we employed all but four of the environmental attitude and action items, in ten indexes. Alpha coefficients vary substantially among the indexes and some – notably indexes measuring participation in organized environmental activity and belief in the sacredness of nature – are quite low. Nonetheless they allow us to explore several aspects of environmental belief, attitudes and (reported) actions.[2]

One index measures dominion-like beliefs, in that it contrasts concern for the environment with concern for the economy. Four indexes measure a wide range of action or policy orientations: performing personal pro-environment activities like recycling, taking part in organized pro-environmental activities, being willing to pay an economic price to protect nature, and approving pro-environment governmental regulation of business and individual behaviours. In addition, we have an index of 'green' lifestyle – defined by such behaviours as eating organic produce, being a vegetarian, and restricting one's driving – that seems to extend the measures of action orientation in a New Age direction. The action items contain an option to be checked if the respondent is unable to take the stated action, so that responses do not suffer the 'availability' problem that Kanagy and Willits may have faced.

Two indexes may possibly tap a stewardship dimension, one that asks degree of belief in animal rights and one that measures the extent of belief that nature is sacred because it was created by God. We are not convinced of the degree of 'stewardship' in either measure. The animal rights movement is highly politically charged, with clear 'liberal' and New Age identification. Also, a stewardship orientation would *not* necessarily lead to a belief in animal rights so much as to a belief that animals should not be unnecessarily harmed. The 'sacredness' of nature is measured by two items that explicitly tie that sacredness to God; they appear to us to be leading questions that might simply signify a nominal respect for a Supreme Being.

Finally, there are indexes that appear on their face *not* to measure dominion *or* stewardship. One of these measures the general belief that human actions will harm nature; the other measures the extent of fear of the effects of various forms of pollution.

Background items and indexes

The GSS contains measures of many phenomena that may affect environmental attitudes. We use 4 measures of knowledge (besides years of education, which is confounded by socialization experiences and is also a social class measure), 17 measures of religious affiliation, culture, practice and belief, and 4 measures of social status. In addition, we employ standard background items: sex, race, age and political orientation.

The original GSS sample was 1606, but NORC employed a split-sample technique, so that not everyone was asked every question. Forty-nine respondents were not asked environmental questions and about a third were not asked religion questions or some of the other background items. Deleting these cases leaves us a sample of 1046.

Knowledge

A respondent's general level of knowledge, especially of environmental issues, may affect stances on those issues. The data set includes four types of measures of knowledge: tests of environmental and scientific knowledge, a vocabulary test, and the interviewer's subjective evaluation of the respondent's comprehension of the survey materials. The measures predict environmental beliefs and attitudes similarly and are moderately correlated. Principal-components analysis of the four measures yielded a one-factor solution, so we reduced each item to a scale of 0-to-1 and summed them to form an index of knowledge (alpha = 0.707).

Social class

We have four measures of social class: years of education, occupational prestige, whether one is a professional, and family income. Again, principal components analysis yielded a one-factor solution so we formed an index of class in the same fashion as with knowledge (alpha = 0.766).

Religion

There are 17 measures of religion/religiosity, including 5 measures of aspects of association, 2 measures of religious activity, and several measures of belief. There are scores on a version of Greeley's (1993) Grace Scale, and on belief in the power of God in the world. Finally, there are 4 measures of religious culture and affect. We use this wide variety of religion items because of the large number of possible religious effects and because of limitations of reliability and validity that plague single-item measures. Inclusion of a sufficiently large set of items allows us to use empirically determined associations to construct indexes. Indeed, principal-components analysis of the set of items yielded a three-factor solution that was readily interpretable after Varimax rotation. We used the results to create indexes of religiosity, excluding items with weaker secondary loadings.[3]

The first index we judge to measure degree of religious *sectarianism,* in that a high score indicates that the person believes the Bible to be true literally, scores low on Greeley's Grace Scale, believes strongly in obedience, is a conservative Protestant, opposes the ban on school prayer, disbelieves in evolution, believes that God is involved in everyday activities, and enjoys gospel music. The second measures fairly *common religiosity* of the 'salt of the earth' variety. It does not tap specific theological underpinnings, but a high score indicates that the person believes in an afterlife, believes in God, believes that faith is very important, prays frequently, and is a Christian. The third index taps level of *participation* in religious organizations. One with a high score belongs to church-related organizations, attends religious services regularly, has faith in religious institutions, and strongly identifies with his or her denomination.[3]

Plan of Analysis

We will first explore zero-order correlations between each religion item (and religion index) and each environmental index. This will give us a first look at which indexes predict which environmental attitudes and actions, as well as which items (if any), provide the bulk of predictive power within each index. Then we will use OLS regression to determine direct effects of the religion indexes. Because of the ease of obtaining significance with large samples, we nominally employ a probability level of 0.01, or an R^2 of 1 per cent, for determination of 'significant' effects. We will note coefficients that fall close to those figures (i.e. $P < 0.02$).

Findings

Zero-order correlations between the various measures of religiosity and scores on the environmentalism indexes are shown in Table 10.1. They support the dominion account in places, though the exceptions demand discussion.

Actions and policy orientations

We will focus first on correlations with scores on the first five indexes, which measure environmental actions or policy orientations. These substantially support the dominion hypothesis. The number of significant relationships varies with the topic, more for personal or organized actions and fewer for policy orientations or green lifestyle, but almost all are in the expected direction. For example, correlations between items forming the sectarianism index and scores on the personal action index are negative, except for the item measuring belief in evolution and scores on the Grace Scale, which are positive. The more traditional or orthodox the belief the less actively 'green' one is likely to be.

Likewise, correlations are stronger for sectarianism items, less so for common religiosity, and insignificant for religious participation. Beliefs are much more important than are common religiosity or religious participation. Two measures of common religiosity, belief in God and belief in the importance of faith, obtain correlations similar to those of items in the sectarianism index; both had, however, obtained secondary loadings on sectarianism. Breaking the trend, frequency of prayer positively predicts cultural greenness (albeit weakly) and does not negatively predict scores on any action index. Also, while being Christian tends to predict nonparticipation in environmental actions, being in a conservative (fundamentalist) church is clearly more important.

There is less complexity if we focus entirely on correlations between environmental action indexes and the religiosity *indexes*. Religious sectarianism is negatively correlated with everything except having a green lifestyle. Common religiosity is negatively

Table 10.1 *Zero-order correlations between religion item/index scores and environmental index scores (Pearson's r)*

	Personal actions	Organized actions	Will bear costs	Approves govt. rule	Cultural 'green'
Belief: Bible	−0.22***	−0.11**	−0.12***	−0.11**	−0.01
Values obedience	−0.23***	−0.08+	−0.05	−0.09*	0.04
Fundamentalist	−0.22***	−0.07	−0.11**	−0.09*	−0.08*
Opposes prayer ban	−0.18***	−0.09*	−0.09*	−0.07+	−0.06
Belief: Evolution	0.19***	0.16***	0.16***	0.16***	0.09*
God is powerful	−0.21***	−0.08*	−0.05	−0.08*	0.03
Likes gospel music	−0.12***	−0.02	−0.05	−0.08+	0.09*
Grace Scale	0.09*	0.05	0.07	−0.02	0.12***
Sectarianism Index	−0.32***	−0.14***	−0.15***	−0.15***	−0.04
Belief: Afterlife	0.03	0.03	0.03	−0.00	0.06
Belief: God	−0.20***	−0.11**	−0.13***	−0.08+	−0.05
Faith is important	−0.17***	−0.08+	−0.07	−0.08*	0.05
Freq. of prayer	−0.05	−0.02	−0.05	−0.07	0.11**
Christian	−0.11**	−0.07	−0.10*	−0.07	−0.04
Common Relig. Index	−0.14***	−0.07	−0.09*	−0.08+	0.03
Church org. member	0.04	0.06	0.01	0.01	0.04
Freq. of attendance	−0.03	−0.03	−0.03	0.01	0.05
Religious salience	−0.04	−0.02	−0.04	−0.04	0.07
Faith in clergy	−0.03	−0.06	−0.04	−0.01	0.01
Participation Index	−0.02	−0.01	−0.03	−0.01	0.06
	Economy central	Hurts nature	Environ. fears	Animal rights	Nature sacred
Belief: Bible	0.24***	0.12***	0.02	0.08+	0.37***
Values obedience	0.27***	0.13***	−0.04	0.04	0.19***
Fundamentalist	0.18***	0.08+	−0.04	0.02	0.21***
Opposes prayer ban	0.23***	0.11**	−0.03	0.03	0.22***
Belief: Evolution	−0.16***	−0.01	0.06	0.07	−0.27***
God is powerful	0.21***	0.18***	0.05	0.13***	0.39***
Likes gospel music	0.21***	0.10*	0.02	0.04	0.27***
Grace Scale	−0.07	−0.04	−0.00	0.08+	−0.11**
Sectarianism Index	0.34***	0.17***	−0.02	0.05	0.43***
Belief: Afterlife	−0.02	−0.02	0.01	−0.03	0.21***
Belief: God	0.20***	0.06	0.01	0.01	0.42***

Table 10.1 (Continued) *Zero-order correlations between religion item/index scores and environmental index scores (Pearson's r)*

	Economy central	Hurts nature	Environ. fears	Animal rights	Nature sacred
Faith is important	0.20***	0.08+	0.06	0.07+	0.48***
Freq. of prayer	0.14***	0.06	0.07	0.02	0.33***
Christian	0.16***	0.01	–0.06	–0.03	0.24***
Common Relig. Index	0.18***	0.05	0.02	0.01	0.46***
Church org. member	0.03	0.02	0.00	–0.10**	0.13***
Freq. of attendance	0.10*	–0.01	–0.01	–0.10*	0.26***
Religious salience	0.14***	0.03	0.00	–0.04	0.29***
Faith in clergy	0.08+	0.01	–0.02	–0.04	0.10**
Participation Index	0.12***	0.02	–0.00	–0.10**	0.28***

N = 1046; mean substitution is used for missing values.
+P < 0.02, *P < 0.01, **P < 0.001, ***P < 0.0001

correlated only with personal actions, and religious participation is correlated with nothing at all.

General orientations

The index that most closely – but not exactly – fits a dominion orientation is the one that considers economic activity as more important than (or even helpful to) the environment. Most items have significant correlations to this, all in the hypothesized direction. All three factor-based indexes of religiosity are correlated with it as well, but the correlation with the sectarianism index has a substantially greater magnitude than do those of the other two indexes.

Everything correlates with the judgement that nature is sacred, and the correlations are, for the most part, the largest. The pattern of correlations is similar to those just discussed, and they raise a problem with interpretation of the meaning of the index. Namely, the religion items that are negatively correlated with pro-environment actions or policy orientations, and are positively associated with ranking the economy as more important than nature, are positively correlated with belief in the sacredness of nature, while those (like belief in evolution or the Grace Scale) that break the pattern are negatively correlated here. Clearly, a stated belief in the sacredness of nature is not associated with any 'pro-nature' actions; quite the *reverse* is true. Because of this, we do not feel confident in assigning to the index any meaning other than a general statement about the grandeur of the Creator.

We find few measures with significant associations to the animal rights index, with no clear pattern. As mentioned above, we did not expect to find substantial associations. Among the indexes of religiosity, only the index of religious participation obtains a significant correlation, a negative one. People who are religiously active are less likely than others to support animal rights, but this is unrelated to religious beliefs.

As we expected, there are no religious correlates with the index measuring worries about pollution. Six of the seven measures that make up the sectarianism index are positively correlated with the belief that human activity is inherently harmful – a sentiment that fits the generally pessimistic beliefs that evangelicals hold about human beings (Wilcox, Linzey and Jelen, 1991). The sectarianism index itself likewise, and unsurprisingly, obtains a positive correlation. The other indexes do not.

Direct religious effects

We now regress the environmentalism indexes across the religion indexes and the measure of knowledge, social class, age, sex, race and political conservatism. This does not allow us to tease out all religious (or other) effects, but by finding direct effects it does let us determine if any religious factors have fundamental effects on environmental actions or attitudes, and it allows us to determine the amount of variance added to explanatory models by the set of religion indexes.

In addition to the findings presented in Table 10.2, we will discuss important associations that emerged in preliminary regression runs in which individual religion items (rather than indexes) were employed. The general set of effects $(R^2, $ etc.) is similar, but this will allow us to focus on some of the most important associations.

We begin with housecleaning, focusing on weak or irrelevant relationships. Note first that the measures of religion add less than one per cent of variance to equations for six of the ten environmental indexes. There are no significant associations and little variance explained for either of the environmental indexes that seem irrelevant to expectations derived from the Lynn White Thesis: those measuring environmental fears and the belief that humans harm nature. Like the famous dog that did not bark in the night, this seems meaningful. Religiosity does not predict simply everything about environmental concerns.

Contrariwise, the religion indexes explain a large amount of variance of the index addressing the sacredness of nature. Recall that we believed scores on the index might be artifacts of direct references to God. Our belief finds support in that preliminary regression runs employing religion *items* found only three items to reach 0.01 significance: ranking faith in God as very important in life (beta = 0.23), believing in God (beta = 0.11) and believing that God is responsible for many outcomes in life (beta = 0.10).

Direct effects on environmental actions and policy orientations

These five indexes that assess environmental actions and policy orientations provide a mix of provocative associations. First only twice, with the indexes of 'personal actions' and 'cultural greenness', is as much as one per cent of variance explained. Religious differences do not account for *much* variance in scores. Indeed, they are utterly without predictive power in the equations predicting willingness to bear environmental costs and approving governmental environmental controls, though we would expect *some* religious effect here.

Still, being sectarian does predict against participating in personal or organized environmental actions or being culturally green. Even here, though, we should note that the effect does not occur through level of belief in the Bible. In regression runs using

Table 10.2 *Regression of environmental index scores across religious index scores (standardized coefficients)*

	Personal actions	Organized actions	Will bear costs	Approves govt. rule	Cultural 'green'
Sectarianism	−0.20***	−0.12*	−0.07	−0.09	−0.13*
Common Religiosity	0.00	0.00	−0.00	−0.01	0.05
Religiously Active	0.11*	0.08	0.04	0.06	0.19+
Adjusted RSQ	22.60%	3.43%	5.18%	5.51%	5.13%
Adjusted RSQ Added	2.40%	0.76%	0.08%	0.34%	1.06%
	Economy central	Hurts nature	Environ. fears	Animal rights	Nature sacred
Sectarianism	0.20***	0.09	−0.07	−0.01	0.17***
Common Religiosity	−0.00	−0.06	0.04	0.03	0.33***
Religiously Active	−0.01	0.02	0.03	−0.11*	0.05
Adjusted RSQ	21.40%	10.76%	9.34%	14.14%	30.16%
Adjusted RSQ Added	2.56%	0.22%	0.11%	0.62%	18.45%

N = 1046; mean substitution is used for missing values. Items controlled are indexes of knowledge and social class, and measures of sex, age, race and political conservatism.
+ $P < 0.02$, *$P < 0.01$, **$P < 0.001$, ***$P < 0.0001$

individual religion items, belief in the Bible had no direct effect on *any* environmental index. This fails to replicate the major finding of Eckberg and Blocker (1989). It does not necessarily mean that orthodox theology plays no role at all, because in the same regression equations belief in human evolution *consistently* predicted scores for the action indexes, even those measuring willingness to bear environmental costs and approving governmental environmental controls (beta = 0.08 to 0.15). That is, disbelief in human evolution, which is conceptually tied to the creation myth in Genesis 1–2, has independent, negative – but again weak – effects on environmental action.

We find weak but positive effects of religious participation on personal environmental action and on cultural greenness, the first of which replicates the findings of Kanagy and Willits (1993) and Guth et al (1993, 1995) and offers some challenges to the dominion thesis. Again, regression equations using individual religion items found frequency of prayer to weakly predict personal pro-environmental actions (beta = 0.10) while being a church organization member positively predicted taking part in organized actions (beta = 0.10).

Environmental beliefs

Only sectarianism predicts belief that economic activity is more important than the environment. In preliminary runs, two items, both of which are part of cultural fundamentalism, maintained independent effects: support for obedience (beta = 0.10) and opposition to the banning of organized prayer in schools (beta = 0.08). These give some support to Greeley's (1993) contention that the harshness of religious symbols plays a role here, but it must be noted that the obedience item had no other independent effects and the Grace Scale had no independent effects at all (and few zero-order correlations). On this index, belief in evolution lost its independent effect, replicating a finding of Woodrum and Hoban (1994).

Turning to the animal rights index, about which we had some questions, only religious activity (negatively) predicts belief in animal rights. In runs using individual items, belief in evolution had a positive direct effect (beta = 0.10) but sentiment that faith in God is very important in life did also (beta = 0.13). We infer from the first effect that people with a Darwinian perspective are more likely to consider people to be part of, rather than above, nature, a position diametrically opposed to the dominion stance in Genesis 1. The second effect, however, may indicate a positive religious effect on environmentalism, though again it is independent of theology.

Discussion

While we have numerous findings, they can be easily summarized. They cannot be as readily explained. With a representative national sample, a large variety of measures of environmental attitudes and actions, and several measures of religious attitudes and behaviour, we have replicated the bulk of earlier findings. First, though we could not support Eckberg and Blocker's (1989) finding of consistent effects of biblical belief on environmental orientations per se, we did find consistent effects of anti-evolution beliefs, which are based on Genesis 1, on several measures of action and policy orientation. Like Guth et al (1993, 1995), we found a larger 'fundamentalism' (we called it 'sectarian') effect on environmental behaviours and attitudes. Like Kanagy and Willits (1993) and Guth et al (1993, 1995), we found positive behavioural effects of religious participation. We find common religiosity to be utterly unimportant in environmental issues. But is there a common thread to these findings?

One possibility – the one that several people have proposed – is that there indeed are contrasting dominion and stewardship effects of Christian theology. Dominion receives some support. A problem with stewardship is that we find no pro-environmentalism effects of Christian *beliefs*; none of our measures of orthodox religious belief shows effects consistent with environmentalism on any index in which we can have confidence. Yet the effect of participation, though limited, appears real, and this is the fourth study to find something like it. When Guth et al (1995, p14) found such an effect they dismissed it as representing 'perhaps, only an institutionally disconnected New Age environmental spirituality'. That could be true, but our salience item specifically mentions denominational affiliation, and we find effects for frequency of prayer and belief that faith in God is important as well. It is plausible that these tap a different element of religious consciousness than one finds in standard measures of belief, one that is characterized by an ethic of responsibility, or perhaps they just tap a propensity to be become 'involved'. In support of this position, we note that church attendance has effects on secular activities much more among those in nonconservative denominations (who are more likely to be pro-environmental) than in conservative ones (see Wilson and Janoski, 1995).

From the original questions that motivated this research, however, two things are certain: we do *not* find stewardship effects of theology, and we do find *some* evidence that points toward dominion effects of theology. If we accept this, then the only question is whether dominion attitudes come from acceptance of Genesis 1, or if there are different (or additional) Biblical roots, as Guth et al suggest. All the 'sectarian' items we employ load onto a single factor and may represent a single orientation; in any event, disentangling Biblical effects cannot be done readily with the present data.

There is, however, the other solution to the religion–environment connection, which is at least implicit in the work of several others (e.g. Weigel, 1977; Greeley, 1993; Guth et al, 1993, 1995; Woodrum and Hoban, 1994). Is it possible that the effect has no Biblical roots at all? This solution suggests that dominion attitudes are fundamentalist or sectarian *instead* of Biblical. Something about religious sectarianism subverts environmentalism. This would account for the ubiquitous fundamentalism effect and could leave room for the positive effect of religious participation on environmental activities. It would also explain why we find *independent* effects of fundamentalist affiliation that do not clearly flow from the dominion hypothesis and why belief in the Bible has no *independent* effects. It would, however, leave open the question of why fundamentalists would take specifically anti-green positions relative to everyone else and independent of background measures. What would make them special on *this* issue?

Greeley's position on the matter does not get much support. He contends that the religion-environmental connection is produced by the trio of religious graciousness or harshness, moral rigidity and conservative politics. We find a direct effect of moral rigidity on one environmental index, and it has a high loading in our principal components analysis. But the Grace Scale shows no independent effects and even fewer significant zero-order associations. All of the relationships in our regression models, further, are independent of effects of political orientation. In data not shown, we repeated our runs without the measure of political orientation. Patterns were almost identical to those reported here. In sum, religious graciousness has little impact on environmental beliefs or actions and religious effects are almost unrelated to general political views. Let us then focus on another church-related issue.

According to our data, those who actively work to protect nature or live in harmony with it tend to be religiously active and nonsectarian. That is, they are active in nonfundamentalist churches and other religious organizations, tend to be nonliteralists on the Bible, to favour free thinking, and to be culturally and religiously nontraditional. Clearly, these are religious liberals, in the US mostly members of the 'Christian Left'.

Active conflict between the religious right and left, between the 'culture of fundamentalism' and the 'culture of modernism', has been a paramount religious issue the past two decades (e.g. Page and Clelland, 1978), to the point of being characterized as 'culture wars' (Hunter, 1991). Religious conservatives are well aware of the liberal 'bias' of environmentalism. Indeed, conservative churches sometimes are suspicious of it (see the discussion in Guth et al, 1995). With theology so intertwined with politics in the present climate, any strictly theological effects on environmentalism could be overwhelmed by the sides-choosing of the moment. The fundamentalism effect could grow from hostility toward religious liberalism as well as from religious dogma. In this scenario, the various measures of sectarianism stand together because each is an indicator of internal solidarity during a time of external conflict.

We cannot at this time nail down the source of the effect of fundamentalism. It could come about because of dominion statements in Genesis 1 (or other powerful religious concepts like end-times theology). It could also be that morality, Biblical inerrancy and 'greenness' have all become politicized, serve as symbols of the two sides in the culture wars and *therefore* are statistically linked in survey research. Disentangling these possibilities will be a difficult task indeed.

Notes

We are indebted to Eric Woodrum, Andrew Greeley and Jim Guth for generous commentaries, suggestions and copies of work in progress, and to the anonymous reviewers.

1   Strictly speaking, White's thesis applies to all Judaeo-Christian theology, and so should apply to Jews as well as Christians. However, White focuses on Christianity. Further, as a practical matter, in the United States, Christians outnumber Jews by almost 50 to 1, and so their beliefs are for the most part of interest to us.

2   The 10 environment indexes are as follows. Item scoring is adjusted so that high scores represent agreement with the sentiment in the index title. Exact wording can be found in Davis and Smith (1993).

   (1) *Engages in Personal 'Green' Activities.* Four items: (a) how often do you recycle, (b) do you do 'what is right for the environment', even if it costs money or takes up time, (c) is it too difficult for you to do much about the environment, (d) have you ever signed a petition about an environmental issue? (alpha = 0.527)

   (2) *Participates in Organized 'Green' Activities.* Two items: (a) are you a member of any environmental group, (b) have you participated in a demonstration on an environmental issue? (alpha = 0.392)

   (3) *Culturally 'Green'.* Three items: (a) how often do you eat organic fruits and vegetables, (b) how often do you refuse to eat meat, (c) how often do you cut back on driving a car for environmental reasons? (alpha = 0.564)

   (4) *Is Willing to Bear Costs to Protect the Environment.* Three items: are you willing to (a) pay much higher prices, (b) pay much higher taxes, and (c) have a lower standard of living to protect the environment? (alpha = 0.833)

   (5) *Approves Government Regulation to Protect the Environment.* Two items: should the government make (a) people, (b) businesses protect the environment? (alpha = 0.642)

   (6) *Believes All Human Actions Hurt Nature.* Three items: (a) Any human change in nature – no matter how scientific – is likely to make things worse, (b) almost everything we do in modern life harms the environment, (c) economic growth always harms the environment. (alpha = 0.587)

   (7) *Believes Humans Take Precedence over the Environment.* Four items: (a) modern science will solve our environmental problems with little change in our way of life, (b) we worry too much about the environment and not enough about prices and jobs, (c) people worry too much about human progress harming the

environment, (d) in order to protect the environment, America needs economic growth. (alpha = 0.589)

(8) *Worries about Pollution.* Seven items: (a) air pollution caused by cars, (b) nuclear power stations, (c) air pollution caused by industry, (d) pesticides and chemicals used in farming, (e) pollution of waterways, or (f) the 'greenhouse' effect, are dangerous: *(i)* in general, *(ii)* for you and your family? (g) Will auto air pollution cause a large increase in ill health? (alpha = 0.910)

(9) *Believes in Animal Rights.* Three items: (a) Animals should have the same moral rights as humans, (b) It is right to use animals for medical testing, (c) Nature would be at peace and harmony if only humans would leave it alone. (alpha = 0.527)

(10)*Considers Nature Is Sacred.* Two items: (a) Nature is sacred because it was created by God, (b) Human beings should respect nature because it was created by God. (alpha = 0.459)

3   The three religiosity indexes are as follows. Item scoring is adjusted so that high scores represent agreement with the sentiment in the index title. Exact wording can be found in Davis and Smith (1993).

(1) *Sectarianism.* Eight items: (a) degree of belief in the Bible, (b) moral rigidity, (c) GSS items coding one a fundamentalist Protestant, (d) opposition to the banning of prayer in public schools, (e) belief in evolution, (f) belief that God controls many important events in life, (g) enjoys gospel music, and (h) a composite measure of religious 'graciousness'. (alpha = 0.732)

(2) *Common Religiosity.* Five items: (a) belief in an afterlife, (b) sentiment that belief in God is among most important traits in a friend, (c) belief in God, (d) frequency of prayer, and (e) being Christian. (alpha = 0.761)

(3) *Religious Participation.* Four items: (a) membership in church-related organizations, (b) frequency of attendance at religious services, (c) salience of religious beliefs, and (d) has faith in organized religion. (alpha = 0.673)

References

1   Berger, P. (1967) *The Sacred Canopy: Elements of a Sociological Theory of Religion.* Doubleday, Garden City, NY
2   Davis, J. A. and Smith, T. W. (1993) General Social Surveys, 1972–1993 [machine-readable data file]. National Opinion Research Center, Chicago
3   Derksen, L. and Gartell, J. (1993) 'The social context of recycling'. *American Sociological Review,* vol 58, pp434–42
4   Eckberg, D. L. and Blocker, T. J. (1989) 'Varieties of religious involvement and environmental concern'. *Journal for the Scientific Study of Religion,* vol 28, pp509–517
5   Greeley, A. (1993) 'Religion and attitudes toward the environment'. *Journal for the Scientific Study of Religion,* vol 32, pp19–28
6   Guth, J. L., Green, J. C., Kellstedt, L. A. and. Smidt, C. E (1995) 'Faith and the environment: religious beliefs and attitudes on environmental policy'. *American Journal of Political Science,* vol 39, pp364–382

7   Guth, J. L., Kellstedt, L. A., Smidt, C. E. and Green, J. C. (1993) 'Theological perspectives and environmentalism among religious activists'. *Journal for the Scientific Study of Religion*, vol 32, pp373–382

8   Hand, C. and Van Liere, K. (1984) 'Religion, mastery-over-nature, and environmental concern'. *Social Forces*, vol 63, pp555–570

9   Hunter, J. D. (1991) *Culture Wars: The Struggle to Define America*. Basic Books, New York

10 Kanagy, C. L. and Willits, F. K. (1993) 'A "greening" of religion?' *Social Science Quarterly*, vol 74, pp674–683

11 Page, A. L. and Clelland, D. A. (1978) 'The Kanawha County textbook controversy'. *Social Forces*, vol 57, pp265–281

12 Shaiko, R. G. (1987) 'Religion, politics and environmental concern'. *Social Science Quarterly*, vol 68, pp244–262

13 Van Liere, K. and. Dunlap, R. E (1980) 'The social bases of environmental concern'. *Public Opinion Quarterly*, vol 44, pp181–197

14 Weigel, R. H. (1977) 'Ideological and demographic correlates of proecology behaviour'. *Journal of Social Psychology*, vol 103, pp39–47

15 White, L. (1967) 'The historical roots of our ecological crisis'. *Science*, vol 155, pp1203–1207

16 Wilcox, C., Linzey, S. and Jelen, T. (1991) 'Reluctant warriors: Premillennialism and politics in the Moral Majority'. *Journal for the Scientific Study of Religion*, vol 30, pp245–258

17 Wilson, J. and Janoski, T. (1995) 'The contribution of religion to volunteer work'. *Sociology of Religion*, vol 56, pp137–152

18 Woodrum, E. and Hoban, T. (1994) 'Theology and religiosity effects on environmentalism'. *Review of Religious Research*, vol 35, pp193–206

11

Measuring Endorsement of the New Ecological Paradigm: A Revised NEP Scale

Riley E. Dunlap, Kent D. Van Liere, Angela G. Mertig and Robert Emmet Jones

Dunlap and Van Liere's New Environmental Paradigm (NEP) Scale, published in 1978, has become a widely used measure of pro-environmental orientation. This article develops a revised NEP Scale designed to improve upon the original one in several respects: (1) It taps a wider range of facets of an ecological worldview, (2) It offers a balanced set of pro- and anti-NEP items, and (3) It avoids outmoded terminology. The new scale, termed the New Ecological Paradigm Scale, consists of 15 items. Results of a 1990 Washington State survey suggest that the items can be treated as an internally consistent summated rating scale and also indicate a modest growth in pro-NEP responses among Washington residents over the 14 years since the original study.

When environmental issues achieved a prominent position on our nation's policy agenda in the 1970s, the major problems receiving attention tended to be air and water pollution, loss of aesthetic values, and resource (especially energy) conservation. Consequently, attempts to measure public concern for environmental quality, or 'environmental concern', focused primarily on such conditions (e.g. Weigel and Weigel, 1978). In recent decades, however, environmental problems have evolved in significant ways. Although localized pollution, especially hazardous waste, continues to be a major issue, environmental problems have generally tended to become more geographically dispersed, less directly observable and more ambiguous in origin. Not only do problems such as ozone depletion, deforestation, loss of biodiversity and climate change cover far wider geographical areas (often reaching the global level), but their causes are complex and synergistic and their solutions complicated and problematic (Stern et al, 1992). Researchers interested in understanding how the public sees environmental problems are gradually paying attention to these newly emerging 'attitude objects' (Stern et al, 1995b), and the number of studies of public perceptions of issues such as global warming is slowly mounting (Dunlap, 1998; O'Connor et al, 1999).

The emergence of global environmental problems as major policy issues symbolizes the growing awareness of the problematic relationship between modern industrialized

Note: Reprinted from *Journal of Social Issues*, vol 56, Dunlap, R. E., Van Liere, K., Mertig, A. and Jones, R. E., 'Measuring endorsement of the New Ecological Paradigm: A revised NEP scale', pp425–442, copyright © (2000), with permission from Blackwell Publishing

societies and the physical environments on which they depend (Stern et al, 1992). Recognition that human activities are altering the ecosystems on which our existence – and that of all other living species – is dependent and growing acknowledgement of the necessity of achieving more sustainable forms of development give credence to suggestions that we are in the midst of a fundamental reevaluation of the underlying worldview that has guided our relationship to the physical environment (e.g. Milbrath, 1984). In particular, suggestions that a more ecologically sound worldview is emerging have gained credibility in the past decade (e.g. Olsen et al, 1992).

In this context, it is not surprising to see that traditional measures of 'environmental concern' are being supplanted by instruments seeking to measure 'ecological consciousness' (Ellis and Thompson, 1997), 'anthropocentrism' (Chandler and Dreger, 1993), and 'anthropocentrism versus ecocentrism' (Thompson and Barton, 1994). The purpose of this article is to provide a revision of the earliest such measure of endorsement of an ecological worldview, the New Environmental Paradigm Scale (Dunlap and Van Liere, 1978).

The New *Environmental* Paradigm Scale

Development of the Scale

Sensing that environmentalists were calling for more far-reaching changes than the development of environmental protection policies and stimulated by Pirages and Ehrlich's (1974) explication of the anti-environmental thrust of our society's dominant social paradigm (DSP), in the mid-1970s Dunlap and Van Liere argued that implicit within environmentalism was a challenge to our fundamental views about nature and humans' relationship to it. Their conceptualization of what they called the New Environmental Paradigm (NEP) focused on beliefs about humanity's ability to upset the balance of nature, the existence of limits to growth for human societies, and humanity's right to rule over the rest of nature. In a 1976 Washington State study Dunlap and Van Liere (1978) found that a set of 12 Likert items measuring these three facets of the new social paradigm or worldview exhibited a good deal of internal consistency (coefficient alpha of 0.81), and strongly discriminated between known environmentalists and the general public. Consequently, they argued that the items could legitimately be treated as a New Environmental Paradigm Scale, and found that endorsement of the NEP was, as expected, negatively related to endorsement of the DSP (Dunlap and Van Liere, 1984). [Dunlap and Van Liere later developed a six-item NEP Scale for use in a national survey for the Continental Group (1982) that has subsequently been used by several researchers, particularly political scientists (Pierce et al, 1992).]

Drawing upon a spate of literature in the late 1970s and early 1980s that explicated more fully the contrast between the emerging environmental paradigm and the dominant social paradigm (e.g. Brown, 1981), subsequent researchers provided far more comprehensive conceptualizations of the NEP and DSP (Cotgrove, 1982; Milbrath, 1984; Olsen et al, 1992). However, their elaborate measuring instruments, encompassing a wide range of both beliefs and values, have proven unwieldy, and the NEP Scale has become the far more widely used measure of an environmental or, as now seems the more appropriate label, 'ecological' worldview. Also, because the emergence of global environmental change has made items like 'The balance of nature is very delicate and easily upset' more relevant now than in the 1970s, and because alternative measures of environmental concern widely used in the 1970s and early 1980s focusing on specific types of environmental problems have become dated (e.g. Weigel and Weigel, 1978), the NEP Scale has also become a popular measure of environmental concern, with endorsement of the NEP treated as reflecting a pro-environmental orientation.

The fact that the NEP Scale is treated as a measure of endorsement of a fundamental paradigm or worldview, as well as of environmental attitudes, beliefs and even values, reflects the ambiguity inherent in measuring these phenomena as well as Dunlap and Van Liere's failure to ground the NEP in social-psychological theories of attitude structure (Stern et al, 1995a). Although attitude theory cautions against categorizing individual items as clear-cut indicators of attitudes *or* beliefs (see e.g. Eagly and Kulesa, 1997), in retrospect it nonetheless seems reasonable to argue that the NEP items primarily tap 'primitive beliefs' about the nature of the earth and humanity's relationship with it. According to Rokeach (1968, p6), primitive beliefs form the inner core of a person's belief system and 'represent his "basic truths" about physical reality, social reality and the nature of the self'. Though not as foundational as the examples used by Rokeach, beliefs about nature and humans' role in it as measured by the NEP items appear to constitute a fundamental component of people's belief systems vis-à-vis the environment.

Social psychologists see these primitive beliefs as influencing a wide range of beliefs and attitudes concerning more specific environmental issues (see Gray, 1985, Chapter 2, and Stern et al, 1995a, for two alternative but complementary models incorporating the NEP as a measure of primitive beliefs). Similarly, political scientists find the NEP beliefs to be a core element in comprehensive environmental belief systems (Pierce et al, 1987; Dalton et al, 1999). A consensus that the NEP items measure such beliefs (Edgell and Nowell, 1989; Gooch, 1995) is emerging, and it seems reasonable to regard a coherent set of these beliefs as constituting a paradigm or worldview that influences attitudes and beliefs toward more specific environmental issues (Dalton et al, 1999). In short, a pro-ecological orientation or 'seeing the world ecologically', reflected by a high score on the NEP Scale, should lead to proenvironmental beliefs and attitudes on a wide range of issues (Stern et al, 1995a; Pierce et al, 1999). Although such beliefs may also influence behaviour, the barriers and opportunities that influence pro-environmental behaviours in specific situations caution against expecting a strong NEP-behaviour relationship (Gardner and Stern, 1996).

Past research and validity of the NEP Scale

Although treated variously as measuring environmental attitudes, beliefs, values and worldview, the NEP Scale has been widely used during the past two decades. It has been used most often with samples of the general public, but it has also been used with samples of specific sectors such as farmers (Albrecht et al, 1982) and members of interest groups (e.g. Edgell and Nowell, 1989; Pierce et al, 1992). It has been used as well to examine the environmental orientations of ethnic minorities in the US (e.g. Caron, 1989; Noe and Snow, 1989–1990) as well as of residents of other nations such as Canada (Edgell and Nowell, 1989), Sweden (Widegren, 1998), the Baltic states (Gooch, 1995),

Turkey (Furman, 1998) and Japan (Pierce et al, 1987). Finally, it has recently been used to compare the environmental orientations of college students in several Latin American nations and Spain with those of American students (Schultz and Zelezny, 1998; Bechtel et al, 1999). In general, these studies have found, as did Dunlap and Van Liere (1978) in their 1976 Washington State survey, a relatively strong endorsement of NEP beliefs across the various samples.

Rather than attempt to summarize the dozens of studies that have employed the NEP items, we will cite selected findings that bear on the validity of the NEP Scale. As noted previously, studies of interest groups such as environmental organizations have consistently found that environmentalists score higher on the NEP Scale than do the general public or members of nonenvironmental interest groups (e.g. Edgell and Nowell, 1989; Pierce et al, 1992; Widegren, 1998). These findings suggest, as did Dunlap and Van Liere's (1978) original study, that the NEP Scale has known-group validity. Similarly, despite the difficulty of predicting behaviours from general attitudes and beliefs, numerous studies have found significant relationships between the NEP Scale and various types of behavioural intentions as well as both self-reported and observed behaviours (e.g. Vining and Ebreo, 1992; Scott and Willits, 1994; Stern et al, 1995a; Schultz and Oskamp, 1996; Blake et al, 1997; Roberts and Bacon, 1997; Tarrant and Cordell, 1997; Schultz and Zelezny, 1998; Ebreo et al, 1999; O'Connor et al, 1999). Such findings clearly indicate that the NEP Scale possesses predictive validity as well. Since both predictive and known-group validity are forms of criterion validity (Zeller and Carmines, 1980, pp79–81), the overall evidence thus suggests that the NEP possesses criterion validity.

Judging the content validity of the NEP Scale is more difficult, especially since the construct of an environmental/ecological paradigm or worldview is inherently somewhat amorphous. A recent study by Kempton et al (1995), however, that employed in-depth, ethnographic interviews in an effort to flesh out the environmental perspectives of Americans is highly relevant in this regard. Although their methods were dramatically different than those employed in the development and construction of the NEP Scale, on the basis of responses to their unstructured interviews Kempton et al (1995, Chapter 3) concluded that three general sets of environmental beliefs play crucial roles in the 'cultural models' by which Americans attempt to make sense of environmental issues: (1) Nature is a limited resource upon which humans rely; (2) Nature is balanced, highly interdependent and complex, and therefore susceptible to human interference; and (3) Materialism and lack of contact with nature have led our society to devalue nature. That Kempton et al found three nearly identical beliefs to those forming the major facets of the NEP Scale – balance of nature, limits to growth and human domination over nature – is strong confirmation of the scale's content validity.

Judging the construct validity of measuring instruments is difficult because it depends on how the measure relates to other measures in ways that are theoretically specified (Zeller and Carmines, 1980, pp80–84). Original claims of the NEP Scale's construct validity (Dunlap and Van Liere, 1978, p16) were limited to the fact that scores on it were related in the expected fashion with personal characteristics such as age (younger people were assumed to be less wedded to traditional worldviews and thus more supportive of the NEP), education (the better educated were assumed to be exposed to more information about environmental issues and to be more capable of comprehending the ecological perspective implicit in the NEP) and political ideology (liberals were assumed to be less committed to the status quo in general and the DSP in particular). Although there have been some exceptions, most studies have continued to find support for the NEP to be negatively related to age and positively related to education and liberalism.

More importantly, studies that have examined the presumed intervening links between these variables and support for the NEP, such as those that have documented the assumed positive relationship between environmental knowledge and endorsement of the NEP (Arcury et al, 1986; Arcury, 1990; Pierce et al, 1992; Furman, 1998) and two that found a negative relationship between right-wing authoritarianism and support for the NEP (Schultz and Stone, 1994; Lefcourt, 1996), are beginning to provide more convincing evidence of the NEP Scale's construct validity. But the most important evidence of the NEP Scale's construct validity comes from studies that have theorized that the NEP forms a primary component, along with fundamental values, of environmental belief systems and then have found this expectation empirically confirmed (Pierce et al, 1987; Stern et al, 1995a). As theoretical models of the sources of environmental attitudes and behaviours that assign a key role to the NEP are developed, tested and confirmed, evidence of the NEP Scale's construct validity should increase.

Dimensionality of the NEP Scale

While the bulk of available evidence converges to suggest the overall validity of the NEP Scale, there is far less consensus on the question of whether the scale measures a single construct or is inherently multidimensional. After a series of US studies (Albrecht et al, 1982; Geller and Lasley, 1985; Noe and Snow, 1990) produced similar results via factor analysis, suggesting that the NEP is composed of three distinct dimensions – balance of nature, limits to growth and human domination of nature – some researchers began to routinely measure each dimension separately (e.g. Arcury, 1990; Vining and Ebreo, 1992; Ebreo et al, 1999). A careful review of studies that have factor-analysed the NEP items, however, reveals considerable inconsistency in the number of dimensions actually obtained: Three studies (Edgell and Nowell, 1989; Noe and Snow, 1990, p24; Lefcourt, 1996) found all items to load on a single factor with at least one of their samples, and several studies have found only two dimensions in one or more of their samples (Noe and Snow, 1989–1990, 1990; Noe and Hammitt, 1992; Scott and Willits, 1994; Gooch, 1995; Bechtel et al, 1999). Although a number of studies have found three dimensions similar to those noted above in one or more samples (Edgell and Nowell, 1989; Noe and Snow, 1989–1990; Shetzer et al, 1991), still others have found as many as four dimensions (Roberts and Bacon, 1997; Furman, 1998).

The above results, combined with the fact that studies finding three dimensions often report some discrepancies in the loadings of individual items, suggest that it may be premature to assume automatically that the 12 NEP items measure three distinct dimensions. We encourage researchers to at least factor-analyse the entire set of items at the outset to determine if the three widely used dimensions do in fact emerge. Factor-analysing 12 items typically yields two or more dimensions, but as the above results indicate, the dimensions are often sample specific. For this reason, some researchers see unidimensionality as an unrealistic goal and settle for a high level of internal consistency, as measured by strong item-total correlations, high loadings on the first *unrotated* factor, and an acceptable (0.7 or higher) value for coefficient alpha, the mean of all possible split-half reliabilities (Zeller and Carmines, 1980, Chapter 3). Although internal consistency is generally a necessary but not a sufficient condition for unidimensionality, it provides a reasonable rationale for combining a set of items into a single measure rather than creating ad hoc dimensions that emerge from various factoring techniques.

The decision to break the NEP items into two or more dimensions should depend upon the results of the individual study. If two or more distinct dimensions that have face validity emerge and are not highly correlated with one another, then it is sensible to employ them as separate variables. If substantively meaningful dimensions do not emerge, however, and the entire set of items (or at least a majority of them) are found to produce an internally consistent measure, then we recommend treating the NEP Scale as a single variable. Although the notion of a worldview or paradigm implies some consistency (in terms of taking pro- or anti-NEP positions) in responses to the NEP items, it is not unreasonable to expect that discernible dimensions will emerge in some samples, as populations vary in terms of how well their belief systems are organized into coherent frameworks (e.g. Pierce et al, 1987; Gooch, 1995; Bechtel et al, 1999; Dalton et al, 1999). Thus, the decision to treat the NEP as a single variable or as multiple variables should not be made beforehand but ought to be based on the results of the particular study. Whether used as a single scale or as a multidimensional measure, the NEP can still be fruitfully employed to examine the structure and coherence of ecological worldviews and the relationships between these worldviews and a range of more specific environmental attitudes, beliefs and behaviours.

Finally, it should also be noted that the apparent multidimensionality of the NEP items may stem in part from a serious flaw in the original 12-item NEP Scale. Only 4 of the 12 items were worded in an anti-NEP direction, *and all 4 focused on anthropocentrism or the belief that nature exists primarily for human use and has no inherent value of its own.* That these items generally form a distinct dimension (often termed 'domination of nature') in factor-analytic studies reporting two or more dimensions may thus represent a methodological artifact, reflecting the direction of their wording relative to the rest of the items (see e.g. Green and Citrin, 1994).

The Study

To address the directionality imbalance in the original NEP Scale and to update and broaden the scale's content, we have developed a revised NEP Scale. In keeping with the growing salience of broad 'ecological' (as opposed to narrower, more specific and less systemic 'environmental') problems facing the modern world, this new and hopefully improved instrument is labelled the 'New *Ecological* Paradigm Scale'.

Data collection

After being pretested with college students, the new set of NEP items was used in a 1990 mail survey of a representative sample of Washington State residents (as was the original

Table 11.1 *Frequency distributions and corrected item-total correlations for New Ecological Paradigm Scale items[1]*

Do you agree or disagree[2] that:	SA[3]	MA	U	MD	SD	(N)	r_{i-t}
1 We are approaching the limit of the number of people the earth can support	27.7%	25.2%	21.0%	16.0%	10.0%	(667)	*0.43*
2 Humans have the right to modify the natural environment to suit their needs	4.1	28.5	9.2	33.9	24.3	(663)	0.35
3 When humans interfere with nature it often produces disastrous consequences	44.6	37.6	4.0	11.2	2.5	(668)	0.42
4 Human ingenuity will ensure that we do NOT make the earth unlivable	7.8	23.5	21.5	24.4	22.7	(664)	0.38
5 Humans are severely abusing the environment	51.3	35.3	2.6	9.3	1.5	(665)	0.53
6 The earth has plenty of natural resources if we just learn how to develop them	24.4	34.8	11.3	17.5	11.9	(663)	0.34
7 Plants and animals have as much right as humans to exist	44.7	32.2	4.7	12.8	5.7	(665)	0.46
8 The balance of nature is strong enough to cope with the impacts of modern industrial nations	1.1	7.4	11.3	30.9	49.4	(664)	0.53
9 Despite our special abilities humans are still subject to the laws of nature	59.6	31.3	5.4	2.9	0.8	(664)	0.33
10 The so-called 'ecological crisis' facing humankind has been greatly exaggerated	3.9	17.9	13.8	25.9	38.5	(665)	0.62
11 The earth is like a spaceship with very limited room and resources	38.0	36.3	7.5	13.4	4.8	(664)	0.51
12 Humans were meant to rule over the rest of nature	13.5	20.4	8.2	23.9	34.0	(661)	0.51
13 The balance of nature is very delicate and easily upset	45.9	32.8	5.9	14.1	1.4	(665)	0.48
14 Humans will eventually learn enough about how nature works to be able to control it	3.2	20.1	24.2	27.9	24.6	(666)	0.35
15 If things continue on their present course, we will soon experience a major ecological catastrophe	34.3	31.0	16.9	14.1	3.6	(667)	0.62

[1] Question wording: 'Listed below are statements about the relationship between humans and the environment. For each one, please indicate whether you STRONGLY AGREE, MILDLY AGREE, are UNSURE, MILDLY DISAGREE or STRONGLY DISAGREE with it'.

[2] Agreement with the eight odd-numbered items and disagreement with the seven even-numbered items indicate pro-NEP responses.

[3] SA = Strongly Agree, MA = Mildly Agree, U = Unsure, MD = Mildly Disagree, and SD = Strongly Disagree.

set of items). A questionnaire covering a wide range of environmental issues was mailed out in early March of that year, and the data collection ended in early May. It proved impossible to contact 145 members of the sample of 1300 (because of their having moved and left no forwarding addresses, being deceased, etc.), and 676 completed questionnaires were received from the remaining 1155 potential respondents, for a completion rate of 58.5 per cent. Given that funding allowed for only two follow-ups, rather than the recommended three (Dillman, 1978), this is a reasonably good overall response rate.

Item construction and modification

Besides achieving a better balance between pro- and anti-NEP statements, we also wanted to broaden the content of the scale beyond the original three facets of balance of nature, limits to growth, and anti-anthropocentrism. The notion of 'human exemptionalism', or the idea that humans – unlike other species – are exempt from the constraints of nature (Dunlap and Catton, 1994), became prominent in the 1980s through the efforts of Julian Simon and other defenders of the DSP. In addition, the emergence of ozone depletion, climate change and human-induced global environmental change in general suggested the importance of including items focusing on the likelihood of potentially catastrophic environmental changes or 'ecocrises' besetting humankind. Consequently, we added items to tap both the exemptionalism and ecocrisis facets. Finally, we wanted to modify the outmoded sexist terminology ('mankind') present in some of the original items and decided to include an 'unsure' category as a midpoint to cut down on item nonresponse.

The set of 15 items shown in Table 11.1 (including 6 from the original NEP Scale, 4 of which are modified very slightly) was constructed to achieve these purposes. Three items were designed to tap each of the five hypothesized facets of an ecological worldview: the reality of limits to growth (1, 6, 11), anti-anthropocentrism (2, 7, 12), the fragility of nature's balance (3, 8, 13), rejection of exemptionalism (4, 9, 14) and the possibility of an ecocrisis (5, 10, 15). (Item 5 was in the original NEP Scale and typically showed up in the 'balance' dimension.) The eight odd-numbered items were worded so that agreement indicates a pro-ecological view and the seven even-numbered ones so that disagreement indicates a pro-ecological worldview.

Results

The percentage distributions for responses to each of the 15 items are shown in Table 11.1. As in past studies, overall there is a tendency for respondents to endorse pro-ecological beliefs, as pluralities and often majorities (sometimes large ones) do so on every item. This is especially true for seeing the balance of nature as being threatened by human activities but is much less true for accepting the idea that there are limits to growth. There is also considerable variation in the proportions being 'unsure' about the various statements, as over 20 per cent are unsure about items 1 (on limits) and 4 and 14 (both on human exemptionalism).

Constructing a New Ecological Paradigm Scale

We were particularly interested in determining if the 15 items can legitimately be treated as measuring a single construct. A high degree of internal consistency is a necessary condition for combining a set of items into a single measure as well as an appropriate (albeit not essential) expectation for item responses constituting a reasonably coherent worldview, so we began by examining the consistency of responses to the 15 items. The last column in Table 11.1 shows the corrected item-total correlations for each item. All of these correlations are reasonably strong, ranging from a low of 0.33 to a high of 0.62. Not surprisingly, then, coefficient alpha is a very respectable 0.83. Furthermore, deletion of any of the 15 items lowers the value of alpha. Thus, the evidence from this initial survey suggests that the set of 15 items can be treated as constituting an internally consistent measuring instrument (Mueller, 1986).

Another means of assessing internal consistency is via principal-components analysis. All 15 items load heavily (from 0.40 to 0.73) on the first unrotated factor, and this factor explains 31.3 per cent of the total variance among the items (compared to only 10 per cent for the second factor extracted). This and the pattern of eigenvalues (4.7, 1.5, 1.2 and 1.1) suggest the presence of one major factor and thus reinforce the prior evidence concerning the internal consistency of the revised NEP Scale (Zeller and Carmines, 1980, Chapter 3).

Because the dimensionality of the original NEP Scale has frequently been investigated, we employed Varimax rotation to create orthogonal dimensions, and the results are shown in Table 11.2. When the four factors with eigenvalues greater than one are subjected to a Varimax rotation, six items load most heavily on the first factor: the three ecocrisis items (5, 10, 15), two balance-of-nature items (3, 13), and one exemptionalism item (9). In addition, three other items that load most heavily on other factors have substantial cross-loadings on the first factor: one anti-anthropocentrism item (7), one limits-to-growth item (11), and one balance-of-nature item (8). These results suggest the first and major factor taps the balance and ecocrisis facets heavily but also incorporates the remaining three facets to some degree. The four items loading most heavily on the second factor include the remaining two exemptionalism items (4, 14), the third balance item (8), and a limits item (6), and the ecocrisis item (10) from the first factor also cross-loads heavily on this factor. Only the marginally important third and fourth factors (with eigenvalues barely above 1.0) consist of items designed to tap the same facet. The remaining two limits items (1, 11) load most heavily on the third factor, whereas the third one (6) loads almost as heavily here as it does on the second factor, and the three anthropocentrism items (2, 7, 12) load most heavily on the fourth factor.

Different researchers will have varying interpretations of the results of this analysis. Because the evidence suggests the presence of one predominant factor, and because the first three factors have items from several facets loading heavily on them, we are not inclined to create four NEP subscales measuring the four factors that emerged from the principal-components analysis and Varimax rotation. Furthermore, because all 15 items load heavily on the first *unrotated* factor, have strong item-total correlations and yield an alpha of 0.83 when combined into a single measure, we think it is appropriate to treat them as constituting a single (revised) NEP Scale. Further, the revised NEP Scale possesses a level of internal consistency that justifies treating it as a measure of a coherent belief system or worldview. Of course, future research on differing samples is needed to

Table **11.2** *Principal components analysis of NEP items with Varimax rotation*

		Factors			
		1	2	3	4
NEP 3	(Balance)	**60**	04	07	19
NEP 5	(Eco-Crisis)	**71**	12	20	09
NEP 9	(Anti-Exempt)	**62**	20	−15	00
NEP 10	(Eco-Crisis)	**54**	**36**	27	22
NEP 13	(Balance)	**60**	00	**33**	14
NEP 15	(Eco-Crisis)	**66**	13	**35**	21
NEP 4	(Anti-Exempt)	19	**74**	05	−05
NEP 6	(Limits)	−18	**54**	**52**	11
NEP 8	(Balance)	**30**	**63**	11	21
NEP 14	(Anti-Exempt)	06	**72**	−03	18
NEP 1	(Limits)	20	−05	**76**	16
NEP 11	(Limits)	**31**	15	**75**	01
NEP 2	(Anti-Anthro)	11	10	−02	**75**
NEP 7	(Anti-Anthro)	**38**	01	10	**63**
NEP 12	(Anti-Anthro)	08	28	26	**71**
Eigenvalue		4.7	1.5	1.2	1.1
Percentage of variance		31.3	10.0	7.8	7.4

Note: Loadings of 0.30 and above are in bold.

confirm the appropriateness of treating the new set of 15 items as a single measure of endorsement of an ecological worldview as opposed to creating two or more dimensions of such a worldview from the NEP items. As noted earlier, differing populations will no doubt vary in the degree to which the NEP beliefs are organized into a highly consistent belief system, and in many cases it will no doubt be more appropriate to treat the NEP as multidimensional.

Predictive and construct validity

Because the original NEP Scale has been subjected to a good deal of testing and has been found to have considerable validity, we are not concerned about obtaining evidence on the validity of the new measure at this stage. However, the 1990 questionnaire included a number of indicators of pro-environmental (or pro-ecological) orientation, and examining the correlations between them and the revised NEP Scale provides at least limited data on the predictive validity of the latter. Scores on the revised NEP Scale correlate significantly ($r = 0.61$) with scores on a 13-item measure of the perceived seriousness of world ecological problems (the higher the NEP score, the more likely the problems are seen as serious); significantly (0.57) with a 4-item measure of support for pro-environmental policies (the higher the NEP score, the more support for the policies); significantly (0.45) with a 4-item measure of the perceived seriousness of state and community air and water pollution (the higher the NEP score, the more likely pollution is viewed as serious); and – most importantly – significantly (0.31) with a 10-item measure of (self-reported) pro-environmental behaviours (more behaviours are reported by those with high NEP scores). These results, showing that the new NEP Scale is related to a wide range of ecological attitudes and behaviours, suggest that it possesses predictive validity.

Researchers have consistently found young, well-educated and politically liberal adults to be more pro-environmental than their counterparts and have offered theoretical explanations for these findings (Jones and Dunlap, 1992). In addition, one would expect to find people with such characteristics more likely to endorse, in particular, an ecological worldview, for the reasons noted previously. Our results fit this pattern, although only political liberalism is substantially ($r = 0.32$) correlated with endorsement of the NEP. Age is slightly (–0.11), albeit significantly, related to endorsement of the NEP, as is education (0.10), both in the expected direction.

Other variables that are significantly ($p < 0.05$) correlated with scores on the revised NEP Scale include political party (0.22), with Democrats having higher NEP scores; occupational sector (0.13), with those employed in primary industries having lower NEP scores; income (–0.10), which is negatively related to endorsement of the NEP; and past residence (0.08), with those raised in urban areas scoring higher on the NEP. Although these correlations are quite modest, they are generally consistent with past studies of correlates of environmental concern in general and the NEP in particular. To the extent that there are sound theoretical reasons for expecting these correlations (Jones and Dunlap, 1992), as there especially are for age, education and ideology, such findings provide some degree of construct validity for the revised NEP Scale.

Trends in endorsement of NEP beliefs

To our knowledge only one previous study has obtained longitudinal data on public endorsement of the NEP. Arcury and Christiansen (1990) compared responses of statewide samples of Kentucky residents to the six-item version of the NEP Scale in 1984 and 1988 (the latter following a severe summer drought) and found an increase in pro-NEP responses. The increase in support for the NEP was significant, however, only in counties that had experienced water use restrictions, leading Arcury and Christiansen (1990, p404) to conclude that 'critical environmental experience can accelerate change in environmental worldview'. A secondary purpose of the present study was to examine possible changes in Washington State residents' endorsement of key elements of an ecological worldview over time. Because the sample frame and data collection techniques were the same for the 1976 and 1990 surveys, we can examine trends in Washingtonians' support for the NEP over the 14-year period.

Table 11.3 presents the relevant data for eight items that were used in both surveys and for which the wording was either identical or changed in only minor ways. (The last two items, reflecting the ecocrisis or ecological catastrophe facet in the revised NEP Scale, were included in the 1976 questionnaire but were not incorporated into the original scale.) It should be emphasized, however, that because 'unsure' was *not* used in the 1976 survey, the 1990 results have been recomputed with that response category deleted (which accounts for the difference between these figures and the results reported in Table 11.1). In general, there was a modest increase in Washington residents' endorsement

Table 11.3 *Trends in responses to selected NEP items by Washington residents,
1976 and 1990*

	1976	1990[1]	Change
Ecological limits			
We are approaching the limit of the number of people the earth can support. (AGREE)	73%	67%	−6%
The earth is like a spaceship with very limited room and resources.[2] (AGREE)	83	80	−3
Balance of nature			
When humans interfere with nature it often produces disastrous consequences. (AGREE)	76	86	+10
The balance of nature is very delicate and easily upset. (AGREE)	80	84	+4
Human domination			
Humans have the right to modify the natural environment to suit their needs. (DISAGREE)	62	64	+2
Ecological catastrophe			
Humans are severely abusing the environment.[3] (AGREE)	79	89	+10
The so-called 'ecological crisis' facing humankind has been greatly exaggerated.[4] (DISAGREE)	57	75	+18
If things continue on their present course, we will soon experience a major ecological catastrophe.[5] (AGREE)	60	78	+18

[1] The 1990 results were computed with 'Unsure' deleted, as that category was not used in 1976.

[2] The 1976 wording was 'The earth is like a spaceship with *only* limited room and resources'.

[3] The 1976 wording was '*Mankind* is severely abusing the environment'.

[4] The 1976 wording was 'The so-called "ecological crisis" facing *mankind* has been greatly exaggerated'.

[5] The 1976 wording was 'If things continue on their present course, *mankind* will soon experience a major ecological catastrophe'.

of elements of the NEP over the 14-year period, reaching 10 per cent on four of the eight items. The largest increase occurred on the two items that most clearly focus on the likelihood of ecological catastrophe, suggesting that the emergence of major problems such as ozone depletion and global warming have had some effect on the public. Interestingly, however, the two items dealing with ecological limits saw a decline in support, perhaps reflecting the impact of the Reagan era (which most definitely rejected the idea of limits to growth) as well as the declining salience of energy shortages.

The overall pattern of increasing endorsement of the NEP in Washington State, especially given the 'ceiling effect' imposed by the relatively strong pro-NEP views expressed in 1976, provides modest support (as does the above-noted complementary trend in Kentucky) for arguments that an ecological worldview is gaining adherents (e.g. Olsen et al, 1992). Presumably, had the original data been obtained in the 1960s, or earlier, rather than in the middle of the so-called environmental decade, the amount of change would have been far more striking (see Dunlap, 1995, for data on long-term trends in public concern for environmental quality).

Conclusion

The results reported in this article suggest that it is appropriate to treat the new set of 15 items designed to measure endorsement of an ecological worldview as constituting a single 'New Ecological Paradigm Scale'. The revised NEP Scale appears to be an improved measuring instrument compared to the original scale, as it (1) provides more comprehensive coverage of key facets of an ecological worldview, (2) avoids the unfortunate lack of balance in item direction of the original scale (where only four items, all dealing with anthropocentrism, were stated in an anti-NEP direction) and (3) removes the outmoded, sexist terminology in some of the original scale's items. The revised NEP Scale has slightly more internal consistency than did the original version (alpha of 0.83 versus 0.81), although this likely stems from its having three more items (as alpha tends to increase with scale length, all other things being equal). Although items were selected to represent five discernible, but interrelated, facets of an ecological worldview, thus maximizing content validity, the results suggest the presence of one dominant factor in the Washington survey.

Of course, future research will be needed to address the issue of the revised NEP Scale's dimensionality, and on some samples a clearer pattern of multidimensionality will no doubt emerge and warrant creation of two or more subscales measuring distinct dimensions of the NEP. A goal for future research will be to compare the degree to which the NEP beliefs are organized coherently across different populations, including comparing patterns of multidimensionality when distinct dimensions emerge, as well as the degree to which resulting belief systems (or worldviews) influence a range of environmental attitudes, beliefs and behaviours.

We also hope to see additional longitudinal research employing the revised NEP Scale. Although they tap primitive beliefs about humanity's relationship with the Earth, the NEP items should be responsive to personal experiences with environmental problems (as reflected by Arcury and Christianson's [1990] Kentucky study) and to information – diffused by government agencies, scientists, environmentalists and the media – concerning the growing seriousness of environmental problems. Despite the inherent complexities involved in cognitive change (see e.g. Eagly and Kulesa, 1997), we suspect that the never-ending emergence of new scientific evidence concerning the deleterious impacts of human activities on environmental quality and the subsequent threats these pose to the welfare of humans (and other species) will generate continual pressure for adoption of a more ecological worldview. The revised NEP Scale should prove useful in tracking possible increases in endorsement of an ecological worldview, as well as in examining the effect of specific experiences and types of information in generating changes in this worldview.

Note

1   This is a revision of a paper presented at the Annual Meeting of the Rural Sociological Society, The Pennsylvania State University, State College, PA, August 1992, Revision of the NEP Scale benefited from Dunlap's long-term collaborative effort

with William R. Catton, Jr, to document the emergence of an ecological paradigm within sociology. The data reported in this article were collected in a survey sponsored by Washington State University's Department of Natural Resource Sciences and Cooperative Extension Service for which Dunlap served as a consultant. Thanks are extended to Robert Howell for facilitating Dunlap's involvement with that survey.

References

1   Albrecht, D., Bultena, G., Hoiberg, E. and Nowak, P. (1982) 'The new environmental paradigm scale'. *Journal of Environmental Education,* vol 13, pp39–43

2   Arcury, T. A. (1990) 'Environmental attitudes and environmental knowledge'. *Human Organization,* vol 49, pp300–304

3   Arcury, T. A. and Christiansen, E. H. (1990) 'Environmental worldview in response to environmental problems: Kentucky 1984 and 1998 compared'. *Environment and Behaviour,* vol 22, pp387–407

4   Arcury, T. A., Johnson, T. P. and Scollay, S. J. (1986) 'Ecological worldview and environmental knowledge: The new environmental paradigm'. *Journal of Environmental Education,* vol 17, pp35–40

5   Bechtel, R. B., Verdugo, V. C. and Pinheiro, J. de Q. (1999) 'Environmental belief systems: United States, Brazil, and Mexico'. *Journal of Cross-Cultural Psychology,* vol 30, pp122–128

6   Blake, D. E., Guppy, N. and Urmetzer, P. (1997) 'Canadian public opinion and environmental action'. *Canadian Journal of Political Science,* vol 30, pp451–472

7   Brown, L. R. (1981) *Building a Sustainable Society.* W. W. Norton, New York

8   Caron, J. A. (1989) 'Environmental perspectives of Blacks: Acceptance of the "new environmental paradigm"'. *Journal of Environmental Education,* vol 20, pp21–26

9   Chandler, E. W. and Dreger, R. M. (1993) 'Anthropocentrism: Construct validity and measurement'. *Journal of Social Behaviour and Personality,* vol 8, pp169–188

10 Continental Group (1982) *Toward Responsible Growth: Economic and Environmental Concern in the Balance.* Author, Stamford, CT

11 Cotgrove, S. (1982) *Catastrophe or Cornucopia.* John Wiley and Sons, New York

12 Dalton, R. J., Gontmacher, Y., Lovrich, N. P. and Pierce, J. C. (1999) 'Environmental attitudes and the new environmental paradigm', in Dalton, R. J., Garb, P. N., Lovrich, P., Pierce, J. C. and Whitely, J. M. (eds) *Critical Masses: Citizens, Nuclear Weapons Production, and Environmental Destruction in the United States and Russia.* MIT Press, Cambridge, MA, pp195–230

13 Dillman, D. A. (1978) *Mail and Telephone Surveys.* Wiley Interscience, New York

14 Dunlap, R. E. (1995) 'Public opinion and environmental policy', in Lester, J. P. (ed) *Environmental Politics and Policy.* Duke University Press, Durham, NC, 2nd ed, pp63–114

15 Dunlap, R. E. (1998) 'Lay perceptions of global risk: Public views of global warming in cross-national context'. *International Sociology,* vol 13, pp473–498

16 Dunlap, R. E. and Catton, Jr. W. R. (1994) 'Toward an ecological sociology', in W. V. D'Antonio, M. Sasaki and Y. Yonebayashi (eds) *Ecology, Society and the Quality of Social Life.* New Brunswick, NJ, Transaction, pp11–31

17 Dunlap, R. E. and Van Liere, K. D. (1978) 'The "new environmental paradigm": A proposed measuring instrument and preliminary results'. *Journal of Environmental Education,* vol 9, pp10–19

18   Dunlap, R. E. and Van Liere, K. D. (1984) 'Commitment to the dominant social paradigm and concern for environmental quality'. *Social Science Quarterly*, vol 65, pp1013–1028

19   Eagly, A. H. and Kulesa, P. (1997) 'Attitudes, attitude structure, and resistance to change', in Bazerman, M. D., Messick, D. M., Tenbrunsel, A. E. and Wade, K. A. (eds) *Environmental Ethics and Behaviour*. New Lexington, San Francisco, pp122–153

20   Ebreo, A., Hershey, J. and Vining, J. (1999) 'Reducing solid waste. Linking recycling to environmentally responsible consumerism'. *Environment and Behaviour*, vol 31, pp107–135

21   Edgell, M. C. R. and Nowell, D. E. (1989) 'The new environmental paradigm scale: Wildlife and environmental beliefs in British Columbia'. *Society and Natural Resources*, vol 2, pp285–296

22   Ellis, R. J. and Thompson, F. (1997) 'Culture and the environment in the Pacific Northwest'. *American Political Science Review*, vol 91, pp885–897

23   Furman, A. (1998) 'A note on environmental concern in a developing country: Results from an Istanbul survey'. *Environment and Behaviour*, vol 30, pp520–534

24   Gardner, G. T. and Stern, P. C. (1996) *Environmental Problems and Human Behaviour*. Allyn and Bacon, Boston

25   Geller, J. M. and Lasley, P. (1985) 'The new environmental paradigm scale: A reexamination'. *Journal of Environmental Education*, vol 17, pp9–12

26   Gooch, G. D. (1995) 'Environmental beliefs and attitudes in Sweden and the Baltic states'. *Environment and Behaviour*, vol 27, pp513–539

27   Gray, D. B. (1985) *Ecological Beliefs and Behaviours: Assessment and Change*. Greenwood Press, Westport, CT

28   Green, D. P. and Citrin, J. (1994) 'Measurement error and the structure of attitudes: Are positive and negative judgements opposites?' *American Journal of Political Science*, vol 38, pp256–281

29   Jones, R. E. and Dunlap, R. E. (1992) 'The social bases of environmental concern: Have they changed over time?' *Rural Sociology*, vol 57, pp28–47

30   Kempton, W., Boster, J. S. and Hartley, J. A. (1995) *Environmental Values in American Culture*. MIT Press, Cambridge, MA

31   Lefcourt, H. M. (1996) 'Perspective-taking humour and authoritarianism as predictors of anthropocentrism'. *Humour*, vol 9, pp57–71.

32   Milbrath, L. W. (1984) *Environmentalists: Vanguard for a New Society*. State University of New York Press, Albany, NY

33   Mueller, D. J. (1986) *Measuring Attitudes: A Handbook for Researchers and Practitioners*. New York: Teachers College Press.

34   Noe, F. P. and Hammitt, W. E. (1992) 'Environmental attitudes and the personal relevance of management actions in a park setting'. *Journal of Environmental Management*, vol 35, pp205–216

35   Noe, F. P. and Snow, R. (1989–90) 'Hispanic cultural influence on environmental concern'. *Journal of Environmental Education*, vol 21, pp27–34.

36   Noe, F. P. and Snow, R. (1990) 'The new environmental paradigm and further scale analysis'. *Journal of Environmental Education*, vol 21, pp20–26

37   O'Connor, R. E., Bord, R. J. and Fisher, A. (1999) 'Risk perceptions, general environmental beliefs, and willingness to address climate change'. *Risk Analysis*, vol 19, pp461–471

38   Olsen, M. E., Lodwick, D. G. and Dunlap, R. E. (1992) *Viewing the World Ecologically*. Westview, Boulder, CO

39   Pierce, J. C., Dalton, R. J. and Zaitsev, A. (1999) 'Public perceptions of environmental conditions', in Dalton, R. J., Garb, P., Lovrich, N. P., Pierce, J. C. and Whitely, J. M. (eds) *Critical Masses: Citizens, Nuclear Weapons Production, and Environmental Destruction in the United States and Russia*. MIT Press, Cambridge, MA, pp97–129

40 Pierce, J. C., Lovrich, Jr, N. P., Tsurutani, T. and Takematsu, A. (1987) 'Environmental Belief Systems Among Japanese and American Elites and Publics'. *Political Behaviour*, vol 9, pp139–159

41 Pierce, J. C., Steger, M. E., Steel, B. S. and Lovrich, N. P. (1992) *Citizens, Political Communication and Interest Groups: Environmental Organizations in Canada and the United States*. Praeger, Westport, CT

42 Pirages, D. C. and Ehrlich, P. R. (1974) *Ark II: Social Response to Environmental Imperatives*. W. H. Freeman, San Francisco

43 Roberts, J. A. and Bacon, D. R. (1997) 'Exploring the subtle relationships between environmental concern and ecologically conscious consumer behaviour'. *Journal of Business Research*, vol 40, pp79–89

44 Rokeach, M. (1968) *Beliefs, Attitudes, and Values*. Jossey-Bass, San Francisco

45 Schultz, P. W. and Oskamp, S. (1996) 'Effort as a moderator of the attitude-behaviour relationship: General environmental concern and recycling'. *Social Psychology Quarterly*, vol 59, pp375–383

46 Schultz, P. W. and Stone, W. F. (1994) 'Authoritarianism and attitudes toward the environment'. *Environment and Behaviour*, vol 26, pp25–37

47 Schultz, P. W. and Zelezny, L. C. (1998) 'Values and proenvironmental behaviour: A five-country survey'. *Journal of Cross-Cultural Psychology*, vol 29, pp540–558

48 Scott, D. and Willits, F. K. (1994) 'Environmental attitudes and behaviour: A Pennsylvania survey'. *Environment and Behaviour*, vol 26, pp239–260

49 Shetzer, L., Stackman, R. W. and Moore, L. F. (1991) 'Business-environment attitudes and the new environmental paradigm'. *Journal of Environmental Education*, vol 22, pp14–21

50 Stern, P. C., Dietz, T. and Guagnano, G. A. (1995a) 'The new ecological paradigm in social-psychological context'. *Environment and Behaviour*, vol 27, pp723–743

51 Stern, P. C., Dietz, T., Kalof, L. and Guagnano, G. A. (1995b) 'Values, beliefs, and proenvironmental attitude formation toward emergent attitude objects'. *Journal of Applied Social Psychology*, vol 25, pp1611–1636

52 Stern, P. C., Young, O. R. and Druckman, D. (1992) *Global Environmental Change: Understanding the Human Dimensions*. National Academy Press, Washington, DC

53 Tarrant, M. A. and Cordell, H. K. (1997) 'The effect of respondent characteristics on general environmental attitude-behaviour correspondence'. *Environment and Behaviour*, vol 29, pp618–637

54 Thompson, S. C. G. and Barton, M. A. (1994) 'Ecocentric and anthropocentric attitudes toward the environment'. *Journal of Environmental Psychology*, vol 14, pp149–158

55 Vining, J. and Ebreo, A. (1992) 'Predicting behaviour from global and specific environmental attitudes and changes in recycling opportunities'. *Journal of Applied Social Psychology*, vol 22, pp1580–1607

56 Weigel, R. H. and Weigel, J. (1978) 'Environmental concern: The development of a measure'. *Environment and Behaviour*, vol 10, pp3–15

57 Widegren, O. (1998) 'The new environmental paradigm and personal norms'. *Environment and Behaviour*, vol 30, pp73–100

58 Zeller, R. A. and Carmines, E. G. (1980) *Measurement in the Social Sciences*. Cambridge University Press, NY

12

Value Orientations, Gender and Environmental Concern

Paul C. Stern, Thomas Dietz and Linda Kalof

Environmental politics has long frustrated participants on all sides. Environmental movement activists accuse corporations and government agencies of trading irreplaceable values for short-term selfish gains, and corporate and government officials accuse environmentalists of irrational desires for a risk-free life. The participants seem to be talking past each other. And the conflicts do not recede in the face of increasing knowledge about the effects of different policy choices on the environment or on other things people value. Part of the problem is that the political actors represent competing interests: Environmental politics is an interchange between potential winners and potential losers. But the other part of the problem is that the actors do not all value the same things. Sometimes, it seems, they do not even see the same world (Dietz et al, 1989).

Beginning with the work of Dunlap and Van Liere (1978, 1984), research on environmental attitudes has assessed the extent to which individuals concerned with the environment view the world in ways that differ fundamentally from those who are less concerned with the environment (see also Cotgrove, 1982; Milbrath, 1984; Inglehart, 1990). Much of this work has emphasized the emergence of a new worldview, or paradigm, associated with environmentalism. The work is consistent with the argument in the social movements literature that environmentalism, like other 'new social movements', aims not at redistributing resources, but rather at a different and in many ways more fundamental restructuring of society (Habermas, 1981; Offe, 1985; Buttel, 1987).

To date, however, the idea that environmentalism represents a new way of thinking has not been linked to a social-psychological model. A number of critics have suggested that the lack of a general theoretical frame may be one reason that research on environmental attitudes and environmentalism is not cumulative (Heberlein, 1981; Stern and Oskamp, 1987). A major exception to this has been a growing literature that attempts to use Schwartz's norm-activation model of altruism to explain actions intended to ameliorate environmental problems (Heberlein and Black, 1976; Van Liere and Dunlap, 1978; Black et al, 1985; Stern et al, 1986; Hopper and Nielsen, 1991). Schwartz's theory of altruism suggests that pro-environmental behaviour becomes more probable when an individual is aware of harmful consequences (AC) to others from a state of the environment and when that person ascribes responsibility (AR) to herself or himself for

Note: Stern, P. C., Dietz, T. and Kalof, L., *Environmental Behaviour*, vol 25, pp322–348, copyright © (1993) by Sage Publications. Reprinted by permission of Sage Publications

changing the offending environmental condition. Under conditions of AC and AR, individuals experience a sense of moral obligation to prevent or mitigate the harmful consequences. This so-called personal norm motivates action.

The Schwartz-derived model treats pro-environmental behaviour as a special case within a social-psychological theory of altruism. It implicitly assumes that people have a general value orientation toward the welfare of others, that is, that they value outcomes that benefit others and can be motivated to act to prevent harm to others. Under appropriate conditions, pro-environmental behaviour will follow from this social or altruistic value orientation. We expand on the Schwartz model by offering an integrative theoretical model of environmental concern. We presume that the value orientation toward human welfare is only one of at least three value orientations that might underlie environmental attitudes and behaviour. The others are the egoistic value orientation that many economic and socio-biological accounts of environmental problems assume to be the predominant motivation for human behaviour (e.g. Olson, 1965; Hardin, 1968), and a biospheric value orientation such as that described and advocated in the writings of 'deep ecologists' and others (Devall and Sessions, 1985; Devall, 1988; Naess, 1989; for reviews and critiques, see Brennan, 1988; Eckersley, 1992). Our preliminary test of the expanded model suggests it has reasonable explanatory power and also sheds some light on gender differences in environmental concern. In addition, our findings suggest that the model can help explain some of the surprising responses to contingent valuation surveys noted by other researchers (Gregory et al, 1992; Irwin et al, (1993)).

Environmentalism and Value Orientations

Schwartz's norm-activation theory (Schwartz, 1968a, 1968b, 1970, 1977), as we have noted, can treat environmentalism as a type of altruism. In the terminology of value theory (Rokeach, 1973), environmental attitudes can flow from a value orientation that reflects concern for the welfare of other human beings. This assumption has proven fruitful. Heberlein (1972; Heberlein and Black, 1976) first showed that this general model is applicable to environmental problems, using littering and purchase of lead-free gasoline as examples. Following these initial studies, the norm-activation approach has been applied to a variety of environmentally significant behaviours, including energy conservation (Black et al, 1985), yard burning (Van Liere and Dunlap, 1978), recycling (Hopper and Nielsen, 1991; Oskamp, et al, 1991) and political support for environmental protection (Stern et al, 1986).

Some studies using the Schwartz model, however, also recognize that the effect of personally held normative beliefs (altruistic personal norms) is partially countered by the effect of perceived costs to the individual engaging in the behaviour these norms prescribe (Black et al, 1985). Such studies in effect recognize that environmentally relevant behaviour can reflect a trade-off between altruistic and egoistic motivations, and therefore that egoistic value orientations as well as social-altruistic ones are implicated in environmental attitudes and behaviour.

A published debate of the 1970s was the first mention in the academic literature of a third value orientation affecting environmental behaviour (Heberlein, 1972, 1977;

Dunlap and Van Liere, 1977a, 1977b). It posed the question of whether pro-environmental behaviour was a case of following the 'golden rule' (treating others as you would have them treat you), as the Schwartz model assumes, or of adherence to a 'land ethic' (Leopold, 1949), a value orientation toward the welfare of *nonhuman* species or the biosphere itself. Heberlein and Dunlap and Van Liere agreed that, at the time they were writing, the golden rule was the most likely basis for environmental concern. Although neither side in the debate was optimistic that the land ethic would become widespread as a value basis for environmental concern and action, Dunlap nevertheless incorporated a number of items that appear to measure adherence to a biospheric ethic in his New Environmental Paradigm scale (Dunlap and Van Liere, 1978). Here we develop a model that incorporates all three value orientations: concern for the welfare of other human beings, which we call the social-altruistic value orientation; concern with nonhuman species or the biosphere, which we call the biospheric orientation; and egoism or self-interest.

In the literature on evolutionary theory, social choice and social psychology, the distinction between egoism and altruism is typically made so that the latter refers to values, attitudes and behaviour toward conspecifics. We maintain the familiar distinction but add to it the recognition that nonegoistic behaviour, including environmentalism, may also be motivated by biospheric values that extend beyond the human species. Such behaviour is altruistic in that it involves self-sacrifice but not in the sense of implying sacrifice for other people.

The three value orientations we identify are the most frequently noted in the Western literature on environmental concern, but they are not the only ones that might be relevant. In the disintegrating Soviet Union of 1989–1990, for example, environmental activism was often rooted in nationalist concerns about exploitation of resources in non-Russian areas by the central, Russian-dominated government. In different cultural contexts, still other value orientations might be salient.

Each value orientation, if present in a pure form, could produce environmental concern under different conditions. For example, if environmental concern were based entirely on self-interest, an individual would favour protecting the environment when and only when doing so would have expected benefits for the individual that would outweigh the expected costs.[1] A prototypical example is the NIMBY ('not in my back yard!') protest, in which individuals become concerned when they perceive that a hazardous industrial process may harm them and their families. Individuals act more or less as would be predicted by various forms of rational-choice theory, and endure costs to protect the environment provided they expect benefits that exceed those costs.[2]

If environmental concerns were based entirely on a social-altruistic value orientation, an individual would bear personal costs to safeguard the environment only when doing so would protect other human beings. For instance, someone with a strong social value orientation might become an environmentalist on learning about potential harm to innocent people, such as children living downwind of an industrial plant over which they have no control, that exposes them to air pollution but gives them no benefits. To the extent that environmentalism is based on a social-altruistic value orientation, environmental concern should be closely correlated with other concerns and actions that are altruistic in the same sense, for example, concerns with the rights of minorities or with poverty. Similarly, we would expect environmentally protective behaviours such as recycling to be common among individuals who also engage in other forms of altruism, such as blood donation or community work. If environmental concern were based entirely on biospheric values, an individual would express and act on moral principles that incorporate concerns with other species and with natural environments. Someone motivated purely by biospheric values would become involved in environmental issues when species extinction or habitat destruction is at stake, but would be relatively unconcerned when the only effects are on people. Echoes of this purist position are heard in the work of deep ecologists and some environmental philosophers, and within the animal rights movement. Biospheric morality extends beyond kin and beyond all of humanity to other species, to places and to the biosphere itself.

Of course, egoistic, humanistic and biospheric value orientations toward the environment are not incompatible; indeed, they may be related. We presume that many people's environmental attitudes reflect some combination of the three orientations.[3]

A Model of Environmental Concern

To investigate the links between value orientations and to assess the relationship of each to environmental behaviour, we develop a model that extends the Schwartzian model. We presume that each value orientation predisposes people to be sensitive to information about certain outcomes (outcomes for things they value). In Schwartz's terms, behaviour depends on awareness of consequences (AC) that are significant in terms of the value orientation. We refer to AC as a belief rather than an awareness, however, because the consequences lie in the future and may therefore not arise. Our general presumption is that people who believe an environmental condition has adverse consequences (AC) for things they value will be predisposed to take action. For someone with a strong social-altruistic orientation, a belief that an environmental condition has adverse consequences for other people will motivate pro-environmental behaviour. In the same way, behaviour can be triggered in someone with strong biospheric values by the belief that an environmental condition has adverse consequences for the biosphere or the nonhuman environment, and in an egoist by a belief that there may be adverse consequences for the self. We refer to these conditions as biospheric AC and egoistic AC, respectively. We consider motivation to act to be the product of beliefs about consequences for a valued object (AC) and the weight or importance of the value orientation toward that object (V), summed across value orientations:

$$M = V_{ego}AC_{ego} + V_{soc}AC_{soc} + V_{bio}AC_{bio}$$

where the subscripts ego, soc, and bio refer to egoistic, social-altruistic and biospheric value weights (V) or consequences (AC). This equation has the form of a regression model in which the V terms are the regression coefficients when an index of motivation to act is regressed on measures of the three AC beliefs. In this study, we measure beliefs about consequences for self, others and the biosphere with scales of survey items, use behavioural-intention statements as the index of motivation to act, and estimate the weights given to each value using regression coefficients. Although the Schwartz model specifies that ascription of responsibility to self (AR) and personal norms mediate between AC and behaviour, we do not measure the intervening variables in this study.

The model can also be expressed in the language of behavioural-decision theory. In this formulation, an individual believes an environmental condition has a set of consequences (AC) for valued things: personal wellbeing, social wellbeing and the health of the biosphere. Each value (V) has a weight for each individual, and according to the axioms of decision theory, the utility of the environmental condition for the individual is described by the equation above. In economic analyses, utilities or preferences have the same theoretical status as the concept of motivation to act in psychology. Indeed, efforts to model preferences or utility functions often took a form similar to that which we are using. The demand for a good, service or state of the world is regressed on its characteristics (defined objectively or in terms of respondents' perceptions or beliefs). The resulting coefficients represent the preference for or utility associated with those characteristics. Similarly in our model, the AC scales measure beliefs about states of the world and the regression coefficients for each AC estimate the preference or value assigned to those states.[4]

Gender and Environmentalism

Theoretical arguments linking gender to altruism or environmental attitudes often invoke or imply gendered differences in value orientations that can be investigated within the present theoretical framework. For example, Gilligan's work on women's moral development suggests that women may be more altruistic than men because of stronger socialization to consider the wishes of others (Gilligan, 1982).[5] In the terms of our model, the argument can be read in either of two ways: that women have a stronger altruistic value orientation than men (i.e. they are more concerned about and affected by consequences to others), or that women are more aware than men of the consequences of events for others and are therefore more likely to develop beliefs about these consequences. The first reading would predict a relatively stronger correlation between social-altruistic AC and behavioural intention among women (compared with the correlation of behaviour with egoistic or biospheric AC); the second reading would predict higher levels of awareness of human consequences (AC_{soc}) among women, but no difference in relative value orientations. Brody's (1984) examination of gender differences in attitudes toward nuclear power provides evidence consistent with the second reading. Using national survey data, he found that women are more concerned about safety issues of nuclear power (higher AC), whereas there is no evidence of gender differences in the effects of safety concerns on support for nuclear power (no difference in weights assigned to AC).

Some ecofeminist writings suggest that women are potentially more environmentalist than men because of a biospheric orientation (Griffin, 1978; Merchant, 1979; Diamond and Orenstein, 1990). This argument may also be read either as a claim that women assign greater weight to biospheric values ('care more' about the biosphere) or as a claim that women, possibly because they are more 'rooted' in the natural environment, are more likely to become aware of the consequences of human activity for the biosphere. The theoretical literature is ambiguous or equivocal on this point.

We note in passing that such gendered differences in values need not be based on 'essentialist' assumptions for which ecofeminist writers have been criticized (Biehl,

1991; Code, 1991; Eckersley, 1992). Concern with others or the biosphere may well derive from cultural and social-structural factors rather than any innate, universal or biological characteristics of women. It has been argued, for example, that women's relationship-centered moral views result from their subordinated or 'minority' status and may therefore also be common among men from socially subordinated groups (e.g. Tronto, 1987). Data regarding race and social class in relation to environmental attitudes are scarce, however. For a review of theoretical arguments and empirical evidence, see Mohai (1985). We presume that if gender differences in value orientations exist with regard to humanistic or biospheric altruism, they are more likely to derive from shared experience than innate differences.

In fact, the empirical research on gender and environmental concern does not report consistent findings (Borden and Francis, 1978; McStay and Dunlap, 1983; Brady, 1984; Arcury et al, 1987; Blocker and Eckberg, 1989; Schahn and Holzer, 1990; Mohai, 1992), and a meta-analysis confirms these inconsistencies (Hines et al, 1986–1987). In some studies, women appear more concerned about the environment, whereas in others the gender relationship disappears or is reversed. Mohai's (1992) recent review suggests that women express more concern than men in local environmental issues and that the difference is smaller for national issues. He also notes that women are less likely than men to take political action to protect the environment. Research findings on gender and altruism are also inconsistent. See, for example, Austin (1979), Deaux and Major (1987), Mills et al, (1989), and, for a meta-analysis, Eagly and Crowley (1986).

Our model offers a theoretical account that could make sense of such inconsistent findings. If there are gendered differences in value orientations or in the tendency to become aware of certain kinds of consequences, gender differences in environmental attitudes would vary with the actual or perceived consequences of particular environmental conditions, and therefore with the environmental problem. This line of argument is consistent with Blocker and Eckberg's (1989) discussion of 'mother' and 'father' effects, and the earlier statements of McStay and Dunlap (1983) and Hamilton (1985). Blocker and Eckberg report a 'mother effect' in which women with children are substantially more concerned about local environmental problems than are men, and a 'father effect' (initially reported by George and Southwell, 1986) in which men with children are more concerned with economic than environmental consequences. These effects suggest that having children may increase parents' attentiveness to consequences bearing on their sex-typed roles in families: for mothers, concern for their children's health; for fathers, concern for the material wellbeing of the family.

Although such interpretations are not yet well supported, these findings and those of Brody (1984) suggest that it may be fruitful to look at gender effects within a model that allows us to assess whether men and women differ in the degree to which they hold beliefs about the consequences of environmental conditions for self-interest, other human beings or nonhuman species or the biosphere, or in the weights they give to egoistic, social-altruistic and biospheric values. A difference in beliefs may reflect gender differences in the degree to which individuals are attuned or attentive to information about particular consequences of environmental problems. A difference in the weight given those beliefs in choosing what actions to take implies a difference in the strengths of value orientations toward self, others and the biosphere.

This article reports a limited test of our theoretical model. Using data from a sample of college undergraduates, we develop scales to measure beliefs about the consequences of pollution and environmental protection for self, others and the biosphere. We then examine the relationship of these scales to three measures of action with regard to the environment – one that measures political action, and two measures of willingness to pay for improved environmental quality. Finally, we examine the relationship of gender to beliefs about consequences, to the three value orientations, and to behavioural intentions.

Data and Methods

Data are from a systematic random sample of undergraduates at a large public university in northern New York State.[6] Table 12.1 reports the items used to form scales of beliefs about the consequences of environmental quality or environmental protection for the self, the welfare of others and the biosphere, as well as the items on the scale of political action. Responses to all items were on 4-point Likert-type scales with categories *strongly disagree, disagree, agree,* and *strongly agree.*[7] The scales were constructed using Armor's (1974) theta scaling procedure. The reliabilities of the AC scales are only moderate, which is not surprising given the small number of items available to construct each scale. Despite measurement error, however, the analysis shows that the scales have significant predictive power.

The political-action scale measures willingness to take four kinds of political action for environmental protection. The two additional measures assess willingness to pay: 'How many extra dollars per year in income tax would you be willing to pay if you knew the extra money would be spent to protect the environment?' and 'How much increase in gasoline prices, in cents per gallon, would you be willing to pay if the money was spent to protect the environment?' To analyse the willingness-to-pay items, we added US$0.50 and US$0.005, respectively, to each response to recode 'zero' responses, and then used the natural logarithm of the recoded value to minimize skew in the distribution.

Our theory implies a regression model. We have analysed it using ordinary least squares. A stochastic regressor or hierarchical model might better reflect our theoretical model, but more traditional techniques seem appropriate for this exploratory effort. Standard diagnostics suggest no problems with outliers in either carriers or residuals and a reasonable degree of normality in the estimated residuals (Dietz et al, 1987; Dietz et al, 1992). The level of collinearity in the model is moderate.[8] We interpret a statistically significant regression coefficient linking a belief scale to a behavioural intention measure as evidence of an effect of belief on behavioural intention, or to put it another way, as evidence of a nonzero weighting of the relevant value orientation. (The model treats each value orientation as the coefficient of association between behavioural intention and belief about a type of consequence of environmental conditions.) We test hypotheses about gender differences in AC beliefs by regressing the belief scales on gender, a procedure equivalent to a difference of means test. We test the hypothesis of gender differences in the value weights by allowing the regression coefficients for each AC belief to differ between men and women and testing for significance of interaction effects.

Table 12.1 Items used in belief and behavioural-intention scales

	Mean	SD	Loading	Theta
Belief in consequences for self (AC$_{ego}$)				.66
Protecting the environment will threaten jobs for people like me	1.66	0.65	-0.78	
Laws to protect the environment limit my choices and personal freedom	1.87	0.64	-0.77	
A clean environment provides me with better opportunities for recreation	3.39	0.56	0.77	
Belief in consequences for others (AC$_{soc}$)				.62
We don't need to worry much about the environment because future generations will be better able to deal with these problems than we are	1.36	0.56	-0.72	
The effects of pollution on public health are worse than we realize	3.25	0.67	0.77	
Pollution generated here harms people all over the earth	3.30	0.56	0.77	
Belief in consequences for the biosphere (AC$_{bio}$)				.56
Claims that current levels of pollution are changing the earth's climate are exaggerated	1.69	0.72	-0.64	
Over the next several decades, thousands of species will become extinct	3.15	0.65	0.81	
The balance of nature is delicate and easily upset	3.21	0.63	0.73	
Political Action				.77
I would participate in a demonstration against companies that are harming the environment	2.80	0.82	0.79	
I would contribute money to environmental organizations	3.02	0.68	0.84	
I would sign a petition in support of tougher environmental laws	3.34	0.63	0.79	
I would take a job with a company I knew was harming the environment	2.03	0.72	-0.66	

Results

Table 12.2 presents the intercorrelations of all the measures we developed in the study.

Table 12.2 *Scale intercorrelations*

	AC_{ego}	AC_{soc}	AC_{bio}	Political action	Gas tax
AC_{ego}					
AC_{soc}	0.57				
AC_{bio}	0.43	0.60			
Political action	0.57	0.59	0.52		
Gas tax	0.25	0.23	0.22	0.39	
Income tax	0.32	0.26	0.27	0.40	0.42

Table 12.3 reports the results of regressions.

Table 12.3 *Regressions of behavioural-intention scales on belief scales*

	Political action scale	Income tax	Gasoline tax
AC_{ego}	0.316**	0.419**	0.204*
AC_{soc}	0.270**	0.089	0.133
AC_{bio}	0.219**	0.280*	0.153
Intercept	−0.014	3.824**	1.631**
R square	0.458	0.122	0.078

$* P < 0.05; ** P < 0.01.$

Model of environmental concern

Table 12.3 shows that belief in each of the three types of consequences significantly predicts willingness to take political action regarding the environment when other beliefs are statistically controlled, despite moderate collinearity among the scales and the measurement error in each. This finding is consistent with the Schwartz model, but implies that beliefs about consequences for self or for the biosphere, and not only about consequences for others, can motivate action on environmental issues. It supports our model of environmental concern as dependent on all three value orientations.

The regression equations for willingness to pay, however, have different implications. Prediction of willingness to pay via either gasoline or income taxes is much weaker than for political behaviour. In each case, willingness to pay is significantly predicted by egoistic AC. Biospheric AC provides some explanatory power with regard to willingness to pay increased income taxes, but not gasoline taxes.

Nothing in our model of environmental concern, nor in other theoretical work in the literature, suggests that behavioural intentions toward a single attitude object should have a different value base for different behaviours.[9] We believe the most likely explanation lies in the possibility that different survey items – in this case, different behavioural intention items – focus the respondents' attention selectively on different value orientations, thereby affecting responses (Dietz and Stern, 1992). We hypothesize that because three value orientations coexist in respondents and may all influence behaviour (as indicated by the data on political behaviour), individual action may depend on the belief or value set that receives attention in a given context. Cialdini (Cialdini et al, 1990, 1991) has demonstrated a number of 'focus effects' of this type in experimental settings. We hypothesize that in a survey, questions about intended political action draw respondents' attention to whatever values spur them to political action on the issue in question – and in environmental politics, the public debate suggests that each of the three value orientations may be involved. Questions about willingness to pay draw respondents' attention to the things on which they spend money, and these things are more likely to pertain to their wellbeing than to social-altruistic or biospheric values. If this argument is correct, a willingness-to-pay question has the effect of focusing attention on the egoistic value orientation.

Our argument is similar to one recently advanced in the literature on contingent valuation surveys, a method of assessing preference that relies on willingness-to-pay questions.[10] Irwin et al (in press) found that respondents' preference orderings were different as a function of the way willingness-to-pay questions were asked. People who were asked to give the dollar prices they were willing to pay to reduce local air pollution and to buy a higher quality camera (they saw pictures of two Denver cityscapes and two cameras) offered more money for the camera. The preference ordering was reversed when people were asked whether they would pay more for the improved air quality or the improved camera. Gregory et al (1992) interpret the findings in terms of cognitive heuristics. The compatibility effect (Slovic et al, 1990) is an over-reliance on attributes that are scaled in the same units as the response: Consumer goods are normally scaled by prices, but air quality is not, so the nonmonetary values of air quality tend to be ignored when people are asked to evaluate it in terms of money. However, when people are asked whether better air quality or an improved camera is worth more to them, they are implicitly asked to marshal arguments for their choices: In this frame, there are many good reasons to favour air quality.

Our findings and those of Irwin et al (in press) support the argument we have made elsewhere (Dietz and Stern 1992) that the focus concept has important implications for interpreting expressions of preference, such as on contingent valuation surveys. Techniques of contingent valuation direct individuals to focus on a monetary calculus for evaluating goods and services. They may thereby give a skewed impression of preferences or at the least a systematically different impression from what would emerge from other measurement techniques. We hypothesize that questions about behaviours that involve financial commitments focus attention on an economic calculus, and thus elicit an egoistic value orientation to a greater degree than general behavioural questions. We expect that in general, biospheric and social-altruistic values will be more predictive of nonfinancial measures of behavioural intent, whereas egoistic values will explain more variance in willingness-to-pay items.

Gender effects

Tables 12.4 and 12.5 examine the effects of gender on political action and the willing-ness-to-pay items. In each case, gender has a significant total effect, with women taking a more pro-environment stance. But when the three beliefs are controlled, the effect of gender drops substantially and is not significant. Table 12.5 indicates that gender is strongly related to each of the three beliefs. Thus the model provides a mechanism for interpreting the effects of gender on environmental action. Women are more likely than men to see environmental quality as having consequences for personal wellbeing, social welfare and the health of the biosphere. When these gender-differentiated belief systems are taken into account, there is no remaining direct effect of gender on either political action or willingness to pay. These findings support the interpretation that when women are more active on environmental issues, it is because of an increased likelihood to make connections between environmental conditions and their values, rather than because they have different value structures from men. The regression analysis in Table 12.4, as well as an analysis-of-covariance F test for gender differences in the slopes relating the belief scales to the dependent variables, indicates that there are no significant gender differences in the weights given each belief.[11]

Table 12.4 *Regressions of behavioural intentions on gender and belief scales*

	Political action scale		Income tax		Gasoline tax	
Gender	0.511**	0.174	0.744**	0.453	0.427*	0.246
AC_{ego}	–	0.326**	–	0.427**	–	0.218*
AC_{soc}	–	0.262**	–	0.019	–	0.066
AC_{bio}	–	0.178**	–	0.289*	–	0.162
Intercept	–0.281**	–0.098	3.381**	3.543**	1.334**	1.434**
R square	0.062	0.461	0.034	0.134	0.020	0.085

* $P < 0.05$; ** $P < 0.01$

Table 12.5 *Regressions of belief scales on gender*

	AC_{ego}	AC_{soc}	AC_{bio}
Gender	0.470**	0.511**	0.278*
Intercept	0.264**	–0.268**	–0.152
R square	0.050	0.064	0.017

* $P < 0.05$; ** $P < 0.01$

Discussion

Our theory is an attempt to integrate three themes in research on environmental concern. The first, and oldest, is the theme of environmentalism as altruism. We expand the Schwartz norm-activation model, which treats environmental concern as altruism toward other human beings, to incorporate both self-interest, or egoism, and concern with other species or the biosphere itself. By allowing the possibility that biospheric values may influence behaviour, we integrate the Schwartz model with the ideas of Dunlap and others about environmental worldviews. In essence, we argue that environmental concern in the US has three distinguishable, although correlated, components – self-interest, concern with others and concern with other species or natural environments.

In our sample, all three types of beliefs have some influence on expressed willingness to take political action. But as suggested by focus theory, the effects of beliefs about consequences beyond the self are much weaker when we ask about willingness to pay taxes to protect the environment – questions that draw attention to the monetary, and thus egoistic, aspects of environmental problems. Some of the anomalies in contingent valuation research and the apparent inconsistencies in the literature on environmental concern may be the result of such focus effects. Different sets of environmental attitude or preference questions draw attention to different value frames and yield differing degrees of measured environmental concern.

It may be that egoistic, social-altruistic and biospheric orientations represent points on a dimension of moral scope or breadth of moral concern. Such is an implication of the kin-selection approach to cultural evolution, which suggests that concern and altruism are a function of closeness of blood kinship. Or it may be that the orientations compete, as is suggested by the criticisms of environmentalists as lacking concern about people. These are empirical issues. The moderate positive correlations we find among AC beliefs suggest that in the area of environmental perception the value orientations may be part of a single perceptual package. Disentangling the relationships among them will require more sophisticated analysis than that performed here.

Gender is the third theme integrated into our work. We provide a social-psychological model for understanding gender differences in environmental concern. Women may hold different beliefs than men about the consequences of environmental conditions and/or they may assign different value weights to each type of consequence. We find that in our student sample gender differences in environmentalism are the result of gender differences in beliefs about the effects of environmental problems. Women apparently are more accepting than men of messages that link environmental conditions to potential harm to themselves, others and other species or the biosphere. We find no substantial male-female differences in the value weights assigned to those beliefs, however. Our findings are consistent with the argument in feminist theory that women tend to see a world of inherent interconnections, whereas men tend to see a world of clearly separate subjects and objects, with events abstracted from their contexts. That argument suggests that men might be less attentive than women to links between the environment and things they value, even if men and women hold the same values.

Our approach suggests that socialization and social structure can shape individual environmental concern either by affecting value orientations or by altering individuals' attentiveness to information. Our results suggest that gender differences involve the latter mechanism. The mother and father effects that have been identified in the literature on gender and environmental concern may depend on such differential awareness. Becoming a parent increases attention to information about things that may affect one's children's wellbeing; gender socialization may lead women to focus on children's health, and men on children's economic wellbeing, with opposite effects on environmental concern.

The model also suggests a mechanism for understanding age, period, and cohort differences in environmental concern (Van Liere and Dunlap, 1980; Dunlap, 1991). We suspect that beliefs about the effects of environmental conditions on the self, others and the biosphere or other species, because they depend to a great degree on secondhand information and are not tightly linked to self-identity, should be changeable on the basis of new information. In contrast, the values that can turn these beliefs into action are much less mutable. Thus we hypothesize that differences in beliefs about the consequences of environmental conditions may be largely period effects based on changing publicity about the consequences of environmental change for the self, others and the biosphere. In contrast, differences in value orientations are more likely to reflect cohort effects that come about from differences in early socialization and the shared formative experiences of cohorts. Age effects are likely to involve both value differences rooted in formative experience and changes in beliefs resulting from different information. This line of thinking implies that the same scientific information will affect environmental concern differently for different cohort and age groups.

Here we have not discussed in any detail how individual concern is shaped by macro-factors, such as social movements and political-economic forces. In earlier articles (Stern et al, 1986; Dietz et al, 1989), we have sketched some links between individual beliefs and values and these macro-forces, and examined how policy actors attempt to shape public attitudes by moulding problem definitions. These processes both influence environmental beliefs and focus attention selectively on certain values, and in this way are conformable with our social-psychological model.

Of course, the present results are quite preliminary. Further empirical work is needed to see if these results generalize to more diverse and representative populations. Further methodological work is needed to improve the measurement of beliefs and the measurement and estimation of value orientations. Further theoretical work is needed to clarify the ways scientific knowledge, political-economic forces, social movements and the processes of public discourse link to individuals' environmental concerns and to integrate a more complete model with a broader social-psychological theory.

Notes

This research was supported in part by the Division of Sponsored Research of the State University of New York, Plattsburgh and by the Northern Virginia Survey Research Laboratory, Department of Sociology and Anthropology, George Mason University. The views expressed herein are not necessarily those of the National Research Council.

1   Theories of genetic kin selection and reciprocal altruism suggest that the calculus of self-interest may include consideration of others when they are either close kin or when repeated contacts make reciprocity likely (Hamilton, 1964; Trivers, 1971). In addition to these approaches grounded in socio-biology, some theorists have suggested that altruism benefits the altruist through mechanisms such as joint utility functions (Buchanan, 1954; Arrow, 1963, 1975) or internal rewards (Cialdini et al, 1987; Schaller and Cialdini, 1988). For the purposes of our analysis, these

intangible internal rewards still produce behaviour that is altruistic in the sense that the material or instrumental costs to the altruist outweigh her or his material or instrumental benefits, while providing benefits to others. The model we develop is consistent with these arguments that all altruism is at some level egoistic, as well as with Schwartz's model. Contrary to many assumptions of socio-biology and rational-choice theory, recent work on cultural evolution demonstrates that the interests of individuals and the collectivity often may coincide and that under a variety of plausible conditions altruism may persist and spread in a culture (Boyd and Richerson, 1985, ch 7; Simon, 1990; Dietz, Burns and Buttel, 1990; Dietz and Burns, 1992).

2 Even in NIMBY protests, free rider problems may occur (Walsh and Warland, 1983). But because NIMBY protests by definition deal with localized issues, the free rider problem is much less severe at the local level than in national or international environmental problems. Note, however, that some participants in NIMBY protests base their actions on more than self-interest.

3 The same is true of environmental-movement organizations. The Greens and the 'new environmental movement' that predated them in the 1970s in the US are strongly concerned with issues of social justice that are a mark of the social-altruistic value orientation. Critics of the environmental movement on the left, however, have until recently vilified environmentalists for 'caring more about whales than poor people', suggesting that the targets of their attacks hold only biospheric and not social-altruistic values. Some of the rhetoric of Earth First! and other militant groups does suggest a limited concern for people compared to the biosphere. Still, the preponderance of environmental organizations and of the environmentally concerned probably hold both social-altruistic and biospheric concerns. For example, Jasper and Nelkin's (1991) account of the animal rights movement indicates that only one branch of the movement, which they label 'fundamentalist', would afford animal welfare a strict equivalence with human welfare, and thus give equal or greater weight to biospheric than to social-altruistic concerns.

4 Of course, it would be possible to use a psychometric approach and develop scales that measure preference or value orientation directly. Further work might move in this direction. The regression approach we use offers the advantage of linking to a standard approach in decision theory. In addition, because our model posits that values are weights assigned to a type of consequence, direct measurement of the values would lead to a multiplicative model, which would greatly increase the effects of measurement error and make statistical estimation more difficult.

5 The same conclusion can also be derived from genetic and cultural models of egoism and altruism, both of which accept that individuals act altruistically toward close kin. Because many environmental threats are long-term and may have greater effects on future generations than on contemporary adults, and because children are more susceptible to many environmental toxins, parents may be more environmentally concerned than nonparents. Further, mothers, who typically are more intimately involved in childraising than fathers, might also be more sensitive to environmental threats to their immediate families. This awareness may provide a causal mechanism for Gilligan's observation of women's greater concern for the other in making moral judgements. In our terms, such concerns with one's children

might easily generalize to concern with other children and with other humans. That is, concerns with family might be precursors to humanistic altruism. This point is raised by Hamilton (1985) and by Blocker and Eckberg (1989).

6   The initial sample was of 553 undergraduates, of whom 349 returned usable surveys, for a response rate of 63 per cent. The survey was conducted by mail in the fall of 1990. The Dillman (1978) protocol with an initial mailing and two follow-up mailings was used to minimize nonresponse.

7   College students tend to exhibit high levels of concern about the environment, and our sample is no exception, as is obvious from the small coefficient of variation for most items used in scaling. The limited variance on most items undoubtedly reduces the reliability of the scales. The high degree of skewness on the items suggests it would not be appropriate to use inferential methods, such as confirmatory factor analysis, in constructing scales. When observed variables are ordinal, polychoric correlations are generally considered the most robust measure of association (Olsson, 1979; Jöreskog and Sörbom, 1988), but the use of these correlations assumes that the latent variables underlying the observed variables have a bivariate normal distribution. An analysis of the 36 polychoric correlation coefficients linking our nine AC indicators leads to rejection of the null hypothesis of bivariate normality at the 0.01 level for two thirds of the pairs. Thus, in this exploratory study we have not applied inferential scaling methods. We believe the content and construct validity of the scales, combined with their moderate reliability, justifies their use in this exploratory effort (Bollen, 1989, pp151–190). Note that measurement error in the independent variables in a regression has complex effects, but in the simplest case the effect is to attenuate regression coefficients. Thus the statistically significant effects we find support our argument for distinct belief domains.

8   The R^2 values for the auxiliary regressions for models including the three belief scales and gender are 0.37, 0.53, 0.39 and 0.08 for egoistic AC, social-altruistic AC, biospheric AC and gender, respectively.

9   There is an argument in the literature that environmentally relevant behaviours are predicted by beliefs and personal norms specific to the behaviour (Black et al, 1985), but no such argument applies to the kind of general environmental beliefs and values measured here. The environmental-attitudes literature on gender often notes a distinction between local and general environmental issues. Such a difference could be based on value orientations, especially egoistic versus social-altruistic values.

10   The very substantial literature on contingent valuation is reviewed in Mitchell and Carson (1989) and Cummings, Brookshire and Schulze (1986). The contingent valuation method is seen by advocates as providing a method of valuing public goods when markets do not provide an adequate mechanism for assigning value to them. The method has become very popular with environmental economists. Mitchell and Carson (1989, pp308–215) list 104 contingent valuation studies in their summary, and each month adds a few more studies or contributions to theory and methods. The method has been criticized on a number of grounds (discussion in Cummings, Brookshire, and Schulze, 1986; Harris, Driver and McLaughlin, 1989; Dietz and Stern, 1992; Slovic, 1992).

11   The F values for a gender difference in belief slopes are 0.9 ($P = 0.44$), 2.3 ($P = 0.08$) and 1.7 ($P = 0.17$) for the political action, gasoline tax and income taxes

items, respectively. The interaction term for self-interest was significant at the 0.05 level in the regressions for the two tax items, with women giving less weight to self-interest than men, as is consistent with the ecofeminist literature. Because the overall F test for interaction effects was not significant, and because a Bonferroni correction for nine hypothesis tests (three interaction terms for each of three equations) suggests a test at the 0.0056 level, we do not discuss this effect further.

References

1 Arcury, T. A., Scollay, S. J. and Johnson, T. P. (1987) 'Sex differences in environmental concern and knowledge'. *Sex Roles*, vol 16, pp463–472

2 Armor, D. J. (1974) 'Theta reliability and factor scaling', in Costner, H. L. (ed) *Sociological Methodology*, San Francisco, Jossey-Bass, pp17–50

3 Arrow, K. (1963) *Social Choice and Individual Values.* Wiley, NY

4 Arrow, K. (1975) 'Gifts and exchanges', in Phelps, E. S. (ed) *Altruism, Mortality, and Economic Theory.* Russell Sage, NY

5 Austin, W. (1979) 'Sex differences in bystander intervention in a theft'. *Journal of Personality and Social Psychology*, vol 37, pp2110–2120

6 Biehl, J. (1991) *Rethinking Ecofeminist Politics.* South End, Boston

7 Black, J. S., Stern, P. C. and Elsworth, J. T. (1985) 'Personal and contextual influences on household energy adaptations'. *Journal of Applied Psychology*, vol 70, pp3–21

8 Blocker, T. J. and Eckberg, D. L (1989) 'Environmental issues as women's issues: General concerns and local hazards'. *Social Science Quarterly*, vol 70, pp586–593

9 Bollen, K. A. (1989) *Structural Equations with Latent Variables.* Academic Press, NY

10 Borden, R. J. and Francis, J. F. (1978) 'Who cares about ecology? Personality and sex differences in environmental concern'. *Journal of Personality*, vol 46, pp190–203.

11 Boyd, R. and Richerson, P. J. (1985) *Culture and the Evolutionary Process.* University of Chicago Press, Chicago, IL

12 Brennan, A. (1988) *Thinking about Nature: An Investigation of Nature, Value and Ecology.* University of Georgia Press, Athens

13 Brody, C. J. (1984) 'Sex differences in support for nuclear power'. *Social Forces*, vol 63, pp209–228

14 Buchanan, J. M. (1954) 'Individual choice in voting and the market'. *Journal of Political Economy*, vol 62, pp334–343

15 Buttel, F. H. (1987) 'New directions in environmental sociology'. *Annual Review of Sociology*, vol 12, pp465–488

16 Cialdini, R. B., Kallgren, C. A. and Reno, R. R. (1991) 'A focus theory of normative conduct A theoretical refinement and reevaluation of the role of norms in human behaviour'. *Advances in Experimental Social Psychology*, vol 24, pp201–234

17 Cialdini, R. B., Reno, R. R. and Kallgren, C. A. (1990) 'A focus theory of normative conduct Recycling the concept of norms to reduce littering in public places'. *Journal of Personality and Social Psychology*, vol 58, pp1015–1026

18 Cialdini, R. B., Schaller, M., Houlihan, D., Arps, K., Fultz, J. and Beaman, A. L. (1987) 'Empathy-based helping: Is it selflessly or selfishly motivated?' *Journal of Personality and Social Psychology*, vol 52, pp749–758

19 Code, L (1991) *What Can She Know? Feminist Theory and the Construction of Knowledge.* Cornell University Press, Ithaca, NY

20 Cotgrove, S. (1982) *Catastrophe or Cornucopia: The Environment, Politics and the Future.* Wiley, New York

21 Cummings, R. G., Brookshire, D. S. and Schulze, W. D. (1986) *Valuing Environmental Goods.* Bowman and Allanheld, Totowa, NJ

22 Deaux, K. and Major, B. (1987) 'Putting gender into context'. *Psychological Review*, vol 94, pp369–389

23 Devall, B. (1988) *Simple in Means, Rich in Ends: Practicing Deep Ecology.* Gibbs M. Smith, Salt Lake City, UT

24 Devall, B. and Sessions, G. (1985) *Deep Ecology: Living as if Nature Mattered.* Gibbs M. Smith, Salt Lake City, UT

25 Diamond, I. and Orenstein, G. F. (1990) *Reweaving the World: The Emergence of Ecofeminism.* Sierra Club Books, San Francisco

26 Dietz, T. and Burns, T. R. (1992) *Human Agency and the Evolutionary Dynamics of Culture.* Swedish Collegium for Advanced Study in the Social Sciences, Uppsala, Sweden

27 Dietz. T., Burns, T. R. and Buttel, F. H. (1990) 'Evolutionary theory in sociology: An examination of current thinking'. *Sociological Forum*, vol 5, pp155–171

28 Dietz. T., Frey, R. S. and Kalof, L (1987) 'Estimation with cross-national data: Robust and resampling estimators'. *American Sociological Review*, vol 52, pp380–390

29 Dietz, T., Kalof, L. and Frey, R. S. (1992) 'On the utility of robust and resampling estimators'. *Rural Sociology*, vol 56, pp461–474

30 Dietz, T. and Stern, P. C. (1992, February) 'Individual preferences and social values'. Paper presented at the annual meeting of the American Association for the Advancement of Science, Chicago, IL

31 Dietz, T., Stern, P. C. and Rycroft, R. W. (1989) 'Definitions of conflict and the legitimation of resources: The case of environmental risk'. *Sociological Forum*, vol 4, pp47–70

32 Dillman, D. R. (1978) *Mail and Telephone Surveys: The Total Design Method.* Wiley, NY

33 Dunlap, R. E. (1991) 'Public opinion in the 1980s: Clear consensus, ambiguous commitment'. *Environment*, vol 33(October), pp10–15, 32–37

34 Dunlap, R. E. and Van Liere, K. D. (1977a) 'Land ethic or golden rule: Comment on "land ethic realized" by Thomas A. Heberlein, JSI, 28(4), 1972'. *Journal of Social Issues*, vol 33, pp200–207

35 Dunlap, R. E. and Van Liere, K. D. (1977b) 'Response to Heberlein's rejoinder'. *Journal of Social Issues*, vol 33, pp211–212

36 Dunlap, R. E. and Van Liere, K. D. (1978) 'The new environmental paradigm: A proposed measuring instrument and preliminary results'. *Journal of Environmental Education*, vol 9, pp10–19

37 Dunlap, R. E. and Van Liere, K. D. (1984) 'Commitment to the dominant social paradigm and concern for environmental quality: An empirical examination'. *Social Science Quarterly*, vol 65, pp1013–1028

38 Eagly, A. H. and Crowley, M. (1986) 'Gender and helping behaviour'. *Psychological Bulletin*, vol 100, pp283–308

39 Eckersley, R. (1992) *Environmentalism and Political Theory: Toward an Ecocentric Approach.* Albany State University of New York Press

40 George, D. and Southwell, P. (1986) 'Opinion on the Diablo Canyon nuclear power plant'. *Social Science Quarterly*, vol 67, pp722–735

41 Gilligan, C. (1982) *In a Different Voice: Psychological Theory and Women's Development.* Harvard University Press, Cambridge, MA

42 Gregory, R., Lichtenstein, S. and Slovic, P. (1992) *Valuing Environmental Resources: A Constructive Approach.* Unpublished manuscript, Decision Research, Eugene, OR

43 Griffin, S. (1978) *Women and Nature: The Roaring inside Her.* Harper and Row, NY

44 Habermas, J. (1981) 'New social movements'. *Telos*, vol 49, pp33–37

45 Hamilton, L. C. (1985) 'Who cares about water pollution? Opinions in a small-town crisis'. *Sociological Inquiry*, vol 55, pp170–181

46 Hamilton, W. D. (1964) 'The genetical evolution of social behaviour, I, II'. *Journal of Theoretical Biology*, vol 7, pp1–52

47 Hardin, G. (1968) 'The tragedy of the commons'. *Science*, vol 162, pp1243–1248.

48 Harris, C. C., Driver, B. L. and McLaughlin. W. J. (1989) 'Improving the contingent valuation method: A psychological perspective'. *Journal of Environmental Economics and Management*, vol 17, pp213–229

49 Heberlein, T. A. (1972) 'The land ethic realized: Some social psychological explanations for changing environmental attitudes'. *Journal of Social Issues*, vol 28, pp79–87

50 Heberlein, T. A. (1977) 'Norm activation and environmental action: A rejoinder to R. E. Dunlap and K. D. Van Liere'. *Journal of Social Issues,* vol 33, pp207–211

51 Heberlein, T. A. (1981) 'Environmental attitudes'. *Zeitschrift für Umweltpolitik*, vol 2, pp241–270

52 Heberlein, T. A. and Black, J. S. (1976) 'Attitudinal specificity and the prediction of behaviour in a field setting'. *Journal of Personality and Social Psychology*, vol 33, pp474–479

53 Hines, J. M., Hungerford, H. R. and Tomera, A. N. (1986–1987) 'Analysis and synthesis of research on responsible environmental behaviour'. *Journal of Environmental Education*, vol 18(2), pp1–8

54 Hopper, J. R. and Nielsen, J. M. (1991) 'Recycling as altruistic behaviour: Normative and behavioural strategies to expand participation in a community recycling program'. *Environment and Behaviour*, vol 23, pp195–220

55 Inglehart, R. (1990) *Culture Shift in Advanced Industrial Society.* Princeton University Press, Princeton, NJ

56 Irwin, J. R., Slovic, P., Lichtenstein, S. and McClelland, G. H. (1993) 'Preference reversals and the measurement of environmental values'. *Journal of Risk and Uncertainty*, vol 6, pp1–13

57 Jasper, J. M. and Nelkin, D. (1991) *The Animal Rights Crusade: The Growth of a Moral Protest.* Free Press, NY

58 Jöreskog, K. G. and Sörbom, D. (1988) *PRELIS: A Program for Multivariate Data Screening and Data Summarization.* Scientific Software, Inc, Mooresville, IN

59 Leopold, A. (1949). *A Sand County Almanac.* Oxford University Press, NY

60 McStay, J. and Dunlap, R. E. (1983) 'Male-female differences in concern for environmental quality'. *International Journal of Women's Studies*, vol 6, pp291–301

61 Merchant, C. (1979) *The Death of Nature: Women, Ecology and the Scientific Revolution.* Harper and Row, NY

62 Milbrath, L. (1984) *Environmentalists: Vanguard for a New Society.* State University of New York Press, Albany

63 Mills, R. S. L., Pedersen, J. and Grusec, J. E. (1989) 'Sex differences in reasoning and emotion about altruism'. *Sex Roles*, vol 20, pp603–621

64 Mitchell, R. C. and Carson, R. T. (1989) *Using Surveys to Value Public Goods: The Contingent Valuation Method.* Resources for the Future, Washington DC

65 Mohai, P. (1985) 'Public concern and elite involvement in environmental-conservation issues'. *Social Science Quarterly*, vol 66, pp820–838.

66 Mohai, P. (1992) 'Men, women, and the environment: An examination of the gender gap in environmental concern and activism'. *Society and Natural Resources*, vol 5, pp1–19

67 Naess, A. (1989) *Ecology, Community and Lifestyle* (D. Rothenberg, Trans). Cambridge University Press, Cambridge

68 Offe, C. (1985) 'New social movements: Challenging the boundaries of institutional politics'. *Social Research*, vol 52, pp817–868

69 Olson, M. (1965) *The Logic of Collective Action*. Harvard University Press, Cambridge, MA

70 Olsson, U. (1979) 'Maximum likelihood estimation of the polychoric correlation coefficient'. *Psychometrika*, vol 44, pp443–460

71 Oskamp, S., Harrington, M. J., Edwards, T. C., Sherwood, D. L., Okuda, S. M. and Swanson, D. C. (1991) 'Factors influencing household recycling behaviour'. *Environment and Behaviour*, vol 23, pp494–519

72 Rokeach, M. (1973) *The Nature of Human Values*. Free Press, NY

73 Schahn, J. and Holzer, E. (1990) 'Studies of individual environmental concern: The role of knowledge, gender and background variables'. *Environment and Behaviour*, vol 22, pp767–786

74 Schaller, M. and Cialdini, R. B. (1988) 'The economics of empathic helping: Support for a mood management motive'. *Journal of Experimental Social Psychology*, vol 24, pp163–181

75 Schwartz, S. H. (1968a) 'Awareness of consequences and the influence of moral norms on interpersonal behaviour'. *Sociometry*, vol 31, pp355–369

76 Schwartz, S. H. (1968b) 'Words, deeds, and the perception of consequences and responsibility in action situations'. *Journal of Personality and Social Psychology*, vol 10, pp232–242

77 Schwartz, S. H. (1970) 'Moral decision making and behaviour', in Macauley, J. and Berkowitz, L. (eds) *Altruism and Helping Behaviour*. Academic Press, NY

78 Schwartz, S. H. (1977) 'Normative influences on altruism', in Berkowitz, L. (ed) *Advances In Experimental Social Psychology*. Academic Press, NY, vol 10, pp221–279

79 Simon, H. A. (1990) 'A mechanism for social selection and successful altruism'. *Science*, vol 250, pp1665–1668

80 Slovic, P. (1992, February) Preference and payment: Psychological issues in valuing environmental impacts. Paper presented at the annual meeting of the American Association of the Advancement of Science, Chicago, IL

81 Slovic. P., Griffin, D. and Tversky, A. (1990) 'Compatibility effects in judgement and choice', in Hogarth R. M. (ed) *Insights in decision making: A tribute to Hillel J. Einhorn*. University of Chicago Press, Chicago, IL, pp5–27

82 Stern, P. C., Dietz, T. and Black, J. S. (1986) 'Support for environmental protection: The role of moral norms'. *Population and Environment*, vol 8, pp204–222

83 Stern, P. C. and Oskamp, S. (1987) 'Managing scarce environmental resources', in Stokols, D. and Altman, I. (eds) *Handbook of Environmental Psychology*, vol 2, Wiley, NY, pp1043–1088

84 Trivers, R. (1971) 'The evolution of reciprocal altruism'. *Quarterly Review of Biology*, vol 46, pp35–57

85 Tronto, J. (1987) 'Beyond gender difference to a theory of care'. *SIGNS: Journal of Women in Culture and Society*, vol 12, pp644–663

86 Van Liere, K. D. and Dunlap, R. E. (1978) 'Moral norms and environmental behaviour: An application of Schwartz's norm-activation model to yard burning'. *Journal of Applied Social Psychology*, vol 8, pp174–188

87 Van Liere, K. D. and Dunlap, R. E. (1980) 'The social bases of environmental concern: A review of hypotheses, explanations and empirical evidence'. *Public Opinion Quarterly*, vol 44, pp181–197

88 Walsh, E. J. and Warland, R. W. (1983) 'Social movement involvement in the wake of a nuclear accident: Activists and free-riders in the Three Mile Island area'. *American Sociological Review*, vol 48, pp764–781

13

Environmental Values:
A Place-Based Theory

Bryan G. Norton and Bruce Hannon

Introduction

Tip O'Neil, the late and popular former congressman from Massachusetts, said, 'All politics is local'. Does it not follow that environmental policy, which must in some real sense politically define a good life in a good environment, is also necessarily local? We wonder whether this insight might help us formulate a general concept of sustainability that is based on a local commitment of citizens to protect their cultural and natural heritage.[1] In this paper, we propose a theory of environmental valuation that is based on a commitment to place. Locally developed and formulated values, when expressed as strident opposition to the siting of solid waste disposal sites, waste treatment plants and nuclear utility plants – what is usually referred to as 'NIMBYism' – are often thought of as a hindrance to formation of a rational environmental policy.[2] If our theory is accepted, however, it follows that any democratically supportable environmental policy has to take NIMBYism, and the sentiments associated with it, into account as givens. Indeed, in accordance with the theory that we propose, local sentiments are embraced as the driving force constituting 'environmental' values. The task, then, is to formulate a multiscalar structure of valuation and policy formation that is based democratically in many local perspectives, and yet capable of embracing the imperative that local behaviour be understood in relation to longer-term and larger-scale environmental problems – regional, national and global.

As a first step, consider the strong argument, originally proposed by Mark Sagoff, that individuals conceptualize and answer questions regarding environmental protection very differently depending on the context in which the questions are posed. Sagoff argues, in particular, that when the context encourages respondents to answer as *citizens* rather than as *consumers*, one can expect quite different answers to questions such as whether to develop or preserve wild landscapes.[3] Common, Blamey and Norton, following Sagoff, have articulated and begun testing the 'Sagoff hypothesis': individuals consider questions arising with regard to their nonuse relationships with nature 'in [the] citizen, as opposed to consumer, mode'.[4] The early and limited evidence apparently supports the Sagoff hypothesis.

Note: Reprinted from *Environmental Ethics*, vol 19, Norton, B. G. and Hannon, B., 'Environmental values: A place-based theory', pp227–245, copyright © (1997), with permission from authors

We believe, however, that the Sagoff hypothesis is better viewed as a proposal to shift paradigms, as advocating a change in how we express and describe environmental values, rather than as an empirical hypothesis. Sagoff's emphasis on political values and community-oriented commitments conflicts with mainstream economists' view of environmental value, which can be modelled in a market system; however, that is as we should expect, given that the Sagoff hypothesis is better understood as a decision to reject the economists' fiction that environmental decisions can be modelled as the decisions of individuals acting in markets. Thus, while the Sagoff hypothesis is in this sense tautological, it is an important tautology because it suggests that we model the behaviour of decision makers and members of the public not simply as they are driven by the limited motives of *Homo economicus*, but also as motivated participants in a process that involves *both* expressing *preferences* in the short run and, on a multigenerational communitarian scale, articulating *aspirations* for future generations.

Although we agree with the Sagoff hypothesis that setting environmental goals must be political, we go beyond that hypothesis (as formuated by Common et al), arguing that those political acts must be contextualized within a multiscaled, but locally centred, political process. Unlike economists who model environmental decisions as faced by a placeless, rational, individual, utility maximizer, *Homo economicus,* who costlessly migrates as necessary, we model environmental decisions as faced by individuals who are deeply influenced both by their individual perspective and by a local, community perspective. We see place-centredness not as a failure of rationality, but as an expression of their commitment to one's own home and community. Our challenge is to accept these expressions of place preference and to integrate them into a larger, regional and global community. Individuals, as we model their choices, conceptualize their environmental decisions as citizens who relate *from* a place, and *outward toward* their surroundings on several scales.

Having touted the legitimacy of local values, but also having recognized the legitimacy of regional and national interests in some cases, how do we decide the correct level, or scale, on which to address any given environmental problem? We answer: at the level of the physical system that corresponds to the temporal scale of the problem as it is formulated in policy discourse.[5] Note that implicit in the recognition of a 'problem' is an evaluation of possible outcomes. Concern that something of value is threatened is the essence of problem recognition and characterization, and the determination of the scale at which a problem will be modelled is an important part of this process. This design is therefore guided by implicit or explicit evaluations. Our approach strives to make the role of values more explicit in modelling environmental problems.

A Place-Based Theory of Environmental Valuation

Our theory rests on the testable hypothesis that some form of territoriality is universal to all human cultures, especially to those aspects of culture that relate people and communities to their ecological, social and cultural context.[6] Hannon has noted, using existing databases, that people desire to be near things they consider 'good' and to be far from things they consider 'bad'.[7] People prefer to live near schools, churches and grocery stores and far from sewage treatment and power plants, landfills and prisons.[8] He therefore proposes, as an empirical hypothesis, that human behaviour exhibits 'geographic discounting'.[9] We formulate this hypothesis as follows: the intensity of one's opposition to unpopular industries and the strength of approbation for desirable land uses, varies inversely with the distance of that activity from one's own geographic 'place'. We wish to be near the things we like and far from the things we fear.

General form of the hypothesis

Although this testable scientific hypothesis serves as the 'skeleton' of our theory, we do not mean to claim that simple measurements of distance will track, on a unit-for-unit basis, changes in environmental valuation. This empirical hypothesis simply establishes that the theory is place-based. The content of true place-based value must be a cultural artifact of local interactions, a dialectic between a culture and its natural context. Simple measurement of distance therefore provides no direct measure of environmental value. For example, communities in the foothills may orient toward the mountains, and identify with the mountain culture, and find 'flatlanders' from the valley (who are physically closer, but culturally different) alien. The definition of communities and their territories is in this sense 'lumpy' as compared to mere distance measures.

It follows that two individuals who live equidistant from a physical point may value that point very differently. Imagine, for example, members of two competing tribes who have shared an uneasy boundary for generations, and suppose that a single canyon at the intersection of their territories is the site of the dominant tribe's greatest victory and of the less dominant tribe's most humiliating defeat, when a decisive battle – perhaps generations ago – established exclusive rights of the dominants to valuable and contested territory. Two individuals, situated in these different cultures, will express very different values for the canyon, even if they happen to live equidistant from the canyon. Our point is not that these values are completely malleable. Although the canyon has specific physical features that must fit into the 'story' of both tribes, the attitudes and images of it will also reflect historical-cultural events, and personal and cultural ties as well as simple distance. These special, culturally determined values are nevertheless shaped upon the basic skeleton of place-centredness.[10] To the extent that we can observe and measure *actual* choices made, deviations from simple geographic distance can therefore represent the extent to which a local culture has contributed to the nature/culture dialectic that has emerged at this place. Presumably, doing so would also allow us, with improved concepts and methods, to rank cultures according to the degree to which the distinctive nature of its culture is intertwined with the actual biogeography of the place.

Environmental values, viewed in this way, are cultural values that are constructed from a given perspective in space and time. The intensity of environmental valuation is highest in the here and now; this intensity is discounted from the home perspective across both time and space. It may be possible to understand this hypothesis as quantifiable in two more specific senses: (a) as a scientific hypothesis relating the physical distance of an object from point of domicile to intensity of value judgements; and (b) as a social-scientific hypothesis that allows us not only to predict how people will value things, but also to measure changes in local preferences as a result of experiences in democratic formulation of management goals. Sustainability planning in a community can be understood as an ongoing, community-based discussion of environmental value as part of an ecosystem management plan. This approach, we argue, will be reflective of local sense of place values to the extent that it identifies and protects the distinctive character of a place and the culture-nature dialectic that emanates from that place.

Spatial discounting should be understood in rough analogy to temporal discounting (whereby it is hypothesized that humans exhibit a nearly universal tendency to favour the present by preferring current enjoyments of positive experiences and seeking to delay unpleasant experiences). If we put these two insights together – the two 'discount rates' plotted as scales in space and time – we create a dynamic geography of the conceptual space in which we construct models of our life in our environment as we perceive it. These models are 'contextual' in the sense that they are constructed from many individual local perspectives, as nested systems and subsystems organized hierarchically.[11]

Place and space

The geographer Yi-Fi Tuan argues that we need a sense of place *and a sense of the space around that place*, for it is the surrounding space that defines our place and shapes our sense of who we are.[12] This insight nicely encapsulates the idea that gaining a sense of place requires, at least, a perspective/home base *and* adoption of an appropriate sense of scale for interpreting events that affect one's experience. The choice of a perspective and associated scales on which to measure success in environmental management will be revealed in our choice of models to characterize environmental problems.[13] We propose to embody this sense of place within a theory of place-relative value formation. To the extent that sense-of-place values exist within a culture, these will be expressed in the structure of the models that we choose to characterize and measure environmental problems. In this sense, our method is frankly value-laden: choice of a spatiotemporal hierarchy, which orients from a home place, involves a choice of what to see, what to model, and what to protect.

Our models are in this quite specific sense 'phenomenological' rather than 'objective'. They reflect the environment as it is experienced from a local perspective and determinatively shaped by local orientation and implicit place-oriented valuations.[14] We hypothesize that (a) environmental values are formed within a phenomenological space which is organized from some place and (b) that development of a full sense of place involves a recognition of the various scales on which one interacts with nature from that place. Mere place preference, if not accompanied by a sense of the space around the place, is incomplete. It is the opposite of hollow – lacking a spatial context it collapses into a simple, meaningless point. Both elements are therefore necessary for a full-fledged sense of place. The larger context is important because that context – which can be changed by many incremental decisions of individuals – is the context in which the future will face the problem of survival.

Speaking more formally, our multiscalar hypothesis states that individuals conceptualize environmental decisions in a context that is further determined by a complex combination of (a) cultural adaptations/mores and (b) geographical orientation, where that orientation is characterized by (i) a 'place' considered as a point of orientation and (ii) by concentric layers, or 'scales' – identifiable, spatially organized subsystems, represented as a complex, hierarchical structure. The multiscalar hypothesis is therefore more specific than is the Blamey-Common-Sagoff hypothesis and has more potential empirical content, in that it asserts the priority of local values and local governmental processes, within a larger, multiscalar system of analysis. This priority represents a commitment to place-based values.

Hierarchy theory

Having argued that there exists a multiplicity, indeed a hierarchy, of spaces around a place, we propose using hierarchy theory, drawn from the scientific study of ecological systems as a set of methodological tools that give shape to the moral and evaluative decision space inhabited by communities.[15] Hierarchy theory is characterized by two central assumptions. First, it is assumed that all observation and measurement is taken from some point in space and time, from inside a dynamic, multiscalar system; second, it is assumed that spatial relations are organized such that smaller systems change and cycle more rapidly than do larger systems. Adopting hierarchy theory ensures that individuals viewing the world from any point within the dynamic will see larger-scale systems as somewhat predictable and relatively 'stable'. Policy is thus discussed within a locally based, multiscalar system that is asymmetric in space-time relations. Those operating at a given level within the system are constrained by the level above them, and develop their dynamic behaviour through interaction with the level below them. Survival of organisms, for example, depends on their adaptation to regularities presented to them by their local environment. At the same time, the cumulative impacts of individuals and cultures eventually impact those larger regularities, changing the context of future adaptations. Models of ecological systems should therefore be designed to represent a single focal level, with dynamics generated by interaction at the next lower level, and constraints imposed by the next higher level. One important, though little understood, phenomenon of hierarchical systems is the possibility of positive feedback loops, which can create destabilization in the face of drastic perturbations, such as fires or smelters. These perturbations can be followed by either regeneration or degeneration. Degeneration is the collapse of cross-scale organization; however, more positively, it is also possible that a minor breakthrough at a smaller, and faster, level can start a new feedback, and transcend a crucial constraint. An extreme example of this process – discussed by Robert O'Neill and co-authors – is the evolution in diatoms of an ability to develop a silicon shell, removing the constraint of predation. As a result, diatoms radiated explosively until they used up most of the silicon in ocean waters. Such examples provide some reason for optimism, because the possibility of creating such radiating effects are greatly enhanced by the introduction of fast-changing cultural experimentation, and even more so by a conscious search for policies that have positive impacts on more than one level of environmental organization *and* have positive feedback loops.[16]

Note that hierarchy theory's assumptions – that we observe, measure and act from a perspective, and that this perspective is embedded within a larger conceptualization of the space around the local place – merely formalize the assertion of Tuan that place identification necessarily requires a sense of the space around the place. Hierarchy theory therefore serves to provide spatial structure and a mathematical method for relating the various scales that are perceived from a local perspective. This mathematical aspect can then provide the skeleton, also, for theorizing about place-based environmental models, values and goals.

Our model therefore represents resource decisions as occurring on several different and somewhat independent scales. We therefore attempt to choose our conceptual model to be isomorphic with the temporal frame in which individuals conceptualize environmental problems. In addition, we want our models to be simple enough to act as exhibits in public discussions designed to formulate a rational environmental policy based on local values.

A triscalar system

To initiate discussion, we focus on three basic scales, each of which corresponds to a temporally distinct *policy* horizon, and each of which orients from an attachment to a home place: (1) locally developed values that express the preferences of individuals, given the established limits and 'rules' – laws and market conditions, for example – within which individual transactions take place; (2) a longer and larger community-oriented scale on which we hope to protect and contribute to our community which might be taken to include the entire *ecological* community; and (3) a global scale with essentially indefinite timescales on which humans express a hope that their own species, even beyond current cultures, will survive and thrive.[17] We seek to formulate many locally based sutainability ethics, and look forward to efforts to integrate each smaller level into the next larger level through a democratic process. We believe that it is only in this way that the local sentiment can be harnessed into a positive force for democratically supported change in our currently destructive cultural practices.

The middle scale, in which we feel concern for our culture, is especially important because it is at this scale that we also feel concern about the culture's interaction with the ecological communities that form its context. This scale corresponds roughly to the scale on which multiple generations of human individuals must relate to populations of other species, which are assembled into ecological communities. To value a Chesapeake waterman and his culture is to value, less directly but no less palpably, crucial bay processes and resources. Human cultures act as one species within a community. Good management requires, in the immortal words of Leopold, learning to 'think like a mountain' – or like a bay.[18] Nonetheless, we cannot avoid the fact that it is humans who must learn to think like mountains and bays, and who must develop the cultural characteristics of caring about these resources.

Local values are in this sense constrained by larger-scale environmental variables that normally change at a slower rate; we assume that successful cultures (ones that have survived for many generations in a particular place) will have evolved some form of control mechanisms to limit the extent to which individual decisions and collective, short-term decisions may alter the ecological context within which a culture evolves and develops.[19] Such practices have 'cultural survival value' because rapid alteration of the habitat of a group results in disintegration of customs and even economic practices such as agricultural techniques. These cultural constraints can be understood either as (a) centrally formulated constraints that are imposed on local cultures by a centralized authority, or they can alternatively be understood as (b) wisdom accrued from generalization based on local knowledge of locally experienced constraints. We will call these two related, but in important ways opposed, processes 'top-down' and 'bottom-up' valuation respectively.

Some Illustrative Examples

Is a locally based sustainability ethic possible? It is unquestionably true that local communities have in many situations degraded their local resources. It might be thought that the local, home-centred attitude that gives rise to NIMBYism is incorrigible. We explore the possibility that a sustainability consciousness can be articulated and defended from a local viewpoint by exhibiting some anecdotes that illustrate important aspects of locally based perspectives on environmental values. While we have no evidence that these anecdotes are representative, we do believe they illustrate – individually and collectively – the complex interactions between place-based and centralized decision structures.

The myth of Erisichthon

In the time before writing, oral traditions contained many stories which warned against the abuse of sacred places, and against excess in altering nature.[20] Unwarranted consumption could lead to insatiable desire, a fate worse than death itself. The Greek story of Erisichthon is one of many entries in that tradition.

When Erisichthon, a rough and godless person, cut into the great oak in the sacred grove of Ceres, blood flowed from the wound. A spirit voice from the tree warned him of his awaiting punishment, but he continued until the great tree had fallen. The mourning spirits of the forest appealed to Ceres that Erisichthon be punished and she consented. Ceres requested Famine to possess Erisichthon. Famine obeyed, cursing Erisichthon, who awoke with a hunger which knew no bounds. The more he ate, the more hungry he became. To obtain the food for his growing hunger, he spent his entire estate and even sold his daughter into slavery. She appealed to Neptune to change her form, allowing her to escape her new master. Upon returning to her father, he only sold her again and again to earn food to sate his unquenchable hunger. It was not enough; Erisichthon finally consumed himself in desperation. Only in death was he free of the vengeance of Ceres.[21]

The myth of Erisichthon shows that storytellers, even before written language, created illustrations of the evils of hubris and lack of realistic limits in the expansion of demand for resources. Erisichthon is faulted for destroying the largest tree – no doubt symbolic of the old-growth forests. At first, it is difficult to understand how Erisichthon could become hungrier the more he ate, but like all good myths, he is not a metaphor for each of us but for all of us together. Stories such as these were common throughout the Mediterranean and Middle East, even among preliterate cultures.[22] Indeed, every major religion of the world recognizes that the right to use the Earth carries with it also an obligation to protect it for future use.[23]

The sacred groves of India

As new areas were settled in India, and land was cleared, a sacred grove was always set aside as the rightful abode of the local spirits who were displaced by development from their traditional homes throughout the forest.[24] As long as local customs were revered within the indigenous, local and mostly animistic versions of Hinduism, the groves were carefully preserved. Only holy men could use the groves, and only for the gathering of ritual herbs and healing potions. Although the groves were carefully protected, in the wake of catastrophe – a fire or flood that destroyed the village, for example – trees could be cut from the sacred groves, but only after consultation with the spirits, and only with their ritually invoked consent. Once the spirits of the place were appeased, the sacred grove could be used to rebuild the village.

When the central authority of the Hindu religion, located in the cities, attempted consolidation and sought control over local worship (including the imposition of a common 'liturgy'), priests were chosen by authorities and sent from the cities into the outlying villages. These priests, whose stated purpose was to unify Hindu worship under central authority, sought also to homogenize ritual and to stamp out local variations because these became symbols of local resistance to centralized authority. Some groves were destroyed intentionally; others suffered from lack of care and attention. The ones that remain represent some of the few refuges for the native species that once inhabited the entire subcontinent.[25]

The example of the sacred groves of India illustrates how local myths and rituals can tie cultural practices to the plants and animals in a region. The local roots of animism and ritual practices maintained the connection between people and their natural history. We can think of the setting aside of the sacred groves, first, as a religiously based act, but also as a recognition of limits in the destruction of nature and as an expression of a bond between a community of people, and with their past, their future and their land. These links are both represented in concrete objects – medicines – and also symbols – materials for rituals – of connection to place. However, the priests from faraway cities did not identify with, or value, these benefits and symbols, corroborating the inverse relationship here suggested between concern and distance.

The intrusion of centralized authority conflicted with these local processes of value formation and, to the extent that local plants and the myths associated with them provide symbols of local experiences and their value, the existence of the sacred groves, and their spiritual occupants, stood in the way of centralized authority. Local values are associated with a particular place, they are forged out of a very intimate relationship with the biotic communities in a region, and their perpetuation is associated by local inhabitants with success in maintaining their sense of spiritual and physical place. These values conflict with geographically broader, centralized and authoritarian values, when these are imposed by centralized authorities.

The Japanese example

Beginning as early as the 1200s, the feudal kings of Japan began to draw their boundaries with greater care, form small armed bands, and test the possibilities of expansion into the arable land of a neighbour. By 1500, these bands had become armies and feudal kingdoms numbering more than 250. The struggle for control of the island was fierce and protracted. Population growth may have been the root cause of the centuries of strife in Japan. About 1600, one family, the Tokugawa of Edo (Tokyo) and the river valley nearby became the victor in this long and nearly continuous war. The leader of this family, the first real Shogun, enacted a comprehensive set of social regulations to govern nearly everyone's life in detail. He expelled the Jesuits and all representatives of Western religions from the country, removed all metal weapons from the peasants (and rifles from the soldiers of the coastal lords), required them to stay in the place of their birth unless permitted to move by their lord, and most importantly of all, he established a rice tax. The tax, and its cotton equivalent, was heavy (between 25 per cent and 35 per cent of total production). The Shogun collected it through his soldiers-turned-administrators who dealt with feudal lords, who in turn dealt with headmen (mayors) of the villages. The tax was based on a quota, established by a survey of the village production capabilities. The villages were regularly surveyed for changes in production and the quota was adjusted accordingly.

Population estimates reveal that the Japanese increased their numbers by about 50 per cent to 30 to 35 million between 1600 and 1720. The population level remained steady until the 1870s, the end of the Tokugawa reign, when the country was forced 'open' by Admiral Perry for the insistent US trade and the need for Asian-based whaling ports. By using the hierarchical method of collection and control, the Shogun could use the detailed information available to the village headmen, and harness the detailed knowledge of the peasants about each other's farming potential. Such information ensured that no family could conceal any significant increase in production. Everyone in the village realized that additional mouths to feed by one's neighbour would reduce their future ability to make contributions to the rice tax. Local ostracism over the appearance of inappropriate family expansion was intense. The method appears to have driven the population to a steady state and held it there for about 150 years, an unprecedented accomplishment.[26]

Because the Shogun apparently sought peaceful economic sustainability for the nation, the Japanese example provides a top-down approach/solution to the problem of resource use, illustrating how resource conservation and limits on the exploitation of resources can be accomplished by a centralized authority, provided the centralized leadership is far-sighted and provided the system is insulated from outside influences. The method of the Shogun has the virtue of not being a hypothetical solution; the costs, however, of this approach to conservation are enormous, measured as losses in individual and local autonomy. Can we, recognizing that resources are limited, achieve a steady-state population and resource protection on the local level with less costs to autonomy?[27]

The Sangamon River episode

In 1967, the US Army Corps of Engineers announced an enlarged version of its plan to dam the Sangamon River at Decatur, Illinois. The new reservoir would back water across one of the few remaining forests in the east central Illinois area at Allerton Park, and that fact was duly noted by one of the local citizens. He was then a graduate student in engineering at nearby University of Illinois, which, as it turns out, held the park in a trust for the people of Illinois. He had been an engineer in nearby industry and earlier, an officer in the Corps of Engineers. He set out to organize a fully documented, multidisciplined attack on the premises for the proposal. The industrial and army experiences had taught him much about management and, over the next eight years, he documented and expanded the written criticism of the plan with the help of other citizens. In short, he engaged in the political and social organizing activities which are now seen as fundamentally necessary for the successful challenge of such a plan. Today the park is federally designated as national natural landmark, the Congress has deauthorized the proposal, and the army has closed the regional office which had promoted the reservoir plan. In 1979, a study by the Brookings Institute called this achievement the paradigmatic exemplar of policy change by citizen action.[28]

The graduate student attributed his environmental awareness, and his determination to defeat the army proposal, to a strong sense of place. His was the fifth generation of his family to have lived in the area since they immigrated to the United States about 1850. Many of them had been farmers and small town businessmen and they had inculcated a strong sense of responsibility to their adopted place. The example of the Sangamon River illustrates how these ideas apply to environmental problems today; it also illustrates the positive role that science can have on policy, if it is developed and applied from a local, place-oriented perspective and in service of local, protectionist values. In the best case, locally based values can motivate a deep understanding of valued places. When coupled with skilful use of political processes, it is possible for locally based values to restrain forces that attempt to impose development from centralized power sources.

We can also speculate that locally motivated, locally originated, mission-oriented science, when combined with a strong sense of place and local activism, can take the place of local myths as a determinant of policy. Science that is used as a 'story' about how a culture has negotiated a lasting niche in an ecosystem guides the development of modern ideas of limits. This line of reasoning suggests two differing functions of science depending on whether science acts in the service of centralized authority, or whether it acts as one element in a local struggle to formulate ecological limits imposed by concern for future generations. Science used in the service of bureaucratic goals of centralized governments can cause homogenization and destruction of local flora, fauna and ecological systems. When science serves local values, however, it is science employed from a local perspective, and seeks to protect local variations as valuable markers of place. Note how this observation supports and complements our earlier argument that choices regarding perspective and scale are intertwined with questions of social values.

Some lessons from these examples

In opposition to these locally determined values, the values that are imposed from the centre are usually based on authority. These values are determined by abstract principles or distant markets more than local appropriateness and they flow down a political and geographical hierarchy. The goals of nationhood can make it politically important to remove local variation. In modern nation states, including the federal system in the US, if local values conflict with values of the centre, the former must give way.

Taking local values seriously may also call into question the contemporary wisdom favouring free trade, international capital markets and the pervasive search for competitive advantage.[29] The world economy, as currently organized, exhibits strong centralist tendencies and may be incompatible with protecting locally developed values and the cultural practices local people have evolved for living as a human community within a distinctive, local, ecological community. According to this analysis, we are tending toward a global victory of *epistēmē* (theory) over *technē* (local practice) with all of the attendant calamities.[30] The ramification of such a victory is often seen today at the community level, as government planners limit access of local, indigenous groups to tribal lands, destroying in turn the traditional, local adaptations to specialized ecological conditions.

In his revealing monograph on the ecological history of colonial New England, William Cronon demonstrates that, while Native Americans had always 'managed' the landscape, the scale of their changes was limited by the tools available to them and by their decentralized culture and nomadic patterns of resource use.[31] The imposition of a European pattern of ownership, the introduction of money, and the idea of 'cash crops' that can be sold in response to world demand, all tended to increase the extent to which values were forced downward through a geographically defined hierarchy. Local communities cannot control economic demand as expressed in world markets; a commitment to exports to bring in foreign exchange greatly narrows the options for development opportunities in less developed regions. The result was homogenization of land use – especially draining of wetlands for hay and grain fields – and destruction of social and biological diversity.

Note that Cronon's history is yet another example of how a centralized value structure can impose itself on the land, destroying diversity of the landscape by pursuing foreign markets. We can call this 'top-down' valuation of nature, and associate it with colonialism and exploitation across political boundaries. We contrast it with 'bottom-up' valuation which originates locally. Centralism and top-down authority can be seen as forcing values downward through a hierarchy, as constraints are enforced from above. Localism and resistance to enforcement of centralized authority in resource use can be seen, however, as fighting to force values up through the hierarchy.

According to our multiscalar theory, creativity, diversity and sustainability result from energy/values being forced up the hierarchy in the face of constraints that are evident at larger scales. The question is whether the constraints will be voluntarily recognized, formulated and accepted at each level, or whether they will be imposed from above, as in the Japanese shogunate. Or, will they be understood by citizens who view their environment from a local viewpoint but see also the importance of protecting larger systems and processes, and of dealing with problems that require attention on larger, regional and national scales as well?

We have developed a general approach to environmental management based on a sense of place; this approach, which emphasizes locally developed values, myths and cultural practices, gives rise to a distinctive approach to environmental valuation. By positing spatial discounting as an analogue to temporal discounting, we have constructed rough mental models of the space in which citizens form their environmental values. We therefore define the task of understanding sustainability as that of developing many local, but ultimately integrated, sustainability ethics, each one of which embodies sensitivity to the particularities of local cultural adaptations and to the wisdom of various uses of local ecosystems. The proposed approach expresses, operationalizes and supports a growing consensus that ecosystem management must include significant attempts to engage local communities in setting goals and discussing proposed 'experiments'.[32]

Embracing the NIMBY in Each of Us

What, then, are we to make of the NIMBY syndrome and the local sentiments associated with it? While we cannot deny that NIMBY sentiments can express themselves in overly selfish and shortsighted ways, we have nevertheless argued that a successful approach to sustainability must be built upon these sentiments which express a local 'sense of place'. Our theory, indeed, implies that a preference for the near is inherent in human behaviour. The goal, then, should be to build an approach to environmental policy that takes NIMBY sentiments into account and channels those sentiments toward a policy of environmental protection that is developed from many local perspectives.

Using our theory as a guide, we are able to draw two general distinctions that help us to separate legitimate exercise of local power from cases where local obstructionism results in environmental policies that undermine the overall public good and local community values.

(1) It is important to distinguish *economic* NIMBYism from true, *place-oriented* NIMBYism. If efforts to stop sitings of undesirable land uses are based on economic motives only, losses to surrounding landowners can be economically compensated. These are losses that will be perceived by other buyers and will affect the resale value of their property. When NIMBYism degenerates into a game to ensure adequate compensation – if, for example, landowners are fully willing to take the best financial settlement and relocate on a comparable property far away – then they are economic, or 'defensive' NIMBYs at best. This behaviour does not rest on an attitude of protection of this specific place for its specific charms; it is a *self*-protective motive. The interest behind it is in protecting the 'investments' of the individual, investments that are as well protected by a generous pay-off as by protection of the integrity of the place in question. If, however, NIMBYs show no interest in compensation, but rather indignation that their home will be violated by decisions made far away, we are more likely to consider their local sentiments to be justified. Our theory helps to understand the distinction between defensive and positive NIMBYism, because it explains the importance of positive sense-of-place values in moving the NIMBY sentiment beyond mere negativism. If the NIMBY sentiment is accompanied by an active search for, and articulation of, positive, local sense-of-place values, then we regard it as headed in the right direction. Indeed, a positive sense of place might be understood as values expressed for natural characteristics of a habitat that cannot be attributed to economic use or exchange value.[33]

(2) Our theory, which integrates local sentiments into larger-scale systems, also allows us to distinguish two importantly different versions of the NIMBY attitude toward surrounding places and municipalities. We distinguish:

NIMBY A: You may not do *x* in my backyard; therefore, do *x* in someone else's backyard.

NIMBY B: You may not do *x* in my backyard; furthermore, if you cannot find some other community that democratically chooses to accept *x*, then *x* will cease.

NIMBY A and NIMBY B are both locally based. NIMBY B, however, differs from NIMBY A in that the former possesses a fuller sense of place, which we have defined as having two inseparable elements. In the words of Tuan, A-type NIMBYs exhibit a sense of place, but no sense of space around the place. In moral and political terms, they have not accepted that their right to self-determination is, if it is a 'right' of *their* community, also a 'right' of *every* community; and conversely, only if self-determination is the right of every community is it the right of their community. Although environmental policy must be local in the sense that each place accepts responsibility for the integrity of its place, local sentiments must be tempered with a sense of surrounding space and inevitable interactions with other regions in addressing environmental problems, and therefore must respect the environmental concerns of other local communities. Because our locally based theory and approach recognizes that the urge to protect one's home place is universal, fairness requires that rejection of a facility in one locale must be accompanied with scepticism of the centralized policies that impose unwanted land uses on any and all communities. Local communities cannot insist on their own self-determination and consistently deny that right to other communities which feel similarly, but from distinct spatial perspectives. This ethical principle provides a moral rule, analogous to the golden rule in human ethics, a sort of universalizability on the community level.

Conclusion

Our theory suggests no less than an about-face in current trends in environmental planning and policy formation. What we are saying, prescriptively, is that we should, whenever possible, shift responsibility for resource use to local levels, and accompany this change with an active and ongoing effort – such as many locally-based ecosystem management plans – to build a positive sense of place.[34] Nevertheless, we also recognize that making an about-face in the flow of environmental values and decision making will require great wisdom, an extraordinary educational effort, and no little time. The important point is that we now begin to think more locally and recognize that the goal of a national environmental policy is to reduce the number of centralized decisions that cannot be implemented in a fully democratic way at the local level. We propose an end to the *ex cathedra* pronouncements of the environmental expert, and urge scientists to emphasize study of local ecosystems and participation in environmental management projects. The time necessary to retool laws and institutions in this direction will at least be matched by the equally slow process of environmental education necessary to ensure that, as local governments and organizations accept responsibility, they will also have built a strong sense of responsibility for the space around their place. It also implies that the formation of environmental policy goals should include a significant element of public education and, by using scientific-conceptual models that are informative to lay persons, it should strive to generate a sustainability path of development from the bottom up. The burden of environmental managers, then, is to communicate to the public and to simultaneously learn from the public, in the development of locally based models for the articulation of local values. This interaction between the public and managers, which is exemplified in the best examples of community-based ecosystem management programmes, must be locally driven and dynamic, and it must provide an open and ongoing forum for the explicit examination and articulation of locally based values.

Notes

1   A number of recent authors have advocated environmental values that are based on a sense of place. See, for example, Kirkpatrick Sale, *Dwellers in the Land* (San Francisco, Sierra Club Books, 1985); David Seamon and Robert Mugerauer, eds *Dwelling, Place, and Environment* (New York, Columbia University Press, 1985); David Ehrenfeld, *Beginning Again* (New York, Oxford University Press, 1993); and Mark Sagoff, 'Environmental economics: An epitaph', *Resources,* vol 111 (Spring 1993), pp2–7; Sagoff, 'Settling America: The concept of place in environmental ethics', *Journal of Energy, Natural Resources and Environmental Law,* vol 12 (1992), pp351–418. These authors continue the exploration of a theme introduced earlier by geographers such as Yi-Fu Tuan, *Topophilia: A Study of Environmental Perception, Attitudes, and Values* (Englewood Cliffs, NJ, Prentice-Hall, 1974), and *Space and Place: The Perspective of Experience* (Minneapolis, University of Minnesota Press, 1977).

2   See Nicholas Freudenberg, *Not in Our Backyards! Community Action for Health and the Environment* (New York, Monthly Review Press, 1984), for a general discussion of NIMBYism. For an update, see Nicholas Freudenberg and Carol Steinsapir, 'Not in our backyards: The grassroots environmental movement' *Society and Natural Resources,* vol 4 (1991), pp235–245.

3   Mark Sagoff, *The Economy of the Earth* (Cambridge, Cambridge University Press, 1988), esp pp50–57.

4   M. S. Common, R. K. Blamey and T. W. Norton, 'Sustainability and environmental valuation'. *Environmental Values,* vol 2 (1993), pp299–334, esp pp316–19.

5   Bryan Norton and Robert Ulanowicz, 'Scale and biodiversity policy: A hierarchical approach', *Ambio,* vol 21 (1992), pp244–249, have argued that biodiversity policy, for example, must be addressed at the scale of the 'landscape ecosystem' because of the long time horizon of the goal of sustaining biodiversity. These arguments are based on the central assumption of hierarchy theory, that systems of large spatial scale change more slowly than do their components, providing a means to correlate spatial and temporal scale. See note 15.

6   Some readers will surely wonder whether we are making the somewhat stronger claim that the tendency to orient from a place is hereditary. While we do not wish to commit ourselves on this point, we are aware that our general theory is susceptible of an interesting hybrid interpretation. It seems plausible that the *tendency to orient from a home-place* is hereditary, given its similarity to evolved behaviours in other animals, such as territoriality. However, our theory, given its local bias and commitment to local adaptations of culture to local habitats, also suggests that particular local practices and the values associated with them are learned in response to local environments. Place-orientating behaviour may therefore be analogous to linguistic behaviour. Just as there seems to be an inborn tendency to learn a language –

to hear and imitate speech as patterned, for example – there may be an innate tendency to perceive and value from a specific local space. Moreover, also in analogy to linguistic behaviour, the multiplicity of self-replicating language systems that co-exist in the world, the content of place-oriented values may similarly be learned in local contexts. This possibility suggests the additional idea that one can, with considerable effort, learn the 'language' of a new culture. What is learned in this process can be thought of as the many bits of wisdom that help an individual culture to live, to reproduce, to 'sustain' itself, in its particular habitat/local niche.

7 Bruce Hannon, 'Sense of place: Geographic discounting by people, animals and plants', *Ecological Economics,* vol 10 (1994), pp157–174; Robert Mitchell and Richard Carson, *Property Rights, Protest, and the Siting of Hazardous Waste Facilities* (Washington, DC, Resources for the Future, 1986), p4; see Hannon, 'The discounting of concern', in *Environmental Economics,* ed Gonzague Fillet and Takeshi Murota (Geneva, R. Leimgruber, 1987).

8 Hannon, 'Sense of Place', p160.

9 Ibid, p159.

10 See Peter Gould and Rodney White, *Mental Maps* (Boston, Allen and Unwin, 1986), for a mathematical model, and interesting commentary, on the attachment to, and evaluation of, possible locations at which to live.

11 See Bryan G. Norton, 'Context and hierarchy in Aldo Leopold's land ethic', *Ecological Economics,* vol 2 (1990), pp119–127, for a discussion of context and perspective as a formative idea of the land ethic.

12 Yi-Fu Tuan, 'Man and nature', Commission on College Geography, Resource Paper 10, Association of American Geographers, Washington, DC, 1971.

13 Norton and Ulanowicz, 'Scale and biodiversity policy'.

14 Seamon and Mugrauer, *Dwelling. Place, and Environment.*

15 It is customary to refer to multilevelled theories of scale as 'hierarchy theory'. See, for example, T. F. H. Allen and Thomas B. Starr, *Hierarchy: Perspectives for Ecological Complexity* (Chicago, University of Chicago Press, 1982); Robert O'Neill, D. L. DeAngelis, J. B. Waide and T. F. H. Allen, *A Hierarchical Concept of Ecosystems* (Princeton, Princeton University Press, 1986); T. F. Allen and Thomas W. Hoekstra, *Toward a Unified Ecology* (New York, Columbia University Press, 1992). For explicit attempts to apply hierarchy theory to practical problems of management and policy, see R. V. O'Neill, 'Hierarchy theory and global climate change', in Thomas Rosswall, Robert G. Woodmansee, and Paul G. Risser, eds, *Scales and Global Change* (New York, John Wiley and Sons, 1988); Bryan G. Norton, 'Context and hierarchy in Aldo Leopold's theory of environmental management', *Ecological Economics,* vol 2 (1990), pp119–27; Norton, *Toward Unity among Environmentalists* (New York, Oxford University Press, 1991); and Norton and Ulanowicz, 'Scale and biodiversity policy'. While we have used the term *hierarchy* ourselves, it is unfortunate that the term is often taken to imply a 'top-down' flow of power and authority even though this implication is expressly not included in the use, by ecologists, of the term. The problem of top-down versus bottom-up authority is discussed below. Because of the confusing implication, we prefer the term *multiscalar analysis,* and use it whenever possible. When it is unavoidable, however, the term *hierarchy* is used in the neutral sense which does not imply one

or the other directional flow of power relationships. For a more detailed treatment of these issues, see Norton, 'Should environmentalists be organicists?' *Topoi*, vol 12 (1993), pp21–30.

16 See O'Neill et al, *A Hierarchical Concept*, pp170–175, for a discussion of the impacts of the bypassing of constraints on multiscaled systems. More generally, see Alan R. Johnson, 'Spatiotemporal hierarchies in ecological theory and modeling', in 'Second international conference on integrating geographic information systems and environmental modeling', Breckenridge, CO, 26 September 1993.

17 This triscalar approach is introduced in 'Reduction *versus* integration: Two approaches to environmental values'. Also see Norton, 'Evaluating ecosystem states: Two paradigms of environmental management'. *Ecological Economics*, vol 14 (1995), pp113–127, and Norton, 'Ecological Integrity and Social Values: At What Scale?' *Ecosystem Health*, vol 1 (1995), pp228–241.

18 Aldo Leopold, *A Sand County Almanac* (New York, Oxford University Press, 1949); Susan Flader, *Thinking like A Mountain: Aldo Leopold and the Evolution of an Ecological Attitude toward Deer, Wolves, and Forests* (Columbia, University of Missouri Press, 1974); Bryan G. Norton, 'The constancy of Leopold's land ethic', *Conservation Biology*, vol 2 (1988), pp93–102; Norton, *Toward Unity*.

19 See Aldo Leopold, 'Some fundamentals of conservation in the southwest', *Environmental Ethics*, vol 1 (1979), pp131–141 (posthumous publication of an essay written in 1923); Leopold, *Sand County Almanac*; Madhav Gadgil, 'Diversity: Cultural and biological', *Tree*, vol 2 (1987), pp369–373; Madhav Gadgil and Fikret Berkes, 'Traditional resource management systems', *Resource Management and Optimization*, vol 8 (1991), pp127–141; Fikret Berkes, Carl Folke and Madhav Gadgil, 'Traditional ecological knowledge, biodiversity, resilience and sustainability', Beijer Discussion Paper Series no. 31, Beijer International Institute of Ecological Economics, Royal Swedish Academy of Sciences, 1993; Madjav Gadgil, 'Ecological organization of Indian society', *Indian Council of Social Science Research Newsletter*, vol 21 (1993), pp1–9; Bryan G. Norton, 'On what we should save: The role of culture in determining conservation targets', in *Systematics and Conservation Evaluation*, eds P. L. Forey, C. J. Humphries and R. I. Vane-Wright (Oxford: Clarendon Press, 1994); See Madhav Gadgil, Fikret Berkes and Carl Folke, 'Indigenous knowledge for biodiversity conservation', for a discussion of factors affecting whether indigenous populations develop conservation constraints in *Ambio*, vol 22 (1993), pp151–156. Also see N. V. Joshi and Madhav Gadgil, 'On the role of refugia in promoting prudent use of biological resources', *Theoretical Population Biology*, vol 40 (1991), pp211–229. For an application of localized thinking to international biodiversity policy, see Jeffrey A. McNeely, 'Reversing the loss of biodiversity: Implementing political, economic, and social measures', presented at 'Symposium on biological diversity: Exploring the complexities', University of Arizona, Tucson, AZ, 25–27 March 1994.

20 John Moore, personal communication.

21 This version is from Thomas Bulfinch, *Bulfinch's Mythology* (New York, Harper and Row, 1970), pp169–171. Bulfinch relied on a Latinized version of the myth, which explains why the gods in this version have Roman names.

22 John Moore, personal communication.

23 Edith Brown Weiss, *In Fairness to Future Generations* (Tokyo and Dobbs Ferry, NY, The United Nations University and Transnational Publishers, 1989), pp17–21.

24 We are indebted to Madhav Gadgil of the Centre for Ecological Sciences of the Indian Institute of Science for both the details of this history and for a most stimulating conversation on the local nature of environmental values in Stockholm, July 1992. The protection of sacred groves was a common practice in many ancient cultures, which suggests that locally expressed religious traditions and distinctive local 'worldviews' have been connected with limits on the scale of alteration of nature in many traditional cultures. See Gadgil, Berkes and Folke, 'Indigenous knowledge for biodiversity conservation'. For an account of the destruction of the Indian forests through centralization under British rule, and of the losing struggles of local indigenous tribes to maintain control over lands that they held by tenure, see Ramachandra Guha and Madhav Gadgil, 'State forestry and social conflict in British India', *Past and Present*, vol 123 (1989), pp141–177, and Madhav Gadgil and Ramachandra Guha, *This Fissured Land: An Ecological History of India* (New Delhi, Oxford University Press, 1992).

25 Gadgil et al, 'Indigenous knowledge for biodiversity conservation', 1993; Gadgil and Berkes, 'Traditional resource management systems'.

26 See Bruce Hannon, 'Energy and Japanese peasant agriculture', *Journal of Social and Biological Structures*, vol 69 (1983), pp207–217, for more detail and further references.

27 See, for example, Robert Heilbroner, *An Inquiry into the Human Prospect* (New York, W. W. Norton, 1974); William Ophuls, *The Politics of Scarcity: A Prologue to a Political Theory of the Steady State* (San Francisco, Freeman, 1977), and *The Politics of Scarcity Revisited: The Unraveling of the American Dream* (New York, Freeman, 1992); Bruce Hannon, 'World shogun', *Journal of Social and Biological Structures* 8 (1985): 329–341; Paul Kennedy, *Preparing for the Twenty-First Century* (New York, Random House, 1993).

28 Daniel A. Mazmanian and Jeanne Nienaber, *Can Organizations Change? Environmental Protection, Citizen Participation, and the Corps of Engineers* (Washington, DC, Brookings Institution, 1979), pp19–24. The local citizen is Bruce Hannon.

29 See Herman Daly and John Cobb, *For the Common Good* (Boston, Beacon Press, 1989), pp209–235, and Herman Daly, 'Problems with free trade: Neoclassical and steady-state perspectives', in Durwood Zaelke, Paul Orbuch, and Robert F. Housman, eds, *Trade and the Environment: Law, Economics, and Policy* (Washington, DC, Island Press, 1993).

30 Stephen Marglin. 'Losing touch: The cultural conditions of worker accommodation and resistance', in Frederique Marglin and Stephen Marglin, eds *Dominating Knowledge* (Oxford, Clarendon Press, 1990); Gadgil et al, 'Indigenous Knowledge for Biodiversity Conservation'.

31 William Cronon, *Changes in the Land: Indians, Colonists, and the Ecology of New England* (New York, Hill and Wang, 1983). Cronon's book was only the first of a new genre of ecological histories, each entry of which showed how the imposition of European land-use patterns and styles of ownership destroyed traditional systems of land and resource use in colonized areas of the New World, transforming the landscape in the process. See, for example, Timothy Silver, *A New Face on the*

Countryside: Indians, Colonists, and Slaves in South Atlantic Forests, 1500–1800 (Cambridge, Cambridge University Press, 1990); Ramon A. Gutierrez, *When Jesus Came, The Corn Mothers Went Away* (Stanford, Stanford University Press, 1991). Also see Gadgil and Berkes, 'Traditional resource management systems', and Guha and Gadgil, 'State forestry and social conflict in British India', for documentation of similar historical patterns in India.

32 Our approach is therefore complementary to the adaptive management approach as proposed and developed by the ecologist C. S. Holling and other colleagues. For discussion of the socio-political aspects of adaptive management, see, especially, Kai Lee, *Compass and Gyroscope* (Covelo, CA, Island Press, 1993), and Lance Gunderson, C. S. Holling and Stephen S. Light, *Barriers and Bridges to the Renewal of Ecosystems and Institutions* (New York, Columbia University Press, 1995).

33 See Bryan Norton and Bruce Hannon, 'Democracy and sense of place values in environmental policy', in Light, A. and Smith, J. (eds) *Philosophies of Place* (New York, Rowman and Littlefield, 1998, pp119–146).

34 Our approach leads us to expect that a culture of high mobility will be less likely to protect the ecological context that gives meaning to local cultural adaptations. See Sagoff, 'Settling America', for a helpful general discussion. But we wonder, optimistically, if it may be possible to encourage a stronger sense of place in local communities, and greater responsibility for local resource use, through public participation in ecosystem management plans and through public education and dialogue. See Norton and Hannon, 'Democracy and sense of place values in environmental policy'. Clearly more research and discussion is warranted here.

Part 4

Judgement and Decision Making Themes in Environmental Values

Introduction

It should by now be apparent that value is a hotly contested term, the reasons for which become most evident in this our final section. The authors in Part 4 explore the gulf that separates the term 'value' from 'valuation' by asking an important set of questions: Are some values easier to elicit and/or measure than others? Are some values labile? Can values be elicited and measured using willingness-to-pay protocols or 'dollar' as the appropriate metric or vehicle for expression? Should values be discussed and measured individually or in collective venues where democratic debate is possible? Finally, can discussions about values be structured in such a way as to reconcile these and other points of debate?

In the first article, Kahneman and Knetsch challenge the assumption that survey respondents accept the premise of a hypothetical market and so treat willingness-to-pay (WTP) surveys as market-like choices. In particular, they find evidence for the arbitrariness of some responses and the linked phenomena of 'embedding' effects. These occur when the dollar amount a survey respondent is willing to pay remains unchanged regardless of whether they are paying for the improvement of one good or all goods in that class (e.g. one national park or all national parks). Moreover, because WTP responses correlate highly with judgements of moral satisfaction associated with contributions to an environmental cause, the authors conclude that WTP studies are actually measuring moral and not financial transactions. That is, the authors posit that assigned dollar values are an index of the commitment to a moral cause (the betterment of national parks) and not the willingness to purchase, in a market-like fashion, a specific improvement.

Baron and Spranca also offer empirical evidence for the resistance of survey respondents to WTP or market expressions of values, although their emphasis and explanation departs markedly from that of Kahneman and Knetsch. Instead, they find evidence for the phenomena of protected values and, borrowing from colleagues Fiske and Tetlock (1997), the linked idea of taboo trade-offs. Depending on the design, valuation exercises involve implicit or explicit trade-offs because they rest on the premise that a lesser valued good can be lost or traded off for a higher valued good. As such, Baron and Spranca find that people are uncomfortable with the dollar-valuation and trade-off act itself. The experience is an uncomfortable one because it forces people to make trade-offs that may give rise to moral and ethical dilemmas that are fundamentally difficult to resolve. For instance, many people are deeply offended by or have a profound psychological aversion to assigning dollar values to morally important goods precisely because they experience such acts as violating norms they seek to protect or regard as sacred. In practice, this lack of a willingness to assign dollar values and hence the ability to trade off a higher-value good for a lower value one produces a pattern of behavioural responses. These include but are not limited to the following problems:

Absolutism, where valuation and trade-off efforts often break down because the posed options trigger respondents into believing that they must sacrifice a deeply held principle (such as assigning prices to something morally important) in order to participate in negotiation or a decision process; *quantitative insensitivity* or the belief that destroying one bird (by willingness to accept compensation for that loss) is unacceptable, hence just as bad morally as destroying many; and *denial* or resistance to the idea that one must face an unpleasant trade-off; thus people deny the trade-off's necessity or suspend decision making until a more palatable option can be found. Finally, trade-off resistance is also linked to *the slippery slope problem* wherein any move in a particular direction, no matter how minor (e.g. that some natural goods can be purchased on the open market), will lead to or is symbolic of devastating future outcomes. This is similar to legal decisions that are established on the basis of minor infractions but are ultimately contentious because they hint at the undermining of such inalienable rights as free speech.

Work of this kind provided the basis for an important concurrent paper by environmental philosopher Mark Sagoff, who was the first to produce a comprehensive analysis of these and linked debates in the valuation field. Reproduced here, the article sets out to explain the critical difference between consumer versus citizen preferences, and in so doing offers a basis for understanding the gulf that divides many approaches. Sagoff finds that much contention can be explained by the tendency to treat value (especially WTP) surveys as expressions of utility, as an answer to the question: What do you as an individual want in order to enhance your individual utility, welfare or wellbeing? He finds that this misrepresents the problem as there is much evidence to suggest that stakeholders are not seeking individual utility, but rather deontological preferences wherein they pursue notions of a good society. Debates about environmental futures generally proceed without reference to wellbeing, thus efforts must focus on the means through which citizen (and not consumer) preferences can be taken into account. Surveys, including WTP, may help us rank preferences but there exists a largely unrecognized need to help participants reflect upon their social preferences. The goal is not to become ever more sophisticated at 'mining' the evidence for pre-existing values, but to provide the opportunity for participants to 'work through evidence and argumentation to reach a considered judgment' (p221 of original article). In particular, informed group deliberation via careful thought, discussion and evidence might serve as a vehicle for constructing citizen preferences as to what is good for society and nature.

The last two papers in this chapter take up the idea of constructed preferences and the move in the field toward deliberative processes. Many advances in both approaches have emerged since these two influential papers by Dietz and Gregory and colleagues first emerged. We chose however to include these two contributions because of their articulation of the problem and the agenda, and because each still very much captures the intent, content and spirit of what has and continues to follow. Gregory developed the idea of constructed valuation processes in conversation with his psychologist colleagues and co-authors, Slovic and Lichtenstein. The paper is a marriage of empirical evidence in psychology for the idea that survey respondents are easily influenced by the elicitation task and the demands of economists for conditions under which use and exchange value can be reasonably identified and traded. Gregory, Lichtenstein and Slovic suggest that we recognize the constructed nature of survey responses and from this position develop a valuation procedure that defensibly helps people articulate and develop (i.e. construct) their values. Drawing on theory from economics and decision analysis, they propose multiple elicitation and decision steps which help people define in collective deliberation their preferences, values and objectives; develop subjectively meaningful scales to measure those objectives; recognize and make any necessary trade-offs across these objectives; and thereafter consider policy alternatives or create new policies aimed at meeting the values or objectives recognized as most important.

We end this volume with the work of Thomas Dietz; it was he who first aptly characterized most deliberation processes as based on either benefit–cost analysis or discursive analysis. Dietz assesses the strengths and weaknesses of these two methods of collective decision making in terms of their theoretical understandings about human nature. While benefit–cost analysis is based on a rational actor model, discursive policy analysis draws on an evolutionary linguistic model of human action. The rational actor model is a simple one: it views the biophysical environment, the humans in that environment and the preferences of those humans as relatively homogeneous, unchanging and similar across different societies and cultures. While one advantage of benefit–cost analysis is that it clarifies what is 'good policy' (those policies that increase welfare in that the benefits to society outweigh the costs), the disadvantages include discounting (very large costs or benefits in the distant future are reduced to zero in the present), ignoring distributional issues (who actually pays the costs and who receives the benefits) and problems with valuing nonmarket goods, such as ecosystems. The evolutionary linguistic model is more complex than the rational actor model, taking into account human cognition, such as language, and its centrality to all human action. This model argues that rules vary with different individuals, and the social environment (such as the family, community or even the market) can be broken down into different structures of local contexts. With multiple environments and multiple rules, individual actors are engaged in a process of communication or a 'discourse', and it is assumed that since different people have different rules in different contexts, it is difficult to predict individual decisions. Policy decisions are made through group interaction and conversation, and structured group processes are used to assign values to anticipated environmental impacts, with a set of rules facilitating fair and effective discussion among all individuals. The goal of discursive analysis is to have a diversity of people draw on a diversity of contexts to assign social value, and if all individuals agree that utility maximization is the rule that should be applied to a policy decision, discursive policy analysis can integrate benefit–cost considerations. The major drawbacks to discursive methods include the inability to guarantee strategies for closure and agreement and, most importantly, a tendency to disregard the influence of power embedded in the structure of language and culture. Nevertheless, Dietz concludes that an evolutionary linguistic model is a good underpinning for normative policy analysis – one that is capable of subsuming, rather than discarding, the rational actor model and allowing for an evolution of valuation rules in a community.

Linda Kalof and Terre Satterfield

References

1   Fiske, A. P. and Tetlock, P. E. (1997) 'Taboo trade-offs: Reactions to transactions that trans-
    gress spheres of justice'. *Political Psychology*, vol 18, pp255–297

14

Valuing Public Goods: The Purchase of Moral Satisfaction

Daniel Kahneman and Jack L. Knetsch

There is substantial demand for a practical technique for measuring the value of non-market goods. Measures of value are required for benefit–cost assessments of public goods, for the analysis of policies that affect the environment, and for realistic estimates of environmental damages resulting from human action, such as oil spills. In recent years the contingent valuation method (CVM) has gained prominence as the major technique for the assessment of the value of environmental amenities. This paper is concerned with a critique of CVM.

The idea of CVM is quite simple: respondents are asked to indicate their value for a public good, usually by specifying the maximum amount they would be willing to pay to obtain or to retain it. The total value of the good is estimated by multiplying the average willingness to pay (WTP) observed in the sample by the number of households in the relevant population. This value is sometimes divided into *use value* and *nonuse value* by comparing the WTP of respondents who expect to enjoy the public good personally (e.g. benefit from improved visibility or from the increased number of fish in a cleaned up stream) to the WTP of respondents who have no such expectations. Specific questions are sometimes added to partition nonuse value further into the value of retaining an option for future use, a bequest value and a pure existence value (Krutilla, 1967).

The accuracy of the CVM is a matter of substantial practical import, not only in benefit–cost assessments but also in litigation over liability and damages. The validity of the technique is taken as a rebuttable presumption in environmental cases brought in the United States under the Comprehensive Environmental Response, Compensation and Liability Act of 1980 (CERCLA). The research on the method has been reviewed in two authoritative volumes, which offer detailed guidelines for its use (Cummings et al, 1986; Mitchell and Carson, 1989; see also Fischhoff and Furby, 1988). Some assessments of CVM have been very favourable, as illustrated by the claims that 'the necessary structure for constructing a hypothetical market for the direct determination of economic values within the Hicksian consumers' surplus framework has been developed' (Brookshire et al, 1982, p173) and that contingent valuation 'is potentially capable of directly measuring a broad range of economic benefits for a wide range of goods, including those not yet supplied, in a manner consistent with economic theory' (Mitchell and

Note: Reprinted from *Journal of Environmental Economics and Management*, vol 22, Kahneman, D. and Knetsch, J. L., 'Valuing public goods: The purchase of moral satisfaction', pp57–70, copyright © (1992), with permission from Elsevier

Carson, 1989, p295). Acceptance of the technique is not universal, however, and some strong reservations about the adequacy of CVM to support specific compensation claims have recently been expressed (Cummings, 1989; d'Arge, 1989; Phillips and Zeckhauser, 1989).

The present article reports an experimental investigation of what is perhaps the most serious shortcoming of CVM: that the assessed value of a public good is demonstrably arbitrary, because willingness to pay for the same good can vary over a wide range depending on whether the good is assessed on its own or embedded as part of a more inclusive package. We next provide evidence for a similar difficulty in the response to payment schedules: WTP estimates can be much larger when the payment is described as a long-term commitment rather than as a one-time outlay. Another study suggests that WTP for public goods is best interpreted as the purchase of moral satisfaction, rather than as a measure of the value associated with a particular public good. Lastly, we examine the categories of expenditures from which contributions to public goods are drawn.

The Embedding Effect

The standard interpretation of CVM results is that the WTP for a good is a measure of the economic value associated with that good, which is fully comparable to values derived from market exchanges and on the basis of which allocative efficiency judgements can be made. However, two related observations that cast doubt on this interpretation have been discussed in the CVM literature. The first is an order effect in WTP responses when the values of several goods are elicited in succession: the same good elicits a higher WTP if it is first in the list rather than valued after others. For example, Tolley and Randall (1983) found that estimates of the value of improved visibility in the Grand Canyon differed by a factor of three depending on whether this item appeared first or third in a survey. Because the order in which goods are mentioned in a survey is purely arbitrary, any effect of this variable raises questions about the validity of responses.

Another problem for CVM is an effect that we call *embedding*, also variously labelled as a part-whole effect, symbolic effect or disaggregation effect (Cummings et al, 1986; Mitchell and Carson, 1989): the same good is assigned a lower value if WTP for it is inferred from WTP for a more inclusive good rather than if the particular good is evaluated on its own. A finding that we obtained some time ago illustrates the embedding effect: the expressed willingness of Toronto residents to pay increased taxes to prevent the drop in fish populations in all Ontario lakes was only slightly higher than the willingness to pay to preserve the fish stocks in only a small area of the province (reported in Kahneman, 1986). It is quite unlikely that the respondents in Toronto viewed saving fish in the Muskoka area as a fully adequate substitute for saving fish in the whole province. The similar WTP observed for separate regions and for the whole of Ontario therefore appears anomalous. Further, the result raises a question about the proper assessment of WTP for a particular region: should this be estimated by the WTP assessment for that region in isolation, or by allocating to it a share of the sum offered for the clean-up of lakes in the entire province?

The embedding problem was noted long ago by investigators who were concerned with the appropriateness of aggregating WTP for several commodities obtained from different samples into an estimate of WTP for the package (Hoehn and Randall, 1982, as summarized in Mitchell and Carson, 1989, pp44–46). Schulze et al stated that '*no* researcher would be willing to defend the summation of CV values that have been obtained in various studies for *many* types of environmental effects; indeed the summation of average CV values for public goods thus far available in the literature would *exhaust* the budget of the average individual' (Schulze et al, 1983, p6; emphases in the original).

The effects of order and embedding observed in assessments of value for public goods are difficult to reconcile with standard value theory. To appreciate why this is so, it is useful to consider the conditions under which assessments of the value of private goods would exhibit these effects. Two generic cases can be identified. The first involves goods which are perfect substitutes for one another and for which satiation is attained by the consumption of one unit. Thus, in the absence of opportunities for storage, resale or altruistic giving, most adults will have zero WTP for a second large ice cream cone offered immediately after the consumption of the first. This is an order effect – the positive value of consuming an initial ice cream cone could be associated with any of those potentially available, but the value of any cone considered immediately thereafter would be zero. The value of ice cream cones under these circumstances also exhibits an embedding effect: WTP for 100 ice cream cones will not be higher than WTP for 1, much as WTP for improved fishing in all of Ontario was little more than WTP for fishing in a small area of that province. Although the notions of substitution and satiation may apply to some environmental goods, they do not readily extend to existence values for beautiful sites, historical landmarks or endangered species. If it is found that WTP to save all threatened historical landmarks in a region is not much higher than WTP to save any single landmark, this can hardly be because each individual landmark provides as much utility as the whole set. Indeed, the uniqueness of the valued goods is the essence of existence value, as this notion has been discussed since Krutilla (1967).

Effects of order and embedding are also expected in another extreme case: goods for which people are willing to pay a large part of their wealth. For example, the sum that an individual will pay to avoid the loss of both an arm and a leg is likely to be much less than the sum of WTP to save each limb separately, because the amount the person is willing to pay to save one limb is almost certain to be high in relation to available wealth, leaving little to prevent the second loss. In this case, order and embedding effects are produced by limited wealth. However, median WTP in CVM studies commonly falls in the range of US$40–100 (d'Arge, 1989), far too small to be severely restrained by wealth.

The problem for the interpretation of CVM results is the following: if the value of a given landmark is much larger when it is evaluated on its own that when it is evaluated as part of a more inclusive package of public goods, which measure is the correct one? The discussions of the problem in the literature provide no agreed principles that would define the proper level of aggregation for the evaluation of a specific good. In the absence of such principles, the results of CVM become arbitrary. This criticism could be fatal. No measuring instrument can be taken seriously if its permitted range of applications yields drastically different measures of the same object.

Embedding a public good

Our first study was conducted to document the embedding effect in a controlled experimental design, focusing on the valuation of a public good that is of personal relevance to respondents: the increased availability of equipment and trained personnel for rescue operations in disasters. Coincidentally, the study was conducted within weeks of the San Francisco earthquake of 1989, a fact that certainly enhanced the relevance of the topic.

Three samples of adults living in the greater Vancouver region in Canada were interviewed by telephone. Samples were evenly split by gender. All calls were made in evening hours. The interviewers introduced themselves as being from a professional polling firm 'conducting interviews on behalf of researchers at Simon Fraser University'. All respondents were initially told:

> The federal and provincial governments provide a wide range of public services that include education, health, police protection, roads and environmental services.

Respondents in one sample were then told to focus on environmental services, which were described as including 'preserving wilderness areas, protecting wildlife, providing parks, preparing for disasters, controlling air pollution, ensuring water quality and routine treatment and disposal of industrial wastes'. They were then asked the following question:

> If you could be sure that extra money collected would lead to significant improvements, what is the most you would be willing to pay each year through higher taxes, prices or user fees, to go into a special fund to improve environmental services?

The evaluation questions were concluded at this point if the respondent's answer was zero. Other respondents were then asked:

> Keeping in mind the services just mentioned, including those related to providing parks, pollution control, preservation of wilderness and wildlife and disposal of industrial wastes, I would like to ask you in particular about improved preparedness for disasters. What part of the total amount that you just mentioned for all environmental services do you think should go specifically to improve preparedness for disasters?

Subjects were allowed to answer by stating a dollar amount, a fraction or a percentage. Where necessary, the interviewer immediately computed the dollar amount of the offered contribution and recorded that value. A third question was asked after some aspects of preparedness for disasters were listed (emergency services in hospitals; maintenance of large stocks of medical supplies, food, fuel and communication equipment; ensuring the availability of equipment and trained personnel for rescue operations; and preparing for clean-up of oil, toxic chemicals or radioactive materials):

> Keeping in mind all aspects of preparedness for disasters, what part of the total amount you allocated to improving preparedness do you think should go specifically to improve the availability of equipment and trained personnel for rescue operations?

Table 14.1 *Willingness to pay for selected classes of goods and allocations of totals to less inclusive groups*

Public good		Sub-sample		
		Group 1 (N = 66) (US$)	*Group 2* (N = 78) (US$)	*Group 3* (N = 74) (US$)
Environmental	Mean	135.91		
services	Median	50.00		
Improve disaster	Mean	29.06	151.60	
preparedness	Median	10.00	50.00	
Improve rescue	Mean	14.12[1]	74.65[2]	122.64
equipment, personnel	Median	1.00	16.00	25.00

[1] Two respondents did not answer this question, reducing N to 64.
[2] Four respondents did not answer this question, reducing N to 74.

The same procedure was followed with the second sample, except that the initial question they answered referred to 'a special fund to improve preparedness for disasters', with a subsequent allocation to 'go specifically to improve the availability of equipment and trained personnel for rescue operations'. Respondents in the third sample were told to focus on preparedness for disasters and were asked to state their willingness to pay 'into a special fund to improve availability of equipment and trained personnel for rescue operations'.

Table 14.1 presents the medians and means of the willingness to pay responses for each of the questions in the three surveys. Zero responses are included in the calculations; respondents who stated a zero response to the initial question were assigned zero responses to subsequent allocation questions.[1] As in other applications of CVM, the data included extremely high responses, in some cases up to 25 per cent of reported household incomes, which probably reflect a misunderstanding of instructions. These responses have considerable effect on the means of WTP, but there is no agreed way to draw a line beyond which responses will be rejected. To avoid this problem, our analyses of WTP results are based on medians, using all responses. The qualitative conclusions are unaffected by this choice of statistics.

The WTP for the public good mentioned in the first question posed to respondents was hardly affected by the inclusiveness of this good. The percentages of positive contributions were 61 per cent for improvements in 'the availability of equipment and trained personnel for rescue operations', 63 per cent for 'preparedness for disasters', and 65 per cent for 'all environmental services'. The median WTP was $25 at the lowest level of inclusiveness and $50 at the two higher levels, but the difference was not significant in a Mann-Whitney test in which the two higher levels were combined. The means of WTP across levels of embedding were also very close, and the differences among them did not approach statistical significance by F test. The pattern is the same as that which we observed in our previous study, in which WTP to preserve fish in all Ontario lakes was only slightly higher than WTP to maintain but a particular few.

The bottom rows of Table 14.1 display the effect of position in the embedding structure on stated WTP for a particular good. The median amounts allocated to 'equipment and trained personnel' vary from $25 when that good is evaluated on its own to $1.50 when the initial question concerns WTP for 'environmental services'. The three values shown in the last row of the table differ markedly from each other in the predicted direction. Group 1 differs significantly from Groups 2 and 3, by both parametric and nonparametric tests. The difference between Groups 2 and 3 only approaches significance.[2]

As in other studies, WTP values were small relative to reported incomes. Pooling over the three samples, the median WTP stated in response to the first question was $37.50 for respondents stating a family income under $20,000 (23 per cent of total sample), $50 for income between $20,000 and $40,000 (39 per cent of total), and $100 for families with incomes in excess of $40,000 (38 per cent of total). The corresponding means were $97, $131 and $230. Clearly, these values are not in the range in which the embedding effect could be explained by constraints of wealth or income.

The results of this study demonstrate a large embedding effect. The key finding is that WTP is approximately constant for public goods that differ greatly in inclusiveness. The inevitable consequence of the insensitivity of WTP to inclusiveness is that estimates of WTP for the same particular good differ – by a factor of 16 for medians or 8 for means – depending on the scope of the initial question. An even larger embedding effect could probably be obtained by asking respondents to make explicit allocations to all the subcategories at each level of embedding: the procedure of the present study, in which respondents make an allocation to a single subordinate good, appears likely to enhance its importance.

The specific good evaluated in the present study is fairly well defined, and the answer is interpretable as a quantity choice: how much extra equipment and personnel would you be willing to pay for? The good also has personal use value for most respondents, because improved availability of equipment and personnel for rescue operations would contribute to their safety and that of their families. The findings therefore extend the evidence for embedding: unlike demonstrations of embedding for existence value, the present results cannot be explained by invoking a concept of symbolic response (Kahneman, 1986; Mitchell and Carson, 1989, p250).

Temporal embedding of payments

The embedding effects discussed so far apply to the specification of the good that is to be acquired. A related effect can arise in the specification of the schedule of payments. The question is whether respondents in a CVM survey are likely to make the appropriate discriminations between a one-time payment and a long-term commitment to a series of payments for a good. The issue is of some importance to the practical implementation of CVM. For example, willingness to pay was assessed in one study by asking people to state the amount that they would be willing to pay annually for 10 years in order to acquire a good, and conventional discount factors were applied to obtain an estimate of the present value of WTP (Rowe et al, 1986).

The issue of whether the participants in a CVM survey actually perform the discount calculations that are imputed to them has not been systematically examined, to our knowledge. The observations of embedding effects in which respondents did not discriminate between goods that vary in inclusiveness suggested the hypothesis that a similar failure of discrimination could be found between payments that vary in temporal inclusiveness. A small study was carried out to examine this hypothesis.

After completion of the main part of the interview, participants in the three groups of the first study were asked one of two versions of the following question. The version presented to each individual was selected at random:

> Now we would like to ask you how much you would be willing to pay (as a one-time payment/every year for a period of five years) to a fund to be used exclusively for a toxic waste treatment facility that would safely take care of all chemical and other toxic wastes in British Columbia.

Median WTP was $20, both in the group that considered a one-time payment (N = 106) and in the group that considered a five-year commitment (N = 100). The corresponding means were $141 and $81. The difference between the means was produced almost entirely by a few extremely high responses in the one-year group. There were five responses stating WTP of $1000 or more in that group, averaging $1800. There were only two such responses in the five-year group, averaging $1300. These extreme responses contribute approximately $54 to the difference of $60 between the means of the two groups. The results provide no reliable indication that the respondents discriminated between payment schedules that differed greatly in total present value.

The significance of embedding

What can be learned from these demonstrations of embedding? It may be useful to state the obvious qualification, that the present results have not established that insensitivity to inclusiveness is a *universal* characteristic of the valuations elicited in CVM studies. No single study could do so. The conservative conclusion from our findings is that future applications of CVM should incorporate an experimental control: the contingent valuation of any public good should routinely be supported by adequate evidence that the estimate is robust to manipulations of embedding, both in the definition of the good and in the specification of the number of payments. Whether this challenge can be met by appropriate CVM techniques is a question that will likely be the subject of further research.

Another defence of CVM against the embedding problem should be mentioned: the observation that different embeddings lead to different valuations of the same good would not be as troubling if there were a way of selecting one of these valuations as the correct one. As noted earlier, however, we were unable to identify in the existing CVM literature any compelling principles that could guide the choice of the appropriate embedding level for the good to be valued, or of a duration for the schedule of payments. Indeed, it is far from obvious that such principles can be found. Should the value of the damaged Alaska shoreline be assessed by WTP to clean up the damage done to it by aggregating separate estimates of WTP to clean up parts of it, or by allocating to the clean-up a fraction of total WTP for environmental improvements? In the absence of agreed answers to such questions, our results suggest that current standards for the use of CVM may allow estimates of the value of a good that differ by more than an order of magnitude, all with an a priori equal claim to validity. As illustrated by the two examples reported here, the designer of a contingent valuation survey may be able to determine the estimated value of any good by the choice of a level of embedding. This potential for manipulation severely undermines the contingent valuation method.

The Purchase of Moral Satisfaction

The results presented in our first study do not support the interpretation of WTP for a public good as a measure of the economic value of this good. It remains a fact, however, that respondents express a willingness to contribute for the acquisition of many public goods, and there is no reason to doubt their sincerity or seriousness. Indeed, some elegant experiments have confirmed the willingness of people to pay for existence value – subjects actually paid to prevent a plant from being destroyed (Boyce et al, 1990). What is the good that respondents are willing to pay to acquire in such experiments or in CVM surveys? We offer the general hypothesis that responses to the CVM question express a willingness to acquire a sense of moral satisfaction (also known as a 'warm glow of giving'; see Andreoni, 1989, 1990a) by a voluntary contribution to the provision of a public good. In attaining this satisfaction, the public good is a means to an end – the consumption is the sense of moral satisfaction associated with the contribution. An interesting feature of the warm glow of moral satisfaction is that it increases with the size of the contribution; for this unusual good, the expenditure is an essential aspect of consumption (Margolis, 1982). The interpretation of the responses to the hypothetical questions used in CVM in terms of moral satisfaction is consistent with Andreoni's economic analyses of actual donations to public goods, both in the field (Andreoni, 1989, 1990a) and in experimental situations (Andreoni, 1990b), which distinguish the utility derived from increasing the total supply of the good from the utility gained in the act of giving.

Public goods differ in the degree of moral satisfaction that they provide to the individual making a contribution. Saving the panda may well be more satisfying for most people than saving an endangered insect and cancer research may be a better cause than research on gum disease. The quality of causes as sources of moral satisfaction will reflect individual tastes and community values. Our first hypothesis is that differences in WTP for various causes can be predicted from independent assessments of the moral satisfaction associated with these causes.

The results of our first study can be explained by invoking the additional hypothesis that moral satisfaction exhibits an embedding effect: the moral satisfaction associated with contributions to an inclusive cause extends with little loss to any significant subset of that cause. A closely related idea is that people may be willing to 'dump their good cause account' on any valued cause (Cummings, 1989). Thus, contributing to the provision of rescue equipment may be as satisfying as contributing to the more inclusive cause of disaster preparedness. Indeed, a narrowly defined cause can be even more satisfying than a cause that includes it: it could be the case, for example, that saving the panda is more appealing than saving endangered species. Different subsets of a cause may vary in their appeal. In general, however, moral satisfaction could be expected to be about the same for an inclusive cause and for representative subsets of it.

An experiment was conducted to test these hypotheses. For the purpose of the experiment, a set of 14 pairs of public goods was constructed (see Table 14.2). Each pair consisted of two causes, one of which was embedded in the other. The items were chosen to include two types of embedding: geographical embedding (e.g. famine relief in Ethiopia or in Africa) and categorical embedding (e.g. research on breast cancer or research on all forms of cancer). The 14 issues were arbitrarily divided into two sets, labelled A and B respectively, including the first 4 and the last 10 issues in Table 14.2

A special telephone survey of adult residents of the Vancouver region was conducted, with respondents randomly assigned into four groups. Respondents in groups 1 ($N = 60$) and 2 ($N = 61$) judged the moral satisfaction associated with the various causes (group 1 judged the inclusive items of set A and the embedded items of set B; group 2 judged the remaining items). After an introduction similar to that used in the surveys described in our first study and an indication that the questions were about 'various causes to which people might be willing to make voluntary contributions', the instructions given to these two groups were:

> Please consider each of the causes separately and independently; that is, assume you are only being asked about the one cause. Indicate the degree of satisfaction you would receive from contributing to each cause on a scale from 0 to 10, with 0 indicating no satisfaction at all and 10 indicating a great deal of personal satisfaction.

Groups 3 ($N = 61$) and 4 ($N = 60$) were matched, respectively, to groups 1 and 2, but they provided measures of WTP for the same sets of causes. After the same introduction and indication of what the questions were about, these respondents received the following instructions:

> Please consider each of the causes separately and independently; that is, assume you are only being asked about the one cause. Indicate the most that you would be willing to pay for each.

The order in which the causes were presented was randomly determined separately for each respondent.

Table 14.2 presents the mean ratings of moral satisfaction and the medians and means of WTP for the 28 public goods included in the study, arranged in pairs. In each case, the embedded good is the first member of the pair. There is as usual a large discrepancy between mean and median WTP, due to extremely large WTP reported by a few individuals in each group. As before, we chose to focus on medians, without discarding any responses. The moral satisfaction ratings, which were made on a bounded scale, are not susceptible to large effects of a few aberrant responses, and the means of the satisfaction ratings were accordingly used in the analysis.

The hypothesis that WTP is predictable from assessments of moral satisfaction was tested by ranking the 14 issues evaluated by each group and by comparing the ranking of these issues by WTP and by moral satisfaction. The rank correlations between the means of satisfaction ratings made by group 1 and the median WTP of group 3 was 0.78 ($P < 0.01$). The corresponding correlation between the responses of groups 2 and 4 was 0.62 ($P < 0.02$). The general hypothesis that WTP can be predicted by ratings of

Table 14.2 *Maximum willingness to pay for various causes and ratings of satisfaction from making contributions*

Cause	Satisfaction Mean	Median	WTP (US$) Mean
Reduce acid rain damage in Muskoka, Ont	7.18	20	40.91
Reduce acid rain damage in eastern Canada	7.25	50	214.55
Restore rural BC museums	4.67	10	32.78
Restore rural Canada museums and heritage buildings	5.79	20	113.47
Improve sport fish stocks in BC fresh water	5.25	10	41.89
Improve sport fish stocks in Canada fresh water	6.61	10	147.16
Protect marmot, a small animal in BC	5.48	1.5	33.27
Protect small animals in BC	6.42	10	141.75
Research on dengue fever, a tropical disease	4.57	0	52.42
Research on tropical diseases	4.97	4	17.83
Protect peregrine falcon, an endangered bird	6.46	25	125.00
Protect endangered birds	6.98	20	59.07
Improve sport facilities in small communities in BC	6.22	10	209.75
Improve sport facilities in small communities in Canada	5.42	10	55.96
Rehabilitate recently released young offenders	5.78	50	233.16
Rehabilitate all recently released criminals	4.97	0	25.04
Habitat for muskrats, wild N American rodent	4.70	0	51.60
Habitat for muskrats, squirrels and other wild N American rodents	4.59	4	52.28
Improve literacy of recent adult BC immigrants	6.30	10	190.53
Improve literacy of adults in BC	7.10	10	56.61
Replant trees in cutover areas in BC	7.80	20	151.70
Replant trees in cutover areas in western Canada	7.53	20	54.74
Increase research on toxic waste disposal	7.87	50	234.12
Increase research on environmental protection	7.44	50	98.77
Famine relief in Ethiopia	6.38	20	157.67
Famine relief in Africa	5.57	25	72.68
Research on breast cancer	8.12	50	243.14
Research on all forms of cancer	8.38	50	162.09

moral satisfaction is strongly supported. As may be seen in Table 14.2, there was only one striking discrepancy in the rankings of issues by WTP and by moral satisfaction: the rehabilitation of young offenders was one of the four causes eliciting the largest monetary contributions, but it ranked very low as a source of moral satisfaction. The discrepancy was not predicted, and any account of it must be speculative. One hypothesis is that the illegitimate context in which the need for public contributions arises makes it difficult to describe these contributions as yielding any kind of satisfaction – including moral satisfaction.

The data of Table 14.2 also allow a test of the effects of inclusiveness (embedding) on both moral satisfaction and WTP. The more inclusive causes have a very slight advantage on both dimensions overall, but the effect is weak and inconsistent: the more inclusive cause is associated with a higher rating of moral satisfaction for 8 of the 14 pairs of causes and with a lower rating for the other 6. Median WTP is higher for the inclusive than for the embedded cause in 6 pairs, identical in 6 others and inferior in the remaining 2 pairs. On the other hand, mean WTP is higher for the embedded cause in 9 of the 14 pairs.

The results of this experiment support the proposed interpretation of willingness to pay for public goods as an expression of willingness to pay to acquire moral satisfaction. With only one salient exception, causes that were judged to provide little moral satisfaction also elicited relatively low WTP. Overall, there was a close correspondence between the rankings of issues by the two measures. Furthermore, the interpretation of WTP as an index of moral satisfaction helps explain the embedding effect: if the inclusiveness of the cause does little to enhance moral satisfaction, increasing inclusiveness should have little effect on WTP, as was indeed observed both in this study and in the earlier section on 'The embedding effect'.

The sources of contributions to public goods

The question posed to respondents in a CVM survey is an unusual one, which has some features of a market survey, an opinion poll and an appeal on behalf of a new charity. Respondents who follow instructions consider the possibility of a significant financial commitment to the provision of a public good. If they are serious about it, such a commitment to a new expenditure entails a corresponding reduction in other categories of spending. To understand the decisions of respondents in CVM surveys it is useful to identify the categories of spending from which they would expect to draw their contributions.

In the budget of most households there already exists a category of spending that is dedicated to obtaining moral satisfaction – voluntary contributions to charity. Spending on charity is far from negligible. For, example, in fiscal year 1988 donations by individuals in the US totalled $86 billion, approximately $350 per capita. The respondent in a CVM study is likely to consider a new contribution in the context of the existing pattern of voluntary donations by the household. It is of interest to find out whether respondents view the proposed payment as a substitute to current charitable giving or as an addition to the moral satisfaction budget, requiring a reduction in other categories of spending. To test these possibilities, participants in the survey of 'The embedding effect' section who had stated a positive WTP for the cause presented to them were asked a series of questions in the following format:

> Suppose you were actually called on to make the contribution to environmental services you indicated earlier. Which expenditure categories do you think this money would mainly come from? What would you spend less on?

Table 14.3 *Percentage of respondents indicating reduced spending in various expenditure categories* (N = 137)

Category	'Reduction'	'Greatest reduction'
Food	19.1	2.3
Charities	34.6	9.3
Holidays	64.2	15.5
Entertainment	76.1	41.1
Savings	46.2	22.5
Other things	65.9	9.3

The expenditure categories mentioned in the questions included food, charities, holidays (vacations), entertainment, savings and 'other things'. After answering this series of questions, respondents who had listed more than one category were asked: 'From which category do you think most of the money would come?' and the relevant list of categories was repeated to them. Table 14.3 presents the results.

The results indicate that added spending on environmental and disaster services would be drawn from discretionary spending, and especially from entertainment. Respondents would not expect to alter their eating habits. More important, they would not withdraw the contribution from current charitable giving. Most respondents apparently viewed the contribution as an addition to the 'good cause' budget, not as a substitute for existing items in that spending category. The observed pattern of responses is the same as would be expected in answers to the question: 'If you made an *extra* contribution to charity, where would it come from?' In the terms of the present analysis, the respondents appear to have considered the contingent valuation question as an opportunity to acquire additional moral satisfaction. Note that if households contribute only to causes that yield high moral satisfaction, the only way to increase the consumption of this good is by increasing contributions – to the currently favoured causes or to equally satisfying causes.

Conclusions

The research reported here had two objectives: to examine the proposition that CVM results are susceptible to an embedding effect that could render them largely arbitrary and consequently useless for practical purposes and to advance the interpretation of what people do in answering CVM questions.

The central result of the first study was that willingness to pay was almost the same for a narrowly defined good (rescue equipment and personnel) and for vastly more inclusive categories (all disaster preparedness, or even all environmental services). Correspondingly, the value assigned to the more specific good varied by an order of magnitude depending on the depth of its embedding in the category for which WTP was initially assessed. This result appears to invalidate a basic assumption of CVM: that standard value theory applies to the measures obtained by this method. As the choice of embedding structure is arbitrary, the estimates of value obtained from CVM surveys will be correspondingly arbitrary.

Our assessment of the validity of the CVM is in marked contrast to that reached by Mitchell and Carson (1989) in their comprehensive review of the literature on this method. Mitchell and Carson recognized the potential severity of the embedding effect, but sounded a hopeful note in their discussion of it (p250), arguing that such an effect is not inevitable. The evidence cited for this conclusion was the observation that WTP to improve water quality nationwide, assessed in a national survey (Mitchell and Carson, 1984), was approximately twice as high as an estimate of WTP to raise the quality of water in the Monongahela River system in Pennsylvania, assessed in a local survey conducted by other investigators using a similar instrument (Desvousges et al, 1983). Given the uncertainties of comparisons across studies and sampling areas, this evidence against embedding is not persuasive.

There was some prior reason to hope that the embedding effect might be restricted to nonuse values, but the present results show that estimates of use value are not generally immune to embedding effects: an essentially complete embedding effect was obtained for disaster preparedness, a public good for which respondents have use value. Our tentative conclusion is that the factor that controls the magnitude of the embedding effect is not the distinction between public goods that have use value and those that only have nonuse value. A more important distinction could be between public goods for which private purchase is conceivable and other goods for which it is not. Access to clean air and the right to fish in a stream could be privately purchased in a market, and sometimes are. The respondents in contingent valuation surveys have some experience in the purchase of such goods and could rely on this experience to determine their willingness to pay (Brookshire et al, 1982). On the other hand, few respondents have experience in individual purchases of improvements in disaster preparedness, air traffic control, maintenance of species or expansion of parks. The only way to procure such goods is by concerted public action, and the decision to make a voluntary contribution to such action has more in common with charity than with the purchase of consumption goods. Note that we do not assert that the CVM is necessarily valid for public goods that could be purchased by individuals. Our point is that the purchase of moral satisfaction is especially plausible as an interpretation of WTP for goods that could not be so purchased, even when these goods have use value.[3]

Students of CVM have long known that the respondents' answers to questions about their willingness to accept compensation for the loss of public goods (WTA) are strongly affected by moral considerations. Participants are prone to respond with indignation to questions about the compensation they would require to accept pollution of the Grand Canyon National Park, or of an unspoiled beach in a remote region. The indignation is expressed by the rejection of the offered transaction as illegitimate, or by absurdly high bids. The practitioners of contingent valuation hoped to avoid the difficulties of assessing WTA by substituting WTP even where WTA is the theoretically appropriate (Freeman, 1979; Cummings et al, 1986). The present results suggest that the adoption of the WTP measure does not really avoid moral concerns because the voluntary contribution to the provision of such goods can be morally satisfying. A treatment that interprets contributions to public goods as equivalent to purchases of consumption goods is inadequate when moral satisfaction is an important part of the welfare gain from the contribution (Andreoni, 1990a). The amount that individuals are willing to pay to acquire moral satisfaction should not be mistaken for a measure of the economic value of public goods.

Notes

This research was supported by Fisheries and Oceans Canada, the Ontario Ministry of the Environment, and the Sloan Foundation. Interviews and preliminary statistical analyses were performed by Campbell-Goodell Consultants, Vancouver, British Columbia. We benefited from conversations with George Akerlof, James Bieke, Brian Binger, Ralph d'Arge, Elizabeth Hoffman, Richard Thaler and Frances van Loo, from a commentary by Glenn Harrison, and from the statistical expertise of Carol Nickerson.

1   Glenn Harrison has suggested that this procedure could bias the results because of the theoretical possibility that a respondent might be willing to pay for a good but not for a bundle that includes it. Note that this objection can be eliminated by informing respondents in advance that they will have an opportunity to allocate each contribution to an inclusive good among its separate constituents. It seems highly implausible that this minor procedural change would significantly alter results. The reasons for refusals to contribute in CVM surveys are commonly quite general (rejection of responsibility, opposition to extra taxes etc.) and therefore likely to apply to the constituents as well as to more inclusive goods.

2   An earlier draft mistakenly stated that all three groups differed significantly from one another.

3   The application of CVM to goods such as hunting licences in limited supply [4] is perhaps best viewed as a special case of market research, because these goods are in all essential respects conventional private goods.

References

1   Andreoni, J. (1989) 'Giving with impure altruism: Applications to charity and Ricardian equivalence'. *Journal of Political Economics*, vol 97, pp1447–1458

2   Andreoni, J. (June 1990a) 'Impure altruism and donations to public goods: A theory of warm-glow giving' *Economical Journal*, vol 100

3   Andreoni, J. (1990b) *An Experimental Test of the Public Goods Crowding-out Hypothesis.* Working paper, University of Wisconsin

4   Bishop, R. C. and Heberlein, T. A. (1979) 'Measuring values of extramarket goods: Are indirect measures biased?' *American Journal of Agricultural Economics*, vol 61, pp926–930

5   Boyce, R. R., Brown, T. C., McClelland, G. D., Peterson, G. L. and Schulze, W. D. (1990) 'An Experimental Examination of Intrinsic Environmental Values', Working Paper, University of Colorado

6   Brookshire, D. S., Thayer, M. A., Schulze, W. D. and d'Arge, R. C. (1982) 'Valuing public goods: A comparison of survey and hedonic approaches'. *American Economic Review*, vol 72, pp165–176

7   Cummings, R. G. (1989) Letter to Office of Environmental Project Review, Department of the Interior, 10 November

8   Cummings, R. G., Brookshire, D. S. and Schulze, W. D. (eds) (1986) *Valuing Environmental Goods: An Assessment of the Contingent Valuation Method*. Rowman and Allanheld, Totawa, NJ

9   d'Arge, R. C. (1989) 'A practical guide to economic valuation of the environment', in *Thirty-fourth Annual Rocky Mountain Mineral Law Institute Proceedings*. Matthew Bendier and Co, NY

10 Desvousges, W. H., Smith, V. K. and McGivney, M. P. (1983) *A Comparison of Alternative Approaches for Estimating Recreation and Related Benefits of Water Quality Improvements*. Report to the US Environmental Protection Agency, Washington, DC

11 Fischhoff, B. and Furby, L. (1988) 'Measuring values: A conceptual framework for interpreting transactions with special reference to contingent valuation of visibility'. *Journal of Risk and Uncertainty*, vol 1, pp147–184

12 Freeman, A. M. (1979) *The Benefits of Environmental Improvement: Theory and Practice*, Johns Hopkins Press, Baltimore

13 Hoehn, J. P. and Randall, A. (1982) *Aggregation and Disaggregation of Program Benefits in a Complex Policy Environment: A Theoretical Framework and Critique of Estimation Methods*. Paper presented at the American Agricultural Economics Association Meetings, Logan, UT

14 Kahneman, D. (1986) 'Comments on the contingent valuation method', in Cummings, R. G., Brookshire, D. S. and Schulze, W. D. (eds) *Valuing Environmental Goods*, Rowman and Allanheld, Totawa, NJ

15 Krutilla, J. V. (1967) 'Conservation reconsidered'. *American Economic Review*, vol 57, pp787–796.

16 Mitchell, R. C. and Carson, R. T. (1984) *A Contingent Valuation Estimate of National Freshwater Benefits*. Report to the US Environmental Protection Agency, Washington, DC

17 Mitchell, R. C. and Carson, R. T. (1989) *Using Surveys to Value Public Goods: The Contingent Valuation Method*. Resources For the Future, Washington, DC

18 Margolis, H. (1982) *Selfishness, Altruism and Rationality*. Cambridge University Press, NY

19 Phillips, C. V. and Zeckhauser, R. J. (1989) 'Contingent valuation of damage to natural resources: How accurate? How appropriate?' *Toxics Law Reporter*, pp520–529

20 Rowe, R. D., Schulze, W. D. and Hurd, D. (1986) *A Survey of Colorado Residents' Attitudes about Cleaning Up Hazardous Waste-Site Problems in Colorado*. Report for the Colorado Attorney General's Office, Denver

21 Schulze, W. D., Cummings, R. G. and Brookshire, D. S. (1983) *Methods Development in Measuring Benefits of Environmental Improvements*. Vol II, Report to the US Environmental Protection Agency, Washington, DC

22 Tolley, George S. and Randall, A. (1983) *Establishing and Valuing the Effects of Improved Visibility in the Eastern United States*. Report to the US Environmental Protection Agency, Washington DC

15

Protected Values

Jonathan Baron and Mark Spranca

Introduction

Some theories of rational decision making require trade-offs among values, including moral values. According to these theories, if we value human life and other goods as well, we will rationally spend some amount of money to reduce risks of death, but not an infinite amount. Some risks are just too small and too costly to reduce. The same goes for all other values, such as those for the protection of nature or individual freedom from interference.

Such willingness to make trade-offs is especially reasonable when we consider what it would mean to be completely committed to some value. It would mean that we could not take any risk of sacrificing this value through our actions or our failures to act. We would thus be obliged to spend our lives looking for actions that could reduce small risks of sacrificing this value. If we had more than one such value, we would be in a serious quandary.

Although the need to make trade-offs is a fact of life, it is not one that everyone is happy with. Some people say that human lives – or human rights, or natural resources – are infinitely more important than other economic goods. These people hold what we call protected values. Some of their values, as they conceive them, are protected against being traded off for other values. People who hold protected values may behaviourally trade them off for other things – by risking lives or by sacrificing nature or human rights – but they are not happy with themselves for doing so, if they are aware of what they are doing. They are caught in binds that force them to violate some important value, but the value is no less important to them because of this behavioural violation.

Why protected values cause problems

We have noted that protected values are typically impossible for individuals to satisfy. Protected values also cause difficulties for institutions, such as government agencies, that try to satisfy the values of many people. If everyone has values that can be traded off, then, in principle, it might be possible to measure the values and arrive at a utilitarian decision that maximizes total value satisfaction, i.e. total utility. At such an optimum, we cannot increase one person's utility without reducing someone else's utility by at least

Note: Reprinted from *Organizational Behaviour and Human Decision Processes*, vol 70, Baron, J. and Spranca, M., 'Protected values', pp1–16, copyright © (1997), with permission from Elsevier

the same amount. Government agencies attempt this sort of optimization when they assess the value of human life in order to determine whether environmental regulations, safety programmes or medical treatments are cost-effective.

Protected values cause trouble for such efforts because they imply that one value is infinitely more important than others. If the value of forests is infinite for some people, we will simply not cut them, and we will have to find substitutes for wood and paper. Even if only a few people place such an infinite value on forests, their values will trump everyone else's values, and everyone else will spend more money and make do with plastic. This is still (theoretically) a utilitarian optimum. But a social decision not to cut any forests because a few people have infinite values for them seems to give excessive weight to those values.

Other problems arise when protected values conflict. If some people have protected values for yew trees while others have protected values for the rights of cancer patients to the drug that is produced from them, no solution seems possible. Of course, a solution is possible. We could honour one side or the other, ignoring the rights of patients or trees. But the choice of the solution would be unaffected by the number of those who favoured patients vs trees.

Such a situation violates apparent normative principles of decision making. For example, it is reasonable to think that, for two options L and T, we either prefer L, prefer T or we are indifferent. In the situation just described, we would be indifferent, since either solution is 'optimal' in the sense that any improvement for one person will make someone else worse off by at least the same amount. Yet, a doubling of the number of people who favoured L or T would not change the decision. This seems to violate a principle of dominance, which could be stated roughly as, 'If we are indifferent between L and T and then get additional reason for L (or T), we should then favour L (or T)'. The same problems arise within an individual who holds conflicting protected values. An additional argument for one option or another will not swing the decision.

To avoid problems of this sort, most normative theories of decision making assume that values can be traded off. That is, for any pair of values, a sufficiently small change in the satisfaction of one value can be compensated by a change in some other value.[1] The values may be held by the same person or by different people. We call values *compensatory* when they are part of such a pair. Economic theory speaks of trade-off functions. Utility theory assumes that each value takes the form of a utility function relating individual utility to the amount of a good or some attribute of the good.

Protected values thus create problems for utilitarian analysis, such as violations of the dominance principle. Economic analysis seems to avoid some of these problems by converting all values to money before comparing them, rather than using utility as that common coin. If we try to assess people's willingness to pay (WTP) to avoid violations of protected values, we often find that it is finite. Realistically, people can pay only so much, so WTP is finite. However, the appropriate measure is sometimes willingness to *accept* (WTA), for example, when individuals have rights to the goods in question. Moreover, in a benefit–cost analysis, the total WTA of all those with rights is the relevant value. If a few people have infinite WTA for a forest, then the forest has infinite economic value. It cannot be cut. When rights conflict, so that we have no choice but to violate one right or another, and when some people have protected values for each of the conflicting rights, we are back to the same problem of dominance violations. We can still make decisions, for example, by voting. But voting need not honour protected values. For example, voting on the siting of hazardous facilities will allow them to be put almost anywhere, even over the ancient burial grounds of native peoples.

The existence of protected values

The seriousness of these problems, and the possibility of solutions to them, may depend on the nature of protected values themselves. This article proposes a theory of protected values and presents some preliminary tests of it. In essence, we propose that protected values derive from rules that prohibit certain actions, rather than values for potential outcomes of these actions. If this is true, then part of the solution to the problem may involve separate measurement of values for actions and outcomes, if it is possible to do this.

People do claim to hold protected values. These values appear in survey responses. In the method of contingent valuation (CV), respondents are asked how much they would pay for some good, such as protection of a wilderness area, or how much they would accept to give up the good. Some respondents refuse to answer such questions sensibly (Mitchell and Carson, 1989). They say 'zero' or 'no amount' because they think that 'we shouldn't put a price on nature'. These responses may reflect people's true values, even if the same people are inconsistent with these values in their behaviour. If some people say that trees have infinite value and you point out to them that they have just sent a fax when they could have used electronic mail, they may admit that they do not really place an infinite value on trees, but they may instead feel guilty at realizing that they have violated one of their values. If we are trying to do what is best for people, we may sometimes do better to try to satisfy the values they hold rather than the values they reveal in their behaviour, for people may sometimes regret their own behaviour. Their behaviour may be inconsistent with their values. Even when people hold conflicting values that are impossible to satisfy jointly in this world, they may wish they lived in a different world. We cannot dismiss these statements with a charge of hypocrisy.

Some philosophers and social theorists defend these refusals to make trade-offs. These defences provide additional evidence of the reality of protected values, at least in the theorists themselves. Schwartz (1986) argues that certain practices should be inviolable, not compromised by trade-offs with anything else. For example, academic standards for giving grades should not be distorted by the desire to pass the quarterback of the football team, regardless of how important it is for the team to win or how few additional examination points are needed. Anderson (1993) argues that economists and utility theorists have a distorted view of the nature of human values. Anderson argues that values cannot be measured quantitatively for the purpose of trading them off. Social decisions, she says, must be reached by a process of discussion. (She does not say how this discussion is to proceed without at least some implicit discussion of the strengths of competing values.)

The purpose of the present theory

Our purpose is to explain the nature of protected values. What are their general properties? How do they participate in judgements?

We do not attempt to settle the philosophical questions about the sense in which protected values are subject to criticism or not (see Baron, 1988, for discussion), although, if we can answer the question of what they are as they commonly occur, that discussion may be able to focus more accurately on its topic.

We also do not concern ourselves with the empirical question of how people resolve conflicts involving protected values. However, our findings may bear on the question of how such formal procedures as benefit–cost analysis could take these values into account without violating the underlying utilitarian theory. The psychological nature of values is central to the question of how we should deal with them. Of course, all we can do is examine some of the most common kinds of protected values in some cultures. We may miss the discovery of values with a different psychological nature, to which philosophical arguments may be relevant that are not relevant to the values we find.

Finally, we do not attempt to answer the question of *which* values are protected or absolute. Others have attempted this, and we have drawn on their work in designing tests of our theory, without necessarily accepting all their conclusions. Andre (1992) provides a taxonomy of 'blocked exchanges', cases in which it is either impossible or immoral to sell something; we focus here on cases in which it is thought to be immoral although possible. Fiske and Tetlock (1997) attempt another analysis in terms of modes of social interaction (see also Tetlock et al, 1996, pp36–39).

Protected values as deontological rules

Our purpose here is to examine the nature of such absolute values as they commonly occur. We present a theory about these values, and some preliminary results. We conclude with a discussion of the implications of these values for utilitarian decision making. We call the values in question 'protected' to emphasize the fact that their defining property is the reluctance of their holders to trade them off with other values. They are at least partially protected from trade-offs. This is what makes them troublesome for utilitarian analysis of decisions. As we pointed out, protected values exist in judgement, but cannot fully exist in action.

We propose that these values express absolute deontological rules, rules that apply to certain behaviour 'whatever the consequences'. An example of such a rule is 'Do not destroy natural processes irreversibly'. Such a rule prohibits the holder from destroying species, even if, for example, the destruction in question would have the effect of saving more species in total. Utilitarianism, utility theory and other forms of consequentialism define right or optimal action in terms of some evaluation of expected consequences. By contrast, deontological rules specify that certain actions should be taken or not taken as a function of a description of the action itself. The description may refer to the way an action is performed, its motives, its antecedent conditions and even its immediate consequences, for example, a direct causal link between the action and extinction of a species. But, if the description includes all the consequences and nothing else, then the rule becomes effectively consequentialist.

When people who try to follow such rules are asked about their values, they are reminded of the rules. So, for example, a person asked about WTA for species destruction will interpret acceptance of the money as complicity in the destruction and will refuse to accept any amount. The use of hypothetical questions does not prevent this interpretation: hypothetical questions are simulations of real questions, and subjects might think that even their answers to hypothetical questions will be known to the experimenter and perhaps reported, so their answers are still real in the sense that they may influence others, just as an opinion poll might do.

Deontological rules are typically agent-relative as opposed to agent-neutral (e.g. Nagel, 1986). Agent-relative rules are those that concern the involvement of a particular person. A rule that parents ought to care for their children is an agent-relative rule, because it concerns particular people. It is not the same as a rule that the children should somehow be cared for, or a rule that we should regard parents caring for their own children as a good consequence. A truly agent-relative rule would hold that X should care about X's child's welfare and Y should care about Y's child's welfare, but X need have no concern either with Y's child *or with ensuring that Y looks out for the welfare of Y's own child.*

Deontological rules typically prohibit harmful actions (e.g. destroying species) rather than harmful omissions under specific and limited conditions (e.g. neglecting one's child or one's job – see Baron, 1996). In general, people think of acts as those that cause relevant outcomes through a chain of causality that involves predictable physical or psychological principles at each step (Baron, 1993). If we fail to prevent some harm because we are out playing tennis at the time it happens, no such link can be made between our behaviour and the harm, although, in another sense, we cause it.

Rules that are agent-relative and that concern harmful actions (or specifically limited harmful omissions) create limited obligations. As a result, deontological rules are easier to think of as absolute. Consequentialist principles, by contrast, can create unlimited obligations unless they can be traded off with other obligations. Consider a consequentialist rule that prohibited trade-offs, such as, 'the destruction of species is infinitely bad'. Such a rule would have to be honoured before any other decision criteria, for omissions as well as commissions. People who took this rule seriously would have to design their lives so that they did as much as possible to preserve species, and to induce others to do the same. Only when they had satisfied this criterion could they apply other criteria. A rule based on consequences does not make a distinction between acts and omissions or between self and others, so the injunction to act to preserve species and to induce others to do so would be as strong as the injunction not to destroy them. A person who took this kind of rule seriously would be a fanatic. Perhaps some fanatics do indeed think this way. Because of the practical difficulty of living this way, however, fanatics are rare.

Deontological rules are not necessarily protected against trade-offs. Indeed, philosophers typically regard them as *prima facie* constraints that can be overridden by other constraints, or by consequentialist considerations. Our suggestion is thus that essentially all protected values are deontological, not that all deontological rules are protected.

Of course, people do have rules based on consequences, but almost all of these rules trade off with other considerations, so that they do not lead to this problem. Moreover, people who hold protected values for some things also hold compensatory values for other things, and these compensatory values trade off in the usual ways. A person who holds a protected value for species may still buy a car by thinking about the trade-offs among price, safety, efficiency etc. Protected values are thus a function of both the value and the person.

Implications

The defining property of protected values is *absoluteness*. Our proposal that these values arise from deontological rules implies directly that three other properties should be present in most cases in which absoluteness is present: quantity insensitivity, agent relativity and moral obligation. These properties need not be perfectly correlated with absoluteness, for other sorts of values may exist that have some of these properties but not all of them.

Absoluteness expresses itself in resistance to trade-offs. People resist trading off protected values with compensatory values, such as their value for money. Typically, people want protected values to trump any decision involving a conflict between a protected and a compensatory value (Baron, 1986). In this sense, protected values are absolute. The resistance to making trade-offs can also express itself in refusals to answer questions about trade-offs. Thus, those with a rule against destroying species may refuse to accept any amount of money in return for allowing such destruction, or they may refuse to say how much they would accept. When asked how much they are willing to pay, they may again try to avoid answering. Potentially such a question creates a conflict with another protected value that people are not so willing to acknowledge, that for their own life. Someone who pays everything to save a species would die from inability to afford the necessities of life. The important implication here is the avoidance of trade-offs of the usual sort. Of course, people with protected values may still answer trade-off questions, with difficulty, in order to oblige the researcher.

Notice that when protected values lead to lexicographic rules – rules that eliminate options by applying one value at a time – these rules are not mere heuristics of the sort found in studies of consumer choices and others without moral components (e.g. Payne et al, 1993). It may be reasonable for people to use a strategy of eliminating apartments if the rent is above a cut-off, even though people know that they might be willing to pay more if everything else were absolutely perfect. This is a heuristic because it is knowingly adopted to save time and effort. Protected values are different. They are treated like commitments.

If absolute values arise from deontological prohibitions, they will tend to have the following properties.

Quantity insensitivity. Quantity of consequences is irrelevant for protected values. Destroying one species through a single act is as bad as destroying a hundred through a single act. The protected value applies to the act, not the result (although a compensatory value may apply to the result as well). One form of quantity insensitivity is insensitivity to probability occurrence.

Some opponents of abortion seem to ignore quantity when they oppose spending government money on international family planning programmes that carry out abortions, even if the money does not pay for the abortions *and even if other expenditures actually reduce the number of abortions performed*. It is not the number of abortions they care about. Another example was the attitude of some abortion opponents to the use of fetal tissue in medical research, which they felt might encourage some women to have abortions: 'In our view, if just one additional fetus were lost because of the allure of directly benefiting another life by the donation of fetal tissue, our department [Health and Human Services] would still be against federal funding... The issue is about whether or not the federal government should administer a policy that encourages induced abortions. However few or many more abortions result from this type of research cannot be erased or outweighed by the potential benefit of the research' (Mason, 1990).

Agent relativity. Protected values are agent relative, as opposed to being agent general. This means that participation of the decision maker is important, as opposed to the consequences themselves. This follows from the assumption that protected values arise as rules about action.

For present purposes (following our earlier discussion), agent relativity includes concern with action rather than omission (and related distinctions such as changing vs not changing the status quo, or causing an outcome vs letting it happen: see Spranca et al, 1991; Ritov and Baron, 1992). Consider again the example of giving aid to family planning programmes that carry out abortions. If the aid is withheld, arguably, the number of abortions will increase. However, those who withhold the aid would not feel responsible for these abortions if they think that they are not responsible for the results of their inaction. If protected values were agent general, people would have infinite responsibility for preventing violation of those values wherever it occurred. The combination of agent-general obligations with quantity-insensitivity for probability would generate obligations to take any action that might do some good, however, improbably. A distinction between acts and omissions is therefore compelled by absoluteness, for practical reasons, even if people might otherwise see these values as agent-general.

Moral obligation. The actions required or prohibited by protected values are seen as moral obligations in the sense of Turiel (1983). Moral obligations are not just conventions or personal preferences. They are seen as universal and independent of what people think. They are also seen as objective obligations: people should try to carry them out even if they do not think they should. This is not to say that compensatory values are always nonmoral. Many are moral too. People who endorse deontological principles, however, may think of objectivity and universality as required in order to prevent trade-offs. If someone thought of a principle as something that did not apply to people in certain situations or to people who did not endorse it, then she would be more free to conclude that she herself was in a situation where it did not apply or that she was no longer bound by it because she no longer endorsed it, and these conclusions would permit her to trade it off with other values.

These three properties follow from the idea of rules concerning actions. However, variants are possible. For example, one variant keeps the action-based aspect while giving up absoluteness. By this variant, we should allocate resources *in proportion* to the tightness of making allocations of various kinds rather than the goodness of the results.[2] Thus, people may believe that the best method of allocating resources is according to the importance of the kind of action paid for by each expenditure rather than according to the effects of the allocation on solving the problem or even according to the size of the problem. Unlike an absolute rule, this rule allows us to allocate some resources to less important actions, but without regard to the consequences.

Two other properties follow from those just listed, along with other assumptions:

Denial of trade-offs by wishful thinking. People may resist the idea that anything must be sacrificed at all for the sake of their value. People generally tend to deny the existence of trade-offs (Jervis, 1976, pp128–142; Montgomery, 1984), and this tendency may be particularly strong when one of the values involved is not supposed to trade off with anything. People may desire to believe that their values do no harm. Thus, opponents of family planning assistance are prone to deny that cutting aid will increase the abortion rate, or have any other undesired effects.

Anger. People may become angry at the thought of violation of a protected value. This is a consequence of its being a moral violation. Tetlock et al (1996) have described both this property and the denial of the need for trade-offs in preliminary data on reluctance to make trade-offs, which anticipates the present work in these respects.

We hypothesize that these five properties will be correlated with absoluteness. These correlations need not to be perfect. Each of the other properties could have other causes aside from absoluteness. However, the correlations should be substantial to the extent to which our proposal is helpful in understanding values in general.

Posturing

When people say that their values are absolute, they may sometimes be simply taking a strong negotiating stance, making 'nonnegotiable demands'. We call this 'posturing'. Environmentalists do not want to be drawn into a debate of how much money a pristine forest is worth. They would rather say that it should simply be preserved, whatever the cost. Still, the fact that philosophical writers defend such absolute values suggests that this is not just a bargaining ploy. Our studies address posturing in a couple of ways, which we shall discuss.

Experiments

We report five experiments. The first three were general surveys of several different values of the sort found to be protected in pilot studies (not reported). The values we examined concerned activities or actions, such as abortion or destruction of natural resources, that some people regard as morally prohibited despite benefits that cause people to engage in them. We hypothesize that opposition to these actions involves protected values in many people. We define a value as protected for a subject when the subject says that the value should not be traded off, i.e. it is absolute. We ask whether such protected values have the other properties we have listed. In particular, we examine correlations between absoluteness and each of the other five properties. The first study also compared conditions in which subjects either did or did not indicate to the experimenter what actions they were rating.

The last two studies concerned sensitivity to quantity, each in the case of a single kind of value: Experiment 4 concerned the prohibition of unnaturally raising IQ through genetic engineering; Experiment 5 concerned endangered species. We are particularly interested in the subjects – however few there are – who are willing to make trade-offs. We asked whether these subjects were less sensitive to quantity when protected values were involved. Quantity was the number of children in Experiment 4 and the probability of saving a species in Experiment 5.

Experiment 1

We presented subjects with 14 different actions and asked 12 questions about each one. The questions corresponded to the hypothesized properties of protected values. The actions were chosen on the basis of pilot studies and prior literature. We tried to select actions so that each action would be prohibited by a protected value for some subjects.

We were also concerned about the effects of posturing. Subjects who felt very strongly about some values might say that they would not trade these values off with anything etc. as a way of impressing the experimenter or others with the strength of their commitment. They may approach the experiment as if it were an opinion poll of sorts. This could make them exaggerate their views for the purpose of influencing others' opinions about the issues or about themselves. To look for such posturing, we compared two conditions. In the 'public' condition, subjects reported the number of each action they were answering about, so that we could tabulate the responses by action. In the 'private' condition, subjects omitted the numbers of the actions, so that we could not tabulate responses. Nobody could know what issue the subject was responding to.

Method

Subjects were 72 students from the University of Pennsylvania and the Philadelphia College of Pharmacy and Science, solicited by advertising and paid US$6/hour for completing this questionnaire and others.

Subjects answered 12 questions about each of 14 actions. The number of each action was printed on a card. The subject had the cards, an answer sheet with a table for the answers, and a list of the actions and the questions. In the private condition, subjects wrote answers without identifying the actions to which they were responding. The instructions for that condition read as follows:

You have a list of actions that some people oppose, numbered 1–14. Some of these are happening now, and others are not. For each action, suppose that those in favour of it were willing to pay a great deal of money. Please answer questions A–L for each action by writing YES, NO or ? (not sure) in the blank on the answer sheet. Use one row for each action.

We are interested in the relations between one answer and another answer. We want you to give your honest opinion about each question. We think you can do that best if there is no possibility that anyone will know which action you are talking about. We would like you to determine the order of the 14 items by shuffling cards with the numbers 1–14 and then answering the items in the order you get. Please DO NOT *write the number of the item you are answering*. This way we cannot tell which action you are responding to.

In the public condition, the last paragraph read: In order to randomize the order, we would like you to determine the order of the 14 items by shuffling cards with the numbers 1–14 and then answering the items in the order you get. *Please write the number of the action you are answering in the leftmost column, so we can tell which action you are responding to.*

The actions were:

1 Destruction of natural forests by human activity, resulting in the extinction of plant and animal species forever
2 Raising the IQ of normal children by giving them (completely safe) drugs
3 Using genetic engineering to make people more intelligent
4 Performing abortions of normal foetuses in the early stages of pregnancy
5 Performing abortions of normal foetuses in the second trimester of pregnancy
6 Fishing in a way that leads to the painful death of dolphins
7 Forcing women to be sterilized because they are retarded
8 Forcing women to have abortions when they have had too many children, for the purpose of population control
9 Putting people in jail for expressing nonviolent political views
10 Letting people sell their organs (for example, a kidney or an eye) for whatever price they can command
11 Refusing to treat someone who needs a kidney transplant because he or she cannot afford it
12 Letting a doctor assist in the suicide of a consenting terminally ill patient
13 Letting a family sell their daughter in a bride auction (that is, the daughter becomes the bride of the highest bidder)
14 Punishing people for expressing nonviolent political opinions

The questions were:

A I do not oppose this
B This should be prohibited no matter how great the benefits from allowing it
C If this is happening now, no more should be allowed no matter how great the benefits from allowing it
D My own role in this matters. If my own government allows this, I have more of an obligation to try to stop it than if some other government does, even if I have equal influence over both governments
E In public discussions of this issue, it is most effective to exaggerate the strength of our opposition to this
F In public discussions of this issue, it is morally right to exaggerate the strength of our opposition to this
G It is impossible for me to think about how much benefit we should demand in order to allow this to happen
H It is equally wrong to allow some of this to happen and to allow twice as much to happen. The amount doesn't matter
I It is worse to allow twice as much to happen than to allow some
J This would be wrong even in a country where everyone thought it was not wrong
K People have an obligation to try to stop this even if they think they do not
L In the real world, there is nothing we can gain by allowing this to happen

Questions B and C (and possibly G) assessed absoluteness; D assessed agent relativity (an issue examined more in subsequent experiments); E and F assessed posturing, the

Table 15.1 *Percentage of subjects endorsing each question for each action*

							Question						
Question	Action	A	B	C	D	E	F	G	H	I	J	K	L
12	Assist suicide	73	28	24	30	50	20	32	47	16	29	28	25
4	Early abortion	53	34	37	54	51	37	40	47	43	44	38	41
2	IQ with drugs	42	56	62	27	50	25	48	56	27	53	49	32
10	Sell organs	37	48	47	50	59	32	45	53	52	45	45	42
3	IQ genetic	37	52	52	26	58	28	38	47	34	59	46	30
7	Sterilize	35	54	52	52	54	37	48	54	37	46	44	29
5	Late abortion	24	54	54	62	64	48	59	66	38	66	53	50
8	Force abortion	15	67	66	60	71	47	54	71	44	66	54	47
9	Free speech	14	74	79	67	67	45	71	76	63	75	69	73
13	Sell daughter	12	73	79	58	77	58	64	79	50	73	63	75
14	Free speech	11	73	82	62	72	55	72	75	53	81	73	64
1	End species	09	83	82	66	73	58	69	54	56	83	63	59
6	Kill dolphins	06	69	72	57	70	54	52	75	58	71	67	64
11	Refuse kidney	06	73	82	73	71	56	64	78	51	94	75	58
	Private actions	31	59	59	58	56	46	50	61	53	59	47	42

willingness to overstate for strategic purposes; H and I were supposed to assess quantity insensitivity; J and K assessed moral obligation; and L assessed denial of trade-offs. Each question was coded as 1 for yes and 0 for no.

Results

Properties of protected values

Subjects generally endorsed hypothesized properties of protected values – quantity insensitivity, denial, moral obligation and agent relativity – more often for absolute values than for other values. We made these comparison within each subject and then averaged the results across subjects.

Table 15.1 shows the percentage of subjects giving positive answers to each question for each of the 14 actions for the public condition only. It is apparent that many subjects endorsed the answers characteristic of protected values.

To evaluate differences among types of values within each subject, we divided each subject's values into those that the subject did not oppose (answered 'yes' to question A), those that the subject opposed but did not consider Absolute ('no' to A, B and C), and those that were Absolute ('no' to A, 'yes' to B and C).[3]

Table 15.2 shows the mean proportions of hypothesized properties, averaged across subjects, as a function of this categorization. For example, a subject who considered five values to be 'absolute' and answered 'yes' to question L for four of these would get a proportion of 80 per cent for the 'Denial' column of the 'Absolute' row. The average across subjects for this cell of Table 15.2 used one such proportion from each subject. Our

Table 15.2 *Percentage of positive responses to each question (or pair of questions) as a function of the answer to the questions about opposition to the action in question and absoluteness, Experiments 1–3*

	Quantity	Denial	Moral	Agent	Posture	Bother	Anger
Experiment 1							
Not opposed	24	18	11	26	25		
Opposed	41*	23*	41	57	46		
Absolute	80	64	79	72*	69		
Experiment 2							
Not opposed	53	7	9	19	20	19	15
Opposed	44*	15*	35	40*	48	45	37
Absolute	74	60	81	70	65*	77	56
Experiment 3							
Not opposed	75	7	9	12	18		
Opposed	46*	19*	60	62	56		
Absolute	52*	55	73*	80	68*		

Note: Significance tests in the table are based on tests across subjects of within-subject differences. In an alternative analysis, correlations tau (τ) were computed for each item across subjects and then tested across the 14 items used in each study. All differences shown as significant in the table (those without asterisks) were significant at the same level or better by this alternative.
*The number listed was not significantly greater ($P < 0.05$) than the number directly above it from the same experiment.

hypotheses concern the difference between the properties of values considered 'Absolute' and values that are merely 'Opposed', but we tested the difference between Not-opposed and Opposed as well.

Some of the properties were averages of two questions. Posture was the average of questions E and F (which correlated highly, mean $\gamma = 0.74$), and Moral was the average of J and K (mean $\gamma = 0.86$). Other properties were responses to single questions: Agent for question D; Denial for L; and Quantity for H. (H did not correlate negatively with I as expected.) We name the variables in this way to facilitate comparison across experiments.

All comparisons between each proportion and the one above it were significant ($P < 0.01$) except those marked with asterisks (which were not significant at $P < 0.05$). In essence, our hypotheses were supported except for the Agent property (agent relativity). Specifically, the proportions of endorsement of each property (Quantity, Denial and Moral) were higher for Absolute values than for Opposed. For Agent, however, subjects felt obliged to stop something even when they were just opposed to it, no matter where it was. Endorsement of Posture was greater for Absolute values than Opposed, but the difference was not significant here.

Public vs private

We found the results just described in both public and private conditions. To compare public and private conditions – a between-subject manipulation – we averaged across issues for each subject. To compare the extent to which values were protected in the two conditions, public and private, we defined a new index for each subject, Protect, as the average of all the items making up Absolute, Quantity, Denial and Moral, plus item G, which correlated with the others. We also computed each subject's mean value of Posture (items E and F, as before) across items.

Condition (public, coded 1, vs private, coded 0) did not correlate significantly with Protect ($r = 0.15$) or Posture ($r = 0.05$). The first correlation is in the direction hypothesized – more properties of protected values for the public condition – but it is small. In addition, the association (measured as a γ coefficient within each subject) between each property (Quantity, Denial, Moral and Agent) and Absolute did not correlate with condition, and the pattern of significant differences among the three value categories was the same for the private group alone as for the combined group (except for Posture, where the difference between Opposed and Not-opposed was no longer significant).

Protect was also uncorrelated with Posture across subjects ($r = 0.10$). This suggests that protected values are not just the result of a tendency to posture, even though items that evoke protected values over all subjects also evoke posturing, as described earlier. The fact that Posture is uncorrelated with Protect and the fact that evidence of protected values is still found in the private condition both indicate that protected values are not simply a matter of posturing.

We found no sex differences in Protect.

Experiment 2

This experiment added questions about emotion, to test the hypothesis that emotion, particularly anger, is related to other properties of protected values (suggested by Tetlock et al, 1996). It also asked whether protected values could be manipulated by presenting items in increasing or decreasing order of tendency to oppose them. Objectionable actions might induce a feeling of anger that would carry over to other items if these came first.

Method

Fifty-five subjects were solicited as in Experiment 1. The actions were the same as those used in Experiment 1, except that item 14 was replace with 'using condoms to prevent the birth of unwanted children in marriage'. Half of the subjects read the new item first and the rest of the items were ordered as in Table 15.1. The other half read the items in the reverse order.

The questions were identical to those used in Experiment 1, except that two questions about emotion were added:

M Thinking about this bothers me

N I get angry when I think about this.

Table 15.3 *Mean percentage of subjects endorsing each question for each action, Experiment 3*

Action	Question											
	A	*B*	*C*	*D*	*E*	*F*	*G*	*H*	*I*	*J*	*L*	*M*
2 Coma unpermitted	08	76	56	58	64	56	69	45	78	68	79	74
9 Kill species	10	71	47	59	78	54	66	56	86	73	65	76
10 Kill dolphins	13	76	50	50	76	51	65	50	74	54	66	79
6 Abortion 3rd	22	50	31	62	71	53	50	29	69	53	78	70
12 Products risk	29	68	49	51	68	58	62	40	69	58	68	71
8 Transplant unpermitted	29	73	22	63	68	55	64	51	66	51	78	69
7 Raise IQ	32	54	28	47	53	43	43	52	49	37	72	49
5 Abortion 2nd	40	42	33	57	68	47	39	23	61	46	70	56
4 Abortion 1st	51	29	26	40	56	31	33	21	49	39	66	42
14 Strike breakers	62	21	19	34	31	22	30	23	24	24	54	37
11 Products forced	68	26	20	40	40	32	19	37	37	23	49	34
3 Assist suicide	71	26	29	44	36	35	27	30	26	26	73	36
13 Nonunion	81	10	13	26	29	14	17	34	18	13	54	18
1 Coma permitted	82	16	06	26	29	25	23	10	21	19	56	29

Note: For Item H, this is the percentage who thought quantity mattered.

Also question I was reworded: 'The amount matters. It is more wrong to allow twice as much to happen than to allow some to happen'.

Results

The order of questions did affect the tendency to oppose the actions (question A: 29 per cent opposition with increasing opposition, 41 per cent with decreasing, $t = 2.56$, $P = 0.013$), but it did not affect Protect, a composite based on all questions except E and F (Posture). This result suggests that some opposition is not based on protected values. Opposition was increased by presenting the most objectionable actions first, but protectedness was unaffected.

Unlike Experiment 1, females were higher in Protect than males ($t = 2.52$, $P = 0.015$) and also higher in their tendency to oppose actions ($t = 3.87$, $P = 0.000$). However, in a logistic regression of sex on these two measures, only the latter was significant. Hence, women are simply more opposed to this set of actions, but given that they are opposed, their values are no more likely to be protected.

The main results of Experiment 1 were replicated, as shown in Table 15.2. The new question I correlated negatively with H, so it was reversed and combined with H to form the Quantity score. All differences in the original items between Absolute and Opposed were significant ($P < 0.02$, one tailed), including Agent, which did not differ significantly in Experiment 1. Questions M (bother) and N (anger), as well, significantly differed between Opposed and Absolute ($P < 0.0005$ for Bother; $P = 0.039$ for Anger, one tailed). We conclude (along with Tetlock et al, 1996) that being angry about an action and bothered by thinking about it are properties of protected values, along with the other properties.

Experiment 3

Experiment 3 used a different set of actions to examine the robustness of some previous findings, particularly those concerned with agent-relativity.

Method

Thirty-nine subjects, solicited as in Experiment 1, completed a questionnaire in which they answered 10 questions about each of 14 actions, in a table. The questionnaire began, 'Below are some actions that could be paid for by your nation's government, with money collected from your taxes. They could also be carried out by private corporations. For each action, please answer questions A–N by writing Yes, No or ? (not sure) in the blank on the table…'

The questions were the same as Experiment 1 except as follows:

C There are no benefits from allowing it, in fact
H You have two choices:
    1 This will happen 100 times
    2 This will happen 200 times
    Which choice is worse, or are they equally bad? (Answer 1, 2 or =.)
I [Same as J in Experiment 1, Moral.]
J [Same as K in Experiment 1, Moral.]
K [was inadvertently misworded in Experiment 1 and is omitted from this report.]
L The government should not pay for this from tax money of those who disapprove of it
M You have an option to buy stock in a company that does this. Another buyer will buy the stock if you don't. This is the last share of a special offer, so your decision does not affect the price of the stock. Is it wrong for you to buy the stock?

The actions were:

1 Doctors causing the death of comatose patients who will never recover, with permission of the patient's family
2 Doctors causing the death of comatose patients who will never recover, against the wishes of the patient's family
3 Doctors assisting in the suicide of a consenting terminally ill patient
4 Aborting normal foetuses in the first three months of pregnancy
5 Aborting normal foetuses in the second three months of pregnancy

6   Aborting normal foetuses in the last three months of pregnancy
7   Raising the IQ of normal children by giving them (completely safe) drugs
8   Taking organs from people who have just died, for transplantation into other peo-
    ple, against the wishes of the dead person's family
9   Cutting down forests for wood in a way that results in the extinction of plant and
    animal species forever
10 Fishing in a way that leads to the painful death of dolphins
11 Selling products for profit made by the forced labour of prisoners
12 Selling products for profit made by workers exposed to hazardous chemicals that
    increase their risk of cancer
13 Selling products for profit made by nonunion labour
14 Selling products for profit made by strike breakers

Results

Table 15.3 shows the mean scores of items, and Table 15.2 shows the differences among
value categories. Of primary interest were three new questions, described here according
to their position in Table 15.2.

Quantity
Question H assessed quantity sensitivity more directly than previous questions. The
new Quality (scored as 1 when quantity did not matter, 1 when 200 times was worse
than 100, and missing otherwise) did not distinguish Absolute and Opposed significantly. It seems as though making the idea of quantity insensitivity explicit by using
numbers, in contrast to the items used in Experiments 1 and 2, reduced the correlations
with other properties of protected values. However, subjects were slightly more willing
to ignore quantity in Absolute than in Opposed, despite the fact that they were in fact
significantly ($P = 0.010$, two tailed) more sensitive to quantity in Opposed than Not-
opposed, presumably because quantity really is irrelevant when no opposition is present.
Possibly, the weak results for this item resulted from ambiguity about its meaning.

Denial
Question C assessed denial of trade-offs. It clearly distinguished Absolute from
Opposed, as did previous Denial items.

Moral
The Moral items were endorsed more often for Absolute than for Opposed, but the
difference was not significant here, as it had been for the same items in Experiments 1
and 2.

Agent
Questions L and M assessed agent-relativity. Table 15.2 (Agent) shows the results for M,
the stock-purchase item, because this is the clearest item for distinguishing personal
involvement from consequences. The consequences are the same because the share will
be bought in any case. Item M (about stock purchase) distinguished Absolute and
Opposed ($P = 0.007$) as did item L (about paying from tax money of opponents, $P =$

0.037), although item D (the original item about obligation to stop one's own government) did not. The results for item M clearly support the relation between absolute values and agent relativity.

Experiment 4

Experiment 4 took a closer look at insensitivity to quantity. In Experiments 1–3, many subjects said that quantity would not matter, but we wanted to find out whether subjects would really show complete insensitivity. We used a procedure based loosely on contingent valuation, with a single value from Experiment 1, the use of genetic engineering to raise IQ. (See Agar, 1995, for discussion of this action.) Subjects indicated their attitude toward raising IQ by indicating whether they would accept a reduction in medical costs in order to allow it and whether they would even pay an increase in order to see it done. We call these WTA (willingness to accept) and WTP (willingness to pay), respectively.

In order to manipulate protectedness, we compared two conditions differing in deviation from normality. In a Low condition, IQ was raised from 75 to 100. This could be seen as a treatment for retardation. In the High condition, IQ was raised from 100 to 125. The Low condition creates or restores normality and the High condition takes the person away from normality, hence, interferes more with nature, perhaps violating a protected value against interference with nature (Spranca, 1992). Alternatively, this factor may be understood in terms of egalitarianism: help those worse off before helping those better off. This principle could also be protected.

The Low-High manipulation was crossed with a manipulation of why the IQ was to be raised. In the Human condition, IQ had been made 25 points lower as a result of exposure to pollution caused by humans. In the Nature condition, IQ differences were simply the result of natural variation.

Method

Subjects were 93 students solicited and paid as in Experiment 1 for completing a questionnaire.

The questionnaire began, 'US residents all pay for each other's medical care, both through insurance payments and through taxes (which fund Medicare, Medic-aid and other government programmes). Suppose that the average person in the US pays $3000 per year for medical care, though all sources. (If you are not a US resident, imagine that you are.) The following cases are made up, but some day they could be real'. One form began with the Low Natural condition, which read as follows:

1. Certain natural genetic defects that cause mental retardation can be detected by tests performed early in pregnancy; if found, an artificially produced gene can be inserted into the foetal tissue through a surgical procedure that is relatively easy and safe. The gene increases average IQ from 75 (retarded) to 100 (normal).

A. Suppose that 10 out of 10,000 people could be helped in this way.

Would you be willing to pay extra in order to make this procedure available to all who wanted it?

(Circle one.) YES NO

If YES, what is the most you would be willing to pay?

$ _____

Would you be willing to allow this to be done if you and others saved money for health costs?

YES NO

If you would be willing to allow it, what is the least that you would have to save per year in order to allow it?

$ _____

B. Suppose that 1 out of 10,000 people could be helped in this way.

[Same questions]

The High Natural condition, which came next, began:

Children expected to have normal IQ can have their IQ increased. A test for normal IQ is done early in pregnancy. If the test is positive, an artificially produced gene can be inserted into the foetal tissue through a surgical procedure that is relatively easy and safe. The gene increases average IQ from 100 (normal) to 125 (superior).

The Low Human condition began:

Certain genetic defects are found to result from exposure to pollution. The pollution is no longer produced, but what was produced before will remain in the environment for centuries and cannot be cleaned up. These defects can be detected by tests performed early in pregnancy. [The rest was identical to the Low Natural condition.]

The High Human condition began:

Pollution is found to cause certain genetic defects that lower the IQ of whose who would be well above average. The pollution is no longer produced, but what was produced before will remain in the environment for centuries and cannot be cleaned up. A test for these defects can be done early in pregnancy. [The rest was identical to the High Natural condition.]

Half of the subjects did the four conditions in the opposite order, and, for these subjects, the order of the WTP and WTA questions ('pay' and 'allow', respectively) were reversed as well.

Results

As expected, many subjects would not accept any amount in the High conditions, especially in the High Natural condition. Conversely, most subjects were willing to pay something in the Low conditions, and the cause of the low IQ did not matter. In those subjects who answered numerically, insensitivity to quantity was more prevalent in the High conditions. (Order of presentation had no effect.)

Many subjects answered both WTA and WTP questions affirmatively. We interpreted this to mean that they were willing to pay something, but, of course, they would also be willing to accept something if it were offered. Thus, we counted WTP in these cases and ignored WTA. We coded the responses in terms of WTP, using negative values for what the subject was willing to accept when she was unwilling to pay anything. If subjects answered 'no' to both questions, we coded that as an extreme negative number

Table 15.4 *WTA and WTP for genetic repair, Experiment 4*

	No amount	WTA > 0	WTP = 0	WTP > 0
Low nature	8.7%	13.0%	4.3%	73.9%
High nature	47.8%	15.2%	5.4%	30.4%
Low human	7.6%	9.8%	3.3%	79.3%
High human	21.7%	24.0%	5.4%	48.9%

Table 15.5 *Numbers of subjects showing a quantity effect or not in each condition, Experiment 4*

	Missing	No effect	Effect
Low nature	8	30	54
High nature	44	19	29
Low human	7	31	54
High human	18	35	39

for purposes of ranking responses. This represents unwillingness to trade off the violation of a value with monetary gain.

Table 15.4 classifies responses by condition, based on the response to the high-quantity condition (10 out of 10,000). In the Low conditions, most subjects were willing to pay something. A Wilcoxon test comparing Human vs Nature in these conditions (using the responses coded as described above) was not significant. Thus, raising low IQ is generally acceptable whatever its cause. All other differences among conditions were significant at $P = 0.000$ by Wilcoxon tests. Thus, raising IQ above normal is unacceptable to many subjects, and few subjects are willing to pay for it. However, this is especially true when the IQ is naturally normal; when IQ is reduced by human pollution, then more people are willing to pay to raise it.

To assess quantity effects, we classified each subject as showing an effect or not in the direction of higher WTP for more children helped (10 vs 1 out of 10,000). Subjects who were unwilling to accept anything in *both* quantity conditions (10 and 1) were counted as missing data.

Table 15.5 shows the number of subjects showing an effect, no effect or missing, in each of the four conditions. Because of the large number of missing data in High Nature, we tested the hypothesis by comparing the proportion of High cases showing sensitivity to quantity (excluding missing data) to the proportion of Low cases. (The proportions for each condition were thus 0, 0.5 or 1.) High showed a significantly smaller proportion of quantity effects than Low ($P = 0.017$, one-tailed Wilcoxon test). Because we assume that the High conditions involve protected values in many subjects, this result supports the hypothesis that protected values are associated with insensitivity to quantity.

Experiment 5

Experiment 5 examines sensitivity to quantity in another way, specifically sensitivity to the probability of success of programmes to save endangered species. Deontological obligations to save species would not be sensitive to the probability of success.

Method

Fifty-eight subjects, solicited as in Experiment 1, were given a questionnaire, which began, 'The Endangered Species Act requires a plan to save each endangered species. These plans often interfere with economic development, so they end up costing money. Imagine you live in a region that will be affected by each of the following plans. For each plan, indicate the most you would be willing to pay in increased prices for goods and services, in per cent, for a 5-year period. You may use fractions or decimals. Say zero if you would not be willing to pay anything. Answer each one of the four subcases (A–D) as if it were the only possible plan.' The four subcases involved respectively: success probability of 0 without the plan and 0.25 with it; 0 without and 0.75 with; 0.50 without and 0.75 with; and 0.75 without and 1.00 with. (Half the subjects did these in the opposite order.)

The six cases were:

1 A species of tree is endangered because too much of it was cut down to make farms. It is useless for wood, but it is unique. No other trees are like it. It cannot be cultivated outside of its natural habitat

2 A species of tree is endangered in your region because too much of it was cut down to make farms. It is useful for wood and valued as an ornamental tree. Because it is valued, it has already been preserved in many arboretums, and it can be cultivated

3 A species of squirrel is endangered because too many trees were cut down to make farms

4 A species of dolphin is endangered because too many dolphins were strangled in nets used to catch tuna

5 A species of tuna is endangered because it has been overfished. People like to eat it

6 A species of tuna is endangered because its natural predators have become more numerous. People like to eat it

The order of these cases was reversed for half of the subjects.

Finally, to measure the extent to which subjects had protected values for each species, each subject 'answered "yes", "no" or "not sure"' [treated as missing data] to the following for each of the six species:

B We should save this species even if there are no tangible benefits to people

F Really no price is too high to save a species like this.

Other questions measuring other aspects of protected values were also included, but, although they correlated with these questions as they should, they were not analysed further.

Results

Protected values were again correlated with insensitivity to quantity. And most of the questions about protected values correlated with each other. (There was no effect of order or sex.)

Across the six cases, the mean answers to the four subcases were, respectively: 13 per cent increase (for 0 to 25 per cent change in probability), 25 per cent (for 0 to 75 per cent), 18 per cent (50 to 75 per cent), and 20 per cent (75 to 100 per cent). All differences were significant ($P < 0.005$ by t test across subjects) except that between the last two conditions. Subjects seemed more concerned with the final probability after the programme was put into effect, rather than the change in probability from before to after. They were also somewhat sensitive to the change, however, as indicated by the greater WTP for the 0–75 per cent change.

Sensitivity to quantity was defined for each species as the log of the ratio of WTP for the 0–75 change to the mean WTP of the 0–25 and 50–75 changes, divided by log(3) so that proportional sensitivity would have a value of 1. The mean sensitivity (averaged across items, then across subjects) was 0.58 (SD 0.31). A protected-value score for each species was defined as the mean of questions B and F. The mean of this score was 0.60 (SD 0.30). The correlation between sensitivity and the protected-value score was computed for each subject across the six items. The mean of this correlation was –0.16 ($P = 0.008$, t test across subjects). Although significant, the measure of this correlation was small. It is clear that many other factors affect sensitivity to quantity. Still, the present experiment supports previous experiments in finding a small but significant relationship between insensitivity and protectedness.

General Discussion

We hypothesized that five properties would correlate with absoluteness, the defining property of protected values: quantity insensitivity, agent relativity, moral obligation, denial of trade-offs and anger. These properties followed from the assumption that protected values derive from deontological prohibitions of action rather than values for consequences. We found these correlations.

Posturing could not account fully for these effects. In particular, they were present even when it was impossible for subjects to communicate which values they were responding to (although subjects could communicate a general tendency toward absolute values). So the tendency to hold protected values appears to exist apart from concerns about self-presentation with respect to particular values.

Experiments 1, 2, 4 and 5 supported the hypothesis that protected values contribute to quantity insensitivity. Value measurements are often insensitive to the quantity of the good being valued (Kahneman and Knetsch, 1992; Diamond et al, 1993; McFadden, 1994; Jones-Lee et al, 1995; Baron and Greene, 1996; Baron, 1997). For example many people will pay no more to save three wilderness areas than they would pay to save one (McFadden, 1994). The same insensitivity is found in judgements of willingness to accept (Baron and Greene, 1996), so the problem is not just one of budget constraints.

We suggest that such insensitivity is more likely when it involves protected values – assuming that people are willing to oblige the researcher by answering the questions – because such values concern the acts involved rather than their consequences. Very likely, however, such values are not the only cause of insensitivity. (Baron and Greene, 1996, suggest others.)

Quantity insensitivity creates problems for value measurement because most social decisions are repeated. Those willing to pay $10 to save one wilderness area might be expected to be willing to do this more than once. So they would be willing to pay about $30 to save three. This would conflict with a stated value of $10 for three. (Baron and Greene, 1996, give other examples of such conflicts.)

The strong relation between Absoluteness and Denial suggests that people want to have their nonutilitarian cake and eat it too. They understand that commitment to protected values could make overall consequences worse in some sense. Rather than simply rejecting their competing, utilitarian intuitions, they deny that this is needed. Perhaps this is true more generally of commitment to deontological rules, absolute or not.

Other properties that we did not examine might also characterize protected values. Irwin (1994) has found that the ratio of willingness to accept to willingness to pay is greater for environmental goods than for consumer goods. She suggested that environmental goods are seen as moral. This difference may result from the belief that taking money to allow immorality is itself immoral. This may be more true of protected values, but it may also be true of moral values in general.

Another implication that we did not test is that protected values should distinguish acts and omissions. Protected values are absolute prohibitions on certain actions. If people tried to follow corresponding prohibitions against omissions that led to the same results, then people would have infinite obligations. Protected values thus depend on the omission-commission distinction. Individuals and situations differ considerably in whether this distinction is relevant to moral judgements or not (Ritov and Baron, 1990; Spranca et al, 1991; Baron, 1992, 1994; Baron and Ritov, 1994). Our theory implies that it will be made more often when protected values are involved.[5]

We have suggested that protected values are a subset of moral values. This idea may have biased our selection of actions. It may be possible to find nonmoral values that are also protected.

Origin of protected values

Why do people have protected values? Several reasons come to mind. Some explanations may be true, or partially true, but insufficient. One of these is self-enhancement. Most people will feel better about themselves knowing that they have a few protected values. Having protected values is a source of self-identity (Williams, 1981). This is true when a culture endorses the idea of 'integrity' as a matter of sticking up for certain values. But where do members of a culture get the idea that integrity is a matter of simple adherence to one value at the expense of others? That is why this explanation, while possibly true, is insufficient.

The same can be said of impression management. For the same reason having protected values enhances one's image to oneself, it enhances one's image in the eyes of others. Politicians are keenly aware of this. To treat a protected value like a compensatory value is political suicide (Tetlock et al, 1996). Yet, if holding protected values makes a good impression, some people must already think of them as admirable.

Holding protected values may increase persuasive power. Many activists believe that they are more likely to achieve their activist goals if they take a hard negotiating stance. Using the rhetoric of protected values makes it easier to justify using hard bargaining strategies. Politicians are aware of this too. Part of this effect is related to impression management. Another part is simply that statements of protected values are the hardest bargaining position that one can take. Our results suggest that the effort to be persuasive is both real and separate from other determinants of protected values. It may be part of their source, but, once started, they seem to take on a life of their own.

Ultimately, the explanation of protected values may lie elsewhere. Two aspects must be explained. One is their absoluteness. The other is their emphasis on action. We have already discussed (in the Introduction) the emphasis on action, and why we think that consequentialist values are not absolute. But we have not said why people adopt absolute rules of action in the first place.

One possibility is that protected values are adopted intentionally and knowingly as rigid, inviolable prescriptive rules. Such prescriptive rules – such as 'do not lie under oath' – are best to follow in practice even though one might imagine a situation in which, if one accepted all the assumptions without question, it would be best to break the rule. People might want such rules to be followed absolutely because they may have good reason to believe that trade-offs, once allowed, will not be honestly made. For example, experience with past abuses – such as the Nazis' use of eugenic arguments – may lead people to think that it is better never to allow something, such as eugenics, than to try to calculate when the benefits exceed the costs. People may adopt such rules because they mistrust others or themselves. People can imagine some *hypothetical* situation in which a trade-off might be allowed, but, as a practical matter, they think that allowing trade-offs would be too risky and that, if they tried to recognize such situations, they would make too many misses and too many false positives. When people are asked about their values, they may reasonably rely on their practical principle rather than on their imagination, since they may distrust potential users of the information they provide, including themselves.

This view of rules as coldly calculated devices for control of self and others is inconsistent with the emotionality we found to be associated with protected values. It seems more likely that such prescriptive rules – regardless of whether they are rationally justifiable in the way just described – take on a life of their own (Hare, 1981). After all, parents and other moral educators typically teach such practical rules without saying whether they are absolute or not. More generally, even if some people understand the rationale just described, they may fail to convey this rationale when they transmit the rules to others. The rules become detached from their justifications. Even when circumstances change so that the rationale – if it was ever valid – is no longer valid, the rule may still be blindly applied (Baron, 1994). Thus, restoring trust in the ability to make some trade-off would not immediately change a protected value into a compensatory one.

We note, however, that our studies did not specifically ask subjects if they could imagine situations in which they would be willing to compromise their values. This would be worthy of further research.

Absolute values, whatever their initial origin, may also appeal to a preference for cognitive simplicity in decision making. It is probably easier to make decisions if we have a few protected values to constrain decision making. Of course, protected values held for this purpose are prescriptive heuristics at best. If people come to hold protected values for this reason, they are elevating rules of thumb into absolutes without adequate reason. They may do this because they have acquired from their culture a concept of moral rules as being like laws, that is, constraints on action that should never be violated.

Alternatively, absolute prohibitions may be at first only temporary phenomena that result from a kind of experience in which one of two competing perceptions becomes dominant and prevents the alternative being noticed, leading to excessive confidence that the alternative is absent (Margolis, 1987). Thus, when faced with a choice between competing harms, one of the harms might become dominant and prevent a person from thinking that the other one is important too. This is especially so when one of the harms results from action. And it is especially so when the options and their results are outside the range of normal experience, where people will have made many choices that sacrificed each of the two competing values. It is possible that such perceptual dominance occurs when subjects confront valuation questions for the first time, but it is also possible that one side or the other has become habitual as a result of prior repetition.

Implications

What are the practical implications of our conclusions for value measurement and social decision making? Value measurement is typically done by policy analysts who are concerned with the utility of consequences. They want to know how people value various consequences, so that they can recommend a policy that maximizes utility. When they question respondents about values, they do not yet know what policies they will recommend, what actions they will ask governments or other institutions to take. If we are correct about the nature of protected values, however, the respondents impose on the value measures some imagined means of producing the consequence, and their stated value for the consequence is contaminated by their value for the imagined means of achieving it. Sometimes this value takes the form of an absolute moral prohibition. Protected values are thus a monkey wrench thrown into the works. They are not about consequences, but rather about the participation of respondents in imagined actions. That is not what the policy analysts need to know, for they need to compare different ways of producing similar outcomes. Respondents' hypotheses about how they would participate might be incorrect.

Practical solutions to this problem must await further research. Perhaps one direction to explore is to separate elicited values into those involving 'means' and those involving 'ends' (Keeney, 1992). This may help respondents, along with further encouragement from analysts, to think about their values for consequences (ends) separately from the values connected with their own participation, since they would have a chance to express those separately.

Another direction is to teach respondents that some prescriptive rules are absolute only because of the practical difficulty of applying compensatory rules. If respondents understand this, then they may be willing to express values as compensatory in hypothetical situations even when they would not be willing to advocate trade-offs in real situations.

The remaining problem of how societies should respond to protected values concerning means is a serious one. For example, we might think that people who place extreme value on not participating in some activity should be excused from paying taxes to fund that activity. However, such a policy would provide incentive for people to say that they had such values even if they did not. It may be that societies simply cannot take all such values into account.

Notes

This research was supported by N.S.F. Grant SBR92–23015. We thank Barbara Gault, Howard Margolis and Carol Nickerson for comments.

Address correspondence and reprint requests to Jonathan Baron, Department of Psychology, University of Pennsylvania, 3815 Walnut St, Philadelphia, PA 19104–6196 [e-mail: baron@psych.upenn.edu].

1   Technically, this amounts to a form of Archimedian axiom (Krantz et al, 1971).
2   This is analogous to, and perhaps a cause of, Andreoni's (1990) 'warm glow' (also Margolis' (1982) theory of altruism).
3   Three subjects were more likely to say 'yes' to B and C when they said 'yes' to A than when they said 'no'. We reversed the answer to A for these subjects. Results were essentially the same with many other analyses that did not depend on this reversal. We also did this for three subjects in Experiment 2 and two in Experiment 3. In addition, in Experiments 1 and 2, we omitted individual items when B and C disagreed.
4   In as yet unpublished work Ritov and Baron have found support for this hypothesis.

References

1   Agar, N. (1995) 'Designing babies: Morally permissible ways to modify the human genome'. *Bioethics*, vol 9, pp1–15
2   Anderson, E. (1993) *Value in Ethics and Economics*. Harvard University Press, Cambridge, MA
3   Andre, J. (1992) 'Blocked exchanges: a taxonomy'. *Ethics*, vol 103, pp29–47
4   Andreoni, J. (1990) 'Impure altruism and donations to public goods: A theory of warm-glow giving'. *Economic Journal*, vol 100, pp464–477
5   Baron, J. (1988) 'Utility, exchange, and commensurability'. *Journal of Thought*, vol 23, pp111–131
6   Baron, J. (1992). 'The effect of normative beliefs on anticipated emotions'. *Journal of Personality and Social Psychology*, vol 63, pp320–330
7   Baron, J. (1993) *Morality and Rational Choice*. Kluwer, Dordrecht
8   Baron, J. (1994) 'Nonconsequentialist decisions (with commentary and reply)'. *Behavioural and Brain Sciences*, vol 17, pp1–42

9   Baron, J. (1996) 'Do no harm', in Messick, D. M. and Tenbrunsel, A. E. (eds) *Codes of Conduct: Behavioural Research into Business Ethics*, Russell Sage Foundation, NY, pp197–213

10   Baron, J. (1997) 'Biases in the quantitative measurement of values for public decisions'. *Psychological Bulletin*

11   Baron, J. and Greene, J. (1996) 'Determinants of insensitivity to quantity in valuation of public goods: contribution, warm glow, budget constraints, availability, and prominence'. *Journal of Experimental Psychology: Applied*, vol 2, pp107–125

12   Baron, J. and Ritov, I. (1994) 'Reference points and omission bias'. *Organizational Behaviour and Human Decision Processes*, vol 59, pp475–498

13   Diamond, P. A., Hausman, J. A., Leonard, G. K. and Denning, M. A. (1993) 'Does CV measure preferences? Some experimental evidence', in Hausman, J. A. (ed) *CV: A Critical Assessment.* North Holland, Amsterdam

14   Fiske, A. P. and Tetlock, P. E. (1997) 'Taboo tradeoffs: Reactions to transactions that transgress spheres of justice'. *Political Psychology*

15   Hare, R. M. (1981) *Moral Thinking: Its Levels, Method and Point.* Oxford University Press (Clarendon Press), Oxford

16   Irwin, J. R. (1994) 'Buying/selling price preference reversals: Preference for environmental changes in buying versus selling modes'. *Organizational Behaviour and Human Decision Processes*, vol 60, pp431–457

17   Jervis, R. (1976) *Perception and Misperception in International Politics.* Princeton University Press, Princeton, NJ

18   Jones-Lee, M. W., Loomes, G. and Philips, P. R. (1995) 'Valuing the prevention of non-fatal road injuries: Contingent valuation vs standard gambles'. *Oxford Economic Papers*, vol 47, pp676 ff

19   Kahneman, D. and Knetsch, J. L. (1992) 'Valuing public goods: The purchase of moral satisfaction'. *Journal of Environmental Economics and Management*, vol 22, pp57–70

20   Keeney, R. L. (1992) *Value-focused Thinking: A Path to Creative Decisionmaking.* Harvard University Press, Cambridge, MA

21   Krantz, D. H., Luce, R. D., Suppes, P. and Tversky, A. (1971) *Foundations of Measurement* (vol 1). Academic Press, NY

22   Margolis, H. (1982) *Selfishness, Altruism, and Rationality: A Theory of Social Choice.* Cambridge University Press, NY

23   Margolis, H. (1987) *Patterns, Thinking, and Cognition: A Theory of Judgement.* University of Chicago Press, Chicago

24   Mason, J. O. (1990) 'Should the fetal tissue research ban be lifted?' *Journal of NIH Research*, vol 2, pp17–18

25   McFadden, D. (1994) 'Contingent valuation and social choice'. *American Journal of Agricultural Economics*, vol 76, pp689–708

26   Mitchell, R. C. and Carson, R. T. (1989) *Using Surveys to Value Public Goods: The Contingent Valuation Method.* Resources for the Future, Washington DC

27   Montgomery, H. (1984) 'Decision rules and the search for dominance structure: Towards a process model of decision making', in Humphreys, P. C., Svenson, O. and Vari, A. (eds) *Analysing and Aiding Decision Processes.* North Holland, Amsterdam

28   Nagel, T. (1986) *The View from Nowhere.* Oxford University Press, NY

29   Payne, J. W., Bettman, J. R. and Johnson, E. J. (1993) *The Adoptive Decision Maker.* Cambridge University Press, NY

30   Ritov, I. and Baron, J. (1990) 'Reluctance to vaccinate: omission bias and ambiguity'. *Journal of Behavioural Decision Making*, vol 3, pp263–277

31   Ritov, I. and Baron, J. (1992) 'Status-quo and omission bias'. *Journal of Risk and Uncertainty*, vol 5, pp49–61

32 Schwartz, B. (1986) *The Battle for Human Nature: Science, Morality, and Modern Life*. Norton, NY

33 Spranca, M. (1992) *The Effect of Naturalness on Desirability and Preference in the Domain of Foods*. Unpublished masters thesis, Department of Psychology, University of California, Berkeley

34 Spranca, M., Minsk, E. and Baron, J. (1991) 'Omission and commission in judgement and choice'. *Journal of Experimental Social Psychology*, vol 27, pp76–105

35 Tetlock, P. E., Lerner, J. and Peterson, R. (1996) 'Revising the value pluralism model: Incorporating social content and context postulates', in Seligman, C., Olson, J. and Zanna, M. (eds) *The Psychology of Values: The Ontario Symposium*, vol 8, Erlbaum, Hillsdale, NJ

36 Turiel, E. (1983) *The Development of Social Knowledge: Morality and Convention*. Cambridge University Press

37 Williams, B. (1981) *Moral Luck: Philosophical Papers 1973–1980*. Cambridge University Press, Cambridge

16

Aggregation and Deliberation in Valuing Environmental Public Goods: A Look Beyond Contingent Pricing

Mark Sagoff

Introduction

This essay seeks to bring together and thus contribute to two programmes of research. The first comprises socio-economic experiments designed to measure the value individuals attach to environmental goods and services that markets fail to price. This effort, which often uses surveys to elicit individual willingness to pay (WTP) for public goods, is associated with the vast literature on contingent valuation methodology (CVM) (Carson et al, 1994). The second research programme is philosophical and analyses the kinds of decisions individuals reach by democratic political processes rather than by market transactions. This research is associated with a large literature concerning discursive and deliberative approaches to the formation of public values enacted in legislation (Fishkin, 1995).

These two fields of research are moving toward a common interest in processes of group learning, discourse and consensus-building. The purpose of this paper is to suggest that each research programme may learn from the other and that their differences may be less important than the direction they share in common.

This essay is organized into the following sections. The first section presents the familiar distinction between 'consumer' and 'citizen' preferences in the context of the even more venerable distinction between utilitarian and deontological approaches in political theory. This section describes the problem citizen preferences pose for CVM insofar as it presupposes a connection between preference satisfaction and individual welfare or wellbeing. The second section describes the pervasive influence citizen preferences exert on CV surveys and on other 'stated preference' methods of socio-economic research.

In the third section, the essay proposes that the two strategies economists initially adopted to deal with citizen preferences, i.e. either denying their existence or connecting them to psychic income, have failed. The fourth part of the essay explains that an

Note: Reprinted from *Ecological Economics*, vol 24, Sagoff, M., 'Aggregation and deliberation in valuing ennvironmental public goods: A look beyond contingent pricing', pp213–230, copyright © (1998), with permission from Elsevier

emerging strategy which emphasizes the constructive as distinct from the diagnostic aspect of CVM may succeed in accounting for these values. The next two sections argue that a constructive, deliberative and discursive turn also goes a long way toward resolving technical problems that have vexed CV research. The paper concludes by suggesting that developments in political theory lend support to the use of CVM as a constructive, deliberative and discursive instrument in estimating the value of public environmental goods. The result is a useful convergence between contemporary moral philosophy and sophisticated methods of socio-economic research.

An Introductory Distinction

Possibly the most venerable – and surely the most familiar – distinction in political theory is drawn between utilitarian and deontological (or Kantian) conceptions of rational choice. March (1994) in his *A Primer on Decision-Making* lays out a standard theoretical understanding of these two points of view. When decision makers adopt the utilitarian approach, they choose among given alternatives 'by evaluating their consequences in terms of prior preferences'. The contemporary utilitarian believes that social wellbeing or welfare, construed in terms of the satisfaction of the preferences ranked by WTP, constitutes the principal goal of environmental policy. 'The basic premises of welfare economics are that the purpose of economic activity is to increase the wellbeing of the individuals that make up the society and that each individual is the best judge of how well-off he or she is in a given situation' (Freeman, 1993).

When they adopt the deontological framework, decision makers 'pursue a logic of appropriateness, fulfilling identities or roles by recognizing situations and following rules that match appropriate behaviour to the situations they encounter' (March, 1994). In this context, individuals typically do not ask, 'what situation will most benefit me as an individual?' but, 'what do we believe is appropriate for us as a society, given our shared principles, beliefs and commitments?' Political institutions provide the context in which citizens debate and legislate conceptions of the common good bounded by civil, political and property rights.

These two conceptions of collective choice differ in the way they interpret disagreement among members of society. The contemporary utilitarian understands disagreement in terms of competition for the use of scarce resources. In a society without resource constraints, all preferences may be satisfied. The Kantian analyses disagreement in terms of the logical opposition of moral or political beliefs (Kant, 1959). In answering the question 'what do we stand for as a nation?' individuals may state logically opposing views of social policy rather than make competing private claims on scarce resources. In this framework for collective choice, the reasoning process 'is one of establishing identities and matching rules to recognized situations' (March, 1994).

These alternative approaches in political theory introduce an equally familiar distinction between consumer and citizen preferences. Consumer preferences, for example, to buy Pepsi rather than Coke, reflect what the individual thinks is good for her or him. Citizen preferences, in contrast, reflect principles the individual believes are implicit in the character, commitments or identity of the community as a whole. While the words

'I want' are likely to introduce a consumer preference, a statement that begins with 'society should...' is likely to express a citizen preference.

Environmental economists, as citizens and as scientists, argue that society should allocate resources to those willing to pay the most for them in order to maximize aggregate social wellbeing. This view expresses an objective policy position, not a consumer preference. Like any policy position, it is to be supported by argument and analysis. One would not assess its objectivity or validity by assessing the WTP of its advocates.

The same distinction between subjective desires and objective beliefs applies to virtually every controversy. Earlier this century, those who opposed child labour, for example, sometimes did so for self-serving reasons. For the most part, however, citizens fought against child labour on objective moral grounds. They believed that in our society, as in any society, children should go to school rather than to the mines. Similarly, when advocating any policy position, whether about campaign reform, the sale of marijuana, abortion or assisted suicide, individuals call on others to agree with their views or, if they disagree, to explain why. Those who oppose the death penalty, for example, usually seek nothing for themselves; they protest capital punishment because they believe it is useless and barbaric, not because they themselves fear being hanged.

To summarize, consumer preferences reflect conceptions of the good life individuals seek for themselves, while citizen preferences reflect conceptions of the good society offered for the consideration and agreement of others. Consumer preferences, having the form 'I want p', are associated with the gains in individual welfare WTP may measure. Citizen preferences, having the form 'we ought to...' or 'society should...', express views the individual holds as one of us about what we stand for. He or she expects other members of the political community to agree or, if they disagree, to explain why. The debate proceeds without reference to personal wellbeing.

Welfare and therefore environmental economists offer one among many positions citizens have defended as approaches to regulation. Other views are also worth considering. For example, libertarians regard pollution as a form of coercion and thus as a violation of rights (Machan, 1984). They argue that society should minimize pollution as a form of trespass or tort rather than optimize it as an economic externality. Libertarians may approve policies, therefore, that require society to reduce or minimize pollution far more than is economically efficient. Libertarians believe it is more important to protect personal and property rights against trespass than to balance benefits and costs.

Members of the Noah movement believe that humanity has a moral obligation to respect and preserve species, even at some cost to itself (Norton et al, 1995). Preservationists in the tradition of John Muir have kept magnificent landscapes from development by making aesthetic, religious and cultural rather than economic arguments. These and other groups saw to it that 'the cornerstones of environmental policy in the United States', such as the Clean Air, Clean Water and Endangered Species Acts, 'explicitly prohibited the weighing of benefits against costs in the setting of environmental standards' (Cropper and Oates, 1992).

Environmental economists have developed careful and sophisticated analyses of the ways environmental policy can handle consumer preferences, i.e. those that reflect judgements individuals make about what benefits them. In discussion or debate about environmental policy, however, citizen preferences loom much larger, since people nearly always argue in terms of what society ought to do rather than in terms of what is good for them. How, then, should policy makers take citizen preferences into account?

As a kind of default strategy, theorists could simply leave it to the individual to act simultaneously within market and political institutions to pursue these different sorts of values. On the other hand, since markets often fail and since political processes, let us say, are not always poetry-in-motion, social scientists have every motivation for trying to design experimental and surrogate instruments and procedures by which these different kinds of values might be expressed, revealed and measured.

In response to this challenge, economists, sociologists and others who seek to strengthen CVM are bringing to the conduct of experiments discursive, information-rich and deliberative research methods to enable subjects to construct informed values or preferences in relation to public environmental goods (Keeney, 1992; Renn et al, 1995a, b; Webler et al, 1995). Political theorists and students of democratic processes, in turn, have begun to emphasize deliberation and consensus-formation, as distinct from the aggregation of individuals' willingness to pay, as the appropriate path to the evaluation of public goods in a democracy (Buell, 1996). These theorists, whether in the social or political sciences, are drawn to some of the same kinds of experiments in their attempts to understand political deliberation in democratic decision making. By analysing similar processes of social learning, exchange and identification, economic analysts and political theorists are developing parallel conceptions of the function of democratic institutions in resolving social conflicts (Elster, 1989; Shklar, 1991; Fishkin, 1995; Sunstein, 1996).

This essay will propose, in the context of recent work both in socio-economic research and political theory, that individuals, rather than serving simply as locations or channels where consumer preferences are found, may participate in a social process in which they construct collective judgements as citizens about the value of a public environmental good. The opportunity for social learning, since it informs consumer and citizen choice, could strengthen CV research. Researchers are beginning to structure the CV experiment as a kind of focus group or jury that might reflect views of the larger society. The outcome of deliberation may then depend less on the addition of individual utilities than on the force of the better argument about the public interest (Habermas, 1982).

The Pervasiveness of Citizen Preferences

From the 1950s to the 1970s, socio-economic approaches to the evaluation of public goods generally adopted the conception of collective choice associated with welfare economics. Traditionally, advocates of this view have held that the 'invisible hand' of the market ideally performs both the function of eliciting preferences and of aggregating welfare. As Kneese and Bower wrote in 1972, economic theory 'developed on the presumption that virtually everything of value is suitable for private ownership with little or no "spillover" to other persons, households and firms when the private property is put to use by its owner'. Kneese and Bower (1972) added: 'of course, it was realized that sometimes adjustments had to be made for "market failure", but these were implicitly, if not explicitly, regarded as minor with respect to the overall allocation'.

Kneese and Bower observed that by the 1960s economists began to recognize that market failures were pervasive and ubiquitous, especially with respect to public goods that possess aesthetic, spiritual or cultural significance, such as endangered species and old-growth forest. As more and more of nature took on historical and cultural value, Kneese and Bower wrote, it became clear 'that the pure private property concept applies satisfactorily to a progressively narrowing range of natural resources and economic activities'. If environmental resources are to be allocated efficiently, they argued, nonmarket mechanisms are needed to allocate them. Economists urged the government to employ experts from their profession to 'correct' market prices for public environmental goods and services. 'Private property and market exchange', Kneese and Bower concluded, 'have little applicability to their allocation, development and conservation'.

If market failure provides 'the most important argument for governmental intervention' (Cowen, 1992) where issues of social equity are secondary, economists must play a central role in policy making. Their expertise is needed to quantify in monetary terms – or attach 'shadow' or 'surrogate market' prices to – environmental goods and services that are not traded under perfectly competitive conditions. This presents a comparatively easy task with respect to common property resources, such as wild fish stocks, that produce the kinds of commodities, such as fish, markets ordinarily price. It is harder to assign shadow prices to the kinds of environmental goods most relevant to this essay, those with moral, aesthetic and cultural significance, such as visibility in the Grand Canyon or wildlife in Prince William Sound. These moral or spiritual assets enlist our political views more than our consumer interests. To allocate (or to preserve) these assets, we traditionally rely on political rather than market institutions and processes.

As economists Cropper and Oates (1992) point out, economists responded in two ways to the need to attach shadow prices to public environmental goods. First, they developed methods 'to infer the value of improved environmental amenities from the prices of the market goods to which they are, in various ways, related'. Second, they 'turned to an approach regarded historically with suspicion in our profession: the direct questioning of individuals about their valuation...'.

This essay is concerned not with methods by which economists 'impute' prices to public environmental goods, but with instruments economists have developed to elicit the stated preferences of individuals with respect to the protection of the natural environment. These surveys generally seek to elicit WTP for public goods with aesthetic or spiritual significance individuals believe society ought to protect. Individuals report that they base their WTP for these goods on their concerns as citizens more than on their wants as consumers. Respondents seem affected less by considerations of their own wellbeing than by 'ethical concerns, altruism, or the desire to do their "fair share" – concerns that indicate they used decision-making processes inconsistent with the neoclassical paradigm', insofar as it seeks to maximize individual welfare or wellbeing (Stevens et al, 1993).

Reviewing several CV protocols, three economists concluded that 'responses to CV questions concerning environmental preservation are dominated by citizen judgements concerning social goals and responsibilities rather than by consumer preferences' (Blarney et al, 1993, unpublished). These responses often reveal 'social or political judgements rather than preferences over consumer bundles' (Blarney et al, 1993, unpublished). The results of one study 'provide an assessment of the frequency and seriousness of these non-economic considerations: They are frequent and they are significant determinants of WTP responses' (Schkade and Payne, 1993).

Researchers found a large range of strategies for constructing stated WTP that had little or nothing to do with respondents' expected utilities (Schkade and Payne, 1994). Edwards (1986) points out with respect to 'bequest' value that choices 'motivated entirely out of an unselfish interest in the wellbeing of others' fail to reflect personal welfare'. A group of economists conclude: 'Whatever CV surveys may be measuring, they are not measuring consumers' economic preferences over environmental amenities. Thus they do not represent values that should be used in cost-benefit analysis or for measuring compensatory damages' (Diamond et al, 1993).

The recently issued Global Biodiversity Assessment acknowledges that nonuse or 'existence' value 'is almost entirely driven by ethical considerations precisely because it is disinterested value' (Perrings et al, 1995). This study notes that 'existence value has been argued to involve a moral "commitment" which is not in any way all self-interested' (Perrings et al, 1995, citing Sen, 1977). The Assessment explains that 'commitment can be defined in terms of a person choosing an act that he believes will yield a lower level of personal welfare to him than an alternative that is also available to him' (Perrings et al, 1995). If the satisfaction of 'existence' values lowers welfare, on which side of the benefit–cost equation should they be entered? The individual does not want less welfare per se, but 'adherence to one's moral commitments will be as important as personal welfare maximization and may conflict with it' (Perrings et al, 1995).

Citizen Preferences and Individual Wellbeing

The pervasive influence of citizen preferences has posed a theoretical problem for CV research. The problem arises in establishing the relevance of WTP, insofar as it measures individual welfare, to citizen preferences, which by definition concern goods or goals other than individual welfare. They also reflect values individuals typically pursue through civic and political association, not through actual or hypothetical market transactions.

Economists have responded to this problem in two distinct ways. Some welfare economists have ruled citizen preferences (other than their own theory) out of consideration. Freeman (1993) states flatly that society 'should make changes in environmental resource allocations only if the results are worth more in terms of individuals' welfare than what is given up by diverting resources and inputs from other uses'. Economists Stokey and Zeckhauser (1978) similarly believe that 'the purpose of public decisions is to promote the welfare of society'. They add that 'the welfare levels of the individual members of society are the building blocks for the welfare of society'. Stokey and Zeckhauser (1978) solve the problem of citizen values by assuming there are none, i.e. that the individual will be motivated only by considerations of personal subjective utility. 'In the United States we usually take the position that it is the individual's own preferences that count, that he is the best judge of his own welfare'.

If individuals are to judge only their own welfare – if they are motivated only by private consumer preferences – who is to provide objective views about public policy? Who is to engage in political deliberation as distinct from actual or hypothetical market transactions? Presumably, only those in the scientific vanguard, who understand the economic foundations of environmental policy, can discuss it objectively. According to this presumption, which Leonard and Zeckhauser (1986) have made explicit, 'consent and the cost-benefit criterion are equivalent and ... cost-benefit analysis can be thought of as a form of 'hypothetical' consent by the community'. What shall we say, then, of individuals who express views of environmental policy inconsistent with the principles of welfare economics? These citizen preferences may influence their replies to CV surveys. Some welfare economists would dismiss such beliefs as irrational. They have concluded that environmental economists 'have failed to get their message across, or that their audience is perversely predisposed against their ideas' (Schelling, 1983).

The ambiguity of the term 'satisfaction' suggests a second way of dealing with the problem of citizen preferences. In a logical sense, to 'satisfy' a preference is to meet or fulfil its terms; this is also the sense in which equations and conditions are 'satisfied'. In a psychological sense, to 'satisfy' a preference or a person refers to a mental state of pleasure or contentment. These two senses of the word 'satisfy' are easily blurred. This being so, it is easy to slide from the logical to the psychological meaning of 'satisfaction'.

In the late 1960s, economists at Resources for the Future, for example, observed that individuals experience psychological satisfaction when they forgo material wellbeing to support policies they believe are intrinsically right. 'There are many people who obtain satisfaction from the mere knowledge that part of wilderness North America remains,' Krutilla (1967) wrote, 'even though they would be appalled by the prospect of being exposed to it.' Building on Krutilla's theoretical insight, economists developed many concepts – including 'existence', 'vicarious benefit', 'bequest' and 'stewardship values' – to capture in welfare terms amounts people are willing to pay for policies of which they strongly approve but from which they do not directly benefit.

Economists seeking to measure these 'nonuse' or 'nonconsumption' values sometimes supposed that WTP correlated with the 'warm glow' individuals expected to obtain in supporting a worthy cause, for example, the protection of a wilderness area they would never visit. This strategy presupposed what had to be proved, namely, that WTP for wilderness preservation 'really' sought to buy psychic satisfaction, avoid feelings of guilt or angst and the like. Krutilla and others assumed that whatever the individual said he wanted to buy, the actual object must be his or her own wellbeing. They thought that individuals, by satisfying their preferences in a logical sense, primarily intended to satisfy themselves in a psychological sense and thus to achieve a higher level of utility.

When citizens say that they are willing to pay for the existence of visibility over the Grand Canyon, whether they will visit it or not, what do they think they are buying? Is it clean air or psychic satisfaction? Surveys that investigate 'nonuse' values never ask how much individuals would pay for the psychic satisfaction or 'warm glow' they expect to experience as a result of various policies. Instead, these surveys inquire about WTP for the policy itself, for example, wilderness protection or the preservation of a species. Wilderness protection and psychic satisfaction are different goods that may be provided separately. For each, therefore, WTP must be separately surveyed.

To understand this, it is helpful to distinguish between pleasure or satisfaction as, (1) the end, object or goal of an action or choice and, (2) the means or mental faculty by which people perceive or appreciate the aesthetic, moral and other normative properties of objects and events. As an object or end of experience, pleasure may be understood as a response to a stimulus, for example, the relief addicts experience when they get their next 'fix'. The entire value of the stimulus, say, morphine, consists in the pleasure or relief from pain it gives. Narcotics, prostitution, gambling and other addictive pursuits, in view of the ferocity of the appetites they feed upon, may deliver the greatest amount of pleasure as a commodity at the lowest cost, at least in the short run. Surgery may also offer a lot of pleasure for the dollar – a nice lobotomy, for instance. These kinds of pleasures, such as the ignorance that is bliss, have no worth. They rob people of their humanity and often make them slaves of their desires.

On the other hand, pleasure may function cognitively to inform us about good and evil. Pleasure (or pain) in this context is not the end but the means – the faculty – by which we perceive the moral and aesthetic qualities of the world. The quiet satisfaction a person takes when contemplating an accomplishment, for example, is a way of perceiving its value, but it is not what gives it value. If pleasure or satisfaction itself were the goal, a good biochemist or hypnotist could provide it at little cost and the Big Lie would be better than the hard truth.

The 19th-century Utilitarian John Stuart Mill understood that pleasures that are inappropriate to their objects are reprehensible. He wrote that 'it is better to be Socrates dissatisfied than a pig satisfied'. Parents know this. They socialize children to enjoy what is valuable rather than to value what is enjoyable. Among those who are socialized, pleasure follows moral judgement and does not substitute for it. If we enjoy what is evil – for example, racism or genocide – that does not make it better. It only makes us worse.

The literature of environmental economics suggests only two approaches to citizen preferences: to dismiss them as irrational or to conflate them with consumer preferences. Some economists, such as Zeckhauser and Leonard, by supposing that their theory of public policy has the hypothetical consent of all citizens, would ignore contrary views (and legislation consistent with them) as perverse or irrational. Like Marxists and others whose science teaches them the truth, they dismiss dissent as ignorance or as wilful irrationality. Other economists in the tradition of Krutilla assume that whatever reasons citizens offer for their WTP, whatever object they describe, and however surveys are worded, the real object of desire must be psychic income or satisfaction. This assumption ties preference satisfaction to expected wellbeing and thus magically transforms views opposed to welfare economics into data for benefit–cost analysis.

A Third Strategy to Account for Citizen Preferences

Economists need not dismiss citizen preferences out of hand, however, nor invoke a special sort of psychic income to explain them. A third strategy for interpreting citizen preferences may be more promising. This approach builds on social choice theory by employing WTP simply to rank or measure preferences relative to one another. No claim is made about the relation of these preferences to welfare or wellbeing in a substantive or psychological sense.

This strategy begins by asserting that the relationship between WTP, wellbeing and preference-satisfaction is a logical, stipulative or formal one. In other words, this strategy makes no psychological claims. Having no psychological dimension, WTP simply orders preferences in relation to each other rather than in relation to some external quantity, such as happiness. If 'welfare' or 'utility' is construed as a formal ordering relation among preferences, as it is in social choice theory, rather than a measure of subjective wellbeing, the distinction between consumer and citizen preferences loses its significance. One could rank preferences without regard to the kinds of preferences they are (Keeney and Raifa, 1980).

This strategy may overcome a familiar criticism of the thesis that links the satisfaction of preferences to welfare or wellbeing. Study after study has shown that after basic needs are met, happiness or contentment do not vary with income and thus with the ability to satisfy preferences (for reviews of the literature, see Kahneman and Varey, 1991; Easterlin, 1995). Studies relating wealth to perceived happiness have found that 'rising prosperity in the USA since 1957 has been accompanied by a falling level of satisfaction. Studies of satisfaction and changing economic conditions have found overall no stable relationship at all' (Argyle, 1986). 'And this is virtually inevitable because the faster preferences actually are met, the faster they escalate' (Rescher, 1980).

The thesis that preference satisfaction correlates with welfare is immune to this kind of empirical refutation as long as economists define 'welfare' in terms of WTP and abandon the attempt to correlate WTP with any conception of wellbeing, not simply denned in terms of it. Many commentators have observed that sophisticated welfare economists use WTP as a formal measure to order preferences without making any inferences about human happiness. As Posner (1981) points out, the 'most important thing to bear in mind about the concept of value – in the welfare economist's sense – is that it is based on what people are willing to pay for something rather than the happiness they would derive from having it'.

We should understand, then, that in contemporary welfare economics, 'welfare' and 'wellbeing' are not causally related to 'preference satisfaction' but are proxies or stand-ins for it. Since 'welfare' and 'preference satisfaction' are logically equivalent, rather than causally related, the proposition, 'society should satisfy preferences to maximize welfare' asserts exactly the same thesis as '$a = a$'. It cannot be refuted because it expresses a stipulated identity. The old adage that 'you get what you pay for' is necessarily true in this instance. 'Wellbeing' is what you always pay for by definition, it has no independent meaning and no connection with happiness as it is ordinarily understood.

One might argue, then, that because WTP refers to or correlates with no substantive, i.e. moral or psychological, conception of wellbeing, it provides a formal, ordering metric to establish the relative weight individuals place on their preferences. To speak crudely, to assess WTP is to ask people to put their money where their mouths are. To express the same thought more politely, WTP serves as a metric to identify the trade-offs individuals would make between what they want for themselves and for society as a whole. As a way to rank preferences – consumer or citizen, self-regarding or other-regarding – WTP may provide a suitable economic measure.

Researchers may establish a ranking of social policies by asking individuals after discussion and deliberation for their WTP for them. For example, researchers could explain the concept of an efficient allocation to a survey group and ask them how much society ought to pay to achieve efficiency in the allocation of environmental goods. In view of the pervasiveness of market failure, efficiency is expensive to achieve. (The current deontological approach to policy, since it is based more on rules than on outcomes, may not incur the same information costs.) The costs involved in determining the 'correct' shadow price for every environmental good and service can be high, especially if everyone's moral and political beliefs must be taken into account. The price of CV surveys is not small and it increases when opposing sides to a controversy each commission their own experiments.

For example, public officials must pay large amounts to fund contingent valuation studies to assess natural resource damage, such as that caused by the *Exxon Valdez* incident. This does not include the large sums various interested parties invest in commissioning their own studies or in litigating the validity of the studies commissioned by their opponents. Exxon has spent vast sums hiring experts to refute damage estimates based on reported willingness to pay for an unfouled environment. When pockets are deep and the political atmosphere is charged, there is no theoretical limit on the amount society may have to pay to achieve closure about the true, scientific or objective value of a sea otter, much less larger public goods. The Exxon corporation was willing to pay huge amounts to many of the nation's best economists to take its side in the Valdez controversy (Hausman, 1993); other litigants were able to attract non-Nobel laureates at somewhat lower prices. More generally, solving technical problems in CVM has become a growth industry, and one may wonder how much of its wealth society must invest to achieve agreement among economists.

Diagnostic and Constructive Elements in CV Research

Traditionally, economists have used CV surveys and other instruments for diagnostic purposes. The purpose of these experiments has been to elicit pre-existent preferences for public goods. This method of eliciting and aggregating individual utilities parallels a conception of democracy as 'a kind of social welfare function which goes from individual preferences to a social preference that embodies the greatest level of preference satisfaction for the whole population' (Christiano, 1995). In this context, discursive group processes may be useful in part because they allow individuals to reflect in an informed and more critical way on their pre-existing preferences.

Recently, social scientists, in response to some of the criticisms restated here, have revised their approach in CV research to treat informed group deliberation as serving not so much a diagnostic as a constructive purpose. The function of this kind of group process is not to plumb more reliably the pre-existing preferences of the respondents but to work through evidence and argument to reach a considered judgement, which may guide policy makers more as a recommendation than as a kind of evidence. Just as the opinion of a jury about the guilt or innocence of a defendant is supposed to be legitimate because of the informed deliberation that produces it, so, too, the process of informed deliberation may add weight to the judgements individuals render about the value of public goods.

One could imagine the possibility that citizen groups might convene as 'juries' to work out through informed deliberation a value or 'price' for particular public goods. Several such juries given the same evidence and information might reach roughly the same judgement. If so, could we say that this consensus represents a kind of knowledge citizens can reach if provided the appropriate context for thought and reflection? The design of these panels might draw upon the strengths of jury processes (Kalven and Zeisel, 1966; Hastie et al, 1983; Hans and Vidmar, 1986; Abramson, 1994). One might also learn from the history of citizen participation in deliberative groups resolving environmental conflicts (Fiorino, 1990) and from work on 'grass roots' deliberation on national issues (Mathews, 1994) and international development (Annis and Hakim, 1988).

Many political theorists believe that deliberation about conceptions of the public interest, as distinct from the articulation and satisfaction of individual subjective utilities, is a defining characteristic of a democratic political process. This view, associated with Rousseau and his contemporary followers (Cohen, 1986, 1989), regards 'the democratic process as an attempt to formulate and reliably choose a conception of the common good with which to guide society' (Christiano, 1995). In this context, individuals might be asked to deliberate not so much about the welfare effect of an environmental policy on them individually as about its appropriateness or desirability for society as a whole, in view of a 'price tag' that is attached to it. Their individual WTP may represent a conception of their 'fair share payment', not a measure of their own welfare loss or gain.

A deliberative and constructive framework for CV research responds to the difficulty for economic theory emphasized in this essay, the penchant of individuals to take concerns other than their own welfare into account when putting hypothetical values on public goods. One might imagine an experiment in which individuals are asked for estimates of WTP based simply on a policy's effects on their own expected welfare or utility and, secondly, based on their moral, religious or political beliefs and commitments. It would be an interesting result if the sign (plus or minus) of the estimates were different, for example, if people thought that protecting the kangaroo rat would affect their own welfare negatively, if at all, but nevertheless were willing as a matter of religious scruple or moral principle to bear a share of the societal cost of maintaining a population of that endangered creature. In that event, a CV study could offer the policy maker two estimates, one related to social welfare, the other to views of social responsibility.

The often-heard objection that benefit–cost approaches are anti-democratic would not seem to apply to research on value formation in a constructive and deliberative setting. Deliberative and discursive processes now being studied may correspond with similar processes that characterize value formation in civil society as well as in consumer markets (Stern and Fineberg, 1996). Accordingly, methods of sociological research now being developed to measure public values by providing opportunities for deliberation may both enlighten and be understood in relation to emerging conceptions of public choice in a democracy (Stern and Dietz, 1994).

Technical Problems Besetting CV Experiments

This paper has proposed that CV research, by adopting a more deliberative, discursive and constructive approach to evaluating environmental public goods, may resolve the objection that CV experiments can deal only with consumer but not with citizen preferences. The move toward group deliberation may also go far toward resolving certain technical problems that vex 'stated preference' methods of valuation. Critics have worried, for example, that the survey vehicle or protocol might influence or bias the response (Samuelson, 1947). The data collected could not then be considered exogenous to – but might be an artefact of – the methods used to collect them. Critics often describe CV surveys as unreliable, for example, because responses vary with the way a survey question is focused or framed. According to these critics, CV surveys can achieve reliable results only under the condition that individuals possess 'a set of coherent preferences for goods, including non-market goods such as clean air and nice views' and that 'these preferences can be recovered' by appropriate survey methods (Kahneman, 1986).

Contrary to this requirement, 'people tend not to have previously well-defined values' about nonmarketed goods (Cummings et al, 1986; Mitchell and Carson, 1989). Accordingly, they 'must construct their responses at the time they are asked an elicitation question, rather than retrieve a previously formed value' (Schkade and Payne, 1993 citing Slovic, Griffin and Tversky, 1990). Schkade and Payne (1993) point out: 'if responses to CV questions are indeed constructed, we would expect them to be highly sensitive to features of the task and context that would influence the process of construction'. Preference-formation does not seem to take place exogenously to the survey but is endogenous to it (Hanemann, 1994).

Experimental results confirm this expectation. The order in which questions are asked, for example, appears to influence the amounts respondents bid (Samples and Hollyer, 1990), as does the information the survey provides (Samples et al, 1986). Preference-reversals are observed across different response modes, such as WTP, ranking and rating (Slovic and Lichtenstein, 1983). Researchers have also found that willingness to accept compensation to forgo an environmental improvement is paradoxically many times greater than willingness to pay for that same improvement (Bishop and Heberlein, 1979; Rowe et al, 1980). Various studies (Kahneman and Knetsch, 1992; Desvousges et al, 1993) demonstrate the 'embedding' effect, a tendency to state much the same WTP for a part of a resource as for the whole. Respondents 'react to an amenity's symbolic meaning instead of to the specific levels of provision described' (Mitchell and Carson, 1989; see also Kahneman and Knetsch, 1992). These anomalies suggest that individuals, lacking relevant preference maps, construct them on the spot (Fischhoff and Furby, 1988; Fischhoff, 1991; Gregory, Lichtenstein and Slovic, 1991). Two economists conclude that 'a fundamental assumption underlying the use of CV, that people have well-articulated values for non-market goods, is simply wrong' (Schkade and Payne, 1993).

Another technical problem that vexes CV surveys has to do with the ambiguity of survey data with respect to preferences. This problem arises because preferences are not observable objects. One might think of them as private mental states or, more accurately, as conceptual constructs of microeconomic theory (Sagoff, 1994). Preference must be inferred from behaviour. Yet behaviour is not self-describing; rather, a person's motions or actions have to be interpreted. To interpret these motions or actions as a choice, one must already ascribe a preference to the agent. Without the ascription of such a motive, the bodily motions would make no sense. An obvious circularity arises. There are as many ways one may describe behaviour as there are preferences one may want to infer from it.

Respondents who are asked to state their WTP to protect a species, for example, might be thought to choose between its 'existence' value and other goods they might buy. In fact, they may frame the opportunity set differently and thus their response may indicate a different kind of choice. They may 'purchase' a clear conscience (Kahneman and Knetsch, 1992) or the approval of the questioner (Bishop et al, 1986). Alternatively, the same expressed WTP may indicate willingness to contribute to a worthy cause (Daum, 1993; Guagnano et al, 1994), to defray a 'fair share' of society's cost (Stevens et al, 1991), to improve the lot of future generations, or 'to avoid violating the rights of others, including non-human species' (Opulach and Grigalunas, 1992). Commentators note that CV surveys can easily misrepresent WTP 'for a good cause as benefits associated with the specific commodity being described' (Opulach and Grigalunas, 1992).

Surveys are intended to function like dipsticks measuring the depth of well-defined preferences in transparent circumstances. A respondent to a survey may have a different choice in mind, however, than the one the researcher ascribes to her or him. He or she may engage in all kinds of strategic or 'gaming' behaviour. 'In reality,' Oppenheim (1966) has written, 'questioning people is more like trying to catch a particularly elusive fish, by hopefully casting different kinds of bait at different depths, without knowing what is going on beneath the surface.'

This problem shows up in CV research because data from surveys, no matter how carefully collected, must be interpreted. This requires the social scientist to make assumptions about the reasons that led subjects to respond as they did. People may overstate WTP for environmental improvements, for example, since 'there is no cost to being wrong and therefore no incentive to undertake the mental effort to be accurate' (Freeman, 1979). The researcher, therefore, is left to figure out what the respondent may have had in mind, in other words, to infer the nature of the behaviour ('strategic bidding') by making an assumption about the underlying preference ('to skew the survey results'). In other words, choice is in fact inferred from preference as much as the other way round.

The Deliberative Turn in CV Research

The deliberative turn in CV research may meet these kinds of objections. Consider, first, the objection that individuals often do not possess well-articulated preference orderings for public goods but must construct them in response to a survey instrument. This will be a problem if the survey purports to reveal a pre-existing, well-articulated preference ordering. It might be an advantage, however, if the research instrument sought a different result, for example, to help respondents construct value judgements. Even if individuals do not have well-articulated preference orderings to begin with, they may nonetheless reach legitimate and reliable value choices in circumstances appropriate to making public choices. These are circumstances in which individuals ideally make choices generally, i.e. as a result of deliberation, reflection and social learning (Estlund, 1990).

To put the same point differently: Socio-economic researchers can make a virtue of necessity by acknowledging that the values that surveys elicit are to some extent artefacts of the survey method. Rather than attempt to eliminate the artifact by ever more refined and subtle controls, they may recognize that the 'elicitation' of preference is inevitably a constructive process. Even if elicited preferences are to some extent artifacts or products of the methods used to elicit them, however, they can be stable and coherent, if these methods enable individuals to arrive at informed and well-considered value judgements.

The objection that preferences are in some way endogenous to the research vehicle loses some of its force, in other words, if the vehicle is conducive to reliable and well-considered preference formation. Researchers may seek ways, therefore, to create fair and open processes of group deliberation, processes which have been thoroughly studied in other contexts (Gunderson, 1995). The use of these processes may produce results which, being more fully considered, are more robust and less susceptible to semantic manipulation, for example, to 'framing', 'focus' and 'embedding' effects.

The recognition that deliberative and discursive processes will enable individuals in groups to construct values rather than express prior preferences may relieve economists of an unnecessary burden, the attempt to elicit responses that are not an artifact of the survey process. Instead they may examine how the dynamics of group deliberation can generate well-considered and informed value choices (Stern, 1991). Plainly, normative, conceptual and theoretical issues must be resolved if practitioners are to succeed in introducing participatory, discursive and deliberative techniques into socio-economic experimental protocols used to measure the value of public environmental goods. Perhaps the easiest of these problems concerns the rules that govern free and equal discussion in the context of group decision making. These rules – along with appropriate institutional contexts – have been studied in the context of conflict-resolution and group dynamics and behaviour (Whyte, 1991). The extensive literature concerning focus groups, for example, should be surveyed for its relevance to new methods and developments in CV research (Morgan, 1993).

The deliberative turn helps to resolve the problem that arises because a person's observable behaviour can be interpreted to embody any number of possible choices. A deliberative approach to CV surveys leaves it to the respondents to clarify among themselves explicitly what they are valuing and why. If it is a particular species or landscape, for example, the deliberative group can pin down for itself precisely which aspects of the 'public good' it values and how much; it can also set up comparative valuations with the appropriate reference classes, i.e. other species and other landscapes. This provides a richer and more meaningful record for the policy maker. The discursive approach also avoids ambiguity in survey questions. The public good and the shadow price, as it were, together become the objects of determination through deliberation.

More difficult questions, which require sustained philosophical analysis, arise concerning the structure of deliberative methods used in the evaluation of public environmental goods. Should the group as a whole strive toward a consensus valuation or vote on alternatives? Should the group seek to determine how much an environmental good is worth to them, or should they try to estimate how much society as a whole should be willing to pay, given some idea of a 'fair share' payment? Still more questions arise if the group is to consider 'equity' considerations, for example, the question of who should pay for reducing pollution or protecting wetlands. The amount people are willing to pay may vary with their beliefs about who ought to pay, for example, for protecting species or reducing pollution. These moral issues are relevant to socio-economic research.

The Relevance of Democratic Theory

Alexander Hamilton, writing in Federalist Paper no 71, declared 'the republican principle demands that the deliberative sense of the community should govern'. Socioeconomic experiments that bring groups of citizens together to deliberate in an informed way over the value of environmental improvements may approximate the ideal dynamics of democratic deliberation. Thus, those who design experimental protocols for eliciting environmental values may have much to learn from the literature about democratic processes of group decision making.

During the past decades political theorists and philosophers have engaged in a lively debate over what is meant by 'the deliberative sense of the community' and how it may come to control the government. In this debate, two conceptions of democracy oppose each other. One treats 'the deliberative sense of the community' simply as the totality of the preferences of its individual members. On this approach, the appropriate function of government is to aggregate these preferences, a task for which voting is a familiar if somewhat inefficient mechanism. The opposing position contends that a 'sense of the community' lies in the considered judgements of its members about the common good. What is central to this conception of democracy is not the act of voting so much as the deliberative process that leads up to it, in which citizens construct and refine their judgement about the common will in dialogue with each other.

In the 1950s and 1960s, political scientists and theorists generally adhered to the first conception of democracy, a 'pluralist' or 'strategic' model of political choice based on conceptions of the individual found in welfare economics (Dahl, 1956; Downs, 1956; Black, 1958; Buchanan and Tullock, 1962). According to this approach, 'man is an egoistic, rational, utility maximizer' (Mueller, 1979) and possesses preference orderings which, if rational, conform to certain well-known formal conditions (Sen, 1970). As Dietz (1994) has written under this rational actor model, 'people try to maximize the benefits they receive relative to the costs they bear. That is, all actors are using the same rule in deciding what action to take – self-interested utility maximization.'

At its simplest, the strategic conception models collective choice on the idea of a social welfare function of the kind famously discussed by Arrow (1951). In this conception, 'individuals are supposed to begin with their diverse ends, desires, goals, or projects and then to promote them as effectively as possible' (Estlund, 1993). Democracy becomes a special case of instrumental rationality (Barry and Hardin, 1982). Many theorists of this school recognized, of course, that a rational person will form his or her own choices in the light of those that others are likely to make, so that this approach to political theory can emphasize cooperation, not just competition. Harsanyi (1982), for example, has argued that social morality arises in this context as a result of rational, utility-maximizing behaviour. In strategic or pluralistic conceptions of democracy, deliberation, consultation, cooperation, learning and morality all may figure prominently. These virtues matter, however, insofar as they help individuals to determine their own best interests and society to serve those interests as fully as resources and technology allow.

Since the 1980s, many political theorists have moved away from the 'strategic' model toward an ideal of democracy as a deliberative and cooperative enterprise (Elster,

1986; Sunstein, 1988; Estlund, 1993). This emphasis on deliberative, discursive and collegial processes of collective choice draws inspiration and support from many sources, including communications theories associated with the Frankfurt School of sociology (Habermas, 1979, 1996; Apel, 1980). A second source is found in the 'civic republican' literature centring in American law schools (Michelman, 1989; Sunstein, 1993b, 1996). A third tradition emphasizes 'civic engagement' in participatory democracy (Putnam, 1993; Mathews, 1994; Fishkin, 1995) and 'civic virtue' (Will, 1992). These positions agree in rejecting the view that political processes fundamentally aggregate prior preferences.

In the models of 'civic republicanism' or 'participatory democracy' that oppose strategic or pluralistic approaches, citizens engage in deliberation not so that each can determine or refine his or her own interests, but so that together they can discover a good that is not simply a function of their individual utilities. Theorists who claim James Madison as the American founder of this tradition cite his defence of a representational system as necessary to 'refine and enlarge the public views by passing them through the medium of a chosen body of citizens, whose wisdom may discern the true interest of their country'. Invoking this tradition, Sunstein (1993a) writes that the goal of a constitutional democracy 'is to ensure discussion and debate ... in a process through which reflection will encourage the emergence of general truths'.

Current research in the theory of democracy suggests that in voting, citizens and their representatives may perform a cognitive task rather than an arithmetic one. Instead of simply aggregating their individual interests, they vote on a common view of their collective interest. In other words, the policy chosen is the one that a majority believes expresses the will of the community as a whole. Those who vote against a resolution are still bound by it, because they participated in the process by which it was chosen. Participation in a political community would then involve a kind of moral commitment to the public interest which participation in a market does not. This accounts for the obligation citizens feel to obey even those statutes they oppose. As long as their views are heard on the merits, rather than balanced on the basis of WTP, citizens retain the 'voice' option of a democracy rather than only the 'exit' option of a market (Hirschman, 1981).

Contingent Valuation and Democracy

Economists and other social scientists initially brought group discussion and deliberation into CVM as ways to overcome problems, such as 'framing' and 'embedding' effects, that beset conventional survey methods (Webler, 1993; Stern and Dietz, 1994). These researchers soon recognized an additional benefit of deliberative methods, namely, that they are more consistent with the larger democratic institutions and processes by which society actually and legitimately makes political trade-offs.

The deliberative and discursive turn in CV research convenes individuals into groups, gives them adequate and appropriate information and encourages them to engage in discussion and deliberation to determine their WTP for a public policy choice (Dietz, 1987, 1988, 1994). (What counts as 'adequate and appropriate' information is a big question and plainly requires a paper in itself.) Such a discursive or deliberative approach may have the same purpose as more conventional survey methods, i.e. to elicit WTP in order to quantify the value of public environmental goods in monetary terms. It may be more reliable, however, because individuals have the opportunity to review their preferences in collaborative discussion with others.

Viewed in the context of the contemporary theory of democracy, moreover, groups of informed citizens convened to deliberate about the value of public goods could serve to guide public policy in another way. They could function not as informants about their personal utilities but as citizen-juries reaching judgements about environmental values on the basis of argument and evidence. Deliberative bodies of citizens could render a judgement, for example, about the value of public environmental goods not simply to them but to society as a whole, along with a statement of the 'fair share' they would pay as members of the community to protect those goods. Individuals joined in groups to consider matters of public policy, in other words, need not stop at stating their WTP as individuals for particular environmental goods or services. They might also explain or express their WTP in terms of a collective judgement (from which some, of course, may dissent) about the value society ought to place on certain resources and the extent to which society as a whole should invest in those goods rather than other public goods and services. In addressing these questions, socio-economic research may draw from a recent model of practical rationality, which gives social deliberation a critical role in resolving conflicts among values (Sherman, 1989). This approach takes the view that practical choice, (1) involves a diversity of competing goods and commitments that lack a (metric) commensurability, (2) depends on context-sensitive perception of what is normatively salient in the particular circumstances (Murdoch, 1970) and (3) requires social deliberation and learning in the choice of ends and means-to-ends, as well as in the distribution of costs and benefits (Sen, 1985, 1987; Nussbaum, 1990, 1995; Richardson, 1994). This approach sees group deliberation not merely as an evidentiary tool or as a mechanism for collective decision making, but as a basic feature of practical rationality. It highlights the importance of group processes for environmental policy making, suggesting a convergence between contemporary moral philosophy and sophisticated empirical research.

Economists and others involved in CV research have responded to the concerns identified here in a variety of ways. Many have developed sophisticated survey protocols, some favouring a dichotomous-choice question format (Hanemann, 1986), others open-ended question formats (Desvousges et al, 1993), referenda methods (Carson et al, 1986; Cameron and Huppert, 1991), bidding games and auctions (Cummings et al, 1986), and other variants in protocol design and analysis (Mitchell and Carson, 1989; Loomis, 1990). While many of these refinements are well worth pursuing, this essay has focused on one methodological innovation that might benefit most from normative and conceptual analysis – the introduction of discursive and deliberative methods of valuation.

The possibility that the dynamics of group discussion and deliberation – as well as access to information – might improve the reliability of socio-economic research into environmental values draws on a large body of established theory in social psychology (Delbecq et al, 1975; Habermas, 1984), social learning (Bandura, 1971), public participation (Fiorino, 1990; Laird, 1993), and group decision making processes (Burns and Überhorst, 1988; Clarke, 1989) in relation to environmental problems. The introduction of a more discursive approach to value elicitation also makes intuitive sense. If individuals do not come to CV surveys with predetermined preferences but must construct them, then the process of construction may legitimately involve social learning, since this is precisely what occurs in other contexts in which people work out their values. In markets, for example, individuals construct preferences for goods over time in response to information and the advice, suggestions and experience of others. If this kind of social learning conditions preference formation in markets, there seems no a priori reason to exclude it from socio-economic research into environmental values in experimental contexts.

Acknowledgements

The author acknowledges with gratitude the generous support of the National Science Foundation, Grant No SBR96-13495, for this research. The Pew Charitable Trusts provided additional support under a generous grant to the Institute for Philosophy and Public Policy to study issues related to civic renewal in America. The views expressed in this paper are those of the author alone and not necessarily of any funding agency.

References

1   Abramson, J. (1994) *We, the Jury: the Jury System and the Ideal of Democracy.* Basic Books, NY
2   Annis, S. and Hakim P. (eds) (1988) *Direct to the Poor: Grassroots Development in Latin America.* Rienner, Boulder, CO
3   Apel, Karl-Otto, (1980) *Towards a Transformation of Philosophy.* Translated by Glyn Adey and David Frisby. Routledge & Kegan Paul, London
4   Argyle, M. (1986) *The Psychology of Happiness.* Methuen, NY
5   Arrow, K. J. (1951) *Social Choice and Individual Values.* Wiley, NY
6   Bandura, A. (1971) *Social Learning Theory: Motivational Trends in Society.* General Learning Press, Morristown, NY
7   Barry, B. and Russell, H. (eds) (1982) *Rational Man and Irrational Society?* Sage, Beverly Hills, CA
8   Bishop, G. F., Tuchfarber, A. J. and Oldendick, R. W. (1986) 'Opinions on fictitious issues: The pressure to answer survey questions'. *Public Opinion Quarterly,* vol 50, pp240–250
9   Bishop, R. C. and Heberlein, T. A. (1979) 'Measuring values of extramarket goods: Are indirect measures biased?' *American Journal of Agricultural Economics* vol 61, pp926–930
10 Black, D. (1958) *The Theory of Elections and Committees.* Cambridge University Press, Cambridge
11 Buchanan, J. M. and Tullock, G. (1962) *The Calculus of Consent, Logical Foundations of Constitutional Democracy.* University of Michigan Press, Ann Arbor, MI
12 Buell, J. (1996) *Sustainable Democracy: Individuality and the Politics of the Environment.* Sage, Thousand Oaks, CA
13 Burns, T. R. and Überhorst, R. (1988) *Creative Democracy: Systemic Conflict Resolution and Policymaking in a World of High Science and Technology.* Praeger, NY

14 Cameron, T. A. and Huppert, D. D. (1991) 'Referendum contingent valuation estimates: Sensitivity to the assignment of offered values'. *Journal of the American Statistical Association*, vol 86, pp910–918

15 Carson, R. T., Hanemann, W. M. and Mitchell, R. C. (1986) *Determining the Demand for Public Goods by Simulating Referendums at Different Tax Prices* (manuscript). University of California, San Diego, CA

16 Carson, R. T. et al (1994) *A Bibliography of Contingent Valuation Studies and Papers*, Natural Resource Damage Assessment, Inc, La Jolla, CA

17 Christiano, T. (1995) 'Voting and democracy'. *Canadian Journal of Philosophy*, vol 25(3), pp395–414

18 Clarke, L. (1989) *Acceptable Risk? Making Decisions in a Toxic Environment*. University of California Press, Berkeley, CA

19 Cohen, J. (1986) 'An epistemic conception of democracy'. *Ethics*, vol 97, pp27–40

20 Cohen, J. (1989) 'Deliberation and democratic legitimacy', in Hamlin, A. and Pettit, P. (eds) *The Good Polity: Normative Analysis of the State*, Blackwell, Oxford

21 Cowen, T. (1992) *Public Goods and Market Failures*. Transaction, New Brunswick, NJ

22 Cropper, M. L. and Oates, W. E. (1992) 'Environmental economics: A survey'. *Journal of Economic Literature*, vol 30, pp 675–740

23 Cummings, R. G., Brookshire, D. S. and Schultze W. D. (eds) (1986) *Valuing Environmental Goods: A State of the Arts Assessment of the Contingent Method*. Rowman & Allanheld, Totowa, NJ

24 Dahl, R. (1956) *A Preface to Democratic Theory*. University of Chicago Press, Chicago, IL

25 Daum, J. (1993) 'Some legal and regulatory aspects of contingent valuation', in Hausman, J. A. (ed) *Contingent Valuation: A Critical Assessment*. North Holland, Amsterdam, pp389–416

26 Delbecq, A. L., van de Ven, A. H. and Gustafson, D. H. (1975) *Group Techniques for Program Planning: A Guide to the Nominal Group and Delphi Process*. Scott-Foresman, Glenview, IL

27 Desvousges, W. H., Red Johnson, F., Dunford, R. W., Boyle, K. J., Hudson, S. P. and Wilson, K. N. (1993) 'Measuring natural resource damages with contingent valuation: Tests of validity and reliability', in Hausman, J. A. (ed) *Contingent Valuation: A Critical Assessment*. North Holland, Amsterdam, pp91–164

28 Diamond, P. A., Hausman, J. A., Leonard, O. K. and Denning, M. A. (1993) 'Does contingent valuation measure preferences? Experimental evidence', in Hausman, J. A. (ed) *Contingent Valuation: A Critical Assessment*. North Holland, Amsterdam, pp41–90

29 Dietz, T. (1987) 'Theory and method in social impact assessment'. *Sociological Inquiry*, vol 57, pp54–69

30 Dietz, T. (1988) 'Social impact assessment as applied human ecology: integrating theory and method', in Borden, R., Jacobs, J. and Young, G.R. (eds) *Human Ecology: Research and Applications*. Society for Human Ecology, College Park, MD, pp220–227

31 Dietz, T. (19940 'What should we do? Human ecology and collective decision making'. *Human Ecology Review*, vol 1(2), pp301–309

32 Downs, A. (1956) *An Economic Theory of Democracy*. Harper and Row, NY

33 Easterlin, R. (1995) 'Will raising the incomes of all increase the happiness of all?' *Journal of Economic Behaviour and Organization*, vol 27, pp35–48.

34 Edwards, S. F. (1986) 'Ethical preferences and the measurement of existence values: Does the neoclassical model fit?' *North-eastern Journal of Agricultural Resource Economics*, vol 15, pp145–159

35 Elster, J. (1986) 'The market and the forum: Three varieties of political theory', in Elster, J. and Hylland, A. (eds) *Foundations of Social Choice Theory*. Cambridge University Press, NY, pp111–112

36 Elster, J. (1989) *Solomonic Judgements: Studies in the Limitations of Rationality.* Cambridge University Press, Cambridge

37 Estlund, D. (1990) 'Democracy without preference'. *Philosophical Review*, vol 99(3), pp397–423

38 Estlund, D. (1993) 'Who's afraid of deliberative democracy'. *Texas Law Review*, vol 71, pp1437–1477

39 Fiorino, D. (1990) *Making Environmental Policy.* University of California Press, Berkeley, CA

40 Fischhoff, B. (1991) 'Value elicitation: Is there anything in there?' *American Psychology*, vol 46, pp835–847

41 Fischhoff, B. and Furby, L. (1988) 'Measuring values: A conceptual framework for interpreting transactions with special reference to contingent valuation of visibility'. *Journal of Risk and Uncertainty*, vol 1, pp147–184

42 Fishkin, J. S. (1995) *The Voice of the People: Public Opinion and Democracy.* Yale University Press, New Haven, CT

43 Freeman, A. M. III. (1979) 'The benefits of environmental improvement: Theory and practice'. *Resources for the Future.* John Hopkins Press, Baltimore, MD

44 Freeman, A. M. III. (1993) 'The Measurement of Environmental and Resource Values'. *Resources for the Future*, Washington, DC

45 Gregory, R., Lichtenstein, S. and Slovic, P. (1991) 'Valuing Environmental Resources: A Constructive Approach', *Journal of Risk and Uncertainty*, vol 7(2), October 1993, pp177–197

46 Guagnano, G. A., Dietz, T. and Stern, P. C. (1994) 'Willingness to pay: A test of the contribution model'. *Psychological Science*, vol 5, pp411–415

47 Gunderson, A. G. (1995) *The Environmental Promise of Democratic Deliberation.* University of Wisconsin Press, Madison, WI

48 Habermas, J. (1979) *Communication and the Evolution of Society.* Beacon Press, Boston

49 Habermas, J. (1982) Critical Debates. Thompson, J. B. and Held, D. (eds). MIT Press, Cambridge, MA

50 Habermas, J. (1984) 'The theory of communicative action', vol 1, *Reason and the Rationalization of Society.* Beacon Press, Boston

51 Habermas, J. (1996) *Justification and Application: Remarks on Discourse Ethics* (C. Cronin, Trans.). MIT Press, Cambridge, MA

52 Hanemann, W. M. (1986) *Implications from Biometrics for the Design of Dichotomous Choice Contingent Valuation Markets.* Paper presented at the United States Department of Agriculture Conference of Research Issues in Resource Decisions Involving Marketed and Nonmarketed Goods, San Diego, California

53 Hanemann, W. M. (1994) 'Valuing the environment through contingent valuation'. *Journal of Economic Perspectives*, vol 8, pp19–43

54 Hans, V. P. and Vidmar, N. (1986) *Judging the Jury.* Plenum, NY

55 Harsanyi, J. (1982) 'Morality and the theory of rational behaviour', in Sen, A. and Williams, B. (eds) *Utilitarianism and Beyond.* Cambridge University Press, Cambridge

56 Hastie, R. Penrod, S. and Pennington, N. (1983) *Inside the Jury.* Harvard University Press, Cambridge, MA

57 Hausman, J. A. (ed) (1993) *Contingent Valuation: A Critical Assessment.* North Holland, Amsterdam

58 Hirschman, A. O. (1981) *Exit, Voice and Loyalty: Responses to Decline in Firms, Organizations and States.* Harvard University Press, Cambridge, MA

59 Kahneman, D. (1986) 'Comments', in Cummings, R. G., Brookshire, D. S. and Schulze, W. D. (eds) *Valuing Environmental Goods: An Assessment of the Contingent Valuation Method.* Rowman & Allanheld, Totowa, NJ

60 Kahneman, D. and Knetsch, J. L. (1992) 'Valuing public goods: The purchase of moral satisfaction'. *Journal of Environmental and Economic Management,* vol 22, pp57–70

61 Kahneman, D. and Varey, C. (1991) 'Notes on the psychology of utility', in Elster, J. and Roemer, J. (eds) *Interpersonal Comparisons of Wellbeing.* Cambridge University Press, New York, pp127–163

62 Kalven, H. and Zeisel, H. (1966) *The American Jury.* Little, Brown, Boston, MA

63 Kant, I. (1959) *Foundations of the Metaphysics of Morals,* L. W. Beck, trans. Bobbs-Merrill, Indianapolis, IN

64 Keeney, R. L. (1992) *Value-Focused Thinking: A Path to Creative Decision Making.* Harvard University Press, Cambridge, MA

65 Keeney, R. L. and Raifa, H. (1980) *Decisions with Multiple Objectives: Preferences and Value Trade-offs.* Wiley, NY

66 Kneese, A. V. and Bower, B. T. (1972) 'Introduction', in Kneese, A. V. and Bower B. T. (eds) *Environmental Quality Analysis.* Johns Hopkins Press, Baltimore, MD

67 Krutilla, J. (1967) 'Conservation reconsidered'. *American Economic Review,* vol 57(4), pp777–786

68 Laird, F. (1993) 'Participatory analysis, democracy and technological decision making'. *Science Technology and Human Values,* vol 18, pp341–361

69 Leonard, H. and Zeckhauser, R. (1986) 'Cost-benefit analysis applied to risks: Its philosophy and legitimacy', in MacLean, D. (ed) *Values at Risk.* Rowman & Littlefield, Totowa, NJ, pp31–48

70 Loomis, J. B. (1990) 'Comparative reliability of the dichotomous choice and open-ended contingent valuation techniques'. *Journal of Environmental and Economic Management,* vol 18, pp78–85

71 Machan, T. (1984) 'Pollution and political theory', in Tom Regan (ed) *Earthbound: New Introductory Essays in Political and Social Philosophy.* Random House, NY, pp74–106

72 March, J. G. (1994) *A Primer in Decision Making.* The Free Press, NY

73 Mathews, D. (1994) *Politics for People: Finding a Responsible Public Voice.* University of Illinois Press, Urbana, IL

74 Michelman, F. (1989) 'Conceptions of democracy in American constitutional argument: The case of pornography regulation'. *Tennessee Law Review,* vol 56, pp293–294

75 Mitchell, R. C. and Carson, R. T. (1989) 'Using surveys to value public goods: The contingent valuation method'. *Resources For the Future,* Washington, DC

76 Morgan, D. (ed) (1993) *Successful Focus Groups: Advancing the State of the Art.* Sage, Newbury Park, CA

77 Mueller, D. (1979) *Public Choice.* Cambridge University Press, NY

78 Murdoch, I. (1970) *The Sovereignty of the Good.* Routledge and Kegan Paul, London

79 Norton, B. G., Hutchins, M., Stevens, E. F. and Maple, T. L. (eds) (1995) *Ethics on the Ark: Zoos, Animal Welfare and Wildlife Conservation.* Smithsonian Institute, Washington, DC

80 Nussbaum, M. (1990) 'The discernment of perception: An Aristotelian conception of private and public rationality', in Nussbaum, M. (ed) *Love's Knowledge: Essays on Philosophy and Literature.* Oxford University Press, NY

81 Nussbaum, M. (1995) *Poetic Justice.* Beacon Press, Boston

82 Oppenheim, A. N. (1966) *Questionnaire Design and Attitude Measurement.* Basic Books, NY

83 Opulach, J. J. and Grigalunas, T. A. (1992) *Ethical Values and Personal Preference as Determinants of Non-use Values: Implications for Natural Resource Damage Assessments.* Department of Resource Economics Staff Paper, University of Rhode Island

84 Perrings, et al (1995) 'Economic values of biodiversity', in Heywood, V. H. (ed) *Global Biodiversity Assessments*. Cambridge University Press, Cambridge, pp823–914

85 Posner, R. (1981) *The Economics of Justice*. Harvard University Press, Cambridge, MA

86 Putnam, R. D., Leonard, R. and Nanetti, R. (1993) *Making Democracy Work: Civic Traditions in Modern Italy*. Princeton University Press, Princeton, NJ

87 Renn, O., Webler, T. and Wiedemann, P. (eds) (1995) *Fairness and Competence in Citizen Participation: Evaluating Models for Environmental Discourse*. Kluwer, Dordrecht

88 Renn, O., Webler, T. and Wiedemann, P. (1995) *Novel Approaches to Public Participation in Environmental Decision Making*. Kluwer, Amsterdam

89 Rescher, N. (1980) *Unpopular Essays on Technological Progress*. University of Pittsburgh Press, Pittsburgh

90 Richardson, H. S. (1994) *Practical Reasoning About Final Ends*. Cambridge University Press, Cambridge

91 Rowe, R.D., d'Arge, R. C. and Brookshire, D.S. (1980) 'An experiment on the economic value of visibility'. *Journal of Environmental and Economic Management*, vol 7, pp1–19

92 Sagoff, M. (1994) 'Should preferences count?' *Land Economics*, vol 70 (2), pp127–144

93 Samples, K., Dixon, J. and Gowen, M. (1986) 'Information disclosure and endangered species evaluation'. *Land Econ.*, vol 62, pp306–312

94 Samples, K. and Hollyer, P. (1990) 'Contingent valuation of wildlife resources in the presence of substitutes and complements', in Johnson, R. L. and Johnson, G. V. (eds) *Economic Valuation of Natural Resources*. Westview Press, Boulder, CO, pp177–192

95 Samuelson, P. (1947) *Foundations of Economic Analysis*. Harvard University Press, Cambridge, MA

96 Schelling, T. C. (1983) 'Preface', in Schelling, T. C. (ed) *Incentives for Environmental Protection*. MIT Press, Cambridge, MA

97 Schkade, D. A. and Payne, J. W. (1993) 'Where do the numbers come from? How people respond to contingent valuation questions', in Hausman, J.A. (ed) *Contingent Valuation: A Critical Assessment*. North Holland Press, Amsterdam, pp271–304

98 Schkade, D. A. and Payne, J. W. (1994) 'How people respond to contingent valuation questions: A verbal protocol analysis of willingness to pay for an environmental regulation'. *Journal of Environmental and Economic Management*, vol 26, pp88–109

99 Sen, A. (1970) *Collective Choice and Social Welfare*. Holden-Day, San Francisco

100 Sen, A. (1977) 'Rational fools: A critique of the Behavioural foundations of economic theory. *Philosophy and Public Affairs*, vol 6(4), pp327–344

101 Sen, A. (1985) 'Wellbeing, agency and freedom: The Dewey Lectures 1984'. *Journal of Philosophy*, vol 82

102 Sen, A. (1987) *On Ethics and Economics*. Blackwell, Oxford

103 Sherman, N. (1989) *The Fabric of Character: Aristotle's Theory of Virtue*. Clarendon Press, Oxford

104 Shklar, J. (1991) *American Citizenship: The Quest for Inclusion*. Harvard University Press, Cambridge, MA

105 Slovic, P. and Lichtenstein, S. (1983) 'Preference reversals: A broader perspective'. *American Economic Review*, vol 73, pp596–605

106 Slovic, P., Griffin, D. and Tversky, A. (1990) 'Compatibility effects in judgement and choice', in Hogarth, R. M. (ed) *Insights in Decision Making: A Tribute to Hillel J. Einhorn*. University of Chicago Press, Chicago

107 Stern, P. C. (1991) 'Learning through conflict: A realistic approach to risk communication'. *Policy Science*, vol 24, pp99–119

108 Stern, P. C. and Dietz, T. (1994) 'The value basis of environmental concern'. *Journal of Social Issues*, vol 50, pp65–84

109 Stern, P. C. and Fineberg, H. V. (eds) (1996) *Understanding Risk: Informing Decisions in a Democratic Society.* National Academy Press, Washington, DC

110 Stevens, T. H., Echeverria, J., Glass, R. J., Hager, T. and Moore, T. A. (1991) 'Measuring the existence value of wildlife: What do CVM estimates really show?' *Land Economics*, vol 67, pp390–400

111 Stevens, T. H., More, T., A. and Glass, R. (1993) 'Measuring the existence value of wildlife: Reply'. *Land Economics*, vol 69, pp309–312

112 Stokey, E. and Zeckhauser, R. (1978) *A Primer for Policy Analysis.* Norton, NY

113 Sunstein, C. (1988) 'Beyond the republican revival'. *Yale Law Journal*, vol 97, pp1539–1570.

114 Sunstein, C. (1993a) *The Partial Constitution.* Harvard University Press, Cambridge, MA

115 Sunstein, C. (1993b) *Democracy and the Problem of Free Speech.* The Free Press, NY

116 Sunstein, C. (1996) 'Earl Warren is dead'. *New Republic*, May 13, pp35–39

117 Webler, T. (1993) 'Habermas put into practice: A democratic discourse for environmental problem solving', in *Crossing Boundaries: New Directions in Human Ecology. Society for Human Ecology*, Salt Lake City, UT

118 Webler, T., Kastenholz, H. and Renn, O. (1995) 'Public Participation in impact assessment: A social learning perspective'. *Environmental Impact Assessment Review*, vol 15, pp443–463

119 Whyte, W. (ed) (1991) *Participatory Action Research.* Sage, Newbury Park, CA

120 Will, G. (1992) *Restoration: Congress, Term Limits and the Recovery of Deliberative Democracy.* The Free Press, NY

17

Valuing Environmental Resources: A Constructive Approach

Robin Gregory, Sarah Lichtenstein and Paul Slovic

Introduction

Contingent valuation (CV) has been used by economists to value public goods for about 25 years. The approach posits a hypothetical market for an unpriced good and asks individuals to state the dollar value they place on a proposed change in its quantity, quality or access. Development of the CV concept has been described in reviews by Cummings et al (1986) and Mitchell and Carson (1989). The approach is now widely used to value many different goods whose quantity or quality might be affected by the decisions of a public agency or private developer. Environmental goods have received particular attention, because they are highly valued by society and entail controversial trade-offs (e.g. manufacturing costs versus pollution, urban development versus wetlands protection) but are not usually sold through markets (Bromley, 1986).

The visibility of CV methods[1] has greatly increased following the 1989 interpretation of CERCLA (the Comprehensive Environmental Response, Compensation, and Liability Act of 1986) by the District of Columbia Circuit Court of Appeals (in *Ohio* vs *United States Department of the Interior*). This decision (a) granted equal standing to expressed and revealed preference evaluation techniques (with willingness to pay measures preferred in all cases), (b) accepted nonuse values as a legitimate component of total resource value, and (c) recognized a 'distinct preference' in CERCLA for restoring damaged natural resources, rather than simply compensating for the losses (Kopp et al, 1990). The court's opinion on these three issues will likely lead to a substantial redrafting of the Department of Interior's rules for natural resource damage assessments.

Interest in CV applications has given rise to much research. Recent studies, for example, have used CV to estimate the value of wetlands protection (Loomis et al, 1991), water quality improvements (Desvousges et al, 1987), groundwater (Mitchell and Carson, 1989), and forest wildlife resources (Walsh et al, 1990).[2] On the other hand, much has been written about problems with CV techniques: they capture attitudinal intentions rather than behaviour (Ajzen and Peterson, 1988), important information is omitted from CV questionnaires (Fischhoff and Furby, 1988), and their results are susceptible to influence from cognitive and contextual biases (Brown and Slovic, 1988).

Note: Reprinted from *Journal of Risk and Uncertainty*, vol 7, Gregory, R., Lichtenstein, S. and Slovic, P., 'Valuing environmental resources: A constructive approach', pp177–197, copyright © (1993), with permission from Kluwer Academic Publishers

One response to these criticisms is to argue that CV methods can provide valid estimates of resource values if studies are done carefully. This is the position taken by many practitioners of CV methods (e.g. Randall et al, 1983; Brookshire and Coursey, 1987) and by the NOAA Panel on Contingent Valuation (Arrow et al, 1993). Several prominent critics of current CV methods also argue for greater care in application; for example, Fischhoff and Furby (1988) provided detailed listings of the information needed to inform CV participants sufficiently about the assigned payment task, the social context for evaluation and the good under consideration.

In contrast, others view these problems as casting doubt on the accuracy of CV responses and the usefulness of even the most carefully conducted CV results in litigation and damage assessments. Indeed, some reject CV as a method for obtaining monetary values of unpriced environmental goods. For example, Phillips and Zeckhauser (1989) questioned whether any CV study will be able to meet standard criteria of reliability and validity. Kahneman and Knetsch (1992) have argued that CV responses denote moral sentiments rather than economic values.

We believe there is a need for monetary assessments of environmental damages and that an evaluation approach based on an individual's expressed preferences is appropriate for this purpose. However, we believe that the holistic measures of monetary value used in current CV methods are flawed because they impose unrealistic cognitive demands upon respondents. In our view, improved methods for valuing nonmarket natural resources can be found by paying closer attention to the multidimensional nature of environmental values and to the constructive nature of human preferences (Gregory and McDaniels, 1987). The underlying assumption of the approach to be discussed in this article is that people have strong feelings, beliefs and values for many things that are not sold through markets (Brown, 1984). However, people's cognitive beliefs about these values typically are not numerically quantified and, most importantly for CV, are not represented monetarily.

The fact that people are not used to thinking about environmental goods in monetary units suggests that a CV approach must function as a kind of tutorial, building the monetary value as it elicits it. We therefore view a CV survey as an active process of value construction (Tversky et al, 1988), rather than as a neutral process of value discovery. Thus, we believe, the designers of a CV study should function not as archaeologists, carefully uncovering what is there, but as architects, working to build a defensible expression of value.

In this article, we first argue that CV methods need to be changed to accommodate the constructive nature of environmental preferences. We then propose criteria to guide the selection of a defensible environmental-values-elicitation method. Next, we examine the possibility of developing a new CV method based on techniques derived from multi-attribute utility theory and decision analysis. Finally, we explain why we believe this new approach will help to solve several of the most vexing problems confronting practitioners and interpreters of environmental policy and valuation studies.

The Constructive Nature of Environmental Preferences

Almost four decades ago, a seminal article by Edwards (1954) introduced psychologists and other Behavioural scientists to theories of decision making and empirical methods for quantifying individuals' preferences. This intellectual enterprise has burgeoned into *behavioural decision theory* (Edwards, 1961; Einhorn and Hogarth, 1981) or *behavioural decision research* (Payne et al, 1992). A major objective of researchers in this field has been to understand the nature of human preferences and values and to develop defensible ways to measure them.

One focus of behavioural decision research has been to clarify the role of judgemental rules of thumb, or heuristics, which are used to simplify complex judgements. These heuristics, such as anchoring on a starting point or relying on easily imaginable information, can be useful and even necessary, but also can lead to systematic biases and errors in judgement (Kahneman et al, 1982). Another focus of this work has been to demonstrate the strong influence of context on measures of preference and value. As a result, decision scientists seeking to elicit values have recognized that order effects, the range and mixture of items being evaluated, the amount and nature of information provided about each item, the method of elicitation, and many other contextual factors can affect the results of any serious elicitation attempt.

This research had lead to a perspective that we shall call 'the constructive nature of preference'. This perspective has strong implications for the theory and practice of CV.

Consider, for example, the phenomenon of preference reversal, which has been studied by psychologists and economists for more than 20 years (Lichtenstein and Slovic, 1971; Grether and Plott, 1979; Tversky et al, 1990). Dozens of empirical studies, using gambles as well as many other stimuli (Slovic et al, 1990), have demonstrated preference reversals: Object A is clearly preferred over Object B under one method of measurement, while B is clearly preferred under a different but presumably equivalent measurement procedure.

Reversals of preference induced by changes in response mode have begun to appear in CV studies. Brown (1984) examined dollar and rating responses of subjects' willingness to pay (WTP) for environmental amenities (air quality and forest scenic quality) and commodities (cameras, cars, stereos and bicycles). Most subjects were willing to pay more for the commodities than for the amenities when giving their answers in dollars, but most rated their willingness to pay for the amenities higher than their willingness to pay for the commodities. Similarly, Viscusi et al (1986) found that people's values for reducing the risks from chemical products were higher when they were given paired comparisons (i.e. choices) than when they were asked to provide WTP values. Irwin et al (1993) conducted several studies showing preference reversals in WTP. These studies involved comparisons of improvements in consumer goods, such as a better camera or a better VCR, with improvements in air quality. Their successful prediction of preference reversals, whereby WTP based on a single-stimulus response favoured improvements in consumer goods and WTP based on a choice response favoured improvements in air quality, was based on two judgement effects found in the decision-making literature: the compatibility effect (Slovic et al, 1990), and the prominence effect (Tversky et al, 1988).

Findings of preference reversals involving environmental values provide strong evidence for the constructive nature of preference. As Tversky et al (1988) observed:

> In the classical analysis, the relation of preference is inferred from observed responses and is assumed to reflect the decision maker's underlying utility or value. But if different elicitation procedures produce different orderings of options, how can preferences and values be defined? And in what sense do they exist? (p383)

The significance of changes in context on a person's expressed preferences supports this constructive view of values. For example, an attribute that would otherwise be of minor importance is more heavily weighed if all the objects are clearly described in terms of that attribute, when other attribute descriptions are incomplete (Slovic and McPhillamy, 1974). Huber (1980) showed that decision processes were influenced by whether information was presented in numerical or verbal form. Gaeth and Shanteau (1984) showed that inclusion of irrelevant information impaired judgement. Many context effects are grouped under the label *framing effects* (Tversky and Kahneman, 1981; Hogarth, 1982). For example, calling a sure loss 'insurance' makes it more palatable (Slovic et al, 1982). Tversky and Kahneman's oft-cited 'Asian disease' problem (1981) showed a reversal of preference when the wording of two public-health problems was framed in terms of 'saving lives' versus a 'loss of life' framing.

Not all the research on context effects applies directly to CV. All, however (and we have cited only a sampling above), reinforce the view that people are not just reporting their values or preferences. Instead, they are constructing them, with whatever help or cues the circumstances provide.

The economists' prevailing response to preference construction is that holistic measures of value can be trusted but separate values for components cannot (e.g. Randall, 1986; Freeman, 1989). Yet this view, that people can aggregate values but cannot partition them, flies in the face of the decision-making literature. This literature tells us that, when faced with complex values, people often resort to simplifying strategies; Payne et al (1992) have oriented their extensive review around this theme. Moreover, simplifying strategies increase when the complexity of the stimuli increases (Johnson et al, 1989). Studies have found that people typically are unaware of their simplifications, and that when people are asked to make holistic judgements about multidimensional stimuli, they typically make use of fewer cues than they say they do (Slovic and Lichtenstein, 1971). In short, the more complex a decision problem, the more likely that expressions of value will be constructed based on only a subset of the available information. Dawes (1977), for example, reviewed both this literature and the findings that simple combinations of judged parts accurately predict known wholes, and recommended just the opposite – namely, trust the values obtained from decomposition procedures more than those obtained from holistic judgements.

An important corollary of the constructive view is that the strong values that people hold for environmental goods are not represented in their minds in monetary form. Consider all the goods that we might want to value in dollar terms. These could be arrayed on a continuum according to the level of market experience that we have with them. At one extreme would be goods such as groceries, for which market experience is great and the strength of our values or preferences can be relatively easily represented by a market price. As we move from groceries to appliances, automobiles and homes, market experience lessens and the ease of representing our preferences monetarily declines as well. For goods such as air or water quality, wilderness areas, endangered species and many other elements of the natural environment, the market no longer applies, and the link between values and money becomes tenuous – so tenuous that it may not exist. Thus, we can have strongly held values that are not at all coded mentally in terms of dollars. Attempts to translate such values into monetary equivalents must take special cognizance of this problem.

One demonstration of the absence of a monetary representation for values comes from a study by Slovic et al (1979) that asked people to evaluate the social seriousness of a death from specified causes (e.g. smoking, alcoholism, nuclear-power accidents) by equating each death with a monetary loss. This was done by asking the respondents to compare a death from each cause to a standard unit of loss to society. In one condition, this standard loss was $1,000,000; in a second condition (with a new group of respondents) this standard loss was $10,000. Respondents were asked to provide a multiplying or dividing factor to indicate how many times greater (or smaller) the specified death (e.g. a cancer death) was in comparison to the standard.

The geometric-mean responses ranged in orderly fashion from smoking and alcohol-caused deaths at the low end, judged less serious than the standard, to death from pesticides and nuclear-power accidents at the extreme high end of the distribution. The correlation between the means in the two conditions, across 34 causes of death, was 0.94. Notably, the mean responses (i.e. the multiplying factors) were almost identical in the two groups, despite the 100-fold difference in the comparison standard. For example, the mean for an alcohol-caused death was 0.91 for the $1,000,000 standard, and 0.89 for the $10,000 standard. In other words, the responses were almost perfectly consistent across the 34 items, but the dollar values implied by the responses differed by a factor of 100. Although there may be other explanations, these results can be interpreted as indicating that the seriousness of deaths from specified causes differed reliably across causes but was not represented monetarily in our respondents' minds.

We believe that the absence of any monetary representation is a principal cause of the *embedding* (or *part/whole*) effect observed by both CV proponents (e.g. Mitchell and Carson, 1989) and critics (Kahneman and Knetsch, 1992), whereby the same good is assigned a lower value when it is inferred from WTP for a more inclusive good than if the good is evaluated on its own. For example, Kahneman and Knetsch report that the willingness of Toronto residents to pay to maintain fishing by cleaning up the lakes in a small area of Ontario was almost as great as their willingness to pay to maintain fishing in all Ontario lakes. They replicated this finding for a diverse set of public goods. Kahneman and Knetsch interpreted their findings as indicating that the 'good' that subjects are willing to pay for in these studies is a 'sense of moral satisfaction' which exhibits an embedding effect – the satisfaction associated with contributing to an inclusive cause extends with little loss to any significant subset of that cause. Alternative explanations are that the subjects in these studies were not sensitive to the differences in the descriptions of the goods or that the subjects had no well-defined monetary representation of value for the goods.

Desirable Features of an Environmental-values-elicitation Approach

What are the characteristics of a good, defensible method for eliciting environmental values? The ultimate criterion is validity: a method clearly measures only what it is supposed to measure. Cronbach and Meehl (1955), in an article that has become a classic to psychologists, discussed four types of validity of which three are relevant to CV methods, namely, predictive, concurrent and constructive validity.[3] *Predictive* and *concurrent* validity refer to the close relationships between the measure and a criterion of known validity (they differ only in timing; predictive validity involves comparison with a future criterion; concurrent validity involves a present criterion). Economic theory posits just such a criterion of known validity, that is, unrestrained market prices at equilibrium. Unfortunately, CV methods are intended for use precisely in those situations for which no market exists.

Construct validity is thus the concept underlying tests of CVs validity. 'A construct is defined implicitly by a network of associations or propositions in which it occurs... Construct validation is possible only when some of the statements in the network lead to predicted relations among observables' (Cronbach and Meehl, pp299–300). Economic theory, in which the construct of contingent valuation is embedded, generously satisfies these requirements.

Construct validity is not sought via one definitive study but in the integration of evidence from many different sources. The finding that CV methods roughly match market values when they are applied, experimentally, to situations in which market values exist (Bishop and Heberlein, 1979; Dickie et al, 1987) is one such piece of evidence favouring construct validity. Other evidence comes from comparisons of different assessment methods, such as comparing risk/risk to risk/money trade-offs (Viscusi et al, 1991) or comparing direct WTP responses to results from travel cost or hedonic (indirect) techniques (e.g. Brookshire et al, 1982; Smith et al, 1986). Such studies have shown agreement among measures within a range of about ±50 per cent (Cummings et al, 1986). Although a 50 per cent margin of error might appal a polluter presented with a bill for damages under CERCLA, such findings do help to build the case for construct validity.

But construct validity also requires negative findings. If the method is valid, variables that *should not* affect the results *do not*. Here conventional CV methods fare poorly. First, there is a widely observed disparity between the maximum amount that people are willing to pay to acquire a good and the minimum amount that they are willing to accept (WTA) to give it up. The observed difference between WTP and WTA is not, as economic theory would predict, small (most persuasively shown by Kahneman et al, 1990; see also Bishop and Heberlein, 1979; Knetsch and Sinden, 1984). Moreover, as noted earlier, the change from a WTP to a choice-response mode induces reversals in the preference ordering of an environmental improvement versus a market-commodity improvement (Irwin et al, 1993). Such findings contradict economic theory and thus seriously threaten the construct validity of WTP-based CV methods.

We are not surprised by these validity-threatening findings, for underlying the search for validity are the assumptions that monetary values for nonmarket goods really do exist and that researchers can find appropriate ways to measure them. In contrast, we hold that such values do *not* exist in monetary form. Instead, they are created during the elicitation process. Thus value formation is intimately tied to the specifics of the elicitation procedures. Following Simon's well-known distinction between procedural and substantive rationality (1978), we therefore present five process criteria that, if satisfied, can be used to defend the goodness of a CV method.[4]

Criterion 1: Accommodate the multidimensionality of value

Early work in behavioural decision research provides abundant evidence that people form judgements on the basis of multiple attributes and dimensions (Hammond et al, 1980). Moreover, there is a robust basis, in both economics and decision theory, for this perspective (Lancaster, 1966; Keeney and Raiffa, 1976). The multidimensionality of values for environmental goods is symbolized by the 'multiple use' concept that guides the resource-management policies of federal agencies such as the US Forest Service. Bishop (1986) presents categories of economic benefits from the environment that include both consumptive and nonconsumptive user benefits, as well as several classes of nonuser values. Environmental philosophers (e.g. Rolston, 1981) have distinguished a large number of dimensions that can be used to characterize environmental goods, including scientific, aesthetic, biodiversity, religious, symbolic and life-support values, in addition to economic and recreational values.

The complexity and multidimensionality of environmental values necessitate that a value-elicitation-method be sensitive to this diversity of values. Yet a good CV method also must recognize the difficulties people have in thinking about such complexities. The experimental evidence previously described indicates that even when all aspects of all alternatives are fully described, people find it difficult to make explicit trade-offs and typically rely on cognitive strategies that result in discounting or neglecting some important aspects.

The typical CV task goes one step further, that is, a holistic response is requested for a single stimulus presented, without either an explicit listing of the relevant dimensions of value or a description of the stimulus on each dimension. Because what is out of sight may be out of mind (Fischhoff et al, 1978), this situation can be expected to lead to the greatest distortions in the expression of multidimensional values. Gregory et al (1992) have shown that open-ended, holistic WTP responses were poorly correlated across a number of market and nonmarket goods, with several value-relevant attributes. Is this so surprising? In most elicitation settings, people have had no experience in thinking about the structure – the multiple dimensions or attributes – of their values. How can people think clearly about the big picture when they cannot distinguish clearly among the components?

We realize that some recent CV studies have used focus groups to examine the multiple attributes of value. Recent CV booklets typically also extensively describe the proposed project or even present two possible projects, not only described in the text but also shown in a paired-comparison chart of attributes (thus aiding the respondent to make a richer consideration). We applaud these improvements. However, the central problem remains: Holistic responses to complex stimuli are not sufficiently sensitive to multidimensionality, because they require respondents to make difficult, unaided trade-offs across attributes.

Criterion 2: Minimize response refusals

Response refusals are a common problem in CV studies (Mitchell and Carson, 1989). Stevens et al (1991), for example, reported that over 80 per cent of the participants in their recent CV survey in Massachusetts said that bald eagles, wild turkeys and Atlantic salmon are very or somewhat important to them, but a majority of respondents (62–64 per cent) would not pay any money to maintain these same populations. Forty per cent of the refusers protested the payment vehicle, and 25 per cent refused to pay for ethical reasons. Irwin et al (1990) and other researchers have reported similar findings. Elegant methods have been proposed for estimating the missing WTP values (McClelland et al, 1991). However, a better CV approach should avoid this vexing problem.

Criterion 3: Exclude irrelevancies

If a CV study were intended to predict, for example, the results of a public vote on funding for a project, then any attribute value that will affect how people vote should properly be expressed in the study. However, contingent valuations are often needed for situations in which some aspects of value, even if strongly held, are legally or ethically irrelevant. For example, we conjecture that an individual's willingness to pay to restore a damaged habitat or to accept compensation for an environmental loss will be strongly affected by the source of the damage (e.g. a natural cause versus a careless spill by a detested chemical company). Legally, however, this attribute (who is to blame) is irrelevant under CERCLA. A good CV method should allow the exclusion of such attributes. This is difficult, if not impossible, for holistic-response methods like WTP or WTA.

Criterion 4: Separate facts from values

Defensible measures of value require respondents who have knowledge of the good under consideration, as well as knowledge of their preferences with regard to the good. For simple goods or for activities with which people have extensive experience, it makes sense to assume that the respondents are competent to assess both facts and values. However, many of the proposed environmental changes that form the subject of CV studies are scientifically complex. In such cases, a good CV method should not require that respondents have a thorough understanding of the scientific complexities in order to express their preferences.

For example, people may value species preservation. Suppose a proposed project will save 100 pairs of a threatened bird species. It is the experts who must provide the translation from the fact of saving 100 pairs of birds to the value-relevant scientific estimate of the associated change in the probability that the bird species will not become extinct. It is not reasonable to assume that respondents will know how to make such translations.

Criterion 5: Ask the right question

The usual CV study asks a WTP question, such as 'How much would you be willing to pay each year in higher prices or increased taxes for...?' or 'Would you be willing to pay US\$X each year in higher prices or increased taxes for...?' (with US\$X varied across respondents). Questions based on willingness to accept (WTA) payment for some loss are less common, because refusal rates are considerably higher, and because average responses seem unduly large (Cummings et al, 1986; Kahneman et al, 1990).

Consider the case where a factory discharges pollutants into a lake, causing environmental damage. The relevant question under CERCLA is: How much should the damager pay? The general answer is that the damager is required under CERCLA to pay that amount necessary to restore or replace the lost resources (Kopp et al, 1990). Let us suppose that this is done to the extent reasonably possible, but that the repair takes some time and is not complete. Then the damager is liable both for losses from the time the damage occurs until the time the repair (whether by nature or by humans) is finished and for losses that cannot be repaired. How should a CV study assess the value of these losses?

This is a typical question and an important one for environmental policy analysis. However, WTP or WTA seems to us inappropriate for this question because it is not the responsibility of the respondent to pay for the damage. There are two separate points here. First, the request to pay for damages to the natural environment brings up the question of an individual's entitlement. If ownership of the resource (e.g. good water quality) forms part of a people's status quo assets, then why should they pay for what they already have a right to? The appropriate response is a refusal to pay. Second, under CERCLA, payment is the responsibility of the damager. Clearly, for some types of environmental damage, such as a widespread degradation of water quality caused by many damagers, the responsibility may effectively fall upon us all. Whether we like it or not, consumer prices or taxes will pay for the clean-up. But even in such cases, it is likely that many people will deny the responsibility. This denial seems to underlie the large percentage of refusals in many CV studies of damaged resources.

In the factory discharge considered here, the damager is clearly liable. Thus, we must consider WTA. However, if you, the respondent, ask for too much money – so that your demand is refused – what will happen? The essence of any WTP or WTA question is a trade-off of some sort between money and a good. But here we are evaluating unrestorable losses. If you are not paid, there will still be a loss; there is no compensating event in the no-exchange alternative that provides a balance against which you can weigh your WTA. Lacking such restraint, why not go for the moon?

It is tempting, in such cases, to ask a different question, such as, 'How much would you pay to avoid a future spill like this one?' But this is, indeed, the wrong question, not only because it denies the true structure of the problem, but also because the respondents are thereby limited by their own ability to pay; whereas the real situation depends upon the damager's ability to pay.

We have now trapped ourselves inside an uncomfortable box. WTP forms of CV questions are inappropriate for CERCLA cases, because they lack the proper structure. WTA forms of CV questions are inappropriate for practical reasons. The usual way out of this conundrum for CV practitioners is to employ WTP questions anyway, perhaps with an apology. However, this apologetic stance strikes us as unfortunate, because there is no reason why *any* measure of people's WTP needs to be obtained directly. Rather, what needs to be known for purposes of CERCLA is the monetary value people place on the damaged good.

This brings us to the central argument for a new approach to eliciting values for environmental resources. If values are constructed during the elicitation process in a way that is strongly determined by context and has profound effects on the resultant evaluations, we should take a deliberate approach to value construction in a manner designed to rationalize the process.

Using Multiattribute Utility Theory in Resource Valuations

We believe that there already exists a sound, formal approach to value construction that can provide the basis for an improved CV method. This approach draws on the techniques and practices of multiattribute utility theory.

Multiattribute utility theory (MAUT) underlies the practice of decision analysis and specifies, axiomatically, the conditions under which one can sensibly attach numbers to values. MAUT and decision analysis are systematic procedures designed to assist people in making choices in the presence of conflicting objectives and uncertainty. They are 'a formalization of common sense for decision problems that are too complex for informal use of common sense' (Keeney, 1982). Detailed descriptions of MAUT and decision analysis are given by Keeney (1980) and by von Winterfeldt and Edwards (1986).

MAUT is essentially a set of axiomatic theories of preference (Keeney and Raiffa, 1976). The central theorem of each theory says that if people can make choices based on their preferences and if these choices satisfy the axioms, then one can (a) assign numbers to utilities or values (we will use these terms as synonymous) and (b) specify a rule for combining the numbers into a summary measure, such that an object with a larger summary measure is preferred over an object with a smaller summary measure. The measurement scale underlying these utilities is not cardinal; it does not have an invariant zero point. But it is stronger than ordinal, because the ordering of differences between the measures, as well as the ordering of the measures, is invariant. Psychologists call such a scale an *interval* scale (Stevens, 1951).

The most helpful aspect of decision analysis is its ability to formally express subjective judgements in the assessment of alternatives and to establish an explicit framework for integrating the multidimensional components of complex values. However, some further development of these techniques will be needed to use decision analysis as the basis for improvements in CV methods. This is because the purpose of MAUT and decision analysis is to promote insight to help decision makers make choices among alternative plans of action. The purpose of a MAUT-based approach to CV would be more specific – namely, to provide dollar-based evaluations of specific nonmarket goods or programmes.

Proposed approach

The general approach required in a multiattribute CV (MAUT/CV) analysis can be described as a sequence of four steps.

1 Structure the problem. In this step, the analyst collects, lists and organizes a description of the problem, identifying all the attributes (that is, all the aspects of the problem that have value to people). The goal is to develop an explicit, comprehensive picture of all factors that contribute significantly to the value of the good or activity. To do so, the analyst will consult both technical experts, to get the facts, and the affected citizenry, to find the link between the facts and the values.

This structuring process differs in two respects from the usual practice of CV. First, the value attributes are made explicit. The usual CV study, in contrast, describes the situation to be evaluated without such an explicit listing. The respondent is assumed to know all attributes of value or to infer them from descriptions in the questionnaire booklet. Second, a MAUT/CV would rely on the affected citizenry to elucidate the attributes of value. This step, which precedes the elicitation of values, has typically been omitted in CV. The value attributes implicit in the usual CV study come from experts in the topic of concern or from the study authors, rather than directly from the affected citizenry (although recently the increasing use of focus groups is mitigating this problem).

In a MAUT/CV, diverse groups of people should be consulted to select the value attributes. These *stakeholders* are defined in an operational sense as groups of people who, for any reason (e.g. place of residence, occupation, favoured activities), share common values or opinions regarding a proposed action (Edwards and von Winterfeldt, 1987). The MAUT/CV analyst might convene three to ten stakeholder groups, each composed of three to seven people; from each group, a values structure is elicited. Careful selection of stakeholder groups ensures that the full range of views is adequately covered. For example, the representatives of an environmental advocacy organization might be expected to present a somewhat different list of attributes than would members of the local Chamber of Commerce, but the views of these two groups are likely to encompass those of many other citizens.

In a complex problem, the expressed attributes will vary in level of generality, and, therefore, often can be structured hierarchically into a value 'tree'. The eventual goal is to find a single hierarchy of values that all the shareholders can agree is complete. This values hierarchy must also be built with due concern for the form of the utility combination rule. The simplest such rule is additive; one adds all the utilities of the lowest-level scales to find the total utility. This combination rule requires value independence: the value of one level of one attribute must not depend upon what the levels are on the other attributes. The decision analyst must probe frequently for value independence; lack of independence may signal an additional, unreported attribute of value.

The finished values hierarchy may have components using causal models, economic models, influence or means/ends diagrams and so forth, showing the linkages between specific measures at the bottom and the abstract attributes at the top. Depending on the situation, some components may have probabilities explicitly built into the model, so that the final utility calculation will be an expected utility.

Suppose that someone wanted to do a MAUT/CV study of the monetary value of the damage resulting from a specific pollutant dumped into Lake Michigan. Technical experts can provide information describing the lake before and after the damage. These descriptions then can be presented to representatives of the people affected by the damage to identify the value attributes. For example, the physical event of the death of a large number of fish might imply aesthetic loss (when the dead fish wash up on the shore), loss of genetic diversity and loss of commercial fishing jobs and profits. These losses indicate the value attributes.

Generic attributes for the lake problem might be Effects on Scenic Beauty, Effects on Genetic Diversity, Human Health Effects, Effects on Commerce and so forth. Each attribute would have subattributes. For example, subattributes influencing Effects on

Commerce might be Real Estate Values (the price of vacation homes would go down if the shore line becomes ugly), Tourist Values and Entitlement (expressing the general public's nonuse value for a beautiful lake). Some or all of these subattributes might be further broken down into sub-subattributes, and so forth, until all relevant values have been listed and organized. At the lowest level, each attribute is described in terms of some specific measure. For example, one subcomponent of Scenic Beauty concerned with shoreline attractiveness might have as its bottom-level measure the number of dead fish per acre of beach.

2 Assess utilities. A typical CV study elicits values from a random sample of the affected citizenry; WTP responses are given by hundreds or thousands of people. In contrast, an approach based in decision analysis would elicit utilities (values) from the stakeholder groups, fewer than 100 people. Depth of value analysis is substituted for breadth of population sampling.

Utilities are assessed for every lowest-level value scale. To start with, it is convenient to assess every utility on a common scale, say, from 0 to 100. For example, the maximum number of dead fish per acre on Lake Michigan beaches as a result of our hypothetical pollutant spill might be assigned a utility score of 100, and the minimum impact level, perhaps 0 dead fish per acre, would be assigned a score of 0. It is essential that this range of outcomes be carefully specified, that the range encompasses all reasonably possible values for the attribute measure, and that this range, once chosen, remains fixed throughout the analysis. Trade-offs are then assessed, using weights or multiplicative factors that rescale the utilities in recognition that not all attributes of value are equally important.

All these value elicitations would be done with numerous consistency checks. If you have told the analyst that a change from 0 to 100 on scale A is twice as good as a change from 0 to 100 on scale B, and that a change from 0 to 100 on scale B is four times as good as such a change on scale C, the analyst will then check to see that you do, indeed, believe that the scale A change is eight times as good as the scale C change.

3 Calculate the total value. Once all the pieces are in place, the combination rule specifies how to calculate the total utility for any particular plan, programme or scenario. This total utility will be expressed using a single arbitrary 'utile' unit of measurement. For contingent valuation, these units must be converted to dollars. In theory, this conversion need only be made at one place in the model. For example, one such conversion might be made in the Lake Michigan pollution example by noting the monetary value and the utility (or, here, disutility) of the loss of one ton of fish to one fishery. Because all utilities, including this one, are measured on a common scale, the monetary worth of all utilities, including the total utility, can be computed from this one conversion. In practice, of course, one would want to find several parts of the model for which both utilities and their monetary equivalents are known (e.g. real estate values, perhaps even the value of a life).

4 Perform sensitivity analysis. The final step required in performing a MAUT/CV analysis would be to recalculate the final utility, using variations in the utilities and trade-offs, to see how sensitive the final answer is to such variations (Merkhofer and Keeney, 1987). Sensitivity analyses performed on a first-draft MAUT/CV might be used to show which aspects should, because of their strong effect upon the total, be subjected to additional stakeholder elicitations or to large-scale sampling of public values.

Different stakeholder groups can be expected to produce different utilities and trade-offs; thus, the total monetary value may differ across groups. Sensitivity analysis will reveal the most important causes of these disagreements. The analyst can then return to each of the stakeholder groups to explore the possibility that small changes in their utilities and trade-offs would be acceptable to the group, yet produce a total value more similar to the total value calculated for other groups. Although there is some encouraging evidence (Gardiner and Edwards, 1975) that the use of MAUT diminishes the disagreement between highly polarized groups, further research is needed to explore the conditions under which a single monetary value can be found that adequately expresses the values of all stakeholders.

Advantages and disadvantages of MAUT/CV

The linkage of MAUT to contingent-valuation approaches will not be an all-purpose panacea. However, we believe that use of a MAUT-based approach to CV offers some strong advantages and possible solutions to several of the most troubling problems confronting environmental researchers. We start by discussing MAUT/CV in terms of the five evaluative criteria discussed above. We then comment on other advantages and disadvantages of a multiattribute CV approach.

1 Accommodates the multidimensionality of value. The judgements required as inputs to a MAUT/CV model will not be easy ones to make. But they are not holistic judgements, requiring the simultaneous integration of many dimensions of value. Thus, it is less likely that important aspects of value will be lost because of cognitive overload. Most importantly, the values that guide a MAUT/CV study will be elicited from a wide range of the potentially affected stakeholders. These stakeholders have a right to express their values as part of an open, constructive decision-aiding process.

2 Minimizes response refusals. MAUT measures value without regard to the problem of who must pay, an issue that can be decided in the voting booth or by the courts. To the extent that this problem underlies response refusals, a multiattribute CV procedure should reduce or eliminate the problem.

One obstacle to incorporating MAUT techniques is an ethical concern, stemming from the quantification of utilities for various goods and activities. Recognizing distinctions among value components and putting numbers on values is not easy, and, to some members of the public, it may be repugnant (MacGregor and Slovic, 1986). The argument can be made that the assignment of numerical values only makes clear the trade-offs that otherwise would be made implicitly rather than explicitly. For some, this logic will be soothing; for others, however, any process requiring quantification is likely to remain questionable.

A further source of response refusals may arise from the extreme stances taken by different groups of stakeholders in a politically potent CV situation. Some stakeholder groups may refuse to participate for political or strategic reasons or because they distrust the agency conducting the study. In such situations, success may rest on the analyst's ability to convince respondents that cooperation in expressing their values will have a genuine impact on the results and that response refusals unfortunately may lead to the omission of their point of view.

3 Excludes irrelevancies. A MAUT/CV model would explicitly list the sources of value. Thus, a MAUT-based CV approach would address the real issues in the problem and permit in-depth examination of the factual and values bases for concern. If irrelevant attributes are proposed in the problem-structuring stage, the analyst can either completely exclude them from the model or include them as separate aspects whose effects on the total value can later be calculated.

4 Separates facts from values. Conducting a multiattribute CV study requires extensive knowledge about the facts of a problem and detailed elicitations of people's values. But the method allows the analyst to distinguish facts from values; stakeholders are asked to determine the components of value; experts then make the factual contributions to understand impact pathways and magnitudes. Thus, the people whose values are sought do not need to understand scientific complexities in order to express their values. Instead, their values are expressed in numerous pieces, with each piece selected to be a readily understandable measure.

5 Asks the right question. There are many occasions when the financial ability of a population of people provides an appropriate and sensible limit on their willingness to pay and thus on their contingent valuation for some situation. This occurs, for example, when tax monies will be dedicated to a specific project. But often people's ability to pay is irrelevant to the contingent valuation problem. One prominent example is CERCLA cases, in which the goal of the valuation enterprise is to determine the monetary payment that must be made by a polluter. Here, MAUT has a distinct advantage in avoiding willingness to pay as a measure of value; it asks the right question: How valuable is this?

6 Other advantages and disadvantages:

Integrates market and nonmarket values. Neither values for which extensive, competitive markets exist nor diffuse, vague, but strongly-held values get an advantage in a MAUT model. Economic models can be subsumed into the model where appropriate. Explicit and simple measures can be sought for vague and diffuse nonmarket values. The strength of the approach is that the model can integrate these different kinds of values.

Lessens the embedding problem. There may be several causes of the embedding problem. Earlier in this article, we suggested that the absence of a monetary representation for a good may be a principal reason for embedding. In this case, the use of a MAUT-based approach to CV should help, because it will assist people to structure their monetary values in a defensible manner. Kahneman and Knetsch (1992) suggest a second cause, which is that people are not really responding to the specific problem but are reporting a general willingness to donate money to good causes. Because spending money is not directly the focus of MAUT elicitations, this source of embedding would not occur.

A third cause for embedding is that people may be trying to respond to the given problem, but are unable to be sufficiently sensitive to its specifications (e.g. 2000 dead fish, not 4000 dead fish) because of its complexity (see Fischhoff et al, 1993; or Loomis et al, 1993). Two characteristics of a MAUT/CV method should increase such sensitivity. First, MAUT elicitation methods are decompositional and therefore do not require people to juggle many aspects of value at the same time. Second, the utility for each attribute is elicited across an entire range; respondents are, for example, asked to provide scale values separately for 2000 fish and for 4000 fish. It is hardly credible that in such a situation the respondents would give the same utility regardless of the number.

Irwin et al (1990) have described a related form of the embedding problem that seems to 'derive from people's beliefs about non-independence'. They report approximately the same WTP for *health* improvements due to cleaner air, *visibility* improvements and *all* improvements, apparently because the respondents assumed that any air cleaning leading to better health inevitably would also lead to better visibility, even though the researchers did not mention it. In the MAUT method, any such beliefs about non-independence would be discovered in the structuring stage; the model would be adjusted to accommodate them.

Flexible in changing circumstances. A MAUT/CV model would elicit a broad range of values for each attribute. As a result, the information would be available, so that the calculations could be redone if the circumstances changed. Changing circumstances that add new elements to the problem, of course, would require further modelling and new elicitations. But in most cases such changes would involve a small portion of the whole analysis, most of which would not need redoing.

Suitable for construction. We have presented the view that people have not formed monetary values for many complex, nonmarket goods such as environmental improvements. Thus, a successful CV method should help the respondents to think carefully and thoroughly about what they value in order to *form* their values. A MAUT/CV approach would provide the setting for such extensive consideration, in both its structuring and its valuing phases.

Every value-elicitation method affects the values being elicited. So a MAUT-based method surely will. We cannot know the exact effects it would exert on people's values. But the process and results of a MAUT/CV would be explicitly recorded and thus open to scrutiny. In contrast to a WTP or a WTA study, one would be far less troubled by wondering what the respondents were and were not taking into consideration when expressing their values.

Cost. As far as we know, MAUT never has been used for contingent valuation of environmental resources. The first few exemplars might cost more than WTP studies now do, because MAUT techniques would have to be adjusted and developed to meet CV applications, whereas WTP techniques already have been extensively developed. After that, we do not know. Recent developments in CV practice (e.g. the use of focus groups and avoidance of collecting data by mail, as urged by Arrow et al, 1993) suggest that the cost of WTP assessments is increasing; this trend may eliminate any cost difference between WTP and MAUT approaches to CV.

A related concern derives from the required expertise: a MAUT/CV analysis would require the analyst to participate in the entire elicitation procedure with each stakeholder group. One of the criticisms often levelled at MAUT techniques is that their application requires as much art as science at a time when resources are scarce and there are few accomplished practitioners. However, the practice of a MAUT/CV effort strikes us as no more demanding or subjective than the practice of conventional CV or, for that matter, benefit–cost analysis (Gregory et al, 1992).

Conclusion

Recent evidence from behavioural decision research casts a perspective on contextual effects that goes beyond bias and challenges traditional views of the nature and stability of environmental preferences and values. According to this view, preferences and values for objects that are unfamiliar and complex are often constructed, rather than revealed, in the elicitation process.

We believe that the concept of constructed preferences has important implications for the dollar-based measurement of environmental values. Environmental resources typically are complex goods that are valued across a number of diverse dimensions and that have not been thought about in quantitative terms, let alone dollar terms. Holistic measures of monetary value, as have been used in most CV studies, ignore these cognitive realities and require people to engage in a task that exceeds their capabilities. We propose that practitioners, rather than giving up on the attempt, adopt explicit value-structuring techniques that will link CV efforts with multiattribute utility theory and decision analysis. This new CV method has the potential to eliminate many of the most vexing problems of conventional CV approaches and provide defensible monetary measures of environmental values.

Notes

The authors gratefully acknowledge that this material is based upon work supported by the Decision, Risk and Management Science Program of the National Science Foundation under Grant Nos SES 88–12707 and SES 90–22952 to Decision Research. We thank Ward Edwards, Charles Howe, John Kadvany, Ralph Keeney, Julie Irwin, John Payne and Detlof von Winterfeldt for their insightful comments on an earlier draft of this manuscript. Any opinions, findings and conclusions or recommendations expressed in this article are those of the authors and do not necessarily reflect the views of the National Science Foundation.

1   Despite the many references in the literature to 'the Contingent Valuation Method' (e.g. Mitchell and Carson, 1989), CV is a conceptual approach which, in application, employs a variety of methods.

2   WTP techniques also are used to value human health and safety (Jones-Lee et al, 1985; Viscusi and Magat, 1987); however, this paper focuses on the evaluation of environmental resources rather than the WTP research on health and safety issues.

3   The fourth, *content* validity, applies only to testing situations. To assess the content validity of a typing test, for example, one would show that the test is an appropriate sample of the universe of typing skills.

4   We do not claim that these are the only criteria to be considered. Several nonprocess criteria also merit consideration, such as legitimacy, standardization (are the same techniques used every time?), and consistency (do similar people respond similarly?). However, our focus in this article is on the key process criteria that will help people to construct their values.

References

1   Ajzen, I. and Peterson, G. L. (1988) 'Contingent value measurement: The price of every-thing and the value of nothing?' in Peterson, George L., Driver, B. L. and Gregory, R. (eds) *Amenity Resource Valuation: Integrating Economics with Other Disciplines.* Venture, State College, PA, pp65–76

2   Arrow, K., Solow, R., Portney, P. R., Learner, E. E., Radner, R. and Schuman, H. (1993) *Report of the NOAA Panel on Contingent Valuation.* National Oceanic and Atmospheric Administration, Washington, DC, January 12

3   Bishop, R. (1986) 'Resource valuation under uncertainty: Theoretical principles for empirical research', *in Advances in Applied Micro-Economics,* JAI Press, Inc, vol 4, pp133–152

4   Bishop, R. and Heberlein, T. (1979) 'Measuring values of extramarket goods: Are indirect measures biased', *American Journal of Agricultural Economics,* vol 61, pp926–930

5   Bromley, D. (ed) (1986). *Natural Resource Economics: Policy Problems and Contemporary Analysis.* Kluwer/Nijhoff Publishing, Boston, MA

6   Brookshire, D. S. and Coursey, D. (1987) 'Measuring the value of a public good: An empirical comparison of elicitation procedures', *American Economic Review,* vol 77, pp554–566

7   Brookshire, D. S., Thayer, M., Schulze, W. D. and d'Arge R. (1982) 'Valuing economic goods: A comparison of survey and hedonic approaches', *American Economic Review,* vol 72, pp165–177

8   Brown, T. C. (1984) 'The concept of value in resource allocation', *Land Economics,* vol 60, pp231–246

9   Brown, T. C. and Slovic, P. (1988) 'Effects of context on economic measures of value', in Peterson, G. L., Driver, B. L. and Gregory, R. (eds) *Integrating Economic and Psychological Knowledge in Valuations of Public Amenity Resources.* Venture, State College, PA, pp23–30

10 Cronbach, L. J. and Meehl, P. M. (1955) 'Construct Validity in Psychological Tests', *Psychological Bulletin,* vol 52, pp281–302

11 Cummings, R. G., Brookshire, D. S. and Schulze, W. D. (1986) *Valuing Environmental Goods: Assessment of the Contingent Valuation Method.* Rowman and Allanheld, Totowa, NJ

12 Dawes, R. M. (1977) 'Predictive models as a guide to preference', *IEEE Transactions on Systems, Man and Cybernetics* SMC-7, pp355–358

13 Desvousges, W., Smith, V. K. and Fisher, A. (1987) 'Option price estimates for water quality improvements: A contingent valuation study for the Monongahela River', *Journal of Environmental Economics and Management,* vol 14, pp248–267

14 Dickie, M., Fisher, A. and Gerking, S. (1987) 'Market transactions and hypothetical demand data: A comparative study', *Journal of the American Statistical Association,* vol 82, pp69–75

15 Edwards, W. (1954) 'The theory of decision making', *Psychological Bulletin,* vol 51, pp380–417

16 Edwards, W. (1961) 'Behavioural decision theory', *Annual Review of Psychology,* vol 12, pp473–498

17 Edwards, W. and von Winterfeldt, D. (1987) 'Public values in risk debates', *Risk Analysis,* vol 7, pp141–158

18 Einhorn, H. J. and Hogarth, R. M. (1981) 'Behavioural decision theory: Processes of judgement and choice', *Annual Review of Psychology,* vol 32, pp53–88

19 Fischhoff, B. and Furby, L. (1988) 'Measuring values: A conceptual framework for interpreting transactions with special reference to contingent valuation of visibility', *Journal of Risk and Uncertainty,* vol 1, pp147–184

20 Fischhoff, B., Quadrel, M. J. and Kamlet, M. et al (1993) 'Embedding effects: Stimulus representation and response mode', *Journal of Risk and Uncertainty,* vol 6(3), pp211–234

21 Fischhoff, B., Slavic, P. and Lichtenstein, S. (1978) 'Fault trees: Sensitivity of estimated failure probabilities to problem representation', *Journal of Experimental Psychology: Human Perception and Performance*, pp330–344

22 Freeman, M. A. (1989) 'Nonuse values in natural resource damage assessments', draft manuscript, in Kopp, R. and Smith, V. K. (eds) *Valuing Natural Assets: 'The Economics of Natural Resource Damage Assessments*. Resources for the Future, Washington, DC

23 Gaeth, G. J. and Shanteau, J. (1984) 'Reducing the influence of irrelevant information on experienced decision makers', *Organizational Behaviour and Human Performance*, vol 33, pp263–282

24 Gardiner, P. C. and Edwards, W. (1975) 'Public values: Multiattribute-utility measurement for social decision making', in Kaplan, M. F. and Schwartz, S. (eds) *Human Judgement and Decision Processes*. Academic Press, NY, pp1–37

25 Gregory, R., Keeney, R. L. and von Winterfeldt, D. (1992) 'Adapting the environmental impact statement process to inform decision makers', *Journal of Policy Analysis and Management*, vol 11, pp58–75

26 Gregory, R., MacGregor, D. and Lichtenstein, S. (1992) 'Assessing the quality of expressed preference measures of value', *Journal of Economic Behaviour and Organization*, vol 17, pp277–292

27 Gregory, R. and McDaniels, T. (1987) 'Valuing environmental losses: What promise does the right measure hold?' *Policy Sciences*, vol 20, pp11–26

28 Grether, D. M. and Plott, C. R. (1979) 'Economic theory of choice and the preference reversal phenomenon', *American Economic Review*, vol 69, pp623–638

29 Hammond, K. R., McClelland, G. H. and Mumpower, J. (1980) *Human Judgement and Decision Making: Theories, Methods, and Procedures*. Praeger, NY

30 Hogarth, R. (ed) (1982) *New Directions for Methodology of Social and Behavioural Science: Question Framing and Response Consistency*. Jossey-Bass, San Francisco, CA

31 Huber, O. (1980) 'The influence of some task variables on cognitive operations in an information-processing decision model', *Acta Psychologica*, vol 45, pp187–196

32 Irwin, J., Schenk, D., McClelland, G. H., Schulze, W. D., Stewart, T. and Thayer, M. (1990) 'Urban visibility. Some experiments on the contingent valuation method', in Mathei, C. V. (ed) *Visibility and Fine Particles*. Air and Waste Management Association, Pittsburgh, PA, pp647–658

33 Irwin, J. R., Slovic, P., Lichtenstein, S. and McClelland, G. H. (1993) 'Preference reversals and the measurement of environmental values', *Journal of Risk and Uncertainty*, vol 6(1), pp5–17

34 Johnson, E. J., Meyer, R. M. and Ghose, S. (1989) 'When choice models fail: Compensatory representations in negatively correlated environments', *Journal of Marketing Research*, vol 26, pp255–270

35 Jones-Lee, M., Hammerton, M. and Phillips, R. (1985) 'The value of safety: Results from a national survey', *Economic Journal*, vol 95, 49–72

36 Kahneman, D. and Knetsch, J. (1992) 'Valuing public goods: The purchase of moral satisfaction', *Journal of Environmental Economics and Management*, vol 22, pp57–70

37 Kahneman, D., Knetsch, J. L. and Thaler, R. H. (1990) 'Experimental tests of the endowment effect and the coase theorem', *Journal of Political Economy*, vol 98, pp1325–1348

38 Kahneman, D., Slovic, P. and Tversky, A. (eds) (1982) *Judgement under Uncertainty: Heuristics and Biases*. Cambridge University Press, NY

39 Keeney, R. L. (1980) *Siting Energy Facilities*. Academic, NY

40 Keeney, R. L. (1982) 'Decision analysis: An overview', *Operations Research*, vol 30, pp803–838

41 Keeney, R. L. and Raiffa, H. (1976) *Decisions with Multiple Objectives*. Wiley, NY

42 Knetsch, J. and Sinden, J. (1984) 'Willingness to pay and compensation demanded', *Quarterly Journal of Economics*, vol 99, pp507–521

43 Kopp, R., Portney, P. and Smith, V. K. (1990) 'Natural resource damages: The economics have shifted after Ohio v. United States Department of the Interior', *Environmental Law Reporter*, vol 4, pp10127–10131

44 Lancaster, K. (1966) 'A new approach to consumer theory', *Journal of Political Economy*, vol 74, pp132–157

45 Lichtenstein, S. and Slovic, P. (1971) 'Reversals of preference between bids and choices in gambling decisions', *Journal of Experimental Psychology*, vol 89, pp46–55

46 Loomis, J., Hanemann, M. and Kanninen, B. (1991) 'Willingness to pay to protect wetlands and reduce wildlife contamination from agricultural drainage', in Dinar, A. and Zilberman, D. (eds) *The Economics and Management of Water and Drainage in Agriculture.* Kluwer Academic, Boston, MA

47 Loomis, J., Lockwood, M. and DeLacy, T. (1993). 'Some empirical evidence on embedding effects in contingent valuation of forest protection', *Journal of Environmental Economics and Management*, vol 25, pp45–55

48 MacGregor, D. and Slovic, P. (1986) 'Perceived acceptance of risk analysis as a decision-making approach', *Risk Analysis*, vol 6, pp245–256

49 McClelland, G., Schulze, W., Waldman, D. I. J. and Schenk, D. (1991) *Sources of Error in Contingent Valuation*, draft manuscript. University of Colorado, Boulder, CO, January

50 Merkhofer, M. W. and Keeney, R. L. (1987) 'A multiattribute utility analysis of alternative sites for the disposal of nuclear waste', *Risk Analysis*, vol 7, pp173–194

51 Mitchell, R. C. and Carson, R. T. (1989) 'Using surveys to value public goods: The contingent valuation method'. *Resources for the Future*, Washington, DC

52 Payne, J. W., Bettman, J. R. and Johnson, E. J. (1992) 'Behavioural decision research: A constructive processing perspective', *Annual Review of Psychology*, vol 43, pp87–132

53 Phillips, C. and Zeckhauser, R. (1989) 'Contingent valuation of damage to natural resources: How accurate? How appropriate?', *Toxics Law Reporter*, October 4, pp520–529

54 Randall, A. (1986) 'Valuation in a policy context', in Bromley, D. (ed) *Natural Resource Economics: Policy Problems and Contemporary Analysis.* Kluwer/Nijhoff Publishing, Boston, MA, pp163–200

55 Rolston, H. (1981) 'Values in nature', *Environmental Ethics*, vol 3, pp115–128

56 Randall, A., Hoehn, J. and Brookshire, D. (1983) 'Contingent valuation surveys for evaluating environmental assets', *Natural Resources Journal*, vol 23, pp635–648

57 Simon, H. (1978) 'Rationality as process and as product of thought', *American Economic Review*, vol 68, pp1–16

58 Slovic, P., Fischhoff, B. and Lichtenstein, S. (1982) 'Response mode, framing, and information-processing effects in risk assessment', in Hogarth, R. (ed) *New Directions for Methodology of Social and Behavioural Science: Question Framing and Response Consistency.* Jossey-Bass, San Francisco, CA, 21–36

59 Slovic, P., Griffin, D. and Tversky, A. (1990) 'Compatibility effects in judgement and choice', in Hogarth, Robin M. (ed) *Insights in Decision Making: A Tribute to Hillel J. Einhom.* University of Chicago Press, Chicago, IL, pp5–27

60 Slovic, P. and Lichtenstein, S. (1971) 'Comparison of bayesian and regression approaches to the study of information processing in judgement', *Organizational Behaviour and Human Performance*, vol 6, pp649–744

61 Slovic, P., Lichtenstein, S. and Fischhoff, B. (1979) 'Images of disaster: Perception and acceptance of risks from nuclear power', in Goodman, G. and Rowe, W. (eds) *Energy Risk Management.* Academic Press, London, pp223–245

62 Slovic, P. and McPhillamy, D. J. (1974) 'Dimensional commensurability and cue utilization in comparative judgement', *Organizational Behaviour and Human Performance*, vol 11, pp172–194

63 Smith, V. K., Desvousges, W. and Fisher, A. (1986) 'A comparison of direct and indirect methods for estimating environmental benefits', *American Journal of Agricultural Economics*, vol 68, pp280–290

64 Stevens, S. S. (1951) 'Mathematics, measurement, and psychophysics', in S. S. Stevens (ed) *Handbook of Experimental Psychology.* Wiley, NY, pp1–49

65 Stevens, Thomas H., Echeverria, Jaime, Glass, Ronald J., Hager, Tim and More, Thomas A. (1991). 'Measuring the existence value of wildlife: What do CVM estimates really show?' *Land Economics*, vol 67, pp390–400

66 Tversky, A. and Kahneman, D. (1981) 'The framing of decisions and the psychology of choice', *Science*, vol 211, pp453–458

67 Tversky, A., Sattath, Sh. and Slovic, P. (1988) 'Contingent weighting in judgement and choice', *Psychological Review*, vol 95, pp371–384

68 Tversky, A., Slovic, P. and Kahneman, D. (1990) 'The causes of preference reversal', *American Economic Review*, vol 80, pp204–217

69 Viscusi, W. K. and Magat, W. A. (1987) *Learning about Risk: Consumer and Worker Responses to Hazard Warning?* Harvard University Press, Cambridge, MA

70 Viscusi, W. K., Magat, W. A. and Huber, J. (1986) 'Informational regulation of consumer health risks: An empirical evaluation of hazard warnings', *Rand Journal of Economics*, vol 17, pp351–365

71 Viscusi, W. K., Magat, W. A. and Huber, J. (1991) 'Pricing environmental health risks: Survey assessment of risk – risk and risk – dollar trade-offs for chronic bronchitis', *Journal of Environmental Economics and Management*, vol 21, pp32–51

72 von Winterfeldt, D. and Edwards, W. (1986) *Decision Analysis and Behavioural Research.* Cambridge University Press, NY

73 Walsh, R. G., Bjonback, R. D., Aiken, R. A. and Rosenthal, D. H. (1990) 'Estimating the public benefits of protecting forest quality', *Journal of Environmental Management*, vol 30, pp175–189

18

What Should We Do?
Human Ecology and Collective
Decision Making

Thomas Dietz

What can human ecology tell us that will lead to better decisions? That is, how might human ecology improve public policy? These questions can be answered only by considering what information is necessary to make sound policy decisions, and how human ecology might provide insights that will lead to better information and better policy.

By public policy I mean any collective decision made by a group of individuals. It could be a decision of a citizens' group to challenge a new development, of a town government to raise property taxes, of a national government to regulate a suspected carcinogen or of an international aid agency to provide funds to build a dam in a developing nation. A policy in this sense is simply a decision by a group of people to undertake some action that will have consequences for people and for the biophysical environment.

What information is needed to make rational decisions about public policy? The first question that must be answered is: 'What will happen?' In making policy decisions, it is essential to know the consequences of implementing the policy. What will happen if the development is challenged, taxes are raised, the compound regulated, the dam built? The answers to such questions are always comparative. That is, the answers take the form of a contrast between what will happen if the development is challenged or not questioned, if taxes are raised or if they are not raised, if the compound is regulated or if it is not, if the dam is built or if it is not. In practice, there are likely to be a number of options under consideration: different strategies for challenge, different levels of taxes, different stringency in regulation, different sizes or locations for a dam. For simplicity in exposition, I'll assume that there are only two options.

Answering such questions about what will happen is the domain of impact analysis (Cramer et al, 1980). It requires positive, or descriptive, knowledge of the human ecological system that will be affected. A model of the system must be constructed in prose, in mathematics or in some other form. The model must be used to project the future of the system with the proposed policy implemented and without the policy implemented. The difference between the two projections is the impact expected from the policy.

Note: Reprinted from *Human Ecology Review*, vol 1, Dietz, T., 'What should we do? Human ecology and collective decision making', pp301–309, copyright © (1994), with permission from Society for Human Ecology

The models and methods used to answer the 'what will happen' question are based on the standard, positivist scientific method. Of course, knowledge models and predictions are always fallible, but the scientific method allows for improvement over time. And in many cases, predictions need not be very precise to be helpful (Cramer et al, 1980; Dietz, 1988).

A second question that must be answered once the consequences of a policy choice have been identified: 'Is this a good idea?' The answer to this question can be obtained by assessing the impacts that were identified in answer to the first question. Each impact must be assigned a value and then the values must be aggregated to determine the policy that seems best.[1] Taking the example of the dam, suppose an impact analysis suggests the dam would increase the production of oranges by providing irrigation water but decrease the number of orangutans by flooding habitat.[2] People may value both orange production and the economic growth that comes with it, or they may value the existence of orangutans, or they may value both. Different people will assign different values to oranges and orangutans. How can a collective decision be reached about whether or not to build the dam? Somehow the value of oranges and orangutans to society must be determined and compared. Politics, economics and policy analysis are the methods by which values are used to make policy decisions (Dietz and Stern, 1993). The first two methods are ancient and the subject of immense literatures. I will focus on the third method, policy analysis.

It is important to recognize that positive, descriptive science does not answer the question of 'is this a good idea?' in any direct way. We may be able to project how many oranges will be grown and how many orangutans lost using traditional scientific methods. But positive science cannot tell us the worth of each. Indeed, a key difference between positive science and normative science is that positive science expressly avoids such value questions. Further, normative, prescriptive analysis can never be wholly scientific since it involves values that are rooted in a different domain of human experience than science (Dietz and Burns, 1994). But systematic scientific thinking can aid us in developing better procedures for making value assessments and thus deciding what policy option is best. That is, human ecology may aid in making more rational decisions by helping to determine what will happen and by helping in the assignment of values to various options.

I want to examine two competing methods of policy analysis and assess their strengths and weaknesses. Each method incorporates a theoretical model of human nature, and the strengths and weaknesses of these methods can be understood in terms of these models. The first, benefit–cost analysis, depends on the rational actor model (RAM). The second, discursive policy analysis, depends on an evolutionary/linguistic model (ELM) of human nature. I will begin by comparing the two models, then discuss the two methods of policy analysis that follow from them, as well as a recent innovation in policy analysis, contingent valuation.

Agents, Systems, the RAM and the ELM

To understand the rational actor and evolutionary/linguistic models, it's helpful to construct a simple description of each model. These descriptions may lack some of the subtlety of the more advanced version of these two models, but they capture their essence. The descriptions are built around the application of evolutionary theory to complex adaptive systems in a number of scientific disciplines.[3]

Agents whose actions are guided by rules are the basis of these models. In human ecology and the social sciences, the agents are individual humans, actors in the social science lexicon. Acting on a rule produces responses from the biophysical environment and from other humans. These reactions provide feedbacks that may favour the use of some rules over others – selection processes. Structure comes in two forms. One is the different social and biophysical environments that yield different responses to rule-guided action. That is, the environment is not homogeneous, but composed of local contexts. The environment is structured. Using a rule in one context may produce a different response than using the same rule would produce in a different context. Structure is also evident in the mix of rules used by any actor. Humans have a need for at least a moderate degree of cognitive consistency, and often use simplification heuristics to reduce the demands of making sense of the biophysical and social world. Thus actors will not have a random collection of rules but will tend to acquire, hold and implement rules that are consistent with each other. This process structures culture.

In the rational actor model, all interactions among actors are strategic or market interactions where the rule used in making decisions is self-interest. Under RAM, people try to maximize the benefits they receive relative to the costs they bear. That is, all actors are using the same rule in deciding what action to take – self-interested utility maximization.[4] Adam Smith (1976 [1804], p446) suggests: 'We are not ready to suspect any person of being defective in selfishness.' In making a decision about a dam project, a rational actor would decide how much they value oranges, how much they value orangutans, multiply those values by the number of oranges to be produced and the number of orangutans to be lost, and support or oppose the dam based on which product was larger.

In the RAM, biophysical environment constrains action, but does not otherwise structure action. Thus the environment is treated as relatively homogeneous. With a homogeneous environment and only one rule of relevance, neither social nor cognitive structure are important. Moreover, the agents themselves are seen as relatively homogeneous and unchanging. As Becker (1976b, p5) has put it: 'Since economists generally have had little to contribute, especially in recent times, to the understanding of how preferences are formed, preferences are assumed not to change substantially over time, nor to be very different between persons in different societies and cultures.'

This model is very simple. It is the dominant paradigm in economics and is of growing influence in the other social sciences. Indeed, the simplicity of the model is one of its appealing features since the model can be used to make explicit deductions about behaviour. Ridley and Low (1993/1994) have discussed the implications of the rational actor model for environmental problems.[5] Jaeger (1994) offers some keen insights into the link between economic institutions and the environment that are directly relevant to understanding the implications of the RAM. Below, I will argue that the rational actor model also has clear implications for policy analysis.

The evolutionary/linguistic model sees human ecology as more complex. Cognition is seen as linguistic and language as close to the core of all human action including decision making. As Mead (1962 [1934], p235) puts it: 'Human society is dependent upon the development of language for its own distinctive form of organization.'[6] The ELM suggests that different actors possess different rules, and that the social environment can be decomposed into different structures or local contexts. One important structure is the market. People who perceive themselves as acting in the market may follow the utility maximization rule. If every one follows that rule, the ELM reduces to the RAM.[7] But other environments exist, such as the family or a community organization. When acting in such a social environment, actors may follow different rules than those they would choose in the market. For example, within the family altruistic rules may be used more often than the rule of self-interest. Because there are multiple environments and multiple rules, actors are constantly attempting to define, redefine and renegotiate with others the contexts in which they are operating and thus the rules that are appropriate for action. This involves communication or discourse, as well as the exchange and instrumental action that typify the market. Because the ELM assumes people will apply different rules in different contexts, the actual decisions someone might make are hard to predict. If an individual frames the dam question in terms of self-interest, then the conclusion she or he would reach would be that expected under the RAM. But if the dam question is framed in the context of the family, considerable weight might be given to the costs and benefits to future generations. The economic advantages of increased orange production in the present might be seen as less important than the ecological value of preserving orangutan habitat for posterity. But despite this complexity compared to the RAM, the ELM also has implications for policy analysis.

Welfare Economics and Benefit–Cost Analysis

What form of policy analysis follows from the rational actor model? One of the most important conclusions that follows from the assumptions of the RAM is that self-interested individuals interacting in a market will eventually produce prices for all goods traded in the market.[8] In addition, the price of a good in a competitive market can be interpreted as the social value associated with a good. The RAM implies that the value of oranges is reflected in the price of oranges, and the value of orangutans is reflected in the price of orangutans.

Benefit–cost analysis follows directly from this line of reasoning. Benefit–cost analysis proceeds by calculating the market value of all impacts associated with a policy and aggregating them into a ratio of benefits to costs.[9] If the ratio of benefits to costs is greater than 1.0, the project is a good idea. If there are several policy options being considered, the one with the highest benefit–cost ratio is preferable.

Benefit–cost analysis has a number of important strengths. First, it offers a clear theory of 'the good'. Those policies are good that increase welfare in the sense that the benefits to society outweigh the costs to society. There is no ambiguity about how to choose among policy alternatives. It has a further theoretical strength in that the welfare economics that underpins benefit–cost analysis is based on an explicit model of human ecology: the RAM. Finally benefit–cost analysis is based on a rigorous and well-defined methodology. Even if any particular benefit–cost analysis has flaws, the application of the technique can improve over time as criticism and research lead to better practice.

The criticisms of benefit–cost analysis can be divided into two categories: internal critiques and external critiques. The internal critiques are part of the learning process in benefit–cost practice. These critiques lead to innovations in the way benefit–cost analysis is done. There are three major lines of internal criticism. First, in environmental problems where the effects of a policy may be very long term, discounting is problematic because it makes very large costs or benefits in the distant future reduce to zero in the present. This may be a practical problem (destroying the earth in the distant future has a negligible current value in the calculation) and it also raises questions of intergenerational equity – the discounting process gives more weight to impacts visited on the present generation than to impacts visited on future generations. Benefit–cost analysis has also been criticized by its students for ignoring distributional issues. Benefit–cost analysis is oblivious to who actually pays the costs and who receives the benefits. There are a number of strategies for including distributional considerations into a benefit–cost analysis, but they are seldom implemented in practice. Finally, benefit–cost analysis has a serious problem in valuing nonmarket goods, such as ecosystem services. The rational actor model justifies the use of market prices for social values. But even if those values are correct, many policies will have impacts on goods and services that are not traded in a market and thus have no market price. In the past, these nonmarket goods and services have been ignored. Recently, the method of contingent valuation has been employed to provide a value estimate for them. Before examining the implications of the evolutionary/linguistic model, in the next section I will briefly discuss contingent valuation.

The external critiques suggest that benefit–cost analysis cannot be fixed even by technical developments to handle distribution, discounting and nonmarket goods.[10] The major external critique comes from those who reject the RAM as an adequate model of human ecology. In brief, this argument suggests that human evolution has favoured linguistic and classificatory abilities over calculative abilities (Dietz and Stern, 1993). Thus we are good at language games and social interaction, but poor at the kinds of arithmetic and algebra required by the RAM. The rejection of the RAM also suggests that market processes do not produce adequate estimates of social values. The RAM assumes people acting with no structure in interactions are unconstrained by power. In fact, markets are highly structured and reflect vast differentials in power and as a result market prices will not reflect true social value but rather will be weighted in favour of those with the power to shape the market.

Contingent Valuation

Contingent valuation is based on a quite venerable method of determining value: ask people what something is worth. Contingent valuation has become very prevalent in the last decade or so as a method of assigning monetary values to nonmarket goods and services so that those values can be included in a benefit–cost or other policy analysis (Mitchell and Carson 1989). In the typical contingent valuation study, a sample of the population is asked a series of questions that are designed to elicit a monetary value associated with various aspects of the environment that are not traded in the market. In the example of the dam, a survey would be conducted asking people how much value (usually in monetary units) they assign to oranges and to orangutans. The average (or some other statistical summary) across respondents to the survey would be the value assigned to oranges and to orangutans.

Contingent valuation can be used to find a social value for almost any nonmarket good or service. It is rigorous and involves an improving practice. It is democratic in that everyone sampled in the survey has the same weight in determining the outcome. But it has two internal weaknesses. First, people often give inconsistent responses. They may offer to pay as much in higher taxes to protect a single lake as they would to protect a group of lakes. They may give different answers if asked how much they would pay to get something than they would if asked how much they would take as compensation for giving something up. While these inconsistencies don't surprise us, they contradict the rational actor model. Second, several studies show that people respond to the typical contingent valuation question as if they were contributing to a good cause – acting altruistically – rather than as if they were buying something in a market – acting selfishly (Guagnano et al, 1994; Kahneman et al, 1993). Again, this contradicts the assumptions of the RAM. In addition, contingent valuation questions are susceptible to question framing effects that focus respondents on one rule set over alternative rule sets that might be applied. That is, question wording can influence whether the respondent answers in terms of personal self-interest or in terms of more altruistic values (Dietz and Stern, 1993; Stern et al, 1993).

Discursive Methods

Discursive methods are those that use conversations or group interaction via language to analyse policy. These approaches are driven by Habermas' notion of communicative rationality (Habermas, 1970, 1984, 1987; Brulle, 1992). A rational decision is one taken by a group where all stakeholders have an ability for competent, unconstrained communication. A fair and competent process produces good policy.

There are two lines of thought exploring this approach to policy evaluation. One is the work of Webler, Renn and their collaborators on discursive decision making (Webler, 1993; Webler et al, 1994; Renn et al, 1995). The other is my own work on discursive methods for impact assessment (Dietz, 1987, 1988; Dietz and Pfund, 1988). Both approaches are based on using structured group processes to assign values to anticipated impacts. Groups are formed that include all major stakeholders. Such groups will include individuals with diverse backgrounds and experience. The rules established for interaction within the group are intended to facilitate effective and fair discussion by limiting the ability of any individual to dominate the group (Dietz and Pfund, 1988).

Recall that the rational actor model assumes all individuals use the utility maximization rule in all contexts. Under the RAM there is no significant environmental or cultural structure that shapes interaction. In contrast, the ELM sees the market as only one of many structures or contexts in which people interact. The rule of self-interest is only one of many rules that people apply in making decisions. The goal of discursive policy analysis is to allow a diversity of people to draw on their experiences in a diversity of contexts to assign values to anticipated policy outcomes. It emphasizes that this should be a reflexive process in which people comment on the valuations proposed by others, and a serious effort is made to understand and examine critically the rules each individual is using.[11]

The discursive process is superior to benefit–cost analysis for two reasons. First, it can subsume benefit–cost analysis. If all participants agree that utility maximization is the rule that should apply and that market values are accurate reflections of social values, then the discursive process would lead to benefit–cost analysis. But the choice of a benefit–cost calculation is the result of a conscious, reflective, collective decision rather than a deduction from the RAM. Second, the discursive process draws on human cognitive strengths, rather than cognitive weaknesses (Dietz and Stern, 1993). We are good at talking and pattern recognition, but quite poor at the calculations required for utility maximization.

Both methods have the advantage that repeated applications and criticism of applications can improve practice. But the discursive method has the added advantage of allowing participants to learn the valuation rules of others and to reflect on their own valuation rules. This allows for an evolution of valuation rules within the community undertaking the process, not just among policy analysts. Indeed, Brulle (1993, 1994a, b) has suggested that social movements such as the environmental movement, in their critique of society, implement a discursive policy method for the whole society, and thus lead to broad social learning.

The discursive method is not without its faults. Two key problems require serious work. First, the discursive method does not guarantee closure and agreement. It is an open-ended process, and that openness may prevent any resolution or conclusion from being reached. Of course, the lack of consensus is in itself important information about the disparate values associated with the policy under consideration. Second, while the group processes used for this approach are intended to facilitate discussion free from the influences of power, power is still embedded in the set of rules that participants bring from their lives to the discussion. As Foucault has emphasized, power is embedded in the structure of language and culture (Foucault 1972; Burchell et al, 1991). The discursive approach has an advantage over less reflexive methods in that it can attempt to uncover the hidden assumptions and biases of language and culture, but it is not immune from them.

What Should We Do to Help Us Answer the Question 'What Should We Do?'

Most human ecologists feel that human ecology should play an important role in policy decisions. For that wish to be realized, human ecologists need to think carefully about the kinds of information needed to guide policy. I've suggested two questions must be answered in making policy decisions: 'What will happen?' and 'Is that a good idea?' The first question can be addressed with standard scientific methodology. The problems are difficult, but the approaches are well mapped.

The second question leads into poorly mapped territory. Much more exploratory work will be required. But some initial forays suggest the general pattern of the land-scape. The dominant approach to normative policy analysis is benefit–cost analysis grounded in welfare economics, and ultimately in the rational actor model. This approach has its merits, but is not sufficient. Truly rational normative analysis will have to be based on a more realistic model of human ecology than the rational actor model, but it must also be a model that subsumes, rather than discards, the rational actor model. An emerging evolutionary/linguistic model takes the rational actor model as a special case that describes human action under some, but not all, circumstances. I have argued that the evolutionary/linguistic model is compatible with discursive policy analysis methods. This provides an alternative approach to normative analysis, but it is one that is not yet well mapped.

Notes

An earlier version of this paper was presented at the 1994 Society and Natural Resources Meeting in Ft Collins, Colorado. I thank R. Brulle, W. Freudenburg, L. Kalof, P. Richerson and J. Taylor for their comments. This work was supported in part by the Northern Virginia Survey Research Labouratory of George Mason University and by US National Science Foundation grant SES92-11591.

1   This discussion avoids the complication that impacts may be uncertain. While uncertainty, and thus risk, is very important in collective decisions, the arguments I make here do not change in character if impacts are considered uncertain. For an overview of the risk literature, see Dietz et al (1995).

2   The idea of comparing oranges and orangutans comes from Bill Freudenburg. Of course, the example is hypothetical, structured to aid exposition rather than provide a realistic analysis of a development project.

3   John Holland (1994) has suggested that seven characteristics define an evolving complex adaptive system. First, such systems exhibit a structure with aggregation of simple components into more complex components. The hierarchy of such components has important implications for the behaviour of both the agents that constitute the smallest units and for the system as a whole. Second, interactions among components lead to nonlinear systems dynamics. Third, flows of matter, energy and information are critical to the behaviour of both agents and the system. Fourth, the agents are themselves heterogeneous with regard to their structural position in flows and hierarchies and with regard to the rules that guide their action. Fifth, recognition and signalling among agents is an important part of systems behaviour. That is, agents recognize their heterogeneity and that recognition shapes behaviour. Sixth, common building blocks (agents and aggregations of agents) are used in multiple ways. Seventh, the agents hold internal models that guide their behaviour, and these models may change in response to experience through learning and evolution. I think it is obvious to any student of human ecology that human-environment systems have all these characteristics. The details of the approach I use here are described in a series of papers that develop an evolutionary

theory of culture, society and agency (Dietz et al, 1990; Burns and Dietz, 1992; Dietz and Burns, 1992).

4   Some economists have suggested that considerations other than narrow self-interest may influence decisions. See for example, Margolis (1982) or Hirschleifer (1987, pp145–193).

5   See also the extensive discussion that follows their argument in *Human Ecology Review* vol 1, no 1.

6   For classic statements on this position, see Mueller-Vollmer (1989), while Lakoff (1989) presents a recent clear articulation.

7   Becker (1976a) has argued that natural selection acting on genes may shape preferences, so that an integration of the RAM with socio-biology may be sufficient to span the social sciences. This is similar to the arguments of Ridley and Low (1993/1994).

8   For simplicity I use the term goods to include both goods and services.

9   Impacts that will occur in the future are discounted into a present value to take account of opportunity costs.

10 Söderbaum (1986, 1993) offers thoughtful critiques of benefit–cost analysis that are compatible with, but somewhat different from, those I propose.

11 How does discursive policy analysis differ from democratic process? In many ways discursive policy analysis is simply an ideal type of democracy. Certainly Habermas' (1970, 1984, 1987) arguments are intended to specify how democracy can realize its potential. The examples discussed here are applications of these principles to policy problems in limited contexts where some of the distortions present in real democracy can be corrected. In a sense, the discursive policy analysis methods have the same relationship to democracy as practiced that benefit–cost analysis has to markets. If the larger, societal level process actually worked as the underpinning theory specifies, there would be no need for the policy analysis implementation of the theory. But when markets and democracies are imperfect implementations of the ideal, focused policy methods can provide useful corrective information.

12 Discursive methods are also subject to the criticism that most human political units are now so large that not all interested parties can participate in the discourse. This is certainly true, and many problems of contemporary democracy may have their roots in the difficulties of democracy for large populations. But here I am focusing on discursive methods of policy analysis, rather than discursive decision making per se. The problem of large populations is less severe for policy analysis in that all important groups can be sampled and the discourse will thus include individuals from all relevant perspectives, contexts and rule sets.

References

1   Becker, G. S. (1976a) 'Altruism, egoism and genetic fitness: Economics and sociobiology'. *Journal of Economic Literature,* vol 14, pp817–826

2   Becker, G. S. (1976b) *The Economic Approach to Human Behaviour.* University of Chicago Press, Chicago

3   Brulle, R. J. (1992) 'Jurgen Habermas: An exegesis for human ecologists'. *Human Ecology Bulletin,* vol 8, pp29–40

4   Brulle, R. J. (1993) 'Environmentalism and human emancipation', in Wright, S. D., Dietz, T., Borden, R., Young, G. and Guagnano, G. (ed) *Human Ecology: Crossing Boundaries,* Fort Collins, Society for Human Ecology, Colorado, pp2–12

5   Brulle, R. J. (1994a) 'Power, discourse and social problems: Social problems from a rhetorical perspective'. *Perspectives on Social Problems* vol 5, pp95–121

6   Brulle, R. J. (1994b) *Environmental Discourse and Social Movements.* Paper presented to the Seventh Meeting of the Society for Human Ecology, East Lansing, Michigan, 23 April

7   Burchell, G., Gordon, C. and Miller, P. (1991) *The Foucault Effect: Studies in Governability.* University of Chicago Press, Chicago

8   Burns, T. R. and Dietz, T. (1992) 'Socio-cultural evolution: Social rule systems, selection and agency'. *International Sociology,* vol 7, pp259–283

9   Cramer, J. C., Dietz, T. and Johnston, R. (1980) 'Social impact assessment of regional plans: A review of methods and a recommended process'. *Policy Sciences,* vol 12, pp61–82

10 Dietz, T. (1987) 'Theory and method in social impact assessment'. *Sociological Inquiry,* vol 57, pp54–69

11 Dietz, T. (1988) 'Social impact assessment as applied human ecology: Integrating theory and method', in Borden, R., Jacobs, J. and Young, G. R. (ed) *Human Ecology: Research and Applications.* Society for Human Ecology, College Park, Maryland, pp220–227

12 Dietz, T. and Burns, T. R. (1992) 'Human agency and the evolutionary dynamics of culture'. *Acta Sociologica,* vol 35, pp187–200

13 Dietz, T. and Burns, T. R. (1994) *Environment, Technology and the Evolution of Democracy.* Paper presented to the 1994 Annual Meeting of the American Sociological Association, Los Angeles, 8 August

14 Dietz, T., Burns, T. R. and Buttel, F. H. (1990) 'Evolutionary theory in sociology: An examination of current thinking'. *Sociological Forum,* vol 5, pp155–171

15 Dietz, T., Frey, R. S. and Rosa, E. A. (1995) 'Risk, technology and society', in Dunlap, R. and Michaelson, W. (ed) *Handbook for Environmental Sociology,* Greenwood Press, Westport, Connecticut, in press

16 Dietz, T. and Pfund, A. (1988) 'An impact identification method for development program evaluation'. *Policy Studies Review,* vol 8, pp137–145

17 Dietz, T., and Stern, P. C. (1993) *Individual Preferences and Social Choice.* Paper presented at the 1993 meeting of the American Association for the Advancement of Science, Chicago, Illinois, 14 February

18 Foucault, M. (1972) *Power/Knowledge.* Pantheon Books, NY

19 Guagnano, G. A., Dietz, T. and Stern, P. C. (1994) 'Willingness to pay for public goods: A test of the contribution model'. *Psychological Science,* vol 5, pp411–415

20 Habermas, J. (1970) *Towards a Rational Society.* Beacon, Boston

21 Habermas, J. (1984) *The Theory of Communicative Action. Part One. Reason and the Rationalization of Society.* Beacon, Boston

22 Habermas, J. (1987) *The Theory of Communicative Action. Part Two. System and Lifeworld: A Critique of Functionalist Reasoning.* Beacon, Boston

23 Hirschleifer, J. (1987) *Economic Behaviour in Adversity.* University of Chicago Press, Chicago

24 Holland, J. (1994) *Complexity Made Simple.* Ulam Memorial Lecture, Santa Fe Institute, Santa Fe, New Mexico, 6 June

25 Jaeger, C. C. (1994) *Taming the Dragon: Transforming Economic Institutions in the Face of Global Change.* Gordon and Breach, Yverdon, Switzerland

26 Kahneman, D., Jacowitz, K., Ritov, I. and Grant, P. (1993) 'Stated willingness to pay for public goods: A psychological perspective'. *Psychological Science*, vol 4, pp310–315

27 Lakoff. G. (1987) *Women, Fires and Dangerous Things: What Categories Reveal about the Mind*. University of Chicago Press, Chicago

28 Margolis, H. (1982) *Selfishness, Altruism and Rationality: A Theory of Social Choice*. Cambridge University Press, NY

29 Mead, G. H. (1962 [1934]) *Mind, Self and Society*. University of Chicago Press, Chicago

30 Mitchell, R. C. and Carson, R. (1989) *Using Surveys to Value Public Goods: The Contingent Valuation Method*. Resources for the Future, Washington, DC

31 Mueller-Vollmer, K. (1989) *The Hermeneutics Reader*. Continuum, NY

32 Renn, O., Webler, T. and Wiedemann, P. (eds) (1995) *Novel Approaches to Public Participation in Environmental Decision Making*. Kluwer, Amsterdam

33 Richerson, P. J. (1977) 'Ecology and human ecology'. *American Ethnologist*, vol 4, pp1–26

34 Ridley, M. and Low, B. S. (1993/1994) 'Can selfishness save the environment?' *Human Ecology Review*, vol 1, pp1–13

35 Smith, A. (1976 [1804]) *A Theory of Moral Sentiments*. Oxford University Press, NY

36 Söderbaum, P. (1986) 'Economics, ethics and environmental problems'. *The Journal of Interdisciplinary Economics*, vol 1, pp139–153

37 Söderbaum, P. (1993) 'Actors, ideology and markets: Neoclassical and institutional perspectives on environmental policy'. *Ecological Economics*, vol 10, pp47–60

38 Stern, P. C., Dietz, T. and Kalof, L. (1993) 'Value orientations, gender and environmental concern'. *Environment and Behaviour*, vol 25, pp322–348

39 Webler, T. (1993) 'Habermas put into practice: A democratic discourse for environmental problem solving', in Wright, S. D., Dietz, T., Borden, R., Young, G. and Guagnano, G. (ed) *Human Ecology: Crossing Boundaries*, Society for Human Ecology, Fort Collins, Colorado, pp60–72

40 Webler, T., Kastenholtz, H. Renn, and O. (1994) 'Can public participation in impact assessment enable social learning?' Paper presented to the Seventh Meeting of the Society for Human Ecology, East Lansing, Michigan, 21 April

Index

materials balance theory 45
MAUT (multiattribute utility theory) 305
  CV using (MAUT/CV) 305–10
meditation 100, 115
Merchant, Carolyn 120
metaphor 93, 131, 141, 213
microeconomics 56
militarization 65, 104, 108, 110
Mill, John Stuart (1806–1873) 19, 43, 86, 280
Mitchell and Carson, 200 (notes), 219 (notes) 241, 294
modern deontology 87
monetary values 6, 23, 44
money 21, 23
moral considerability 63–4
moral obligation 188–9, 252, 255, 256–7, *256,*
  257, 264, 266
moral reciprocity 70
moral satisfaction 227, 279–80, 285
  purchase of 3–4, 10, 232, 238–42, *240,* 243
moral sentiments 73–4, 75, 297
moral standing 63–4
moral values 57, 267
moralistic values 66, 138–41
'mother effect' 193, 199
Muir, John (1838–1914) 3, 63, 102, 106, 275
multiattribute utility theory *see* MAUT
multinational corporate industry 118
mysticism 70, 97, 106

Naess, Arne 64–5, 103, 113, 115, 118–19
  see also deep ecology
National Oceanic and Atmospheric Administration
  see NOAA
national parks 105, 107–8
Native Americans 139, 217
nationalism 108
natural capital 54
natural selection 26, 74
naturalistic values 66, 133–4
nature 63, 84, 131–2, 138–9, 141–2, 173, 176
  appreciation of 145–6, 147
  experience of 93, 133, 134–5
  harmony with 83, 84–5, 85, 92–3, 93, 98
  intrinsic value 81, 84, 85–6
  scientific experience of 134, 135
  scientific understanding of 93
  as symbol 137–8
  women's role in mediating 113–14
  see also dominion over nature
nay-saying 11
needs 20, 64–5, 90–1, 93–4, 98, 144–5
negativistic values 66, 141–2
neo-classical economics 41, 49, 50, 51, 54
NEP (New Environmental Paradigm) Scale 172,
  173–7, 178, 180, 181, 189, 190
New Ecological Paradigm Scale 153, 172, 177–84,
  178–9, 180, 183
NIMBYism ('not in my backyard') 190, 201, 207,
  213, 218–19
NOAA (National Oceanic and Atmospheric
  Administration) panel 9–10, 12, 46, 297

no growth economy 108
no harm principle 90
nonanthropocentric value theory (axiology) 63,
  63–4, 67, 68, 73
nonanthropocentrism 81, 82–6, 84–5, 86, 93
nonhuman entities 53–4, 55, 57, 69, 85, 88,
  98, 119
  intrinsic value 75, 81, 84–5, 85–6
nonindividualism 81, 86–8
nonmarket goods 6, 229, 284
nonmarket valuation 10
nonmonetary values 297, 299–300
Norgaard, Richard 49, 50–1, 54–5
norm-activation theory 188–9, 191, 196, 198
normative policy analysis 247, 322–3
'not in my backyard' attitude *see* NIMBYism
nuclear holocaust 73, 104

Occam's razor 94
Ohmann, Richard 126
ontological 94, 117, 120
open-ended questions 10, 13
optimal control theory 45
optimization 23, 24, 25
order effect, WTP questions 232, 258, 258–9,
  259, 284
Orientalism 107, 111
other, the 106, 107, 115, 201
outdoor experiences 133–4
overconsumption 65, 104, 110
overpopulation 87, 118

parental–filial care 74, 193, 199, 319
Parfit's paradox 87–8, 89–90
parochialism 73, 116
participation, religious 153, 161–62, *163–4,* 164
participatory democracy 36–7, 286–8
passenger pigeon 144
passions 73
passive-use values 3, 7–8, 8–9
passivist 101
patriarchy 113–15
  deep ecology 119–20
patricentric attitude 122
patriotism 74
payment schedules 232
PCE (personal consumption expenditures) 27
peace movement 110
peasants 105, 109, 114, 215
personal norms, altruistic 189
phenomenology 118, 210
place 152
place-based theory of environmental valuation
  154–5, 208–12
plant life 53, 64, 69–71, 74, 103, 139, 214
Plato (427–347 BCE) 71–2
pleasure 279–80
policy analysis 317, 319–20, 322–3
policy change 215–16
political action 193, *194,* 195, *196,* 197–9, *198*
political structures 65, 104, 109